THE **EGG BOWL**

William G. Barner

with Danny McKenzie and Jeff Roberson

University Press of Mississippi / Jackson

THE EGG BOWL

Mississippi State vs. Ole Miss

The University Press of Mississippi is the scholarly publishing agency of the
Mississippi Institutions of Higher Learning: Alcorn State University,
Delta State University, Jackson State University, Mississippi State University,
Mississippi University for Women, Mississippi Valley State University,
University of Mississippi, and University of Southern Mississippi.

Designed by Todd Lape

www.upress.state.ms.us

The University Press of Mississippi is a member of the Association of University
Presses.

Trade paperback ISBN 978-1-4968-4973-1
Epub single ISBN 978-1-4968-5302-8
Epub institutional ISBN 978-1-4968-5303-5
PDF single ISBN 978-1-4968-5304-2
PDF institutional ISBN 978-1-4968-5305-9

British Library Cataloging-in-Publication Data available

[This] maelstrom of mayhem . . . combines the tragic
overtones of Russian drama with comedy straight out of
[a] Gilbert and Sullivan [opera]—blends the delicacy of
a fairy ballet with the blind violence of a rogue elephant.

—WALTER STEWART, *Memphis Commercial Appeal*

The overt emotion and deep intensity of football rivalries
such as Ole Miss and Mississippi State are "a collision of passions."

—TONY BARNHART, *Southern Fried Football*

"A rivalry?" exclaimed one veteran observer.
"Ole Miss and Mississippi State are *war*!"

To every Rebel fan and every Bulldog fan

And to every player, every coach, and every
athletic official at both Ole Miss and Mississippi State

Your emotion and enthusiasm have made this the
South's fiercest rivalry—absolutely the South's greatest

CONTENTS

The Games

Appendixes

ACKNOWLEDGMENTS

No volume of historic significance would be possible without assistance from a great number of people. Among the most valuable have been hardworking newspaper writers, game statisticians, and members of the media relations departments at both Ole Miss and Mississippi State, the real keepers of sports memorabilia, facts, and figures. The record would not have been complete without the concentrated efforts of the staffs of the student publications at both schools—the *Reflector* and the *Reveille* at State and the *Daily Mississippian* and the *Ole Miss* at the University of Mississippi. These devoted contributors have greatly increased the depth of knowledge regarding this rivalry.

A great debt of gratitude goes to the staff writers at various publications whose rich legacy of excitement, drama, and comedy marks these games: the *Biloxi Sun Herald*, *Birmingham Age-Herald*, *Birmingham News*, *Clarksdale Press Register*, *Columbus Dispatch*, *Columbus Weekly Commercial*, *Delta Democrat Times*, *Greenwood Daily Commonwealth*, *Greenwood Morning Star*, *Jackson Clarion-Ledger*, *Jackson Daily News*, *Memphis Commercial Appeal*, *Memphis Press-Scimitar*, *Meridian Star*, *Meridian Times*, *Natchez Democrat*, *New Orleans Times-Picayune*, *Northeast Mississippi Daily Journal*, *Oxford Eagle*, *SEC Record Book*, and *Starkville News*.

The research staffs at Ole Miss's J. D. Williams Library and State's Mitchell Memorial Library opened their collections of memorabilia and microfilm. Kind librarians also offered assistance in Columbus, Greenwood, Clarksdale, and Tupelo, where some of the games were played. The late Billy Gates, former sports information director at Ole Miss, laid the basis for almost all statistical facts with his historical data. Deep appreciation goes to the media relations directors at both schools: Langston Rogers at Ole Miss graciously opened his office for research and personally burrowed through dusty old files to make

these accounts more accurate, and Mike Nemeth at State provided vital play-by-play accounts and supplied great action photos. David Hargrove at Ole Miss and Betty Self and Hilda Scholtes at State patiently, intently, and repeatedly conducted research in the school archives. Bill Cromartie of Gridiron Publishers, my fellow writer and friend, has published seven books on national football rivalries; he suggested this history, and his books are inspiring models for this volume.
WGB

Thanks to Josh McCoy, Ole Miss athletics department photographer, for his many contributions to the book. Thanks to Ben King, sports journalist in Oxford, Miss., for his assistance in compiling facts for the appendices and for assisting in researching statistical information.
JR

Thanks to Thomas Wells and his photography crew at the *Northeast Mississippi Daily Journal*; to Daniel Snowden of the University of Mississippi; and to Mike Nemeth, John Cade, and Joe Galbraith at Mississippi State University. Their help with Egg Bowl photographs was invaluable. And a special thanks to Langston Rogers, the recently retired (and deservedly so) senior associate athletics director for media relations at Ole Miss. After twenty-eight years at Ole Miss and another seventeen before that at Delta State University, Rogers has secured a place on any list of Mississippi sports legends.
DM

MILESTONES OF MAYHEM

1893   First football team organized at University of Mississippi;
        first game on campus on November 11: Mississippi 56,
        Southwestern Baptist University 0.

1895   First football team organized at the Agricultural &
        Mechanical College of Mississippi; first game in Jackson,
        Tennessee, on November 16: Southwestern Baptist 21,
        Mississippi A&M 0.

1897   Yellow fever epidemic forces both Mississippi schools to open
        late, causing cancellation of football season.

1898   University resumes football.

1901   A&M resumes football; first A&M–University football game,
        Monday, October 28 at Starkville Fairgrounds; A&M wins
        17–0 for its first-ever football victory.

1902   First University victory over A&M, 21–0 in Starkville.

1903   First University–A&M game in Oxford; first tie, 6–6.

1904   First off-campus game; in Columbus, the University wins
        17–5.

1905   First game in Jackson; first Thanksgiving Day meeting;
        A&M wins 11–0; postgame celebration results in adoption of
        a Bulldog as A&M mascot.

1906   First field goals and first forward passes.

1910   New rule divides game into four quarters rather than two
        equal halves.

1911   Aggies earn first postseason invitation, a New Year's Day
        game in Cuba against the Havana Athletic Club; A&M wins,
        12–0.

1912–14 Three-year hiatus.

1915   Aggies win, 65–0, for largest margin of victory in this rivalry;
        first passing touchdown scored.

1918	A&M and Ole Miss meet twice in a single season because of restrictions on wartime travel; Aggies win 34–0 in Starkville, 13–0 in Oxford.
1921	Ole Miss receives first postseason invitation, losing 14–0 to Cuba's Havana Athletic Club.
1924	A&M wins 20–0 for the school's one hundredth victory all time and Ole Miss's one hundredth defeat.
1926	Fans engage in postgame "Battle of Starkville."
1927	First Battle of the Golden Egg; Ole Miss wins 20–12.
1930	Women are admitted to A&M for the first time since 1912.
1932	Mississippi A&M becomes Mississippi State College.
1933	The two Mississippi schools join eleven other colleges to form the Southeastern Conference.
1935	State obtains first live Bulldog mascot; Ole Miss gets first major postseason bid, losing to Catholic University in the Orange Bowl, 20–19.
1936	Sportswriters select Rebels as Ole Miss nickname; State receives first major postseason bid, losing to Duquesne in the Orange Bowl, 13–12.
1941	State downs Ole Miss 6–0 for first Southeastern Conference crown.
1943	Wartime travel restrictions force cancellation of season.
1946	Maroons score their one hundredth touchdown in the rivalry, winning 20–0.
1947	Ole Miss takes its first Southeastern Conference crown; Rebels beat Texas Christian, 13–9, in the first Delta Bowl.
1949	College football adopts two-platoon play.
1951	Showboat Boykin scores all seven Ole Miss touchdowns in 49–7 win to set one-game National Collegiate Athletic Association scoring record.
1952	Ole Miss posts undefeated season (8–0–2) and goes to its first Sugar Bowl, losing to Georgia Tech, 24–7.
1958	State becomes Mississippi State University.
1959	Ole Miss finishes the season with a 9–1 record and No. 1 national ranking in four rating systems.
1960	Undefeated Rebels repeat as national champions and beat Rice 14–6 in the Sugar Bowl to finish 10–0–1.
1961	State readopts Bulldog nickname.

1962	Ole Miss records 10–0 season mark, including 17–13 victory over Arkansas in Sugar Bowl, finishes No. 3 in both wire-service polls.
1964	First televised State–Ole Miss game; Bulldogs break a seventeen-year drought with 20–17 victory.
1969	Rebels win 48–22 in a game that features the series' most combined total plays, most yards, most first downs, and most pass attempts.
1971	Rebs score 42 points in one quarter, win 48–0.
1972	Rebels take a 51–14 victory for their highest point total in the rivalry.
1978	Jackson newspapers dub the game the Egg Bowl.
1980	The largest crowd ever, 62,250, watches game at newly expanded Mississippi Memorial Stadium in Jackson.
1991	After eighteen games in Jackson, home-and-home campus play resumes in Starkville.
1992	For the first time in twenty-seven years, both teams receive postseason bowl bids: Ole Miss beats Air Force 13–0 in Liberty Bowl; State drops 21–17 decision to North Carolina in Peach Bowl.
1998	State wins 28–6 for its first Southeastern Conference Western Division crown, goes on to play for conference championship.
2000	Rebels win 45–30, the rivalry's highest combined point total.
2003	Rivalry's one-hundredth game, Ole Miss is co-champion of SEC's western division.
2006	Despite disappointing season records of only 3 wins each, a crowd of 57,685 sees the Rebels win 20–17 on a punt return.

THE GOLDEN EGG

I t is one of the most beautiful trophies in college football.

Admired, cherished, loved, the Golden Egg is appropriately named—a gold football atop a shiny gold column on a dark wood base. This three-foot emblem of victory serves as the supreme symbol of superiority in a lengthy rivalry whose roots reflect the early years of football itself. On this handsome trophy is engraved the score of the annual football battle between the University of Mississippi and Mississippi State University, a contest officially known as the Battle of the Golden Egg and more recently termed the Egg Bowl by fans and the media alike.

Only fifteen Division I-A in-state rivalries nationwide have seen more games than Ole Miss and State's 103. But the Golden Egg trophy, conceived in 1927, is the fifth-oldest in Division I-A, trailing only the Territorial Cup (Arizona–Arizona State, created in 1899), the Little Brown Jug (Michigan-Minnesota, 1909), the Illibuck (Illinois–Ohio State, 1925), and the Old Oaken Bucket (Indiana-Purdue, 1926).

While players and occasionally fans have inflicted bodily harm on each other to gain possession of the trophy, the treasured Egg has also suffered—damaged, hidden, even ignored. In fact, the Egg had its genesis in a battle among the fans. In Starkville in 1926, Ole Miss defeated A&M for the first time in thirteen games stretching over sixteen years. Jubilant Ole Miss fans rushed onto Scott Field and began attacking the goalposts. An A&M player challenged his school's supporters to join the fray, and Aggie fans and students defended their honor with weapons including cane-bottom chairs. "A few chairs had to be sacrificed over [some] heads," pointed out the A&M yearbook, the *Reveille*, "to persuade [Ole Miss fans] that was entirely the wrong attitude."

Officials at both schools were genuinely shocked and vowed to prevent such violence from occurring again. Since fans' desire for souvenirs had been at the root of the free-for-all, administrators attempted to find a way to provide the winning school's backers with those souvenirs without bloodshed. The various suggestions bandied about included the idea of shipping the goalposts to the winning school, with the loser footing the bill. Members of Iota Sigma, an Ole Miss fraternity dedicated to promoting school spirit, proposed the creation of an award that would symbolize the rivalry—a special football-shaped trophy that would be presented as the highlight of a dignified postgame ceremony. The name of the new trophy: the Golden Egg.

In a meeting at A&M College on November 9, 1927, just fifteen days before the upcoming game in Oxford, a two-man delegation from Ole Miss met a six-man committee from A&M, and the group enthusiastically approved the creation of a golden football trophy as a calming factor. The award would feature a regulation-size, gold-plated football (slightly more oval than the regulation football of today) mounted on a short, rounded pedestal. One side of the pedestal would bear the inscription "The Golden Egg," while the other side would read "Presented by Ole Miss and A&M Student Bodies, 1927." The two schools would share the $250 cost of creating the trophy. The score of each game would be engraved on the Egg, and the winning school would keep the Egg in a place of honor for a year. (In case of a tie, each school would have possession of the Egg for six months, with the previous year's loser receiving it first.) The joint resolution called for an amicable new spirit "in order to effect a better understanding in athletic relations, to foster clean sportsmanship, and to promote a lasting tradition." To characterize this new approach, student newspapers—Ole Miss's *Mississippian* and A&M's *College Reflector*—jointly called for "a healthy rivalry, free from strife or bitterness." Added the *College Reflector*, "The spirit of rivalry should be . . . intensified by the cleaner sportsmanship which will result." On November 14, the agreement was officially presented to the students at Ole Miss, who were encouraged to provide funds for the new trophy, with contributors who gave as little as 25¢ receiving tags to wear proudly on their shirts.

Fourteen thousand fans—one of the largest crowds in years—packed the stands in Oxford on Thanksgiving afternoon, November 24, 1927, for the first Battle of the Golden Egg, won by Ole Miss, 20–12. As thousands stayed on for the historic, dignified presentation, each student body stood and sang its alma mater. Team captains and the head of each school met in the center of the field. A&M President B. M. Walker presented the Egg to the University's chancellor, Alfred Hume, who in turn presented the trophy to Ole Miss captain Austin Applewhite. While fans cheered, reported the *Mississippian*, "a score of students" carried Applewhite and the shiny new Egg off the field. A new day had dawned "to promote a lasting tradition," and "sincere handshaking" was noted among players, with "not a single demonstration of violence." The new symbol of friendly competition quickly became each school's most cherished possession.

Despite the original resolution, sharing the Egg has not always been a gracious act. In 1929, the schools tied, and as the agreement dictated, the Aggies (losers the previous year) took the Egg first. But A&M refused to surrender the trophy, and Ole Miss never got its six months with the Egg. Similarly, after 1964's upset victory that ended the Bulldogs' long drought, State kept the Egg for two years on the premise that it had been "too long without it."

The trophy has undergone a number of changes over the years. In the mid-1930s, a new, dark base was added, and a 1935 photo shows the base adorned with ribbons representing the colors of the two schools. Until 1950, the score of each year's contest was engraved on the Egg itself. With no more room available on the trophy, however, a circular gold base was added for subsequent scores. In the spring of 1958, the trophy was replated, with the two schools splitting the bill. The Egg was also replated in 1974, but someone apparently neglected to tell its keepers: for a while, officials feared that the trophy had been lost, but a Gulfport jeweler announced that he was refurbishing the Egg. By 1981 the Golden Egg was again showing the ravages of neglect. Mishandling in overly enthusiastic postgame celebrations had left the trophy badly dented. The Egg toppled off its platform, and the entire trophy easily came apart. Repairs were undertaken, with Ole Miss and State sharing the four-thousand-dollar cost. The dents were removed, the Egg was replated, and dark walnut trim was added to the rounded base. After the 1992 game, the "new" base added in the early 1950s had no more room for game results. To handle additional scores, a square, five-inch wood platform was added, with brass plates on each side to hold additional scores for many years to come.

Presentation of the Egg remained a highlight of each game through the 1930s and 1940s, but interest waned during the 1950s and 1960s, and few fans paid attention to the Egg's presentation. In 1978, however, Tom Patterson, executive sports editor of the *Jackson Clarion-Ledger/Daily News*, sought to breathe new life into coverage of the Battle of the Golden Egg. The paper printed daily reports about each team during the week before the game, and game-day coverage bore the bold headline, "Egg Bowl." And so the game has been known ever since. Today the Golden Egg again holds a prominent place of honor at both schools. The Egg annually appears on the sideline, and after each year's contest, the governor presents the trophy to the winning school.

THE EGG BOWL

A GREAT RIVALRY BEGINS

In the dry autumn of 1901, cotton was still king, and from the Delta fields to the hill country, farmers were busy gathering their big-money crop. More than forty-one hundred cotton gins awaited the harvest. Mississippi's population was 1.5 million, and Democratic Governor Andrew H. Longino was attempting to attract industry to help diversify the economy of his mostly agricultural state. Construction on the new capitol in Jackson had just begun.

Enrollment at both the University of Mississippi and Mississippi Agricultural & Mechanical College was small. The University, which had opened on November 6, 1848, was in its forty-ninth year, having closed during the Civil War. Enrollment was 257. A&M had opened on October 6, 1880, and was in its twenty-second year. Enrollment was 517—all male. As a land-grant college, a military regimen was required. Students wore gray cadet uniforms and marched to classes, and a bugle announced most routines.

Rutgers and Princeton had played the nation's first intercollegiate football game in 1867, but acceptance of the sport by southern colleges was slow to come. Baseball drew the most headlines. Gradually, however, colleges in the South began forming teams and crowd interest developed. Kentucky claims the Southeast's first football game, played in 1881, but then dropped the sport for ten years. In 1890, Vanderbilt first played. In 1892, Georgia, Georgia Tech, and Auburn fielded their inaugural teams. The University of Mississippi organized its first team in 1893, at the same time as Alabama, Louisiana State, and Tulane. Mississippi Agricultural & Mechanical College organized a team for intercollegiate play in 1895. Tennessee's first season was 1896. Florida's first was 1906. Very few schedules were made before school began, and teams usually played between four and six games per season. Coaches, most often hired on a onetime basis, usually left soon after season's end.

A professor in the Classics Department organized the University of Mississippi team. Dr. Alexander L. Bondurant so admired the strong competitive spirit of football teams he saw in the East that he introduced the game to an enthusiastic group of athletes and set up an intensive training program. Bondurant also hired the first coach and chose as team colors the cardinal red of Harvard and the navy blue of Yale: "It was well to have the spirit of these two good colleges," he wrote years later. The University's first game, against Southwestern Baptist University (now Union University), occurred on November 11, 1893, at Oxford's University Park, a baseball field that stood just west of the site of present-day Vaught-Hemingway Stadium. The Red and Blue easily won a 56–0 victory.

The first taste of football at the Agricultural & Mechanical College was informal, consisting of intramural class play and occasional student-faculty games. Agriculture student W. M. Matthews of Harrisburg, Texas, organized the first A&M school team. Like the Mississippi squad, A&M played its first game against Southwestern Baptist: on November 16, 1895, the Aggies traveled to Jackson, Tennessee, where they absorbed a 21–0 defeat. En route, Matthews received the honor of choosing the team colors, declaring without hesitation, "Maroon and white." A&M played only one other game that year, four the next. Despite an exchange of letters, A&M and the University could not agree on a meeting date, so a game between the new arrivals remained merely talk.

An 1897 yellow fever epidemic delayed the opening of both A&M and the University and resulted in the cancellation of the football season. Though the University resumed play in 1898, A&M did not field a team for three more years. In 1901, with support of college president Jack Hardy, A&M revived its football team. An alumnus and professor of military science, I. D. Sessums, brought in L. B. Harvey, a halfback from Georgetown College in Kentucky, to serve as player-coach. And Sessums persuaded the football team from the University of Mississippi to stop off on its way back from a game against the University of Alabama in Tuscaloosa and square off against the A&M squad.

A&M fielded a young, inexperienced team, excited about resuming a football program that had lapsed for four years. The Aggies had never won a game. They had never even scored a point. Their best effort had been a scoreless tie in the season's opener. The University was in its eighth season, having posted an overall record of 18–14, including 1–1 in this still-young season.

The first contest between A&M and the University was on Monday, October 28, 1901, on an improvised gridiron located on the infield of a racetrack at a fairground in Starkville. The field measured 110 yards, and teams had three attempts to gain the required five yards for a first down. A touchdown was worth five points. Though one newspaper reported the game "well attended," most likely it attracted few spectators other than the A&M cadets. Very few Mississippians knew much about football, and no high school in the state adopted the game until 1905. Football uniforms were mostly catch-as-catch-can—a few regular football pants and shirts but often baseball uniforms or heavy turtlenecks. There also was a scattering of shin guards and nose guards. With no helmets, players often let hair grow long, particularly because ladies admired the "football topknot." There were few rules against rough play; with little or no padding, serious injury was all too common and death was not unknown. On the day of this contest, an Ohio State player died from injuries sustained in a game several days earlier.

Coaching the University was Daniel S. Martin, a 1900 Auburn University graduate. He had come in to finish the season after the unexpected departure of Coach William Sibley, a Virginia graduate who reported difficulty in getting enough players to come out for football. Captaining the University squad was right end Fred W. Elmer; A&M was headed by right tackle J. C. Mahoney, who at two hundred pounds was unusually large for that time. Officiating were umpire Fountain Cocke of Columbus, and referee W. S. Davis, an A&M student.

Since this inauspicious beginning, the two teams have faced off 103 times in seven different cities—Starkville, Oxford, Jackson, Columbus, Tupelo, Clarksdale, and Greenwood. An estimated thirty-five hundred players have given their all before roughly 2.8 million highly enthusiastic, sincerely prejudiced fans in what they proudly call the South's Fiercest Football Rivalry.

1901

The First Feud, the First Protest, the First Delay, and Finally the First Game

1901 SCHEDULES

Mississippi 2–4

RESULT	DATE	PF	OPPONENT	PA	LOCATION
W	October 19	6	Memphis University School	0	Oxford
L	October 26	0	Alabama	41	Tuscaloosa
L	October 28	0	Mississippi A&M	17	Starkville
W	November 2	17	Southwestern Baptist*	0	Oxford
L	November 7	0	Louisiana State	46	Baton Rouge
L	November 28	11	Tulane	25	New Orleans

Mississippi A&M 2–2–1

RESULT	DATE	PF	OPPONENT	PA	LOCATION
T	October 26	0	Christian Brothers	0	Memphis
W	October 28	17	Mississippi	0	Starkville
W	November 2	11	Meridian Athletic Club	5	Meridian
L	November 9	6	Tulane	24	New Orleans
L	November 16	0	Alabama	45	Tuscaloosa

* Now Union

It was only fitting that A&M and the University should meet. But after years of delay, the game had to wait another forty minutes from the scheduled 3:30 kickoff as the two teams debated the eligibility of A&M's Norvin E. (Billy) Green, who had played for the University's squad the previous year. According to the *College Reflector*, "After we agreed to take Green out they kicked against [left end F. D.] Harris saying he was from Chattanooga and was being paid to play, and a number of other things—all of which are false." Harris eventually was approved, and at long last, the Aggies kicked off.

The first A&M–University football game was under way. Finally.

The kickoff went to University fullback Guy Dean, who was tackled before he reached midfield. A fumble soon followed, and the Aggies recovered

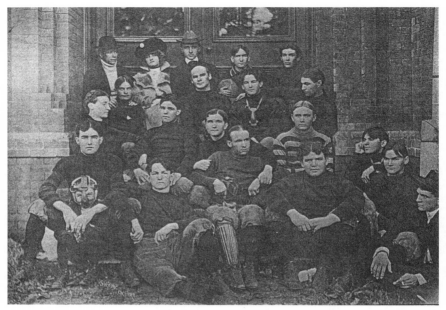

These sixteen players represented the University in the first football game with A&M. Though no identifications were listed, on the top row is Dan Martin, left, who coached the University in the first two rivalry
games, then coached A&M in the next four. In the center is Dr. A. L. Bondurant, who introduced football at
the University. No photo of the 1901 Aggie team is known to exist. University of Mississippi Archives.

the ball. After "several good gains," the *Reflector* reported, left halfback and
coach L. B. Harvey "bucked center for four yards . . . and the first touchdown."
With each touchdown worth five points and Harvey "kicking goal" for the
extra point, the score stood at 6–0.

The rules stated that the scoring team would receive the ensuing kickoff,
and Aggie tackle R. S. Wilson returned the ball 40 yards to the Mississippi
50 (the center of the 110-yard field was the 55). H. H. Pearson gained 15 yards,
Wilson added 5 yards, and J. C. Mahoney tacked on 10 before Harvey galloped
around right end for 18. Harvey probably would have scored but fumbled when
hit by Mississippi's captain, Fred W. Elmer. Pearson snatched up the loose ball
and burst the remaining 2 yards for the score. Though Harvey missed the goal
after, the Aggies had an 11–0 advantage.

After the University covered a fumble, Stone and Elmer picked up 15
yards. However, the Red and Blue failed to get another first down, and the ball
went over to the Aggies. The Aggies drove downfield, and Harvey scored his
team's third touchdown of the day on a 30-yard gallop. He ran the point after
to put his team up 17–0 at the half.

The A&M student newspaper headlined the first football clash between the Aggies and "the University boys" in this manner. *College Reflector,* 1901.

Although the rules dictated two equal halves, the delay in starting and the onset of darkness combined to cut the second half to only six minutes. No more scoring occurred, and A&M had the first victory in school history.

Despite the Aggie victory, the *College Reflector* declared, "The University boys . . . played the dirtiest game of ball that we have seen. They would do anything to put our men out so long as the referee was not looking." Retorted the *University of Mississippi Magazine*, "To one who has never indulged in any exercise more violent than . . . the milking of the patient cow, football seems a brutal sport. Our bucolic friend of the Agricultural College should confine himself to mumble-peg and townball."

It would obviously be a long and intense rivalry.

1902

Oktibbeha State
Fairgrounds,
Starkville

No Feuding. No Fussing. Just Plain, Tough Football

1902 SCHEDULES

Mississippi 4–3

RESULT	DATE	PF	OPPONENT	PA	LOCATION
L	October 11	0	Vanderbilt	29	Nashville
W	October 18	38	Cumberland	0	Oxford
W	October 25	21	Mississippi A&M	0	Starkville
W	November 1	42	Memphis University School	0	Oxford
L	November 8	0	Louisiana State	6	New Orleans
L	November 15	10	Tennessee	11	Memphis
W	November 27	10	Tulane	0	New Orleans

Mississippi A&M 1–4–1

RESULT	DATE	PF	OPPONENT	PA	LOCATION
L	October 17	6	Cumberland	15	Starkville
L	October 25	0	Mississippi	21	Starkville
T	November 1	11	Tulane	11	New Orleans
L	November 8	0	Alabama	27	Tuscaloosa
W	November 15	26	Howard*	0	Birmingham
L	November 27	0	Louisiana State	6	Starkville

* Now Samford

After serious feuding had marred the first game, A&M and the University did an about-face in 1902. On an unseasonably warm Saturday, October 25, the two teams played a straightforward game of football. No arguments. No delays. "Everything moved off smoothly," declared the *Memphis Commercial Appeal*, "without friction or fussing." And it was a "clean, hard game," declared A&M's *College Reflector*. Added the Memphis story, "None of the players sustained any serious injury."

Coach Dan S. Martin was in his second year at Mississippi, while recent Auburn graduate Jerry Gwin was at the Aggies' helm—and refereed the game. The University had its ties to the officials as well: umpire J. W. S. Rhea had assisted Dr. A. L. Bondurant when he organized the first team in Oxford in 1893.

As in 1901, the contest was held in the infield of the Starkville fairgrounds racetrack, although this time, according to the *Commercial Appeal*, a "large and enthusiastic crowd" was in attendance. The school in Oxford, already beginning to be known as Ole Miss, after the yearbook, led 6–0 at halftime and won the contest by a score of 21–0. Extant newspaper accounts of the game give few details, although Mississippi apparently dominated. Halfback John M. Foster reeled off a 65-yard run, while Fred W. Elmer recorded a 40-yard dash and Clyde Connor "plunged through the line at will," according to the Memphis paper.

Captain John M. Foster, whose 65-yard breakaway was one of the long runs that kept the University offense moving and led to victory. *Ole Miss*.

Though regulations called for two twenty-five-minute halves, the second half was called with two and a half minutes remaining, the newspaper explained, "to enable the visitors to catch their train." No complaints were reported from the Aggies, however; they had "had enough," the paper declared, "and were more than willing for [the University players] to go."

A sharp line of cadets appear before the A&M Main Dormitory in 1902. Eventually known endearingly as "Old Main," at one time the building was the nation's largest dormitory under one roof. Mississippi State University Photo.

GAME 3

University Park,
Oxford

1903

The Red and Blue Shades the Aggies' Perfect Record

1903 SCHEDULES

Mississippi 2–1–1

RESULT	DATE	PF	OPPONENT	PA	LOCATION
L	October 24	0	Vanderbilt	33	Nashville
W	November 7	17	Tennessee Medical College	0	Memphis
T	November 14	6	Mississippi A&M	6	Oxford
W	November 21	11	Louisiana State	0	New Orleans

Mississippi A&M 3–0–2

RESULT	DATE	PF	OPPONENT	PA	LOCATION
W	October 16	11	Alabama	0	Columbus
W	October 24	43	Meridian Athletic Club	0	Meridian
W	November 7	11	Louisiana State	0	Starkville
T	November 14	6	Mississippi	6	Oxford
T	December 5	0	Tulane	0	New Orleans

When they arrived in Oxford, the Mississippi A&M Aggies carried a record any team would envy: undefeated, untied, unscored on. When they left old University Park, only one of those celebrated claims survived. Mississippi scored with less than a minute remaining to earn a narrow 6–6 tie, the only points the high-flying Aggies would surrender all year. A&M posted its first undefeated season. The next would not come until 1940.

Interest in the A&M–University game had soared: "Big Game for Oxford," headlined the weekly *Jackson Clarion-Ledger* more than two weeks before game day, Saturday, November 14. Red and blue bunting appeared everywhere in Oxford, which was hosting its first contest between the Aggies and the Red and Blue. "The national football flower—the chrysanthemum," said the *Memphis Commercial Appeal*, "will be worn in a shade of red by more fastidious rooters." Both teams, said one pregame report, "contain the best

The T Formation is not so new, after all. University players used the T in 1903. In four-point stances are, from left, linemen Leo Shumacker, Marion Reiley, Edward L. Dent, Thomas J. Hopkins, Allen P. Dodd, Edgar Moss, and Frank Fair; backs are quarterback Thomas B. Watkins, right halfback Fred Elmer, fullback J. S. Yerger, and left halfback Oman L. Kimbrough. University of Mississippi Archives.

material they have had for several seasons" and are "expected to maintain the state's reputation on the athletic field."

Now coaching at Starkville was Dan S. Martin, who had directed the University in its first two games against A&M. The University squad was led by new coach Mike Harvey, a teammate of Martin's at Auburn. The Aggies had left Starkville in high spirits, the Memphis paper reported. "Never has a team and supporters been more confident of victory. The Aggies expect their physical condition to prove better than the Oxford players."

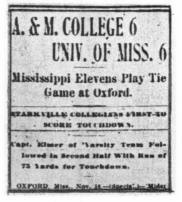

A. & M. COLLEGE 6

UNIV. OF MISS. 6

Mississippi Elevens Play Tie Game at Oxford.

STARKVILLE COLLEGIANS FIRST TO SCORE TOUCHDOWN.

Capt. Elmer of 'Varsity Team Followed in Second Half With Run of 75 Yards for Touchdown.

OXFORD, Miss., Nov. 14.—(Special.)—Midst

The first tie in the series rated a sizable headline in the *Commercial Appeal*, November 15, 1903.

The game was scheduled for 3:30 at University Park, a baseball field located just west of the site of present-day Vaught-Hemingway Stadium. The field was so dusty, complained A&M's *College Reflector*, that "the boys were almost choking." Both teams still had mismatched uniforms, and both coaches served as officials, an ideal way for them to watch the game closely. However, *University Magazine* complained that Martin took advantage of the situation, spending "considerable time" measuring for downs "in order to wind his men."

On an early possession, the Red and Blue drove deep into Aggie territory. But, said the *Reflector*, guard Hugh Overstreet "broke through the line and tackled [halfback Orman] Kimbrough so hard that he fumbled." Near the end of the first half, the heavier A&M line began to have its way with the University men, and despite the University players' vow that they "would rather die" than see A&M score, Aggie right halfback C. S. Fugler was pushed over the goal line with just two minutes to go in the half. At the time, aiding a runner or even tossing him over the line was legal. Norvin E. (Billy) Green kicked the extra point to give A&M a 6–0 edge.

Neither team threatened seriously through most of the second half. With less than a minute remaining, however, Mississippi right halfback Fred Elmer circled right end and galloped 70 yards for the touchdown. "Hundreds went wild," reported the *Commercial Appeal*. Edgar Moss kicked "an easy goal" to knot the count at 6–6. And there the game ended, the first tie between the two schools.

1904

GAME 4

Mississippi and West
Alabama Fairgrounds,
Columbus

Columbus Gets Its "Good Game"

1904 SCHEDULES

Mississippi 4–3

RESULT	DATE	PF	OPPONENT	PA	LOCATION
L	October 15	0	Vanderbilt	69	Nashville
W	October 22	17	Mississippi A&M	5	Columbus
W	October 29	114	Southwestern Baptist*	0	Oxford
L	November 5	0	Louisiana State	5	Baton Rouge
W	November 12	42	Tennessee Medical College	0	Jackson
W	November 19	12	Nashville	5	Memphis
L	November 24	0	Tulane	22	New Orleans

Mississippi A&M 2–5

RESULT	DATE	PF	OPPONENT	PA	LOCATION
L	October 1	0	Vanderbilt	61	Columbus
L	October 15	0	Alabama	6	Columbus
L	October 22	5	Mississippi	17	Columbus
L	October 29	0	Tulane	10	New Orleans
W	November 11	59	Tennessee Medical College	0	Starkville
L	November 18	5	Cumberland	27	Starkville
W	November 25	32	Industrial Institute and College of Louisiana**	5	Starkville

* Now Union
** Now Louisiana Tech

O n Thursday, October 18, 1904, the *Columbus Weekly Commercial* reported that a football game would be held as part of the Mississippi and West Alabama Fair. No teams were announced, but "a good game is assured," the paper reported. When fans learned that the participants would be A&M and the University, alumni began placing bets and packing picnic baskets.

The Aggies entered the game with two big questions. Coach Dan Martin had suffered a bout of typhoid fever and had not arrived on campus until just ten days before the season opener, limiting the team's preparation. Second, the Southern Intercollegiate Athletic Association had banned A&M captain Norvin E. (Billy) Green after he staged a protest during the previous week's game against Alabama in Columbus. Hugh Overstreet replaced Green as the Aggie captain; nevertheless, Green was on the field, sharing the officiating duties with Will Ulmer of Oxford.

Saturday, October 22, saw two thousand excited fans watching from carriages or standing on the sidelines, pressing as close as possible to the makeshift gridiron laid out at the fairgrounds. The game marked the first off-campus contest between the squads, and neither team arrived in Columbus until just hours before kickoff. In addition to enthusiastic alumni of both schools, the crowd included substantial numbers of A&M cadets, who had poured into Columbus by train and even by horseback. The *Columbus Weekly Dispatch* reported that "white and maroon . . . were in evidence everywhere on the streets," and the A&M boys "received . . . many social courtesies." Female students from the Industrial Institute and College (later Mississippi State College for Women, now Mississippi University for Women) had been given a holiday on Friday and came to the game on Saturday—with chaperones, of course.

The University gained a 17–5 victory as the heavier Oxford players, averaging 149 pounds, "outplayed their rivals at almost every point." Two first-half touchdowns and extra points gave the University a 12–0 lead at the break. A&M closed the gap with a second-half touchdown but missed the extra point, and the Red and Blue added another touchdown for the day's final points. Said the *Weekly Dispatch*, "The game was a pretty one from start to finish, though the last half was much more exciting. Both sides played fiercely." The *Reflector* praised the play of the University's Cleveland Huggins and declared that those who "held the laurels for A and M" were J. G. Russell, R. S. Wilson, and Hugh Overstreet.

1905

GAME 5

Mississippi State
Fairgrounds, Jackson

The First Bulldogs Prove Their Mettle

1905 SCHEDULES

Mississippi 0–2

RESULT	DATE	PF	OPPONENT	PA	LOCATION
L	November 20	0	Cumberland	18	Oxford
L	November 30	0	Mississippi A&M	11	Jackson

Mississippi A&M 3–4

RESULT	DATE	PF	OPPONENT	PA	LOCATION
L	October 14	0	Alabama	34	Tuscaloosa
W	October 20	38	Marion Military Institute	0	Marion
L	October 27	0	Auburn	18	Columbus
W	November 11	44	Howard*	0	Starkville
L	November 18	5	Cumberland	27	Starkville
W	November 30	11	Mississippi	0	Jackson
L	December 1	0	Louisiana State	15	Baton Rouge

* Now Samford

I t was a spectators' game. Literally. On Thanksgiving Day, November 30, the University and A&M were meeting in Jackson for the first time, and the fans' unbridled enthusiasm proved almost overwhelming. With no ropes to bar the way, the crowd poured out onto the playing field for a closer look at what, for many, was their first college game. The curious got so close that they even "crowded the players," reported the *Daily Clarion-Ledger*. At one point, the University captain refused to continue until the field was cleared.

The problem was the poor view from the grandstand, which was situated at one end of the field, beyond an end zone, making much of the play seem far distant. Moreover, the grandstand accommodated only about a quarter of the five thousand in attendance. Neither police nor the pleas of Governor James K. Vardaman could influence the members of the crowd, whose conduct grew worse in the second half.

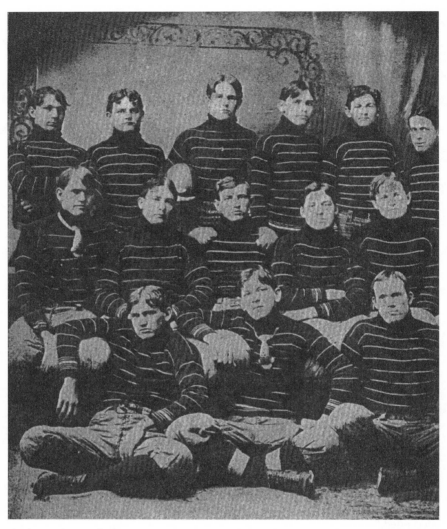

First known photograph of an A&M team. Among these triumphant Aggies are the starting eleven who played every down against the University and inspired a victory celebration that led to adoption of "Bulldogs" as team nickname. No identifications were listed, but Captain Hal McGeorge is top row, third from left. *Reveille*.

In addition to spectator interference, the game suffered from deplorable field conditions, with mud making fast play almost impossible. A Jackson reporter called the game "one of the most uninteresting and unsatisfactory . . . played by college teams." It "drug on in a lifeless kind of way," and its ending came "to the relief of all." Nevertheless, the game was a money-maker, netting the schools $594, a tidy sum in those years. A&M and the University would return to Jackson.

Both teams came to Mississippi's capital on the afternoon before the game. The Aggies, staying at the Martin and Gaddis Building, immediately went to look over the fairgrounds field. The University team stayed at the Edwards Hotel. Special trains brought students from both schools on the morning of the game. The Aggie cadets left at 4:30 in the morning. Six hours later, they marched up Capitol Street to the governor's mansion for an address by Governor Vardaman. Scheduled for three o'clock, kickoff occurred fifteen minutes late.

The University won the toss and chose the north goal. Cadet captain Hal McGeorge's kickoff went 40 yards. Richard C. Beckett took the ball at his 17 and returned it to the 19. Cleveland Huggins gained 5 yards but then lost the ball. The Red and Blue stopped the Aggie threat at the 2, setting the tone for what would be a back-and-forth first half played mostly in Mississippi territory.

The Aggies took a 6–0 lead when right tackle H. H. Cutrer crossed the goal line to cap a drive that included a double lateral play. McGeorge tossed the ball to halfback R. K. McIntosh, who ran around left end before lateraling to halfback V. B. Alexander, who ran for 25 yards. McGeorge added the extra point.

The Cadets scored again early in the second half after Alexander recorded another 25-yard triple play. The drive also featured carries by ends Joe Whitaker and E. D. DeBaum, while tackle H. D. Tate did the scoring honors with a 12-yard run into a corner of the end zone. Coach Dan Martin of A&M, said the *Daily Clarion-Ledger*, "made frequent attempts to go on the field in violation of the rules to coach his men. Sometimes he was stopped, and occasionally succeeded."

The Red and Blue's only chance for a score came on a threat led by quarterback James A. Finley and halfbacks John R. Shields and James B. Perkins Jr. But Cleve Huggins missed a field goal on a drop-kick attempt.

The game ended at 5:25 after two hours and ten minutes of intensive play. A&M took the 11–0 victory on "sheer strength and giant force," the *Clarion-Ledger* analyzed, because the University "was in poor condition, lacking in skill and science, lighter than their opponents." "A&M had better teamwork, better interference and formed its plays quicker." Huggins's kicking, said the paper, was the University's only claim to superiority.

Perhaps more significant for the Starkville school, the game saw the birth of its new nickname. "The A&M boys, 700 strong," reported the *Memphis Commercial Appeal*, "marched through the principal streets, bearing a big pine coffin on their shoulders and preceded by a brass band playing the funeral dirge for 'Ole Miss.'" The coffin was decorated in University colors, with a bulldog pup sitting on top. From then on, the Mississippi State squad was known as the Bulldogs. The Aggie tradition of conducting funeral services for Ole Miss continued as late as 1941, when the Maroon Band played a funeral dirge as part of its halftime show.

Five days before this game, high school football came to Mississippi. A team from Yazoo City scored a single touchdown to beat a visiting squad from Winona, 5–0.

The 1905 season also resulted in other major developments. Fourteen men had been killed while playing football during the year, and seventy-one had died over the preceding five years. Such shocking brutality resulted in public outrage, with President Theodore Roosevelt among those demanding changes to the game. A poem in A&M's student newspaper, the *College Reflector*, illustrated the public attitude.

FOOTBALL DAYS
The football days have come again, the gladdest of the year;
One side of Willie's nose is gone, and Tom has lost an ear;
Heaped on the field the players jab and punch and claw and tear;
They knock the breath of those beneath and gouge without a care.

In response to the public outcry, representatives of sixty-two major colleges met in New York in December 1905 and approved a series of rule changes to open up and speed up the game. Most importantly, the forward pass would now be legal. In addition, teams would have to cover 10 yards rather than 5 to get a first down, although they still had only three downs to do so. The time of each half was reduced from thirty-five to thirty minutes, and each team had to have six players on the line of scrimmage at all times.

These changes did not take long to make themselves felt in the annual contest between Mississippi and A&M. In fact, the forward pass would prove decisive in the very next game between the two schools.

1906

GAME 6

Mississippi State
Fairgrounds, Jackson

Passing Fancy

Mississippi 4–2

RESULT	DATE	PF	OPPONENT	PA	LOCATION
W	October 4	16	Maryville	6	Oxford
L	October 13	0	Vanderbilt	29	Nashville
W	October 20	9	Louisiana State	0	Baton Rouge
W	November 3	17	Tulane	0	New Orleans
L	November 12	0	Sewanee	24	Memphis
W	November 29	29	Mississippi A&M	5	Jackson

Mississippi A&M 2–2–1

RESULT	DATE	PF	OPPONENT	PA	LOCATION
W	September 29	30	Howard*	0	Starkville
W	October 13	62	Marion Military Institute	0	Starkville
T	October 27	0	Louisiana State	0	Columbus
L	November 3	4	Alabama	16	Starkville
L	November 29	5	Mississippi	29	Jackson

* Now Samford

F or the second consecutive year, A&M and the University met in Jackson on Thanksgiving afternoon. For the first time, however, the game marked the end of the season for not one but both teams. On this sunny afternoon, some five thousand fans jammed the grandstand as part of the Mississippi Industrial Exposition. Though many of the spectators watched from the sidelines, none of the crowd-control problems that had marred the previous year's game recurred. Special trains brought students from Oxford and Starkville. The A&M cadets and girls from the Industrial Institute and College (later Mississippi State College for Women, now Mississippi University for Women) filled thirteen coaches, the Jackson paper reported, and two more cars were picked up in Durant. Attendance by "the ladies" was "especially large," reported the *Jackson Evening News*. "Every vehicle in town

In the year that passing was legalized in college football, the first to be completed in a University–A&M game was a toss from Ole Miss's Cleve Huggins (standing, right) to Jim Elmer (standing, fourth from left). Players are, from left, kneeling, Andrew Wood and A. H. (Gus) McDonnell; standing, G. H. Robertson, G. C. Bates, D. G. Wettlin, Jim Elmer, W. N. McLeod, Clyde Conner, Jim Cunningham, E. L. Meaders, Captain Huggins. *Ole Miss.*

has been engaged for the ladies," the paper continued, "and the college colors are everywhere apparent, ribbon stocks . . . in the local stores being well-nigh exhausted."

Tom S. Hammond of Michigan served as Mississippi's coach; Cleve Huggins was captain. Captain for the Aggies was center O. B. Wooten, serving in place of Hal McGeorge, who had broken his collarbone against Louisiana State and was serving as head linesman for the game. Dan Martin was in his fourth and last year as A&M's coach.

At 3:10 P.M., Mississippi's James C. Elmer kicked off from the south goal. Despite a weight advantage of nearly ten pounds that would seem to have dictated a strong ground game, the University was eager to try the newly approved forward pass. On its second possession, the Oxford team attempted the first pass in an A&M–University game. The rules stated that an incomplete pass resulted in a turnover, and that is exactly what happened: A&M had possession of the ball on its own 12 yard line. Undaunted, the Red and Blue

The Aggie squad of 1906 included two complete teams, ready for action. Though no identifications are listed, Dan Martin, top right, coached A&M teams between 1903 and 1906 and previously was coach at Ole Miss for the rivalry's first two games. *Reveille*.

tried another pass on its next possession, and this time, the play succeeded, as Huggins connected with Elmer for a 15-yard gain, the first completed forward pass in the history of the rivalry. With a new rule requiring ten yards for a first down and still only three downs to make it, use of the forward pass became almost a requirement.

The Red and Blue crossed the goal line less than ten minutes into the game, capitalizing on an A&M fumble. D. G. Wettlin smashed 25 yards for the touchdown, and Huggins's kick made the score 6–0. The University launched three more threats, including the first field goal attempt in a clash between these two teams, but none succeeded in early play. As with the forward pass, however, the second time was the charm for a field goal, and Elmer kicked from the 19 for the rivalry's first successful field goal. With field goals worth four points, the halftime score read 10–0.

The Aggies' only pass attempt came early in the second half. The throw fell incomplete, giving the ball to the University squad, and Elmer's second field goal followed shortly. This one, from the 25, made the score 14–0.

Mississippi quickly scored again on Gus McDonnell's 70-yard breakaway, with Cunningham and Huggins paving the way. McDonnell's run "set the crowd wild with enthusiasm"—so wild, declared the *Jackson Evening News*, that "the wire fence on the west side of the gridiron was broken down by the mad rush of the frenzied enthusiasts." Elmer kicked the point after to put his team up 20–0. S. T. Pilkinton counted Mississippi's next touchdown when he snatched up teammate Huggins's punt on the A&M 25 and dashed into the end zone, but Elmer missed the extra point.

With one wire fence down, the other fence was soon to go. When A&M launched its only foray of the day into Mississippi territory, left halfback J. F. Montgomery capped the drive from midfield with a long touchdown run; in the ensuing celebration, said the *Evening News*, "the A&M contingent, which had been rather silent throughout the contest, grew so enthusiastic that the wire fence on the east side went down in the pell-mell rush." The try for goal failed, and the score stood at 25–5.

A third field goal set a rivalry record not equaled for 70 years. Elmer's 45-yard kick went through, the *Daily Clarion-Ledger* wrote, "at the very instant that the timekeeper called the game," making the final score 29–5. As dusk descended, wrote the *Clarion-Ledger* reporter, "a big laughing moon, early rising as if to watch the close of the struggle, pulled itself gently from the eastern horizon and cast a silvery glow over the assembled throng."

The forward pass had made the difference. Mississippi had completed five of the nine passes it attempted, while A&M's only throw had fallen incomplete. In this game, wrote the *Clarion-Ledger*, "the new rules were seen better than they have . . . been demonstrated . . . and . . . proved interesting for those familiar with the technical points."

1907

Knee-Deep in Rivalry
(and Sky-High over the Coffee)

1907 SCHEDULES

Mississippi 0–6

RESULT	DATE	PF	OPPONENT	PA	LOCATION
L	October 12	0	Alabama	20	Columbus
L	October 19	6	Missouri Normal*	12	Oxford
L	October 26	0	Sewanee	65	Memphis
L	November 9	0	Vanderbilt	60	Memphis
L	November 16	0	Louisiana State	23	Jackson
L	November 28	0	Mississippi A&M	15	Jackson

Mississippi A&M 6–3

RESULT	DATE	PF	OPPONENT	PA	LOCATION
W	October 2	7	Southwestern**	0	Starkville
L	October 10	0	Sewanee	38	Sewanee
W	October 12	12	Howard***	5	Birmingham
W	October 19	80	Union	0	Starkville
W	October 24	75	Mercer	0	Columbus
W	October 30	6	Drury	0	Starkville
L	November 9	11	Louisiana State	23	Baton Rouge
L	November 16	4	Tennessee	11	Memphis
W	November 28	15	Mississippi	0	Jackson

* Now Southeast Missouri
** Now Rhodes
*** Now Samford

Torrential rains hit Jackson prior to the Thanksgiving 1907 clash between A&M and Ole Miss, creating an atmosphere that must have been more like a circus than the real three-ring show that had just vacated the field. Players slipped and slid, even disappearing at times into the water that flowed nearly knee-deep across the sloping field. Officials had to hold the ball in place so that it wouldn't float off before the center could snap it. The fairgrounds' management had tried in vain to fill many of the holes created by the circus tent stakes, but a Thanksgiving morning game between

Great Game of Football Was Played in Mud and Water, But Great Crowd of Wet Spectators Enjoyed the Fun.

Perhaps the writer of this headline knew about the whiskey in the coffee pot that helped spectators— and Ole Miss players, too—survive the mud and misery of a wet Thanksgiving afternoon at the state fairgrounds. *Daily Clarion-Ledger*, November 29, 1907.

Jackson High and Chamberlain-Hunt Academy had done even more damage. Spectators, too, were mired in the muck and mud. "Foot passengers waded . . . to their shoetops," reported the *Jackson Clarion-Ledger*, "and were a bedraggled sight."

Nevertheless, the Jackson paper opined, the conditions did not seem to bother the players, "those sturdy youngsters who were to take all the risks of broken bones . . . and death by strangulation in the pools of . . . uncertain depths." While the heavier Aggies were favored, the paper declared that they "were no fuller of bull-dog determination than the University." The Red and Blue was struggling, with just two players back from last year (including captain and right end Andrew Wood) plus the problems of adjusting to a new coach, Frank Mason—"a Harvard man," as the newspaper pointed out. A&M had Fred John Furman, a 1905 graduate of Cornell who also served as a history and civics instructor. One of the Aggie stars was the coach's brother, Harry (Little) Furman, who had scored seven touchdowns each in two of the team's earlier games that season.

A&M captain Hal McGeorge, the only man to serve three years in that role, kicked off the game at 2:30 on a cold, wet Thanksgiving afternoon. A&M threatened early when a Mississippi punt went only to its 25, but a fumble ended the drive. The University then recovered a punt on the Aggie 20 but could gain only 2 yards. Another Mississippi threat that fizzled saw Ike Knox and W. L. Pfeffer carrying and quarterback Roy W. Carruth passing to Chuck Trotter, the only completion by either team in this second year of legitimate forward passes. By this time, "contestants had been soused in water up to their ears," the *Daily Clarion-Ledger* observed, "and were wet and fighting muddy."

The half ended 0–0. When the University kicked off to begin the second half, the players wore an obvious glow. Coach Mason had a large urn of coffee on the sidelines for his team and the few spectators lucky enough to be standing by. To take the chill out of the damp day, Mason poured in a generous portion of "cold medicine"—about ninety proof. On the field, however, conditions were so bad that officials occasionally halted the game so that players could "wipe the mud and water off and find out who everyone was," recalled spectator Marshall T. (Jake) Adams many years later.

The Aggies finally broke through with a long drive that started on the Mississippi 54 and was capped by McGeorge's 1-yard run. A&M missed the extra point but added another touchdown minutes later when McGeorge snapped up a blocked Mississippi field goal attempt and raced 80 yards for the touchdown while Aggie cadets wildly cheered. Another quick score followed a blocked punt on the University 10. E. D. McEnnis bucked over from the four to put A&M up 15–0, and there the game ended.

The only player to serve as captain at A&M for three consecutive years, Hal McGeorge counted two touchdowns in the wet and wild game of 1907. One was an 80-yard run with a blocked field goal attempt. Mississippi State University Photo.

It took the crowd "an hour to get through the sticky mud" on the hill in back of the old Capitol, the *Clarion-Ledger* said. "A great float, capable of holding forty or fifty men was soon filled with college boys. But the team gave out, the harness broke, and the occupants were forced to disembark in the muddiest and wettest section of the road." While the paper declared no hard feelings after the game and "no rowdyism," "the University boys got off the field . . . as soon as possible to escape the jibing . . . of the victors." While the University players blamed their coach, Mason was just as unhappy with his team: "They changed players . . . every day or two," he told the newspaper, and he "could not do anything with them." The paper continued, "Asked if his team was going to leave town last night, the coach said, 'Yes, the team is going north at 11 o'clock; I'm going in another direction, and hope I will never see them again.'" Not surprisingly, Mississippi had a new coach the following year.

Mason's complaint that the team "changed players . . . every day" may have been a reference to the practice of using ringers, or paid players, which was not uncommon at the time. (In addition to Mississippi, other schools accused of using ringers included Vanderbilt, Sewanee, Georgia, and Georgia Tech.) Such charges nearly resulted in the abolition of football at Ole Miss; however, a faculty vote saved the sport, and chancellor A. A. Kincannon declared firmly that ringers would never again be used.

1908

GAME 8

Mississippi State
Fairgrounds, Jackson

Aggies Out-Quick 'Em

1908 SCHEDULES

Mississippi 3–5

RESULT	DATE	PF	OPPONENT	PA	LOCATION
W	October 3	30	Memphis University School	0	Oxford
L	October 10	0	Arkansas	3	Fayetteville
W	October 17	17	Missouri Normal*	0	Memphis
L	October 24	0	Vanderbilt	29	Nashville
W	October 29	41	Mississippi College	0	Jackson
L	October 31	0	Tulane	10	New Orleans
L	November 10	5	Southwestern Presbyterian**	9	Oxford
L	November 26	6	Mississippi A&M	44	Jackson

Mississippi A&M 3–4

RESULT	DATE	PF	OPPONENT	PA	LOCATION
W	October 10	47	Industrial Institute and College of Louisiana***	0	Starkville
L	October 17	0	Georgia Tech	23	Atlanta
L	October 23	5	Southwestern Presbyterian**	6	Columbus
W	October 31	12	Transylvania	5	Starkville
L	November 7	0	Louisiana State	50	Baton Rouge
L	November 14	0	Tulane	23	New Orleans
W	November 26	44	Mississippi	6	Jackson

* Now Southeast Missouri
** Now Rhodes
*** Now Louisiana Tech

In sharp contrast to the mud-bedeviled 1907 game, the 1908 affair highlighted the lightning-fast Mississippi A&M Aggie attack, which produced an easy 44–6 victory and made the Aggies the first team to win consecutive games in the rivalry. At A&M, Fred Furman was in his second year at the helm, while Ole Miss was coached by Frank Kyle, a Vanderbilt graduate. The faculty committee had refused to approve Kyle, but team manager Martin Van Buren Miller hired him for a year anyway.

In 1908, when A&M made it two in a row over Ole Miss for the first time, celebrating students saw to it that no Aggie player's feet touched the ground from the time he left Jackson until deposited back in his dormitory room. "Little" Furman is believed seated on the left (with ball). Quarterback DeWitt Billingsley is seated fifth from the right. *Reveille*.

Game day found railroads offering attractive student rates to Jackson. A round-trip ticket cost just twenty-five cents more than regular one-way fare. The University special rolled in at 10:30, while the Starkville train arrived half an hour later. Alumni greeted each train, and the Aggie cadets demonstrated their military drills on the street. After a morning drizzle, Thanksgiving afternoon was beautiful and sunny, and the field was dry and firm.

More than an hour before the game, fans began streaming in, and by the 2:30 kickoff, the crowd had reached four to five thousand. Two players, A&M starting quarterback DeWitt Billingsley and University halfback Chuck Trotter, had been teammates at Winona in 1905 and had participated in the state's first high school football game when their team went to Yazoo City and absorbed a 5–0 defeat. According to Billingsley, the 1908 game was hectic. The rules permitted the ball to be snapped as soon as the linemen got into a three-point stance, and the Aggies ran Mississippi dizzy: "The ball didn't have to be set down by an official on each play," he explained. "The play was stopped as soon as the runner stopped running, or as soon as the runner hollered to the official he was down. I started calling signals as soon as we got off the ground. We were running off plays before they had a chance to get up and figure what was going on."

The Aggies—heavier by thirty pounds a man—scored eight touchdowns that afternoon, four of them by team captain Harry (Little) Furman, brother of the coach, for an individual Maroon record against Ole Miss not equaled for ninety-seven years. The game featured few forward passes of the fat, egg-shaped ball, as A&M completed one of two attempts and Ole Miss two of seven. Both scored early on the same type of play when they tried onside kicks at their opponent's goal and recovered in the end zone. After that it was all Cadets, as they scored 38 straight points for the rout. One Aggie drive went 105 yards on the 110-yard field, the longest drive in this rivalry. Four players—E. Garrison, Little Furman, H. T. Pollard, and C. M. Rose—contributed consistent runs to the drive, with Furman dashing the final 3 yards for the touchdown. Said the University's *Varsity Voice*, A&M's defense "was well nigh perfect."

In the wake of the stunning victory, Aggie cadets "took the town," the *Daily Clarion-Ledger* reported, "and police gave them all the rope they wanted." In Starkville the celebration went on unchecked. On the team's return, cheering cadets carried each player from the train and put him in a horse-drawn vehicle, but the crowd then unhitched the horses and literally pulled the players back to the campus before carrying each man to his room. Some grateful fans wrote Billingsley's name on the water tower.

1909

University Gets Its Kicks

1909 SCHEDULES

Mississippi 4–3–2

RESULT	DATE	PF	OPPONENT	PA	LOCATION
W	October 2	18	Memphis University School	0	Oxford
W	October 5	15	Tennessee Medical College	0	Oxford
L	October 9	0	Louisiana State	10	Baton Rouge
L	October 16	0	Tulane	5	New Orleans
T	October 23	0	Alabama	0	Jackson
L	October 30	0	Vanderbilt	17	Nashville
T	November 13	12	Henderson State	12	Arkadelphia
W	November 18	45	Union	0	Oxford
W	November 25	9	Mississippi A&M	5	Jackson

Mississippi A&M 5–4

RESULT	DATE	PF	OPPONENT	PA	LOCATION
W	October 2	21	Birmingham College*	0	Starkville
W	October 9	34	Cumberland	6	Starkville
L	October 16	0	Louisiana State	15	Baton Rouge
W	October 22	31	Southwestern Presbyterian**	0	Columbus
L	October 30	0	Tulane	2	New Orleans
W	November 2	25	Union	0	Columbus
L	November 8	0	Howard***	6	Birmingham
W	November 13	37	Chattanooga	6	Starkville
L	November 25	5	Mississippi	9	Jackson

* Now Birmingham-Southern
** Now Rhodes
*** Now Samford

The 1909 contest was a watershed of sorts in the Ole Miss–A&M rivalry. The year saw the arrival of two of the most prominent men ever to coach these two teams. William Dean Chadwick came to Starkville to begin what would become a twenty-one-year association with the school, serving as football coach for five years before taking over as director of athletics. And Dr. Nathan P. Stauffer arrived in Oxford to begin a three-year career as head coach and medical faculty instructor.

On this beautiful Thanksgiving afternoon, five thousand enthusiasts paid two dollars each to enter the Jackson fairgrounds behind the old Capitol, including an estimated five hundred A&M cadets (more than half the student body) and more than three hundred Ole Miss students. The University students, wrote the *Clarion-Ledger*, came down the hill to the fairgrounds "marching 200 strong . . . with the lock step and hand on the shoulder of the man in front. [A] brass band played Dixie." The Aggies arrived in twos, fours, and small groups, "but their band accompanied the team and made the welkin ring." Many spectators brought "a startling variety of noise-making instruments," a reporter wrote. "The gray uniform of the 'Farmer Boys' was in evidence everywhere," the *Daily Clarion-Ledger* reported, "while the red ribbons of the University . . . were noticeable all over the city." Fans "were . . . guying each other in a good natured way . . . and betting their money freely," with University supporters "willing to put up money in any quantity." Buggies and automobiles "lavishly decorated with college colors" surrounded the field. Players arrived "in the biggest wagons they could find in the city. Hundreds of the young lady friends . . . were there to encourage the boys to deeds of valor, and every one of them seemed ready to break his neck if necessary to carry their banner to victory."

A&M kicked off to open the game, and in two and half minutes the University had a 6–0 lead on a touchdown by John (Scotchy) McCall and an extra point kick by Steve Mitchell. A&M replied with an unsuccessful field goal try by W. J. (Blondy) Williams, who played all four years without a helmet. Early in the second half, Williams recovered a fumble and then scored for the Aggies. Though the attempt to "kick goal" failed, A&M had closed to within 1 point at 6–5.

But Mississippi iced the game with a field goal. When Church Lee punted for the University, teammate J. B. Causey recovered the kick on the Aggie 11 yard line. A new rule made each field goal worth 3 points rather than 4, and Kenneth Haxton kicked at a difficult angle from the 20 to give his team the 9–5 victory.

The *Jackson Clarion-Ledger* lauded players on both teams. Mississippi tackle Earl Kinnebrew was "the particular star of his team," while the Red and Blue's Lee exhibited "as pretty punting as was ever seen on the Jackson gridiron," and John Shields's end runs were "hard to beat." For A&M, said the paper, H. T. Pollard's "tackle over tackle and end runs have made his name famous over Southern college grounds," and Williams "was the star of first magnitude."

1910

A Collision of Two Mighty Machines

1910 SCHEDULES

Mississippi 7–1

RESULT	DATE	PF	OPPONENT	PA	LOCATION
W	October 1	10	Central High School	0	Oxford
W	October 5	2	Tennessee Medical College	0	Oxford
W	October 13	16	Tulane	0	New Orleans
W	October 21	24	Mississippi College	0	Clinton
L	October 29	2	Vanderbilt	9	Nashville
W	November 5	16	Alabama	0	Greenville
W	November 12	44	Tennessee Medical College	0	Memphis
W	November 24	30	Mississippi A&M	0	Jackson

Mississippi A&M 7–2

RESULT	DATE	PF	OPPONENT	PA	LOCATION
W	October 1	24	Mississippi College	0	Starkville
L	October 8	0	Auburn	6	Auburn
W	October 15	6	Memphis University School	0	Starkville
W	October 21	3	Louisiana State	0	Columbus
W	October 31	48	Tennessee	0	Starkville
W	November 5	10	Tulane	0	New Orleans
W	November 12	46	Birmingham College*	0	Starkville
W	November 18	82	Howard**	0	Starkville
L	November 24	0	Mississippi	30	Jackson

* Now Birmingham-Southern
** Now Samford

E xcitement reached a fever pitch as five thousand fans jammed the fairgrounds on a sunny Thanksgiving afternoon for the clash of two behemoths. Each team had lost only once, and both defenses were stifling, having produced shutouts in all of A&M's seven wins and all six of those by the University. Credit for such impressive performances went to the two second-year coaches. A&M's W. D. Chadwick fielded a fast team averaging 27 points per game, earning them the nickname Chadwick's Scoring

Machine. Dr. Nathan P. Stauffer's Red and Blue squad was averaging 16 points a game.

What appeared on paper to be the makings of a close contest turned out surprisingly one-sided in reality, however, as the heavier Mississippians used their weight advantage to shut down Chadwick's Scoring Machine in a 30–0 victory, Ole Miss's largest margin of victory to date in the rivalry. Such an uncompetitive game was "totally unexpected," the *Commercial Appeal* declared, and "even the most enthusiastic adherents . . . never thought it would go over twelve at the outside. At no time," added the paper, "was the Mississippi goal in danger."

The Red and Blue might have benefited from the fact that Stauffer served as head linesman a week earlier when the Aggies walloped Howard, 82–0. According to the Memphis paper, Stauffer was watching play so intently that the referee had to remind the good doctor of his duties. The opportunity to scout his team's upcoming opponent certainly didn't hurt.

Pregame betting favored the University, the *Commercial Appeal* reported, and "A&M money was scarce." The trains carrying the two schools' supporters arrived in Jackson in early afternoon, making "things lively around the depot," the *Daily Clarion-Ledger* noted. Bands played, and each group marched across the street to the Edwards House to "let out several of their yells. The

Coach W. D. Chadwick's A&M team and Dr. Nathan P. Stauffer's Ole Miss team were the best their schools had ever produced at the time. When their teams met in Jackson with just one loss each, they had given up only one touchdown apiece all year. Mississippi State University Photo and University of Mississippi Archives.

boys from Starkville outnumbered those from Oxford, but the University . . . made up what they lacked in number with noise." Continued the paper, "The teams arrived [at the fairgrounds] at half past two, and just as soon as they could run over the field they began playing." Among the significant new rules in place, for the first time play was divided into four quarters, rather than two halves, and seven rather than six men were required on the line. The line was Ole Miss's strength. A&M had the better backfield. A&M was playing without one of its star tackles, captain H. T. Pollard, who had been ruled ineligible because of his alleged participation in a track meet in 1906. Quarterback W. J. (Blondy) Williams took over as captain, while the Ole Miss captain was halfback John W. (Scotchy) McCall.

A blocked punt deep in A&M territory led to the first score, as left tackle Fred Carter deflected the ball and then recovered in the end zone. Steve Mitchell's kick made it 6–0. Another Aggie punting miscue led to the second Mississippi touchdown, and the Red and Blue added another touchdown to take an 18–0 advantage at the half.

After the break, Mississippi picked up where it had left off, covering 65 yards in two plays for its next touchdown, then converting yet another Aggie punting error into 6 more points to go up by 30. The Aggies tried to come back late in the game. After a short punt, they had the ball on the Mississippi 32. Alternating carries, right halfback George Cole and fullback Morley Jennings, A&M's first four-letter man, took the ball to the 6, but Williams's drop kick was blocked. Two other Aggie threats also came to naught, and the Red and Blue had the shutout.

The *Jackson Clarion-Ledger* noted the "pleasant" manner in which the game had been played: "There seemed to be a better spirit between the boys this year . . . few if any fights." Nevertheless, Mississippi fans came out in force to celebrate their second straight victory over A&M. Said the *Commercial Appeal*, "Enthusiasm of the university men . . . headed by a brass band, is rampant." Little did Red and Blue backers know that sixteen years would pass before they would have another chance to celebrate a win over the Aggies.

1911

GAME 11

Mississippi State
Fairgrounds, Jackson

Even Collapsing Stands Can't Stop a Fierce Battle

1911 SCHEDULES

Mississippi 6–3

RESULT	DATE	PF	OPPONENT	PA	LOCATION
W	September 30	42	Central High School	0	Oxford
W	October 5	41	Southwestern Presbyterian*	0	Oxford
W	October 13	15	Industrial Institute and College of Louisiana**	0	Oxford
W	October 24	24	Henderson-Brown***	11	Arkadelphia
L	October 27	0	Texas A&M	17	College Station
W	October 30	28	Mississippi College	0	Jackson
W	November 4	34	Mercer	0	Macon
L	November 18	0	Vanderbilt	21	Nashville
L	November 30	0	Mississippi A&M	6	Jackson

Mississippi A&M 7–2–1

RESULT	DATE	PF	OPPONENT	PA	LOCATION
W	September 29	27	Mississippi College	6	Starkville
W	October 7	30	Southwestern Presbyterian*	0	Starkville
W	October 14	48	Howard+	0	Starkville
T	October 21	6	Alabama	6	Columbus
L	October 28	5	Auburn	11	Birmingham
W	November 3	62	Birmingham College++	0	Starkville
W	November 11	6	Louisiana State	0	Gulfport
L	November 20	4	Tulane	5	Starkville
W	November 30	6	Mississippi	0	Jackson
W	January 1, 1912	12	Havana Athletic Club	0	Cuba

* Now Rhodes.
** Now Louisiana Tech
*** Now Henderson State
+ Now Samford
++ Now Birmingham-Southern

The wooden bleachers on the east side of the state fairgrounds playing field were a splendid new addition, erected earlier in the week. Double last year's capacity, they were one hundred feet long and at least eighteen rows high. Some fifteen hundred fans jammed in, anticipat-

MANY HURT IN COLLAPSE OF STAND

More Than Sixty Persons Injured In Disaster At the Football Game Thursday.

NO DEATHS FOLLOW YESTERDAY'S CRASH.

which Hon. William Hemingway, of this city, is president. While the association ostensibly had charge of awarding the contract, in

Headline from the *Clarion-Ledger*, December 1, 1911.

ing an afternoon of exciting football. Across the way another fifteen hundred to two thousand filled the other stands, which gave fans a closer view of the playing field than had ever before existed. The racetrack grandstand off to the side, which until now had been the major seating area, was almost empty. Fans preferred the closer seats, even though they had to pay an extra twenty-five cents for the privilege.

As the two teams readied for kickoff, with the ball already in place, fans stood and cheered. Suddenly, a shout and then a loud creaking sound erupted from the new east stands. The great frame bleachers swayed uncontrollably, and before the eyes of horrified onlookers across the field, the entire east side stands collapsed into a mass of broken timbers while agonizing screams pierced the air. At least sixty persons were injured, many of them seriously—broken bones, wrenched backs, dislocated shoulders, crushed feet. Somewhat incredibly, as rescuers rushed from the west side stands to help the injured, the players appeared not to notice the disaster. The game proceeded without pause.

As tragic as the incident was, it had its light moments. "'Where's my hat?' was a query heard on all sides," reported the Jackson newspaper. "One old chap was seen . . . pulling away planks," the writer said, "trying to find a half-smoked cigar." Also, "While Mr. Joe Robinson was . . . loading injured into his automobile, somebody stole his handsome overcoat." And a plump lady was heard whispering to a friend that her corset strings "bursted."

It was a scoreless battle through the first half and into the second. On Mississippi's second possession of the third quarter, however, the Red and Blue fumbled near its own 20 yard line. Aggie left end W. J. (Chick) Magee quickly

In top photo an Ole Miss player, left, fades for a pass. In center the Aggies, in striped sleeves, down an Ole Miss runner while others rush to join the play. At bottom a University player attempts a block of an A&M punt as a white-shirted official watches. Photos by Robb & Conant, Jackson. From collection of H. L. (Sonny) Hill Jr.

grabbed the ball and, as the *Memphis Commercial Appeal* put it, "with 21 frantic players on his trail, went over for a touchdown." When it was announced that Magee was a Jackson boy, said the paper, rivalry was forgotten for a moment: "Spectators, irrespective of partisan feeling, gave him round after round of enthusiastic cheers." Morley Jennings "kicked an easy goal" to give his team a 6–0 lead. In the fourth quarter, A&M missed a field goal and Ole Miss threatened twice. The Red and Blue's last scoring chance ended on the goal line when time ran out, and A&M had its narrow victory.

The *Commercial Appeal* described the Aggie touchdown as "a fluke" but insisted that "A&M won the game on merit." The Aggie starters had played the entire game, while Mississippi used only two of its second-stringers. The defensive pose of the "farm boys" in the first half, the paper described, "left [the team] in fine fettle . . . and they made the finish in super style." The guard work of A&M's A. H. Allen and S. W. Rhodes and the end play of Chick Magee and Hunter Kimball were "superb," the paper continued, adding compliments about the play of Mississippi left halfback Frank Shields and quarterback Vivian Randolph.

The season ended with A&M's first postseason invitation. The Havana Athletic Club offered the Aggies an all-expense-paid trip to Cuba, where on January 1, 1912, A&M won 12–0. The postseason news for the University of Mississippi was not as good. The following spring, a professor in the medical department, where coach Nathan P. Stauffer taught, charged that he had used paid players, a particularly serious accusation in light of the fact that chancellor A. A. Kincannon had declared in 1907 that the University would never again use such ringers. In response to the latest charges, the Southern Intercollegiate Athletic Association banned eight players, and Stauffer resigned and returned to Pennsylvania to practice medicine. Although an Ole Miss faculty committee subsequently cleared Stauffer and most of the players of any wrongdoing, none of them returned to the team.

1912–1914

Time-Out for a Feud of Another Kind

1912 SCHEDULES

Mississippi 5–3

RESULT	DATE	PF	OPPONENT	PA	LOCATION
W	October 5	34	Central High School	0	Oxford
W	October 12	1	Castle Heights Military Inst.*	0	Oxford
W	October 19	10	Louisiana State	7	Baton Rouge
L	October 26	0	Vanderbilt	24	Nashville
W	November 1	12	Mississippi College	0	Oxford
L	November 9	9	Alabama	10	Tuscaloosa
L	November 13	14	Texas	53	Houston
W	November 16	47	Tennessee Medical College	6	Memphis

Mississippi A&M 4–3

RESULT	DATE	PF	OPPONENT	PA	LOCATION
W	October 4	19	Mississippi College	0	Starkville
W	October 12	38	Tennessee Medical College	0	Starkville
W	October 18	7	Alabama	0	Aberdeen
L	October 26	0	Auburn	7	Birmingham
W	November 2	7	Louisiana State	0	Baton Rouge
L	November 9	24	Tulane	27	New Orleans
L	November 16	7	Texas A&M	41	Houston

* Forfeit

One of the most dynamic bombshells ever to burst over the Ole Miss–A&M series exploded the week of the big game in 1912. Five days before the contest in Jackson, the Southern Intercollegiate Athletic Association (SIAA) declared Mississippi quarterback Ralph Fletcher ineligible because he had appeared in a freshman game at the University of Chicago and had not waited the required year before playing at Mississippi. Rumors swirled. Ole Miss would play, Ole Miss wouldn't. In hopes of saving the game, Jackson mayor A. C. Crowder and editor Frederick Sullens of the *Jackson Daily News* sent a telegram to the Red and Blue: play the game, the city leaders

1913 SCHEDULES

Mississippi 6–3–1

RESULT	DATE	PF	OPPONENT	PA	LOCATION
L	October 8	0	Virginia Military Institute	14	Lexington
L	October 11	14	Virginia Tech	34	Blacksburg
W	October 15	7	Virginia Medical College	6	Richmond
W	October 23	46	Union	0	Oxford
W	November 1	26	Industrial Institute and College of Louisiana*	0	Oxford
L	November 7	6	Hendrix	8	Conway
W	November 15	21	Arkansas	10	Little Rock
W	November 22	7	Cumberland	0	Memphis
T	November 27	0	Ouachita Baptist	0	Arkadelphia
W	November 27	13	Mississippi Normal**	7	Hattiesburg

Mississippi A&M 6–1–1

RESULT	DATE	PF	OPPONENT	PA	LOCATION
W	October 4	66	Howard***	0	Starkville
W	October 10	1	Mississippi College+	0	Starkville
W	October 17	31	Transylvania	0	Columbus
L	October 25	0	Auburn	34	Birmingham
W	November 1	6	Texas A&M	0	College Station
W	November 8	32	Tulane	0	Starkville
T	November 15	0	Louisiana State	0	Starkville
W	November 27	7	Alabama	0	Birmingham

* Now Louisiana Tech
** Now Southern Mississippi
*** Now Samford
+ Forfeit

urged. Otherwise, "we gravely fear for organized football in Mississippi." But the Ole Miss players stood firm: the SIAA had "hounded" them in a season-long investigation—so much that they were "demoralized" by the charges. If Fletch couldn't play, neither would the rest of the team. University chancellor A. A. Kincannon made the decision official. In view of the weeklong student unrest and the players' adamant reaction, Ole Miss would not play. While expressing "profound regret and indignation," the student newspaper, the *Mississippian*, offered solid support for the refusal to play despite the fact that the game "means more than any on the calendar." The A&M community expressed far less concern. The Aggies would have been willing to play, the *College Reflector* wrote later, if the school first made a formal protest to the SIAA "to keep clear of the trouble."

"The trouble" had begun for Ole Miss the previous spring, with the charges that Coach Nathan Stauffer had used ringers. The SIAA had banned

1914 SCHEDULES

Ole Miss 5–4–1

RESULT	DATE	PF	OPPONENT	PA	LOCATION
W	October 3	20	Arkansas A&M*	0	Oxford
W	October 10	14	Southwestern Presbyterian**	0	Oxford
W	October 17	21	Louisiana State	0	Baton Rouge
T	October 28	7	Mississippi College	7	Jackson
L	October 31	0	Ouachita Baptist	7	Memphis
W	November 7	21	Tulane	6	New Orleans
W	November 14	13	Arkansas	7	Little Rock
L	November 17	7	Texas	66	Austin
L	November 20	0	Southwestern	18	Georgetown
L	November 26	7	Texas A&M	14	Dallas

Mississippi A&M 6–2

RESULT	DATE	PF	OPPONENT	PA	LOCATION
W	October 3	54	Marion Military Institute	0	Starkville
W	October 10	77	Cumberland	0	Starkville
L	October 17	13	Kentucky	19	Lexington
L	October 24	0	Auburn	19	Birmingham
W	October 31	9	Georgia	0	Athens
W	November 7	66	Mercer	0	Starkville
W	November 14	61	Tulane	0	Jackson
W	November 26	9	Alabama	0	Birmingham

* Now Arkansas State
** Now Rhodes

eight of the University's players even though, the *Mississippian* declared, they had not "violated any law . . . respected among the other institutions." Boldly increasing its attack, the paper declared that the SIAA had made Ole Miss "a scapegoat" as the association spent a year checking "this man and that . . . to see if he had . . . done something [to] bar him." "Fletcher's ineligibility," it added, "was the final blow. Provoked thus, indignation is righteous."

The refusal to play deeply affected the University. The SIAA suspended Mississippi for a year, and both Fletcher and new coach Leo DeTray, a graduate of Chicago, where Fletcher was accused of having played, left Oxford. More significantly, the lucrative gate provided by the Jackson game obviously was important to the school's financial bottom line. In December, when Ole Miss awarded varsity letters, the usual sweaters were not presented, the *Mississippian* explained, "owing to depletion in the . . . treasury . . . by the cancellation of the annual Thanksgiving game."

In December 1913, acting in response to a July request from A&M vice president B. M. Walker, who argued that a one-year suspension was sufficient punishment, the SIAA reinstated the University of Mississippi. However, the decision came too late for the 1913 season, when the Aggies filled their schedule with SIAA-eligible teams. Moreover, according to A&M's *College Reflector*, the team's Thanksgiving Day game against Alabama in Birmingham was "a better source of revenue" than the Ole Miss game would have been. "A. and M. can easily get along without the University. Whether they can do without A. and M. is a question to be answered."

Ole Miss replaced its annual game with A&M with two games on the same day on two fields hundreds of miles apart. One squad of lettermen won a game over Mississippi Normal (now Southern Miss) in Hattiesburg, while another squad of lettermen played to a scoreless tie with Ouachita Baptist in Arkadelphia, Arkansas.

The pieces appeared to be in place for a resumption of the rivalry during the 1914 season, but once again, it was not to be. At its December 1913 meeting, the SIAA authorized small colleges (those with fewer than four hundred male students) to use "first-year men" (freshmen) during the 1914 season. Ole Miss qualified as a small college, while A&M did not. The *College Reflector* quickly called the new rule "discriminatory." It would put the Aggies at a disadvantage against small schools such as Ole Miss. In addition, the paper argued, the best athletes would not enter A&M or any other larger school if football eligibility began in their sophomore year, leaving them only three years of college play. The Aggies, therefore, refused to schedule Ole Miss in 1914. The University's *Mississippian* launched a vigorous campaign to persuade A&M to reconsider, even suggesting that the two teams meet in a postseason game, but to no avail. In 1914, the schools faced off in basketball, in baseball, and even in a debate match, but not on the gridiron.

At its December 1914 meeting, the SIAA revised the first-year rule, allowing schools to choose whether to use freshmen. Those that elected to do so were placed in one category, with other schools in a separate grouping. Both Mississippi and A&M chose to allow freshmen to play during the following fall. The SIAA also revised the rule that had tripped up Ralph Fletcher, permitting transfers immediately to play varsity football at their new schools unless they had already played on the varsity at their old institutions.

In February 1915, with major disputes apparently resolved, the schools finally reached an agreement to resume the rivalry.

1915

65–0

1915 SCHEDULES

Ole Miss 2–6

RESULT	DATE	PF	OPPONENT	PA	LOCATION
L	October 1	0	Arkansas A&M*	10	Oxford
W	October 8	13	Southwestern Presbyterian	6	Oxford
L	October 15	0	Louisiana State	28	Oxford
L	October 23	0	Vanderbilt	91	Memphis
W	October 30	32	Hendrix	7	Oxford
L	November 6	0	Mississippi A&M	65	Tupelo
L	November 13	6	Mississippi College	74	Jackson
L	November 25	0	Alabama	53	Birmingham

Mississippi A&M 5–2–1

RESULT	DATE	PF	OPPONENT	PA	LOCATION
W	October 2	12	Mississippi College	0	Jackson
T	October 9	0	Transylvania	0	Starkville
W	October 16	12	Kentucky	0	Starkville
L	October 23	0	Auburn	26	Birmingham
L	October 30	0	Louisiana State	10	Baton Rouge
W	November 6	65	Mississippi	0	Tupelo
W	November 13	14	Tennessee	0	Knoxville
W	November 25	7	Texas A&M	0	Dallas

* Now Arkansas State

The long hiatus in relations between A&M and Ole Miss emphasized one undeniable truth: absence had not made the heart grow fonder. In fact, just the opposite may have been true, with the passage of three years merely intensifying the hatred between the fans and the players. The Aggies responded more vigorously, rolling for ten touchdowns and an overwhelming 65–0 victory, still the most one-sided in rivalry annals.

Fans had anticipated this clash since the preceding February, when the schools announced that rivalry play would resume. The location was yet to be

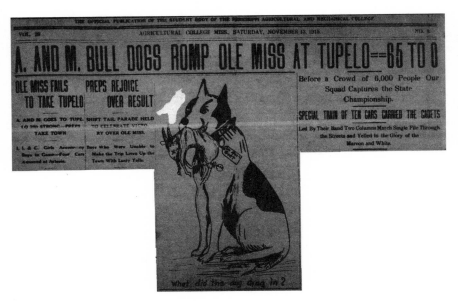

THE OFFICIAL PUBLICATION OF THE STUDENT BODY OF THE MISSISSIPPI AGRICULTURAL AND MECHANICAL COLLEGE

VOL. 20   AGRICULTURAL COLLEGE MISS. SATURDAY, NOVEMBER 13, 1915.   NO. 2

A. AND M. BULL DOGS ROMP OLE MISS AT TUPELO==65 TO 0

OLE MISS FAILS TO TAKE TUPELO

PREPS REJOICE OVER RESULT

A. AND M. GOES TO TUPL. 10 700 STRONG—PREPS TAKE TOWN

SHIRT TAIL PARADE HELD TO CELEBRATE VICTO- RY OVER OLE MISS.

I. I. & C. Girls Accompany Boys to Game—Four Cars Assigned at Artesia.

Boys Who Were Unable to Make the Trip Liven Up the Town With Lusty Yells.

Before a Crowd of 6,000 People Our Squad Captures the State Championship.

SPECIAL TRAIN OF TEN CARS CARRIED THE CADETS

Led By Their Band Two Columns March Single File Through the Streets and Yelled to the Glory of the Maroon and White.

What did the dog drag in?

Headline from *College Reflector,* November 13, 1915.

determined, with Jackson, Meridian, Greenville, and Columbus among the bidders to host the game. Resumption, said the *Mississippian,* was "a cause for rejoicing by students of both schools. It is to be regretted that anything ever arose . . . that should cause them to sever their athletic relations."

Tupelo won the nod as the site for the game, with strong efforts by the city's Businessmen's Club. Railroads offered students discounted tickets, and the price of admission to the field at the fairgrounds on East Main was seventy-five cents. Seven hundred A&M cadets paid $1.50 to ride the train from Starkville, as did three hundred women from the Industrial Institute and College (later Mississippi State College for Women, now Mississippi University for Women). The Oxford train brought three hundred Ole Miss fans, including some from Holly Springs and women from Presbyterian College. Both student groups marched to the center of town, the cadets in twin columns singing, "There'll be a Hot Time in Tupelo Tonight." The Red and Blue squad was led by a native of the city, Fred A. Robins, who had gradu- ated from Vanderbilt, while the Aggie coach was E. C. (Billy) Hayes. Betting was heavy, the *Memphis Commercial Appeal* reported, with A&M the three to one favorite. The Aggie defense had surrendered only 36 points in its five games to date, while Ole Miss had given up an average of 28 points in each of its five previous games.

This contest was the first between the two schools under the rules enacted three years earlier. Touchdowns now counted six points, rather than five. The field had been shortened from 110 to 100 yards, and each team now had four downs rather than three to cover 10 yards for a first down. Both Mississippi and A&M used freshmen, whose eligibility had been so controversial over the previous three years, with Ole Miss relying heavily on first-year players. The referee was T. C. Carter of Tupelo, while the field judge was Mississippi College football coach Dana X. Bible, who went on to coaching fame at Louisiana State, Texas A&M, Nebraska, and Texas.

Approximately six thousand fans jammed the fairgrounds, and 178 automobiles were admitted. The game started "promptly at 2:30m" on an "ideal plat in front of the grandstand," according to the *Tupelo Journal*. Things went quickly downhill for the Mississippians, and at halftime they trailed 33–0. During the break, the dispirited University team sat on the sidelines at about midfield,

Against Ole Miss in 1915 Dudy Noble scored two touchdowns, passed for three more, then closed his collegiate career with fourteen letters in four sports. Later he was head football coach at Ole Miss, then at State—one of just two men to have held coaching reins at both schools. For forty years (1919–1959) he was associated with the Mississippi State athletics as instructor, coach, and athletic director. Mississippi State University Photo.

while the A&M Band was parading, followed by the cadet corps and two mascots—a bulldog for the Aggies, a goat for Ole Miss. Some cadets carried a coffin "to bury Ole Miss." As the goat and the bulldog neared the Ole Miss players, the *Commercial Appeal* reported, the bulldog "picked out a massive Mississippian and endeavored to try his hand in helping the Maroons dispose of their opponents." When the handler showed no sign of pulling the dog away, another Ole Miss player raised his arm as if to strike the handler. Pandemonium resulted. As the marching corps broke ranks, cadets rushed in to do battle and quickly surrounded the players. Fortunately, "prompt action on the part of the coach prevented trouble," said the paper. The A&M student newspaper, the *College Reflector*, declared that the problem had started when the goat was frightened by the bulldog and jumped into the cluster of Ole Miss players. Whatever the cause, a quick return to peace allowed the *Tupelo Journal* to boast, "There was not a case of disorder, not a drunk in the entire crowd and not an accident to mar the pleasures of the day. Mississippi should feel proud of both bodies of students."

Unfortunately for the Oxford team, the second half brought more A&M dominance, as the heavier, more experienced Aggies ripped the lighter Ole Miss team to pieces, allowing the Red and Blue only one first down all day. The Aggies kept the ball 75 percent of the time, the *Commercial Appeal* reported, punted just six times (three because of penalties), and used only seven substitutes. Ole Miss was "outweighed, outclassed and outgeneraled at every stage," said the *Jackson Daily News*. Declared the *Commercial Appeal*, the result was "a procession toward and over the Red and Blue goal." Seven players figured in the point making. The Memphis paper cited defensive play by A&M's M. J. Shaw, who also caught a touchdown pass; T. L. Gaddy, who had two touchdown grabs and kicked three extra points; K. L. Spurlock; and captain E. R. (Dub) Rainey. C. R. (Dudy) Noble, who went on to serve twenty-six years as athletic director at Starkville, ran for two touchdowns and passed for three more. For Ole Miss, the *Tupelo Journal* cited William Finger, D. A. Dawson, Paul (Tex) Neely, and Allen Collete.

At A&M, news of the victory prompted a wild celebration. With shirttails out, four hundred cadets marched behind a band equipped with tin pans, tin cans, and cowbells. The jubilant crowd built a bonfire and then stormed the local "picture show."

1916

On to Tupelo

1916 SCHEDULES

Ole Miss 3–6

RESULT	DATE	PF	OPPONENT	PA	LOCATION
W	September 30	30	Union	0	Oxford
W	October 7	20	Arkansas A&M*	0	Oxford
W	October 14	61	Hendrix	0	Oxford
L	October 21	0	Vanderbilt	35	Nashville
L	October 28	0	Alabama	27	Tuscaloosa
L	November 3	0	Mississippi A&M	36	Tupelo
L	November 11	3	Transylvania	13	Lexington
L	November 18	0	Louisiana State	41	Baton Rouge
L	November 30	14	Mississippi College	36	Jackson

Mississippi A&M 4–4–1

RESULT	DATE	PF	OPPONENT	PA	LOCATION
L	October 6	6	Mississippi College	13	Aberdeen
W	October 14	33	Chattanooga	0	Chattanooga
W	October 21	13	Transylvania	0	Starkville
L	October 28	3	Auburn	7	Birmingham
W	November 3	36	Mississippi	0	Tupelo
L	November 11	3	Louisiana State	13	Starkville
L	November 18	3	Kentucky	13	Lexington
T	November 20	7	Maryville	7	Maryville
W	November 30	20	Arkansas	7	Memphis

* Now Arkansas State

The student newspapers cried, "On to Tupelo!" And on they came—five hundred from A&M and three hundred from the University—for their second consecutive meeting there. "A most gala air," the *Commercial Appeal* observed, was lent by "the presence of Aggie students in their uniforms, headed by a cadet band, together with a dozen different bevies of fair students from neighboring colleges." Enthusiasm of the University supporters, however, hinged more on a grim determination to avenge the previous year's humiliating defeat.

Scott Field would be named for A&M track star and football end Don M. Scott (1915–16), in recognition of his performances in the 1920 and 1924 Olympics. *Reveille.*

No such luck. Despite the *Commercial Appeal*'s pregame assessment that the Aggie backfield "lacks the dash and brilliancy for quick scoring," the A&M gridders tallied two early touchdowns and a field goal and rolled to a relatively easy 36–0 victory.

Kickoff was at 2:40 before a crowd of five thousand on an unusually hot November 3—a Friday. The train from Oxford had arrived at 11 A.M., and the band immediately led the students, two abreast, to Main Street. The A&M cadets' train arrived later, with more than a third of the student body aboard. The cadets marched to Main Street over the same route, "led by their famous 40-piece band," said the *Mississippian* in an unusual compliment to its opponent. At 1:30 the University students formed at the Confederate Monument on Main Street, then moved three blocks to the fairgrounds on East Main, "where they occupied the half of the grandstand opposite the A&M boys," reported the student newspaper. The cadet band led the corps in just afterward.

Otto Schwill was the Aggies' star, scoring three touchdowns and adding two extra points and a field goal for a total of 23 points, a single-game rivalry record that teammate Hubert Howell tied the following year. Schwill's 8 points a year earlier gave him 31 for his career against Ole Miss, a team record that stood for eighty-five years. Ole Miss had two good chances to score in early going but could convert neither, and A&M had its second straight shutout. Both teams had stuck mainly to the ground game, with A&M completing three of its eight pass attempts and Ole Miss successful on none of its five tries. Despite an embarrassing 165 yards in penalties—90 yards against the Aggies and 75 yards against the Red and Blue—the *Commercial Appeal* called the game cleanly fought.

Otto Schwill scored 23 points in the 1916 game, a one-time Aggie record in games with Ole Miss until tied the next year. In addition, Schwill's 31 career total in games against Ole Miss was a Maroon rivalry record that held for eighty-five years, until 2001. Mississippi State University Photo.

1917

GAME 14

Tupelo Fairgrounds

Wartime Is Victory Time for the Aggie Team

1917 SCHEDULES

Ole Miss 1–4–1

RESULT	DATE	PF	OPPONENT	PA	LOCATION
T	October 6	0	Arkansas A&M*	0	Oxford
L	October 13	7	Louisiana State	52	Oxford
L	October 27	0	Alabama	64	Tuscaloosa
L	November 3	14	Mississippi A&M	41	Tupelo
L	November 10	7	Sewanee	69	Sewanee
W	November 29	21	Mississippi College	0	Jackson

Mississippi A&M 6–1

RESULT	DATE	PF	OPPONENT	PA	LOCATION
W	October 5	18	Marion Military Institute	6	Starkville
W	October 13	68	Mississippi College	0	Starkville
L	October 27	6	Auburn	13	Birmingham
W	November 3	41	Mississippi	14	Tupelo
W	November 10	14	Kentucky	0	Starkville
W	November 17	9	Louisiana State	0	Baton Rouge
W	November 29	7	Haskell Institute	6	Memphis

* Now Arkansas State

With wartime restrictions on travel, attendance fell dramatically for the A&M–Ole Miss game's third appearance in Tupelo. Before a crowd of only one thousand, A&M won handily to complete its sweep of the three meetings.

A&M had a new coach, Stanley L. Robinson, who had been a member of Colgate's 1915 national championship team and had most recently coached at Vermont. Ole Miss also was led by a first-year coach, but he was a veteran of the Aggie–Red and Blue rivalry. Mississippi had hired C. R. (Dudy) Noble, one of A&M's most prominent four-sport lettermen and formerly coach at Mississippi College, where he had won the state championship by beating A&M, Ole Miss, and Millsaps. Noble later returned to his alma mater as baseball coach and athletic director.

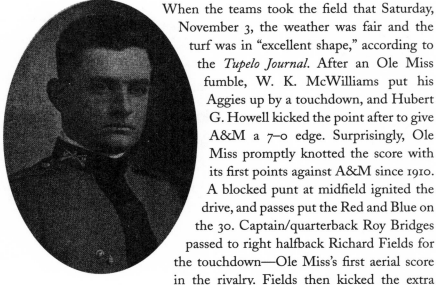

When the teams took the field that Saturday, November 3, the weather was fair and the turf was in "excellent shape," according to the *Tupelo Journal.* After an Ole Miss fumble, W. K. McWilliams put his Aggies up by a touchdown, and Hubert G. Howell kicked the point after to give A&M a 7–0 edge. Surprisingly, Ole Miss promptly knotted the score with its first points against A&M since 1910. A blocked punt at midfield ignited the drive, and passes put the Red and Blue on the 30. Captain/quarterback Roy Bridges passed to right halfback Richard Fields for the touchdown—Ole Miss's first aerial score in the rivalry. Fields then kicked the extra point. 7–7.

When he scored 23 points in the 1917 game, Hubert Howell tied the Maroon record against Ole Miss set the year before by teammate Otto Schwill. Their joint record held for eighty-eight years, until topped in the 2005 game. Mississippi State University Photo.

That's when the A&M cadets took up their singsong chant, "Touchdown, Aggies. Touchdown, Aggies." The players responded, reeling off 20 straight points before Bridges crossed the goal line to make the score 27–14 going into the fourth quarter. The Aggies added two more late touchdowns to take the 41–14 victory. Howell kicked five extra points and added three touchdowns, tying Otto Schwill's school record for points against Ole Miss in a game, individual records that stood until 2005.

Mississippi's defense, the Memphis paper summarized, "was ineffective against splits and cross bucks." The bright spots for the Red and Blue included Bridges, W. H. Sisler, and Charles R. Mayfield, while the Aggies had been led by the play of McWilliams, Howell, R. L. (Dutch) Leonard, M. C. Billingsley, R. N. Henley, and J. A. Oswalt.

1918

Gotcha! Twice!

1918 SCHEDULES

Ole Miss 1–3

RESULT	DATE	PF	OPPONENT	PA	LOCATION
L	November 9	0	Payne Field	6	West Point
W	November 16	39	Union	0	Oxford
L	November 28	0	Mississippi A&M	34	Starkville
L	December 7	0	Mississippi A&M	13	Oxford

Mississippi A&M 3–2

RESULT	DATE	PF	OPPONENT	PA	LOCATION
L	November 2	6	Payne Field	7	Starkville
W	November 9	12	Camp Shelby	0	Starkville
L	November 16	0	Park Field	6	Starkville
W	November 28	34	Mississippi	0	Starkville
W	December 7	13	Mississippi	0	Oxford

World War I sharply curtailed travel and many other activities. It was a sad time in America. Not only were young men fighting—and dying—overseas, but a devastating flu epidemic struck down forty million more at home and around the world. Worldwide events curtailed the football season, and A&M played only five games in 1918, Ole Miss just four. Neither school played a game until November.

Athletic directors W. D. Chadwick of A&M and C. R. (Dudy) Noble of Ole Miss announced that their schools would not only continue their rivalry but would play twice during the season, once in Starkville and once in Oxford. The games were returning to campus play for the first time in fifteen years, declared the *Commercial Appeal*, because of "lack of interest on the part of the towns." Team captains were Ole Miss halfback Edward H. (Red) Ray and A&M center M. E. Kelly, one of the few regulars on a team struck hard by graduation and the call to service.

FIRST GAME [New Athletic Field, Starkville]

A&M and Ole Miss battled for the first time in 1918 on Thanksgiving Day, less than two weeks after the end of the war, in what the *Commercial Appeal* referred to as "a relatively minor operation." A&M coach Stanley Robinson, who had spent much of the year in naval aviation service, returned just a few days before the game. The contest was the first ever between the two schools on the A&M campus, since earlier games in Starkville had taken place at the county fairgrounds. The game was also the first on what was known as the school's "new athletic field." Two years later, Aggie officials named the facility for one of the school's most outstanding athletes, Don Scott, who had played on the football team in 1915–16 and who went on to star in track at the 1920 and 1924 Olympics. The field was subsequently renamed Davis Wade Stadium/Scott Field.

A&M won the toss this cool day and chose to receive. Both teams threatened early, but A&M was stopped on the Ole Miss 10, and Ole Miss fumbled on the Aggie 25. The Aggies then broke through with a 75-yard drive, capped by halfback E. H. McNair's touchdown and missed extra point. McNair added another touchdown on a 25-yard end run at the beginning of the second period, and this time he successfully "kicked goal" to give the Aggies a 13–0 advantage. By halftime, A&M had extended its lead to 20–0, adding another touchdown in the third quarter before Ole Miss launched its only threat. Mississippi right end Dixon Kirk took a 35-yard pass to midfield, but the Aggies intercepted the ball on the next play, soon scoring another touchdown and icing the 34–0 win. "The Ole Miss running attack was unable to gain ground against the Maroon defense," the Memphis paper declared, "and the visitors would generally try three plays and kick."

SECOND GAME [Football Field, Oxford]

Nine days later, the Ole Miss team sought revenge on its home field. According to the student newspaper, the *Mississippian*, "practically the whole school" turned out for the rematch in Oxford on December 7, a beautiful, warm Saturday. The game marked the rivalry's first on Ole Miss's new playing field, which was begun with student labor during the 1914–15 school year and was later dubbed Vaught-Hemingway Stadium/Hollingsworth Field.

Once again, the Aggies jumped out to an early lead, taking a 13–0 edge at halftime on touchdowns by E. H. McNair and R. Mallory and an extra point by C. E. Russell. Mississippi came alive after the break. The Red and Blue took the second half kickoff and marched straight downfield. Deep in A&M territory, however, a fourth-down toss failed to connect, ending the team's first serious threat. Ole Miss again seemed poised to score on its next possession, but it too came to naught, and the game ended with the Aggies the 13–0 victors.

The Ole Miss student newspaper praised the play of Edward H. (Red) Ray, who was knocked out several times yet "came back for more." Reflecting the tenor of the times, *Mississippian* also described quarterback A. B. Carney's tackles as "deadly as German gas." In addition to Ray, the *Memphis Commercial Appeal* lauded the Red and Blue's L. B. Morris and R. H. Lake and the "heavy work" of A&M's McNair, Mallory, and P. M. Hough.

1919

Open the Windows and Let 'Er Rip

1919 SCHEDULES

Ole Miss 4–4

RESULT	DATE	PF	OPPONENT	PA	LOCATION
W	October 4	32	Arkansas A&M*	0	Oxford
L	October 11	0	Alabama	49	Tuscaloosa
L	October 18	0	Louisiana State	13	Baton Rouge
L	October 25	12	Tulane	27	New Orleans
W	October 31	25	Union	6	Oxford
L	November 8	0	Mississippi A&M	33	Clarksdale
W	November 15	30	Southwestern Presbyterian**	0	Oxford
W	November 27	6	Mississippi College	0	Jackson

Mississippi A&M 6–2

RESULT	DATE	PF	OPPONENT	PA	LOCATION
W	October 4	12	Spring Hill	6	Starkville
W	October 11	56	Mississippi College	7	Starkville
W	October 18	6	Tennessee	0	Knoxville
W	October 25	39	Howard***	0	Starkville
W	November 1	6	Louisiana State	0	Starkville
W	November 8	33	Mississippi	0	Clarksdale
L	November 15	0	Auburn	7	Birmingham
L	November 27	6	Alabama	14	Birmingham

* Now Arkansas State
** Now Rhodes
*** Now Samford

With the Great War over, interest in the annual A&M–University clash again rose, and Greenville, Tupelo, and Clarksdale all sought to host the 1919 contest. With strong support from local alumni, Clarksdale won out, and some three thousand fans poured into town this November 8. The morning drizzle gave way to an ideal afternoon with just enough chill to give the teams "added pep," one paper declared. Game site was the new Elizabeth Dorr High School on West Second Street (completed at a cost of one hundred thousand dollars), with play taking place directly in front of the building on a field "covered in a velvety grass," said A&M's *College Reflector*. One goalpost stood practically on the bank of the Sunflower River, giving rise to fears that the ball might sail into the water. Even worse, the other goalpost was located directly in front of the new building, leading to the specter of balls smashing into the school windows. The obvious solution: Open the windows and let 'er rip! While most spectators stood, large numbers of cars were parked around the field, and drivers celebrated exciting plays with their horns. "Deafening," said the Ole Miss paper. According to the *Reflector*, fans of both teams "were in abundance," and "many of the fair sex were present and gave a dash of color to the game." Captains were A&M right guard R. N. Henley and Ole Miss right end Edmund Cowart.

The favored Aggies outweighed the Red and Blue by about thirty pounds per man and tore into the lighter Mississippi line. Five A&M players scored touchdowns in what turned out to be a 33–0 victory.

H. S. Cassell ran two yards for the first Aggie score, and Frank Perry's four carries took him over the goal for touchdown No. 2 before R. N. Henley blocked a punt and recovered for a score. R. K. Quekemyer grabbed a fumble at the goal for touchdown No. 4, and Henry Allen took a 35-yard pass from C. E. Russell for the final score. Cassell and Russell kicked the extra points.

"Ole Miss was outplayed all the way around," reported the *Commercial Appeal*, and fumbles hurt badly: "Several good chances were by lost by . . . inability to hold the pigskin." The Red and Blue did not have a first down until early in the fourth quarter, and their only scoring chances occurred on two late field goal attempts. As the game ended, Clarksdale school officials heaved a sigh of relief: no broken windows.

GAME 18

Greenwood
Baseball Park

1920

20 in '20

1920 SCHEDULES

Ole Miss 4–3

RESULT	DATE	PF	OPPONENT	PA	LOCATION
W	October 2	33	Arkansas A&M*	0	Oxford
W	October 9	54	Mississippi Normal**	0	Hattiesburg
L	October 16	6	Birmingham-Southern	27	Birmingham
L	October 23	0	Tulane	32	Oxford
W	October 29	86	Union	0	Oxford
L	November 6	0	Mississippi A&M	20	Greenwood
W	November 12	38	Southwestern Presbyterian***	6	Oxford

Mississippi A&M 5–3

RESULT	DATE	PF	OPPONENT	PA	LOCATION
W	October 2	27	Mississippi College	0	Starkville
L	October 9	0	Indiana	24	Bloomington
W	October 16	33	Southern Military Academy	0	Starkville
W	October 23	12	Louisiana State	7	Baton Rouge
W	October 30	13	Tennessee	7	Starkville
W	November 6	20	Mississippi	0	Greenwood
L	November 13	0	Tulane	6	New Orleans
L	November 25	7	Alabama	24	Birmingham

* Now Arkansas State
** Now Southern Mississippi
*** Now Rhodes

The eighteenth meeting of Mississippi A&M and the University of Mississippi saw the rivalry's first appearance in Greenwood, a tribute to the hard work of that city's ambitious Chamber of Commerce. Declared one newspaper, the "citizens of Greenwood are crazy over football," and "a record breaking crowd" was assured. For days prior to the contest, the *Greenwood Daily Commonwealth* promoted the game with headlines across the top of page 1.

Headline from the *Greenwood Daily Commonwealth*, November 5, 1920.

Greenwood alumni proudly met their favorite teams as they arrived by train the afternoon before the game. Odds initially favoring the Aggies dropped on the announcement that A&M stars Stennis (Judge) Little, G. F. McGowan, and Gene Barnett were injured. According to reports, new Aggie coach Fred J. Holtkamp "is finding it difficult rounding up a set of backs."

Game day, Saturday, November 6, was warm. According to the Ole Miss student newspaper, the *Mississippian*, a special train brought "one third of the student body" from Oxford. Though the Aggies did not send a special, a telegraphed play-by-play account was constantly updated in the chapel, and students followed the action on a large board simulating the field. Backers of both schools sang and yelled their way through downtown Greenwood all morning, and long before the 2:30 kickoff, excited fans were filling the base-ball park at the foot of Dewey Street, four blocks west of the business district. Though grandstand capacity was only fifteen hundred, by kickoff the crowd had ballooned to three times that number. General admission was $1.10, a spot in the grandstand was $1.25, and box seats cost $1.50, as did automobiles. The goalposts were decorated in each school's colors. Captains were Ole Miss's Rufus H. Creekmore and A&M's M. C. Billingsley, the brother of DeWitt Billingsley, the Maroons' star quarterback in 1908 and 1909.

After nervously exchanging fumbles through the first quarter, the teams settled down in the second, and the Aggies soon scored, with quarterback Noll Davis, the only first-string player in the Aggie backfield lineup, doing the honors. A&M added a second touchdown on a long Davis-to-Billingsley pass to take a 14–0 lead at the half.

Both student groups performed snake dances during halftime and gave "a demonstration of their cheering ability," the *Daily Commonwealth* reported.

In addition, the home county's "Jack Rabbit" Kearney, an A&M cheerleader, "made a big hit with the crowd with one of his dances . . . on a platform in front of the grandstand."

Third period action saw the Aggies gaining "considerable ground around the ends and off tackle," the *Memphis Commercial Appeal* reported. "Ole Miss tried a number of forward passes and trick plays which were uniformly broken up by the Maroons' defense." An electrifying punt return for touchdown by freshman guard Pat Wilson in the fourth quarter gave the Aggies' their final touchdown in the 20–0 win, their fourth straight shutout against Ole Miss.

The *Greenwood Daily Commonwealth* gave mixed ratings to the two teams: "Some brilliant work," the paper declared, "interspersed with ragged work on the part of both elevens," which seemed "unable to hold onto the elusive pigskin." The *Mississippian* placed responsibility for the defeat on the lines—"the much greater weight" of the Aggie line "and the fact that our line was much weakened by the recent expulsion of several of the strongest men on the team."

1921

Football and All That Jazz

1921 SCHEDULES

Ole Miss 3–6

RESULT	DATE	PF	OPPONENT	PA	LOCATION
W	October 1	82	West Tennessee Normal*	0	Oxford
L	October 8	0	Tulane	26	New Orleans
W	October 15	49	Millsaps	0	Oxford
W	October 22	35	Southwestern Presbyterian**	0	Oxford
L	October 29	0	Mississippi A&M	21	Greenwood
L	November 5	7	Mississippi College	27	Vicksburg
L	November 12	0	Louisiana State	21	Baton Rouge
L	November 19	6	Tennessee Medical College	24	Memphis
L	December 31	0	Havana University	14	Cuba

Mississippi A&M 4–4–1

RESULT	DATE	PF	OPPONENT	PA	LOCATION
W	October 1	20	Birmingham-Southern	7	Starkville
W	October 8	21	Ouachita Baptist	6	Starkville
W	October 15	14	Mississippi College	13	Jackson
L	October 22	0	Tulane	7	New Orleans
W	October 29	21	Mississippi	0	Greenwood
L	November 5	7	Tennessee	14	Memphis
L	November 11	7	Texas	54	Austin
T	November 24	7	Alabama	7	Birmingham
L	December 3	14	Louisiana State	17	Starkville

* Now University of Memphis
** Now Rhodes

The twenties were roaring, the Jazz Age was rolling, and Delta young people were upholding their reputation as fun loving. It was a colorful day for Greenwood as A&M and Ole Miss fans returned to see their teams square off again on the local baseball field. Streamers for both schools fluttered from automobiles, and fans showed off team colors. Special trains brought 100 students from A&M and 450 from the University, and enthusi-

Ole Miss, with the ball, goes against the Aggies in a tense moment on the neutral Greenwood baseball field. *Ole Miss*.

The traditional handshake between opposing captains—Howard Robinson, Ole Miss, left, and "Judge" Little, A&M, opened the second of two games in Greenwood. *Ole Miss*.

astic alumni met each group. Ole Miss students marched from the station and halted between the post office and Irving Hotel on Howard, the main business street, to give fifteen rahs for Greenwood and another fifteen for Ole Miss. Coaches pronounced their teams "in the pink of condition," and fans anticipated a good game. The Aggies were led by halfback Stennis (Judge) Little, while fullback Howard Robinson captained the Ole Miss squad.

By three o'clock the baseball park at the foot of Dewey Street was overflowing with five thousand fans—more than three times capacity—and the goalposts again were decorated in team colors. While the Aggie cadets were in bleachers that flanked the grandstand, most of Ole Miss's male students showed their support by following the action from the sideline. Each student section showed its sportsmanship by giving fifteen rahs for the opponent.

Twice in the first half, the heavier Ole Miss team halted A&M deep in Mississippi territory, but the Aggies went up by a second-period touchdown when Little converted a fourth and goal. Ole Miss immediately threatened, but the drive stalled, and A&M clung to its lead at halftime.

In the third period, A&M had a first down on the Ole Miss 34 yard line when the ball was centered through the quarterback's legs. Ole Miss tackle

Shed Davis grabbed the loose ball and raced 56 yards toward the Aggie goal. But end L. W. (Pete) Noble, brother of former lettermen Pickens and C. R. (Dudy) Noble, caught Davis on the 10, and Ole Miss then fumbled the ball away on its third play from scrimmage. Back came the Aggies, who strung together a 90-yard drive to take a two-touchdown lead. Little added his third touchdown of the day early in the final quarter, and the Aggies had a 21–0 triumph. They had now stretched their dominance to five games without allowing their most bitter rivals to score a single point.

The *Daily Commonwealth* praised Little as "almost unstoppable," adding that he had "reeled off . . . gain after gain around the wing positions." The paper ascribed "the greater part of the University's gains" to Calvin Barbour's "sweeping end runs from a trick formation."

Although Ole Miss finished the year with only a 3–5 record, the Havana Athletic Club (the same organization that had invited the Aggies to play a postseason contest after the 1911 campaign) invited Mississippi to come play in Cuba on December 31, 1921. With its touchdowns nullified by penalties, Ole Miss went down to the Cubans, 14–0.

1922

Hot Time in the Old Town

1922 SCHEDULES

Ole Miss 4–5–1

RESULT	DATE	PF	OPPONENT	PA	LOCATION
T	September 30	0	Union	0	Oxford
L	October 7	0	Centre	55	Danville
W	October 14	23	Southwestern Presbyterian*	0	Oxford
L	October 21	13	Mississippi A&M	19	Jackson
L	October 28	0	Tennessee	49	Knoxville
W	November 4	6	Birmingham-Southern	0	Oxford
W	November 11	13	Hendrix	7	Oxford
L	November 18	0	Tennessee Medical College	32	Memphis
L	November 25	13	Camp Benning	14	Columbus, GA
W	November 30	19	Millsaps	7	Jackson

Mississippi A&M 3–4–2

RESULT	DATE	PF	OPPONENT	PA	LOCATION
W	October 7	14	Birmingham-Southern	0	Starkville
T	October 14	0	Howard**	0	Starkville
W	October 21	19	Mississippi	13	Jackson
L	October 28	0	Tulane	26	New Orleans
T	November 4	7	Ouachita Baptist	7	Starkville
L	November 11	3	Tennessee	31	Memphis
W	November 18	7	Louisiana State	0	Baton Rouge
L	November 25	6	Drake	48	Starkville
L	November 30	0	Alabama	59	Birmingham

* Now Rhodes
** Now Samford

I t was State Fair Week, and the big game was back in Jackson for the first time in eleven years. Some fifteen thousand fans poured into town to help make this the largest crowd yet. Special trains brought students from Starkville and Oxford. Hotels were crowded, and many Jackson homes welcomed out-of-town visitors.

Both schools came into the October 21 game with first-year coaches. R. A. Cowell, an Illinois alumnus, was at the Ole Miss helm, while former A&M star and Ole Miss coach C. R. (Dudy) Noble was in his only full season as the Aggies' head football coach. Both A&M and Ole Miss had left the Southern Intercollegiate Athletic Association and were in their first year as members of the Southern Conference. Team captains were Aggie center S. H. Blair and Ole Miss quarterback Calvin Barbour.

Neither squad threatened in the first quarter. Ole Miss had an apparent safety nullified by a penalty before A&M reeled off 19 quick second-quarter points on fullback Gene Barnett's three touchdowns.

Gene Barnett scored all three touchdowns as A&M built a 19–0 lead before Ole Miss snapped back in a narrow 19–13 ball game. Barnett would also have a touchdown in the 1923 game. *Reveille*.

His first, a short jab, capped a 49-yard drive. Another short push for touchdown came after a 45-yard drive. Barnett's third score, from the 4, came after he, J. E. (Jazz) Luckett, and C. B. (Buck) Cameron had set up the threat with good runs.

When the Red and Blue retaliated with two touchdowns early in the fourth quarter, its fans went wild over their first points in the rivalry since 1917. William E. (Dooley) Akin capped a 70-yard drive with a short smack for score, and Barbour broke away for a 50-yard touchdown sprint. At 19–13, Ole Miss was hoping for a major upset. But victory was not to be. Despite a fumble recovery that put Ole Miss on the A&M 30 with about two minutes to play, the Red and Blue could reach only the 5 yard line. The Aggies held, and the A&M winning streak against Ole Miss was now ten.

1923

Push versus Pass

1923 SCHEDULES

Ole Miss 4–6

RESULT	DATE	PF	OPPONENT	PA	LOCATION
W	September 29	14	Bethel	6	Oxford
L	October 6	0	Alabama	56	Tuscaloosa
W	October 13	33	Southwestern Presbyterian*	0	Oxford
L	October 20	6	Mississippi A&M	13	Jackson
L	October 27	3	St. Louis	28	St. Louis
W	November 3	6	Birmingham-Southern	0	Oxford
L	November 10	0	Mississippi College	6	Meridian
L	November 17	0	Tulane	19	New Orleans
L	November 24	0	Tennessee	10	Knoxville
W	December 1	19	Camp Benning	7	Columbus

Mississippi A&M 5–2–2

RESULT	DATE	PF	OPPONENT	PA	LOCATION
W	October 6	28	Millsaps	6	Starkville
W	October 13	6	Ouachita Baptist	0	Starkville
W	October 20	13	Mississippi	6	Jackson
L	October 27	3	Tennessee	7	Memphis
T	November 3	0	Vanderbilt	0	Nashville
W	November 10	6	Union	0	Starkville
L	November 17	0	Illinois	27	Champaign
T	November 24	13	Florida	13	Jacksonville
W	December 1	14	Louisiana State	7	Starkville

* Now Rhodes

I t was the brute strength of the A&M ground game against the passing skills of Ole Miss. Push versus pass.

As the closing feature of the state fair, the game was back in Jackson and a big attraction. Students stepped off special trains aglow with optimism. Ole Miss's delegation displayed its enthusiasm with a parade up Capitol Street. Alumni led, followed by the band and students carrying banners of each of

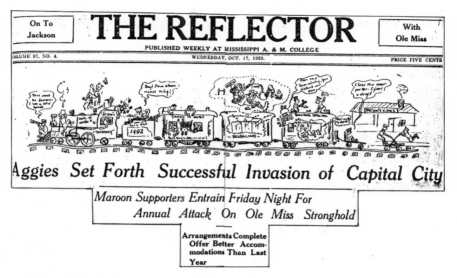

On To Jackson

THE REFLECTOR

PUBLISHED WEEKLY AT MISSISSIPPI A. & M. COLLEGE

With Ole Miss

VOLUME 37, NO. 4.   WEDNESDAY, OCT. 17, 1923.   PRICE FIVE CENTS

Aggies Set Forth Successful Invasion of Capital City

Maroon Supporters Entrain Friday Night For
Annual Attack On Ole Miss Stronghold

Arrangements Complete
Offer Better Accom-
modations Than Last
Year

Headline and cartoon from *College Reflector,* October 17, 1923.

the schools of the University as they sang the "Gridiron Chorus"—"the song of Ole Miss," according to the student newspaper, the *Mississippian.* The fairgrounds field was livened by the spirited music of both bands and the vigorous cheers of eight thousand "thrilled fans"—about half the size of the previous year's crowd. Second-year coach R. A. Cowell's Ole Miss squad arrived with a new nickname, the Southerners, selected by the student newspaper. New A&M coach Earl C. Abell reportedly told Cowell that the Aggies would be "satisfied with a seven-point victory." His team was undefeated, having won its first two games of the young season.

After a prompt 2:25 kickoff, the Aggie ground game produced a 13–0 half-time lead. Gene Barnett, continuing his touchdown assault from the previous year, capped a 55-yard Aggie drive with a buck from the 3, and L. W. (Pete) Noble notched the second A&M touchdown when he snatched up an Ole Miss fumble and ran the ball into the end zone. After the break, Ole Miss capitalized on an A&M fumble. At the end of a drive that relied heavily on the aerial game, Charlie Allen scored on a 4-yard run to cut the lead to 13–6. There the game ended, and Abell had his 7-point victory.

Push had beaten pass. The Aggies had the upper hand on the ground, where they more than doubled the Southerners' yardage—244 to 104. Through the air, Ole Miss had a decided advantage, completing eight of sixteen attempts for 127 yards compared to A&M's 16 yards on two of seven.

1924

Here's a Dozen, Cousin!

1924 SCHEDULES

Ole Miss 4–5

RESULT	DATE	PF	OPPONENT	PA	LOCATION
W	October 4	10	Arkansas A&M*	7	Oxford
W	October 11	7	Southwestern Presbyterian**	0	Oxford
L	October 18	0	Mississippi A&M	20	Jackson
L	October 25	0	Arkansas	20	Little Rock
L	November 1	0	Alabama	61	Montgomery
L	November 8	0	Sewanee	21	Memphis
L	November 15	2	Furman	7	Greenville
W	November 22	10	Mississippi College	6	Oxford
W	November 27	7	Millsaps	0	Jackson

Mississippi A&M 5–4

RESULT	DATE	PF	OPPONENT	PA	LOCATIONS
W	October 4	28	Millsaps	6	Starkville
L	October 11	0	Ouachita Baptist	12	Starkville
W	October 18	20	Mississippi	0	Jackson
W	October 25	7	Tennessee	2	Memphis
W	November 1	14	Tulane	6	New Orleans
L	November 8	0	Vanderbilt	18	Nashville
W	November 15	7	Mississippi College	6	Starkville
L	November 22	0	Florida	27	Montgomery
L	November 27	6	Washington University	12	St. Louis

* Now Arkansas State
** Now Rhodes

"History repeats," wrote the *Memphis Commercial Appeal*. "And so do the Mississippi Aggies in their annual game with the Ole Miss eleven." The teams' third consecutive matchup in Jackson produced A&M's twelfth consecutive victory in rivalry play. "Ole Miss was simply outplayed in every department," the Memphis paper summarized, "and local fans who figured things about even got a severe jolt. The

The Aggies threaten on the Ole Miss goal. Notice the proximity of the posts to the goal line. Three years later football rules moved the posts to a safer spot back of the end zone. Mississippi State University Photo.

Aggies showed much more drive than was expected." The *Jackson Clarion-Ledger* echoed the assessment: "Just plain outplayed and outclassed, that was all." The 20–0 blanking marked the Aggies' twelfth shutout win in the rivalry's twenty-two games.

The eight thousand or so fans who flocked to the state fairgrounds watched Earl C. Abell's A&M squad threaten in the first quarter with a 59-yard drive that fizzled on the 1-yard line. By halftime, the Aggies had built themselves a 10–0 lead on a 35-yard field goal by H. L. (Hook) Stone and a touchdown pass from team captain J. C. (Spec) Young to R. P. (Doc) Patty.

The Aggies opened the second half with a 75-yard scoring drive capped by another Stone field goal, this one from 40 yards out. Down 13–0, Ole Miss, led by coach Chester Barnard in his only season in Oxford, launched its only serious drive of the day, but a fumble put an end to the threat, and the Maroons added a fourth-quarter touchdown by Young at the end of a 50-yard drive that sealed the victory.

GAME 23

1925

Mississippi State
Fairgrounds, Jackson

Strange but True

1925 SCHEDULES

Ole Miss 5–5

RESULT	DATE	PF	OPPONENT	PA	LOCATION
W	September 26	53	Arkansas A&M*	0	Oxford
L	October 3	0	Texas	25	Austin
L	October 10	7	Tulane	26	New Orleans
W	October 17	7	Union	6	Oxford
L	October 24	0	Mississippi A&M	6	Jackson
L	October 31	0	Vanderbilt	7	Nashville
L	November 7	9	Sewanee	10	Chattanooga
W	November 14	19	Mississippi College	7	Clinton
W	November 21	31	Southwestern**	0	Oxford
W	November 26	21	Millsaps	0	Jackson

Mississippi A&M 3–4–1

RESULT	DATE	PF	OPPONENT	PA	LOCATION
W	October 3	34	Millsaps	0	Starkville
T	October 10	3	Ouachita Baptist	3	Starkville
L	October 17	3	Tulane	25	New Orleans
W	October 24	6	Mississippi	0	Jackson
L	October 31	0	Alabama	6	Tuscaloosa
W	November 7	46	Mississippi College	0	Starkville
L	November 14	9	Tennessee	14	Knoxville
L	November 21	0	Florida	12	Tampa

* Now Arkansas State
** Now Rhodes

The Aggies managed only one first down all day, completed just two of their four passes, and punted twelve times. A recipe for defeat? Nope. They won the game, 6–0.

Strange but true.

Game day in Jackson began with rain, but the weather did little to dampen the enthusiasm of the crowds watching the schools parade down Capitol

Street. Although the sun came out just before game time, neither team had much success in early play on the muddy field. The game turned into a fierce line battle, with passing entirely absent until the fourth quarter and A&M punters R. P. (Doc) Patty and P. E. Stephens dueling against Ole Miss's Sollie Cohen and Van Martin.

The Bulldogs' lone first down came in the third quarter; Ole Miss managed five first downs but couldn't score. The Aggies got their big chance when they blocked a punt midway through the fourth quarter and recovered on the Ole Miss 20. After two rushing attempts resulted in no gain, Jim (Old Man) Meeks completed the Aggies' first pass of the day, a 5-yard toss to H. L. (Hook) Stone. But the goal was still 15 yards away, and A&M was facing fourth down. Meeks connected with left end J. W. (Doc) Unger, who evaded three tacklers to cross the goal. Though Stone missed the extra-point kick, the Aggies had their victory. Despite the mud, the game was unusually clean—the two teams combined for just 15 penalty yards (10 for Ole Miss, 5 for A&M), still the all-time low for the rivalry.

In their first twenty-three meetings, Ole Miss and A&M had faced off eleven times in Jackson, with the Aggies taking eight victories. With the exception of the 1934 contest, however, the two teams would not return to the capital city for forty-eight years. There were just too many problems, most notably housing and grandstand seating. According to the *Mississippian*, "Jackson seems unable to accommodate the visitors to the fair and the two student bodies at the same time." In 1923, the Ole Miss student paper reported, the Aggies had been forced to spend the night in their Pullman cars because of lack of housing. Moreover, the fairgrounds had no dressing rooms, meaning that the teams had to change at their hotels, and players frequently took taxis or jogged to the field. And fans had to pay twice—once for admission to the state fair and then again to get into the game. Finally, there was the question of public apathy. "A general . . . indifference appeared," the *Mississippian* continued, "as to whether the game should be played in Jackson." The games would be coming back to campus.

1926

The Battle of Starkville

1926 SCHEDULES

Ole Miss 5–4

RESULT	DATE	PF	OPPONENT	PA	LOCATION
W	September 25	28	Arkansas A&M*	0	Oxford
L	October 2	6	Arkansas	21	Fayetteville
W	October 9	12	Florida	7	Gainesville
W	October 16	13	Loyola of Chicago	7	Oxford
L	October 23	15	Drake	33	Des Moines
L	October 30	0	Tulane	6	New Orleans
W	November 6	32	Southwestern**	27	Memphis
L	November 13	0	Louisiana State	3	Baton Rouge
W	November 25	7	Mississippi A&M	6	Starkville

Mississippi A&M 5–4

RESULT	DATE	PF	OPPONENT	PA	LOCATION
W	September 25	19	Birmingham-Southern	7	Birmingham
W	October 2	41	Mississippi College	0	Starkville
L	October 9	7	Alabama	26	Meridian
W	October 16	34	Millsaps	0	Starkville
W	October 23	7	Louisiana State	6	Jackson
L	October 30	0	Tennessee	33	Starkville
W	November 6	14	Tulane	0	New Orleans
L	November 13	6	Indiana	19	Bloomington
L	November 25	6	Mississippi	7	Starkville

* Now Arkansas State
** Now Rhodes

After thirteen straight losses to A&M, Ole Miss's dream of victory came true on Thanksgiving Day 1926, and it came on the toe of a senior player who had never before attempted an extra-point kick. Ole Miss 7, A&M 6.

As game day neared, enthusiasm spiraled among fans of both schools. Special trains brought spectators from Oxford and Columbus, Jackson and Greenville. Hotel and boardinghouse space was at capacity, and the Starkville

— THE SPIRIT OF 7 TO 6 —

An Ole Miss student artist depicts the results of the Big Game—his team's upset win, the fans' postgame fight for the goal posts, and the victory celebration that followed. *Ole Miss.*

Chamber of Commerce began placing fans in private homes. Box seats were $3.00, reserved seats $2.50, and student tickets $1.00. The crowd of eleven thousand eagerly snapped up even standing-room space. But hospitality was not universal: "Welcome, Ole Miss," A&M's *Reflector* announced, "the fun is at your expense." Coach Homer Hazel's Ole Miss team left Oxford wearing heavy growths of beard, having vowed not to shave until A&M was beaten. Observed a Jackson paper, "University supporters are hoping whiskers, mixed with jam-up football, will give them a triumph." Yet both coaches showed "cautious optimism." A&M's Bernie Bierman told the *New Orleans Times-Picayune*, "Ole Miss has the best team she has ever had, and her eleven will be hard to beat. However, I think my boys are capable of turning the trick." A day of slow rain had turned Scott Field into "a sea of mud," and Hazel predicted that the conditions would "play a large part in any victory or defeat." The Aggies agreed. Mud, they said, would "cramp their style."

Both scores came during the turbulent second quarter. Ole Miss took the lead on a six-play drive from midfield initiated by three consecutive passes by quarterback Harvey (Hubby) Walker. The score came when fullback Lacey Biles powered 3 yards for the score. Ole Miss captain Webster (Webb) Burke, who had never before attempted an extra-point kick and who was suffering from a jammed toe, booted the ball straight through the uprights, giving his team the 7–0 edge.

Bierman's Aggies responded with a 69-yard march that covered ten minutes of play and included only one pass. The touchdown came on a 4-yard fourth-down run by halfback R. R. Biggers. The Ole Miss line rushed the extra-point attempt, and W. B. Ricks missed the kick. The score stood at 7–6, Ole Miss.

Both teams threatened in the second half. Ole Miss reached the A&M 15, and the Aggies got to Ole Miss's 40. Ole Miss had its long-awaited victory. At the final whistle, both sides sent up huge roars. As the A&M players walked slowly off the field with heads bowed, wrote one newsman, the Aggie student section stood and sang the alma mater. On the east side, pandemonium reigned. Unleashing years of pent-up emotion, Ole Miss fans rushed "like madmen onto the field," Burke recalled in 1957, and began attacking the goalposts. As fights broke out between fans from the two schools, players on both sides stayed out of the melee.

Writers credited the play of Ole Miss's Biles, Walker, T. J. Lilly, tackle Robert Davis, guard T. J. Price, and tackle Mitch Salloum. For A&M, credit went to Biggers, fullback Jim (Old Man) Meeks, quarterback Clyde (Heifer) Stuart, and center/captain E. B. Jones.

The Battle of Starkville continued in print. A&M's *Reflector* claimed that the University players used unfair tactics, denounced stories complimenting clean play by Ole Miss, and charged that "only a band of hoodlums" would have swarmed onto the field to secure souvenirs. The *Mississippian* retorted that Aggie fans had responded to the Ole Miss celebration "with malice aforethought . . . with the intent of staging a 'free for all.'" Despite such heated charges and countercharges, fans on both sides were shocked by the violence among the spectators, but from that fight, the Golden Egg was born.

1927

Scramble for an Egg

1927 SCHEDULES

Ole Miss 5–3–1

RESULT	DATE	PF	OPPONENT	PA	LOCATION
W	September 24	58	Ozarks	0	Oxford
L	October 1	7	Tulane	19	New Orleans
T	October 7	0	Hendrix	0	Oxford
L	October 15	7	Tennessee	21	Knoxville
W	October 22	39	Southwestern*	0	Memphis
W	October 29	28	Sewanee	14	Sewanee
W	November 5	12	Louisiana State	7	Oxford
L	November 11	6	Loyola of Chicago	7	Jackson
W	November 24	20	Mississippi A&M	12	Oxford

Mississippi A&M 5–3

RESULT	DATE	PF	OPPONENT	PA	LOCATION
W	October 1	27	Birmingham-Southern	0	Starkville
W	October 8	14	Louisiana Tech	0	Starkville
W	October 15	13	Tulane	6	New Orleans
L	October 22	7	Louisiana State	9	Jackson
L	October 29	7	Alabama	13	Tuscaloosa
W	November 12	7	Auburn	6	Birmingham
W	November 18	6	Millsaps	0	Starkville
L	November 24	12	Mississippi	20	Oxford

* Now Rhodes

The first Battle of the Golden Egg, on Thanksgiving Day 1927, proved to be the biggest game yet. New concrete stands had just been completed on the east (visitor's) side. End zone bleachers had been erected by volunteer student labor to give the Oxford stadium "a bowl effect," bragged the *Mississippian*. In addition to the fourteen thousand spectators packed into the stands, a large overflow filled the surrounding hillsides, making this the largest audience yet for a rivalry game. At least four special trains had brought

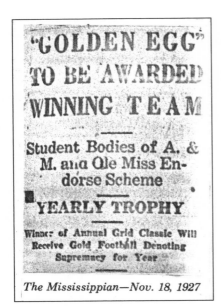

Headline from the *Mississippian*, November 18, 1927.

Game program.

fans to Oxford. The ten-car train from A&M had left at six o'clock in the morning ($5.99 round trip) and was met at the station just off the campus by a large crowd of Ole Miss students offering "a hearty welcome," reported the A&M *Reflector*. Oxford restaurants planned for extra business. Student marshals were posted on campus to control the anticipated heavy automobile traffic.

A light rain was falling at the two o'clock kickoff. For the second time in four years, the game pitted push against pass, but this time it was Ole Miss's running attack against A&M's aerial exploits. Ole Miss was especially strong on the right, with V. K. Smith at guard, Thaddeus (Pie) Vann at tackle, and captain Austin (Ap) Applewhite anchoring the end. The Aggies were captained by center Bill Brunson.

The lighter Aggie team jumped to a 6–0 lead on a touchdown pass from quarterback Gene Chadwick (son of the A&M athletic director) to fullback Willie Wells. The Red and Blue ground game snapped right back in the second quarter with a 51-yard scoring drive capped by fullback Sollie Cohen's 1-yard scoring plunge. Lee T. (Cowboy) Woodruff faked the kick and ran the extra point, giving Ole Miss a 7–6 edge, a lead it would never relinquish.

The rain ended while the Maroon Band was performing at the break, and the sun shone on Ole Miss in the second half. The home team drove straight

Fullback Dutch Stone scores A&M's second touchdown before a packed Thanksgiving Day crowd watching the first Battle of the Golden Egg. Mississippi State University Photo.

for a touchdown, with Woodruff scoring from the 6, and then converted an interception into another 6 points on a run by right halfback Reuben (Rube) Wilcox. The Red and Blue had a commanding 20–6 lead.

The Aggies added a third-quarter touchdown with Chadwick's passing attack that set up L. H. (Dutch) Stone's one-yard plunge and closed the gap to just 8 points but could get no closer, and the University had its second straight victory over A&M, 20–12. Once again, push had proved superior to pass: the Red and Blue totaled eighteen first downs to the Aggies' fourteen; A&M completed nine of fifteen passes, Ole Miss one of four.

The first presentation of the Golden Egg was a dignified ceremony far removed from the previous year's game-ending brouhaha. In the new competitive spirit, wrote A&M's *Reflector*, University students "didn't rub it in." Further displaying a new cooperative spirit, the editor of the *Mississippian* suggested that the two schools be consolidated into a single institution "with increased facilities, better teaching staff, enlarged personnel of students." Moreover, mused the writer, "What a football team that school will put out, a combination unbeatable by any aggregation in the country." In his inaugural address delivered the following January, Governor Theodore G. Bilbo included just such a proposal to merge A&M and the University of Mississippi. The idea soon died in the face of vehement opposition from alumni of both schools, the University's chancellor, and citizens of Oxford, who held a protest meeting.

1928

Tad, Toe, Touchdown

1928 SCHEDULES

Ole Miss 5–4

RESULT	DATE	PF	OPPONENT	PA	LOCATION
W	September 29	25	Arkansas	0	Oxford
L	October 6	0	Alabama	27	Tuscaloosa
L	October 13	12	Tennessee	13	Knoxville
W	October 20	19	Auburn	0	Birmingham
L	October 27	14	Loyola of New Orleans	34	New Orleans
W	November 3	26	Clemson	7	Oxford
L	November 10	6	Louisiana State	19	Baton Rouge
W	November 17	34	Southwestern*	2	Memphis
W	November 29	20	Mississippi A&M	19	Starkville

Mississippi A&M 2–4–2

RESULT	DATE	PF	OPPONENT	PA	LOCATION
W	September 29	20	Ouachita Baptist	6	Starkville
L	October 6	6	Tulane	51	Jackson
L	October 13	0	Alabama	46	Starkville
L	October 20	0	Louisiana State	31	Jackson
T	November 3	6	Michigan State	6	East Lansing
T	November 10	6	Centenary	6	Starkville
W	November 17	13	Auburn	0	Birmingham
L	November 29	19	Mississippi	20	Starkville

* Now Rhodes

Though the 1928 Battle of the Golden Egg featured two have-nots battling for their biggest win of the season, the game was "perhaps the most desperate and thrilling . . . ever staged between these two teams," the *Memphis Commercial Appeal* boldly declared. Despite the fact that both teams had mediocre records—the Maroons at 2–3–2 and the Red and Blue at 4–4—temporary bleachers had to be erected to handle the fourteen thousand fans who descended on Starkville for the game. Special trains rolled in from Oxford, Columbus, McComb, and Greenville.

"Woodruff comes through," the student yearbook notes. The dark-shirted Ole Miss visitors and white-shirted Aggies clash in tense rivalry action during the 1928 game in Starkville. *Ole Miss.*

Ole Miss coach Homer Hazel's squad scored on its third possession of the game, a 59-yard drive that ended with fullback Lee T. (Cowboy) Woodruff running 4 yards for the touchdown. Claude M. (Tadpole) Smith's point-after kick was no good, and the Red and Blue was up, 6–0.

A&M quarterback E. R. Allen retaliated, engineering a 78-yard scoring march that enabled the Aggies to knot the game on Dallas Vandevere's 3-yard fourth-down end run. The half ended with the score tied after Ole Miss's Reuben (Rube) Wilcox kicked a spectacular 80-yard punt, still the rivalry's longest.

Coach J. W. Hancock's Aggies jumped out in front right after the half with an 85-yard drive on which quarterback W. A. (Pap) Pappenheimer and G. L. Carley shared ball-carrying duties. After Pappenheimer's 9-yard touchdown run and O. L. (Shorty) Smith's kick, the Aggies had a 13–6 advantage.

But the lead was brief. Ole Miss tied the game soon after Tad Smith, "a poison thorn in the bruised flesh of the Aggies," according to the *Jackson Clarion-Ledger*, returned an A&M punt to the Aggie 15. Two plays later, Gerald Walker hit left end for the score. Lee T. (Cowboy) Woodruff knotted the count with a buck over center.

In the fourth quarter, Smith reeled off a 40-yard touchdown run behind Woodruff's interference and followed up with the extra-point kick to put the University up 20–13. The kick turned out to be the difference in the game.

Only a minute remained when the Aggies started their comeback, and they covered the 67 yards in only two plays. Vandevere's pass to J. C. Harris reached the Mississippi 31; his second hit captain W. H. Pickens for a 20-yard pass/run that shrank the Ole Miss lead to a single point. Pickens's kick failed, however, and the Red and Blue had its third straight victory over A&M, 20–19—and its second 1-point win in the rivalry in three years.

1929

GAME 27

Ole Miss Field, Oxford

Much Ado about Nothing

1929 SCHEDULES

Ole Miss 1–6–2

RESULT	DATE	PF	OPPONENT	PA	LOCATION
L	September 28	7	Vanderbilt	19	Nashville
L	October 5	7	Alabama	22	Tuscaloosa
L	October 12	7	Tennessee	52	Knoxville
W	October 18	26	Loyola of New Orleans	24	New Orleans
L	October 26	0	Southern Methodist	52	Dallas
T	November 2	6	Sewanee	6	Oxford
L	November 9	7	Purdue	27	West Lafayette
L	November 16	6	Louisiana State	13	Baton Rouge
T	November 28	7	Mississippi A&M	7	Oxford

Mississippi A&M 1–5–2

RESULT	DATE	PF	OPPONENT	PA	LOCATION
L	September 27	0	Henderson State	7	Starkville
L	October 5	13	Georgia Tech	27	Atlanta
L	October 12	0	Tulane	34	New Orleans
L	October 19	6	Louisiana State	31	Jackson
W	November 2	6	Mississippi College	0	Starkville
L	November 9	19	Michigan State	33	Jackson
T	November 16	0	Millsaps	0	Starkville
T	November 28	7	Mississippi	7	Oxford

I f the 1928 Ole Miss–A&M contest was a battle of mediocre teams, the next rivalry game pitted two downright bad squads against each other. However, "past records can be forgotten," said one pregame story: "Victory means a successful season for the winner."

Thousands of fans flocked to Oxford for the game, encouraged by the announcement by the city's mayor that all highways were in fine condition: "Good gravel all the way." A special train from Starkville brought five hundred Maroon fans. Another train from McComb picked up fans in Jackson, Canton, and Durant. Private planes arrived from Baton Rouge and Ft. Worth.

KYZAR
HALF

Sam Kyzer scored for Ole Miss on an off-tackle plunge in the fourth period. *Ole Miss*.

Ole Miss was playing under a proud new nickname, the Mississippi Flood, which had beaten out the Rebels, the Democrats, and the Ole Marsters in a contest sponsored by the school's student newspaper, the *Mississippian*. The Flood held a secret practice the day before the Thanksgiving game, and for the fourth year the players let their whiskers grow "to assure victory."

November 30 dawned wet and windy. In an attempt to dry the field, the Ole Miss subs burned the ground with gasoline, but part of the south end remained "almost ankle deep" in water. Nevertheless, twelve thousand fans braved the weather, showing "lots of pep"—perhaps, one observer noted, because a few were not "duly sober." One fellow was "a countryman," he explained, "full of corn." Governor Theodore G. Bilbo sat in a box seat on the 50. The four Ole Miss cheerleaders were "working like maniacs," according to one newspaper account, and the Ole Miss crowd sang, "Hail, Hail, the Gang's All Here." The reporter judged the teams "well matched" and observed that the "A&M boys on the side line look like they are praying, and shaking hands."

Ole Miss fielded a heavier team, but, the *Mississippian* acknowledged, "any advantage that the University has in weight, A&M offsets in speed and trickery." The Flood stayed primarily with the ground game, while A&M relied on passes, but neither team could gain much of an advantage where it counted—on the scoreboard. When the Aggies' C. Pittman fell on a fumbled punt in the second quarter, his team took the ball on the Mississippi 22. Two plays and an extra point later, A&M had a 7–0 lead. Eddie Thompson passed to right halfback R. L. Lenoir at the goal and eager defenders pushed Lenoir into the end zone. Thompson combined with R. H. Culpepper for the extra point. "They are surely raising H—— behind me now," wrote a *Clarion-Ledger* reporter from the A&M side.

Clouds moved in during the third quarter, and rain became a threat. Ole Miss's score came in the fourth when the Flood capitalized on an Aggie miscue as Wallace Bowles recovered a fumble on the A&M 45. Sam Kyzer got the touchdown after five plays had brought the ball to the 4. Marshall Bentley kicked the extra point to even the score at 7. "This crowd is going crazy," the reporter declared. Though both squads threatened, the two frustrated teams had to settle for their first tie since 1903. A&M had its first possession of the Golden Egg, and though the ground rules called for each team to have the Egg for six months in case of a tie, A&M refused to give up the trophy, retaining it until the squads met again in 1930.

1930

Noble in for Cagle

1930 SCHEDULES

Ole Miss 3–5–1

RESULT	DATE	PF	OPPONENT	PA	LOCATION
W	September 26	64	Union	0	Oxford
L	October 4	0	Alabama	64	Tuscaloosa
L	October 11	0	Tennessee	27	Knoxville
L	October 18	7	Sewanee	13	Oxford
T	October 25	0	Chicago	0	Chicago
L	November 1	0	Vanderbilt	24	Nashville
L	November 8	0	Louisiana State	6	Baton Rouge
W	November 14	37	Southwestern*	6	Oxford
W	November 27	20	Mississippi A&M	0	Starkville

Mississippi A&M 2–7

RESULT	DATE	PF	OPPONENT	PA	LOCATION
L	September 27	0	Southwestern*	14	Starkville
L	October 4	12	Mississippi College	13	Jackson
L	October 11	13	Millsaps	19	Starkville
W	October 18	8	Louisiana State	6	Jackson
L	October 25	0	North Carolina State	14	Raleigh
L	November 1	0	Tulane	53	New Orleans
L	November 8	7	Henderson State	25	Starkville
W	November 15	7	Auburn	6	Birmingham
L	November 27	0	Mississippi	20	Starkville

* Now Rhodes

For the second time in his career, C. R. (Dudy) Noble was coaching a Maroon squad against Ole Miss. With almost no warning, the task had fallen his way when Chris (Red) Cagle resigned as A&M's coach just before the most important game on the schedule. Cagle, an all-American the year earlier at Army, was barely older than his players. Disappointed that his team had won just two games, Cagle resigned to play professional football. Noble's players faced a Mississippi squad in its first year under coach

M

Official Souvenir Program
UNIVERSITY OF MISSISSIPPI
vs
MISSISSIPPI A. & M. COLLEGE

Thursday,

Nov. 27

1930

Thanksgiving

Kick-off

2 P. M.

A. & M. College, Mississippi
Price Twenty-five Cents

Game program.

Edgar Lee Walker, who had played under the famous Pop Warner at Stanford and who brought Warner's razzle-dazzle of reverses, fakes, and triple passes to Oxford.

A special train left Oxford at six o'clock Thanksgiving morning for the five-hour ride to Starkville, where kickoff was scheduled for two o'clock. Student game tickets were $1.00. Guests and parents paid $2.50 for reserved seats, $3.00 for box seats. The afternoon was crisp and sunny, and enthusiasm

Already a star in his two years at halfback, Neal Biggers scored Ole Miss's second touchdown, then kicked the extra point. Biggers would also serve as captain of the 1931 team. *Ole Miss*.

was high among the eight thousand fans. Captain of the home-field Maroons was Miller Matthews. Dick Peeples captained the Flood.

The Aggies were well prepared to face the Warner system and stopped many of the double and triple handoffs. Ole Miss found success running at the Aggie center, however. The Maroons made several threats but succumbed to mistakes, including fumbles that opened the way for two Ole Miss touchdowns. The Flood offense was paced by fullback Guy Turnbow, a "Goliath" (in the words of the *Memphis Commercial Appeal*) whose running, passing, and kicking led to all of the Ole Miss touchdowns and who would become the first Ole Miss player to score in three consecutive rivalry games when he counted one touchdown and kicked an extra point.

The Flood took a 20–0 halftime lead. The first touchdown was set up by a punt recovery on the A&M 35. Sam Kyzer skirted left end from the 5 for the score. Turnbow kicked the point. An Aggie punt went out on the A&M 30, and Neal Biggers capped the drive with a plunge from the 1, then kicked the point after. The third touchdown was easy. When an Aggie fumble rolled backward and Ole Miss recovered on the 1, Turnbow burst through on the third play. It was Ole Miss's first shutout victory since 1910. In addition to Turnbow, the *Commercial Appeal* lauded the play of both sides' backs and centers—Ole Miss's Peeples and George Boutwell and A&M's Eddie Thompson, George Carley, Bob Herrington, and Philip Gousset.

1931

Rivalry Is Everything

1931 SCHEDULES

Ole Miss 2–6–1

RESULT	DATE	PF	OPPONENT	PA	LOCATION
W	September 19	13	Western Kentucky	6	Oxford
L	September 26	0	Tulane	31	New Orleans
L	October 3	6	Alabama	55	Tuscaloosa
L	October 10	0	Tennessee	38	Knoxville
T	October 24	20	Southwestern*	20	Memphis
L	October 30	6	Marquette	13	Milwaukee
L	November 7	0	Sewanee	7	Oxford
L	November 14	3	Louisiana State	26	Jackson
W	November 26	25	Mississippi A&M	14	Oxford

Mississippi A&M 2–6

RESULT	DATE	PF	OPPONENT	PA	LOCATION
W	September 26	10	Millsaps	7	Jackson
L	October 3	2	Mississippi College	6	Starkville
L	October 10	0	Alabama	53	Meridian
L	October 17	0	Louisiana State	31	Baton Rouge
L	October 31	7	Tulane	59	New Orleans
L	November 7	0	North Carolina State	6	Starkville
W	November 14	14	Southwestern*	0	Starkville
L	November 26	14	Mississippi	25	Oxford

* Now Rhodes

Neither the Aggies nor the Flood had much to brag about in 1931. A&M, under new coach Ray Dauber and captain Philip Gousset, had recorded only a pair of victories, while Ole Miss, captained by Neal Biggers and led by second-year coach Ed Walker, had managed only a single win and a tie. Yet the rivalry remained strong, and ten thousand converged on Oxford for the Thanksgiving afternoon game, with students paying $1.00 per ticket and others paying $2.50.

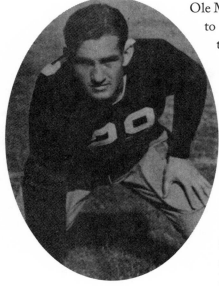

Moments after scoring on a line smash, Ole Miss's Brad White brought the crowd to its feet when he dashed 60 yards down the sideline for another touchdown. White also would score in the 1932 game. *Ole Miss.*

Ole Miss used the flashy Pop Warner system to score twice in the second quarter and twice more in the third. Guy Turnbow scored the first Ole Miss touchdown. The second score came on one of the Warner system's triple hand-offs, with Turnbow handing off to Zollie Swor and Swor lateraling to Kirk Haynes, who dashed 20 yards into the end zone. Ole Miss turned the second-half kickoff into a scoring drive, with Brad White doing the honors and then repeating the feat with a 60-yard sideline run that made the score 25–0. Bob Herrington launched a sensational 65-yard punt that pinned Ole Miss on its own 6-inch line, and the A&M defense refused to allow the Flood to escape the shadow of their goal. The preceding year's star, Turnbow, punted the ball out of the end zone as far as the Ole Miss 35, and Herrington returned the ball 10 yards. A few plays later, Herrington scored; then he kicked the extra point to cut the deficit to 18. In the fourth quarter, Ole Miss missed a chance to pad its lead, losing a fumble on the A&M 3. The Aggies added another score on a 50-yard drive to close the gap to 25–14. John Marble scored on the sixth play of the series, and Ralph Brown added the point after. But the Aggies could get no closer, and the Flood had their fifth win in their last six games against their archrivals.

1932

Now It's *State* versus Ole Miss

1932 SCHEDULES

Ole Miss 5–6

RESULT	DATE	PF	OPPONENT	PA	LOCATION
W	September 24	49	Mississippi Teachers*	0	Oxford
L	October 1	0	Tennessee	33	Knoxville
W	October 8	26	Howard**	6	Oxford
L	October 15	6	Centenary	13	Shreveport
L	October 22	13	Alabama	24	Tuscaloosa
L	October 29	7	Auburn	14	Montgomery
L	November 5	0	Minnesota	26	Minneapolis
W	November 12	27	Sewanee	6	Oxford
W	November 19	7	Southwestern***	0	Memphis
W	November 24	13	Mississippi State	0	Starkville
L	December 3	0	Tulsa	26	Tulsa

Mississippi State 3–5

RESULT	DATE	PF	OPPONENT	PA	LOCATION
L	October 1	0	Alabama	53	Montgomery
W	October 8	18	Mississippi College	7	Jackson
L	October 15	0	Louisiana State	24	Monroe
W	October 22	9	Millsaps	8	Starkville
L	October 27	0	Indiana	19	Bloomington
L	November 5	0	Tennessee	31	Knoxville
W	November 12	6	Southwestern***	0	Starkville
L	November 24	0	Mississippi	13	Starkville

* Now Southern Mississippi
** Now Samford
*** Now Rhodes

A cting in response to a petition from the school's student body, the Mississippi Legislature changed the name of Mississippi A&M to Mississippi State College. Thenceforth, the rivalry would be between Ole Miss and State—or State and Ole Miss, depending on your loyalty. Unfortunately for the newly named Mississippi State Maroons and their coach, Ray Dauber, the name change did not bring a new outcome in the Battle of the Golden Egg, and they went down again to the Flood, 13–0.

In preparation for the Thanksgiving contest, the Ole Miss squad spent the night en route and arrived in Starkville on Wednesday afternoon. The University's coach, Homer Hazel, "refused to comment on the probable outcome," the *Commercial Appeal* reported, but believed "his charges amply able to render a good account of themselves" behind captain Lee Trapp, a guard. Injuries plagued the Maroons, who would be playing without wingback Orlie Price and quarterbacks C. T. (Chick) Burch, Frank Waits, and Carl Sikes. Subbing at quarterback would be team captain Elmer Tutor, who had been moved from halfback. The good news was that for the first time in nearly a month, A&M's entire front wall was healthy, with Buford Taylor and William (Beef) Maxwell back at tackle.

The Scott Field playing surface had been improved in preparation for the game, and while the stands had been enlarged to accommodate ten thousand, the stadium was only just over half full. In the crowd was the state's new governor, Mike Connor.

The contest remained scoreless through the first half, but each team threatened early in the third quarter. Tutor completed a 34-yard pass to Leslie Horne but followed up by throwing an interception to Pete Ruby, who returned the ball to midfield. Jack Burke, Earl Hutson, and Brad White advanced the ball to State's 11, but two incomplete passes stopped the drive. Ole Miss broke through early in the final period. A penalty on a State punt gave Ole Miss the ball at the Maroon 35. Sharing the ball-carrying responsibilities, Hutson, White, and George Gunter picked up good yardage, with Gunter crossing the goal line and Guy Turnbow adding the extra point for a 7–0 lead. Shortly thereafter, Chester Curtis increased the Ole Miss cushion with a rousing 53-yard punt return for a touchdown. Although Turnbow's point-after attempt was no good, Ole Miss had the victory.

1933

GAME 31

Ole Miss Field, Oxford

The Rain Doesn't Let Up, and Neither Does the Rivalry

1933 SCHEDULES

Ole Miss 6–3–2

RESULT	DATE	PF	OPPONENT	PA	LOCATION
T	September 23	6	Southwestern*	6	Memphis
W	September 30	45	Mississippi Teachers**	0	Oxford
T	October 7	0	Alabama	0	Birmingham
W	October 14	7	Marquette	0	Milwaukee
W	October 21	41	Sewanee	0	Oxford
W	October 28	13	Clemson	0	Meridian
W	November 4	12	Birmingham-Southern	0	Oxford
L	November 11	6	Tennessee	35	Knoxville
L	November 18	0	Louisiana State	31	Baton Rouge
L	November 25	6	Centenary	7	Jackson
W	December 2	31	Mississippi State	0	Oxford

Mississippi State 3–6–1

RESULT	DATE	PF	OPPONENT	PA	LOCATION
W	September 30	12	Millsaps	0	Starkville
L	October 7	0	Tennessee	20	Knoxville
L	October 14	0	Alabama	18	Tuscaloosa
T	October 21	7	Vanderbilt	7	Nashville
L	October 27	0	Southwestern*	6	Memphis
W	November 4	18	Mississippi College	0	Starkville
L	November 11	0	Tulane	33	New Orleans
W	November 18	26	Sewanee	13	Starkville
L	November 25	6	Louisiana State	21	Monroe
L	December 2	0	Mississippi	31	Oxford

* Now Rhodes
** Now Southern Mississippi

Half an hour before kickoff, the drenching rain began, and the chill only added to players' and fans' discomfort. Yet most of the seventy-five hundred stuck it out. When the water soaked their laps so they could no longer bear to sit, many simply moved down to follow the action from the sidelines. "It was remarkable in a way," wrote Early Maxwell of the

Memphis Commercial Appeal, "how the crowd lasted . . . how the bands . . . 'whooped' it up until the final whistle."

State was under new coach Ross McKechnie, a U.S. Army captain and former halfback at Washington who had succeeded Ray Dauber when he departed for an assistantship at Tulane. The two quarterbacks, Ole Miss's Pete Ruby and State's Bob Herrington, served as captains.

Ole Miss coach Ed Walker prepared to meet an aerial attack, but the rain severely weakened State's passing game, and the Maroons never mustered a serious threat. Wet conditions failed to slow the Ole Miss ground game, which produced five touchdowns for a 31–0 victory, the Red and Blue's highest point total to date against its Starkville foes. After a scoreless first quarter, Ole Miss's first scoring drive saw Earl Hutson take the ball in from the 4. George Gunter then smacked over from the 12. Pete Ruby hit center for 6 more points before the game's most sensational play of the day: Gunter, threatened in punt formation, galloped 70 yards to score. Rab Rodgers counted the last touchdown with two minutes to play.

According to Maxwell, it "was a case of too much Ole Miss power." The home team dominated thoroughly, outgaining the Maroons by nearly 270 yards (340 versus 69) and racking up fourteen first downs to State's three.

The 1933 game was the first between Ole Miss and State under the banner of the new Southeastern Conference. The preceding December, the two schools had joined eleven other members of the cumbersome Southern Conference in breaking away to form the new league. Ole Miss finished its first conference slate with a 2–2–1 record, good for a tie for sixth place; the 1–5–1 Maroons finished twelfth.

1934

Breaks? Or Tough Football?

1934 SCHEDULES

Ole Miss 4–5–1

RESULT	DATE	PF	OPPONENT	PA	LOCATION
W	September 29	44	West Tennessee Teachers*	0	Oxford
W	October 5	19	Southwestern**	0	Clarksdale
L	October 13	0	Tennessee	27	Knoxville
L	October 20	6	Howard***	7	Oxford
W	October 27	19	Sewanee	6	Oxford
L	November 3	0	Tulane	15	New Orleans
T	November 10	13	Florida	13	Gainesville
L	November 17	0	Louisiana State	14	Jackson
L	November 24	6	Centenary	13	Shreveport
W	December 1	7	Mississippi State	3	Jackson

Mississippi State 4–6

RESULT	DATE	PF	OPPONENT	PA	LOCATION
W	September 21	13	Howard***	7	Birmingham
L	September 29	0	Vanderbilt	7	Nashville
L	October 5	6	Millsaps	7	Starkville
L	October 13	0	Alabama	41	Tuscaloosa
W	October 20	21	Southwestern**	6	Memphis
W	October 26	13	Mississippi College	6	Starkville
L	November 3	3	Louisiana State	25	Baton Rouge
L	November 10	0	Tennessee	14	Knoxville
W	November 17	20	Loyola	6	New Orleans
L	December 1	3	Mississippi	7	Jackson

* Now University of Memphis
** Now Rhodes
*** Now Samford

Though it was technically State's home game, the 1934 Battle of the Golden Egg marked the series' return to Jackson for the first time in nine years. Although the contest drew a crowd of eleven thousand—the largest in five years—the two teams would not play again in the capital city until 1973. Mississippi governor Martin S. Connor and Jackson mayor Walter A.

Mississippi State students present a solid show of support in a pregame parade on Capitol Street in Jackson. Signs urge the Maroons to "Dam That Flood" and beat the "Shyster Lawyers." *Reveille.*

Scott started off the festivities by leading a morning parade up Capitol Street. In addition to the politicos, the procession featured officials, student groups, and bands from both schools as well as the Jackson Boys Band, representatives from Millsaps and Belhaven Colleges, the Jackson High School Band, the National Guard Band, the Shrine Band, and the Boy Scouts.

High-spirited practices marked preparations for the game. Ole Miss coach Ed Walker closed the week's practices so that the team could work in secret on new plays from punt formation to offset State's kicking superiority. Coach Ross McKechnie's Maroons polished their offense. Analysts called the Maroons and the Red and Blue evenly matched, and Walker agreed, telling one newspaper that "breaks" might decide the outcome.

It was an old-fashioned defensive ball game, as the teams battled through three scoreless quarters before unleashing fireworks during a frenzied final period. When the smoke cleared, Ole Miss emerged with a narrow 7–3 victory. State moved the ball inside the

December 1, 1934

Ole Miss 7, Mississippi State 3

	State	Ole Miss
First downs	9	11
Total yards	190	127
Net yards rushing	121	119
Passing yards	69	8
Passes		
(Att-Comp-Int)	13-6-4	2-2-0
Penalties/yards	8/80	5/55

State's Charles (Pee Wee) Armstrong, background, arches a high pass as Ole Miss tacklers close in. Armstrong's accurate tosses were a constant threat to the Flood for three years. *Reveille*.

Ole Miss 35 on seven different possessions, but eight penalties for 80 yards plus four interceptions thwarted the Maroons. The Starkville gridders managed to draw first blood with a 40-yard field goal by captain Jesse Haley, but this only seemed to energize the Ole Miss players, who became, in the words of the *Jackson Clarion-Ledger*, "a bunch of mauling moleskin maniacs." They immediately surged 65 yards in six plays—four runs and two passes—for the winning points. Rab Rodgers scored from the 3 on a reverse, then held as Earl Hutson kicked the point.

Rodgers set a rivalry record—since tied but never surpassed—with three interceptions on the day, the last one coming with less than five minutes remaining to ice the game. Overall, Ole Miss grabbed four pickoffs, the most in a single Ole Miss–State game until 1972.

GAME 33

Ole Miss Field, Oxford

1935

Give 'Em the Razzle-Dazzle

1935 SCHEDULES

Ole Miss 9–3

RESULT	DATE	PF	OPPONENT	PA	LOCATION
W	September 20	20	Millsaps	0	Jackson
W	September 28	92	West Tennessee Teachers*	0	Oxford
W	October 5	33	Southwestern**	0	Oxford
W	October 11	33	Sewanee	0	Clarksdale
W	October 19	27	Florida	6	Oxford
L	October 26	7	Marquette	33	Milwaukee
W	November 1	21	St. Louis	7	St. Louis
L	November 9	13	Tennessee	14	Memphis
W	November 16	26	Centre	0	Danville
W	November 23	6	Centenary	0	Jackson
W	November 30	14	Mississippi State	6	Oxford
L	January 1, 1936	19	Catholic University	20	Orange Bowl

Mississippi State 8–3

RESULT	DATE	PF	OPPONENT	PA	LOCATION
W	September 20	19	Howard***	7	Starkville
L	September 28	9	Vanderbilt	14	Nashville
W	October 4	45	Millsaps	0	Starkville
W	October 12	20	Alabama	7	Tuscaloosa
W	October 18	6	Loyola	0	New Orleans
W	October 26	7	Xavier	0	Cincinnati
W	November 2	13	Army	7	West Point
L	November 9	13	Louisiana State	28	Baton Rouge
W	November 15	27	Mississippi Teachers+	0	Hattiesburg
W	November 23	25	Sewanee	0	Starkville
L	November 30	6	Mississippi	14	Oxford

* Now University of Memphis
** Now Rhodes
*** Now Samford
+ Now Southern Mississippi

For the first time in twenty-five years, both Ole Miss and State brought winning records into their annual meeting. A total of 14,500 fans came to Oxford to see two teams in a powerful display of the deceptive razzle-dazzle system popularized by Glenn (Pop) Warner at Stanford. In the first of his three seasons at State after a successful coaching career at Army, Ralph Sasse had given the Maroons their first winning record in nine seasons. As inspiration, Sasse obtained State's first live Bulldog mascot, named Tol. Ole Miss's Ed Walker was back for his sixth coaching campaign.

When State couldn't move with the opening kickoff, Ole Miss launched a 67-yard scoring drive covering ten plays, most of which featured the brotherly running duo of Clarence (Big) and Ray (Little) Hapes. Big Hapes recorded the touchdown on a plunge from the 2, Bill Richardson made the extra-point kick, and Ole Miss had a 7–0 lead.

With opening of the second quarter, Sasse sent in Charles (Pee Wee) Armstrong, playing with two broken ribs, to get something going for the Maroons, who had the ball on their own 32. Armstrong connected with Fred Walters on a 15-yard pass, and Walters raced down the sideline to the Ole Miss 9. Armstrong and Walters had combined to give State one of its all-time great victories when the Maroons knocked off undefeated Army 13–7 earlier in the season. But the Maroons could get only 4 more yards before the Ole Miss line stiffened, and a four-way onslaught of Richardson, Claude (Red) Jackson, Frank (Bruiser) Kinard, and James (Buster) Poole threw Armstrong back to the 20. Poole and Kinard "tore into the backfield" all afternoon, wrote the *Birmingham Age-Herald*. Ole Miss's 7–0 advantage was safe for now.

That lead remained unchanged into the fourth quarter, when Armstrong and the Maroons started clicking again, mounting an 80-yard touchdown march. Bill Steadman's touchdown run brought State to within 1 point, but Maroon hearts fell when the extra-point kick hit the upright. Little Hapes, whom Birmingham sportswriter Bob Phillips dubbed "the original swivel-hipped, single-footed, toe-dancing ball carrier," took the ensuing kickoff at the 8 and disappeared into a knot of Maroons, only to emerge and flash 92 yards for the first kickoff return for touchdown in the rivalry's thirty-three games. State almost duplicated the feat on the next play, as Armstrong took

November 30, 1935
Ole Miss 14, Mississippi State 6

	State	Ole Miss
First downs	11	10
Total yards	293	176
Net yards rushing	187	173
Passing yards	106	3
Passes		
(Att-Comp-Int)	12-3-1	3-1-0
Punts/average yards	11/36	11/49
Penalties/yards	7/65	4/60

Dave Bernard's kick on the 5 and charged up the middle. He gained 55 yards and was almost loose before Rab Rodgers and Bill Richardson nailed him on the Ole Miss 40. With the 14–6 win, Ole Miss took its sixth straight victory in the Battle of the Golden Egg and its ninth triumph in the last ten games in the rivalry.

As a reward for its 9–2 season mark, Ole Miss received an invitation to play 8–1 Catholic University at the Orange Bowl on New Year's Day 1936. Down 20–6 at the half, Ole Miss held Catholic without a single first down in the final two periods and scored twice in the fourth quarter but came up 1 point short in a 20–19 loss. Despite the outcome, the game was a big financial success for Ole Miss, netting the school's thin sports budget fifteen hundred dollars.

1936

GAME 34

Scott Field, Starkville

Ike Puts Rebels in a Pickle

1936 SCHEDULES

Ole Miss 5–5–2

RESULT	DATE	PF	OPPONENT	PA	LOCATION
W	September 19	45	Union	0	Oxford
L	September 26	6	Tulane	7	New Orleans
L	October 2	7	Temple	12	Philadelphia
T	October 9	0	George Washington	0	Washington, D.C.
L	October 17	0	Louisiana State	13	Baton Rouge
W	October 24	14	Catholic	0	Oxford
W	October 31	24	Centenary	7	Shreveport
W	November 7	34	Loyola of New Orleans	0	Oxford
L	November 14	0	Marquette	33	Milwaukee
L	November 21	6	Mississippi State	26	Starkville
W	November 27	14	Miami	0	Miami
T	December 5	0	Tennessee	0	Memphis

Mississippi State 7–3–1

RESULT	DATE	PF	OPPONENT	PA	LOCATION
W	September 26	20	Millsaps	0	Starkville
W	October 3	35	Howard*	0	Starkville
L	October 10	0	Alabama	7	Tuscaloosa
W	October 17	32	Loyola of New Orleans	0	Meridian
T	October 24	0	Texas Christian	0	Dallas
W	October 31	68	Sewanee	0	Jackson
L	November 7	0	Louisiana State	12	Baton Rouge
W	November 21	26	Mississippi	6	Starkville
W	November 28	32	Mercer	0	Starkville
W	December 5	7	Florida	0	Gainesville
L	January 1, 1937	12	Duquesne	13	Orange Bowl

* Now Samford

After ten lean years, State was ready to end its losing streak in rivalry play and take its first full possession of the Golden Egg. Major Ralph Sasse's Maroons, at 4–2–1, had already notched four shutouts on their way to a winning season that would include six such pastings, while Ole Miss

A 26–6 win earns State its first full possession of the Golden Egg. From the left, State coach Major Ralph Sasse, State student president Bob Caldwell, Ole Miss chancellor A. B. Butts, Ole Miss student president Paul B. Johnson Jr., and State president G. D. (Duke) Humphrey. Mississippi State University Photo.

was an unremarkable 4–4–1. The largest crowd to date—twenty thousand fans—began pouring into Scott Field two hours before kickoff. Spectators arrived in Starkville on a half dozen special trains as well as at least two planes. Lines of cars packed the gravel roads leading to town.

Ole Miss was appearing under a new nickname, Rebels, chosen by southern sportswriters in a poll conducted by *Mississippian* sports editor Billy Gates. Other suggested nicknames were Confederates, Raiders, Stonewalls, and simply Ole Miss. The new Rebels were led by captain Marvin Hutson, while cocaptains Charles (Pee Wee) Armstrong and Frank Keenan headed the State squad.

The Maroons struck first, capitalizing on a Rebel punt that reached only the Ole Miss 24 for a 7–0 lead. Bill Steadman crossed the goal line for the score, while Ike Pickle added the extra point, aided by an offside call against Ole Miss. Short Rebel punts gave the Maroons two more first-quarter opportunities, but both were halted, with the teams "fighting every inch," according to the *Jackson Clarion-Ledger*. The punting duel continued in the second quarter, and the half ended with the Maroons holding their one-touchdown lead. Ole Miss had yet to complete a pass or cross midfield.

November 21, 1936
Mississippi State 26, Ole Miss 6

	State	Ole Miss
First downs	7	5
Total yards	170	121
Net yards rushing	74	74
Passing yards	96	47
Passes (Att-Comp-Int)	13-5-0	13-2-1
Punting average	39.0	34.0
Yards penalized	25	49

The Rebels scored a touchdown on their second possession of the third quarter as halfback Dave Bernard raced 30 yards on a short pass from Herb Baumsten. When Ole Miss missed the extra point, the Maroons had the slimmest of leads, 7–6.

Ole Miss again crossed the 50 yard line on its next possession but could not convert the opportunity into more points, and the floodgates opened in the fourth quarter. Pickle put his team up 14–6 on his touchdown and extra point, and in the words of the *Clarion-Ledger*, "Maroon fans are going wild." State added two more touchdowns on a Bob Hardison run and a 70-yard pass and run play between an injured Pee Wee Armstrong, making his first appearance of the day, and Dennis Cross. At 26–6, State had ended its long losing streak against Ole Miss.

According to Purser Hewitt in the *Clarion-Ledger*, "The game produced everything from sheer brilliance of attack . . . to the highly dramatic and thrill-filled heroics of the final touchdown. Pickle was the spearhead of a precise, alert Maroon attack. [The Rebels] lost to a team mentally determined to win."

With a 7–2–1 record, State accepted its first major bowl bid and met Duquesne in the Orange Bowl on January 1. The Maroons built a 12–7 halftime lead but gave up a 72-yard fourth-quarter pass that gave the Dukes the 13–12 win.

1937

State Launches a Crusade

1937 SCHEDULES

Ole Miss 4–5–1

RESULT	DATE	PF	OPPONENT	PA	LOCATION
W	September 25	13	Louisiana Tech	0	Oxford
T	October 1	0	Temple	0	Philadelphia
W	October 9	21	St. Louis	0	Oxford
L	October 16	0	Louisiana State	13	Baton Rouge
W	October 23	46	Ouachita Baptist	0	Oxford
L	October 30	7	Tulane	14	New Orleans
W	November 5	27	George Washington	6	Washington, D.C.
L	November 13	6	Arkansas	32	Memphis
L	November 25	7	Mississippi State	9	Oxford
L	December 4	0	Tennessee	32	Memphis

Mississippi State 5–4–1

RESULT	DATE	PF	OPPONENT	PA	LOCATION
W	September 25	39	Delta State	0	Starkville
W	October 2	38	Howard*	0	Starkville
L	October 9	0	Texas A&M	14	Tyler
L	October 16	7	Auburn	33	Birmingham
W	October 23	14	Florida	13	Starkville
T	October 30	0	Centenary	0	Shreveport
L	November 6	0	Louisiana State	41	Baton Rouge
W	November 12	12	Sewanee	0	Starkville
W	November 25	9	Mississippi	7	Oxford
L	December 4	0	Duquesne	9	Starkville

* Now Samford

Coming off their stellar 1936 season, the Maroons were expecting great things in 1937. One national magazine even picked State to win the national championship. But things did not go as planned, and in November, with the team mired at 3–3–1, coach Ralph Sasse unexpectedly resigned. The players rallied around the three assistants who took over the team,

Bill Steadman blasts for the touchdown in State's 9–7 victory, just a split second before hits by Bill Williams and Robert Kincade. Steadman was the first Maroon to score touchdowns in three consecutive games with Ole Miss. *Reveille*.

and a thousand students marched to the athletic dormitory in a show of support. To inspire the Maroons, assistant coach Jimmy Stokes placed the Golden Egg on a pedestal in the athletic dorm. The result was what David Bloom of the *Memphis Commercial Appeal* dubbed "a crusade for college and team."

Rebel coach Ed Walker was continuing to use the Pop Warner system, and he took his squad to face his old mentor. Taking the first chartered flight by any college football team, Ole Miss traveled to Philadelphia, where the Rebels recorded a 0–0 tie against Warner's Temple team. The Rebel players continued their now ten-year-old tradition by growing beards "for luck" against State.

November 25, 1937
Mississippi State 9, Ole Miss 7

	State	Ole Miss
Total plays	56	50
Total yards	283	220
Rushes/net yards	41/158	31/96
Passing yards	125	124
Passes		
(Att-Comp-Int)	15-9-2	19-11-2
Punts/average yards	11/37	10/36
Fumbles/lost	2/0	0/0

Ole Miss had just about completed its new west (home) stands prior to the Thanksgiving Day game, and the stadium could now hold fourteen thousand fans. The Maroons appeared disarmingly relaxed as they followed team captain Bill Steadman onto the field. The Rebels were captained by left tackle Frank (Bruiser) Kinard, one of four brothers who have played for Ole Miss.

With both teams banking on top-notch passers—State's Bernie Ward and Ole Miss's Parker Hall—aerial fireworks seemed almost certain.

But as has so often been the case in the Battle of the Golden Egg, things did not go as expected. Early in the game, Maroon right tackle Oren Pittman charged in and sacked Hall for the rivalry's first safety and a 2–0 State lead. The Maroons extended their lead with a touchdown by fullback Bill Steadman, who thus became the first Maroon to score a touchdown in three consecutive games against Ole Miss. Ward kicked the extra point, and it was 9–0.

Ole Miss threatened early in the third quarter but could not score. When State took over but failed to move the ball, Ole Miss turned a Maroon punt into a touchdown with an odd play: State's Shag Goolsby downed the kick on the Ole Miss 22 but neglected to hold the ball for the official's whistle. As players crowded around the ball, quick-thinking Ray (Little) Hapes snatched it up and raced 78 yards (a series record that still stands) for a touchdown while the defenders stood and watched what they thought were merely Hapes's antics. Kinard's kick brought the Rebels to within 2 points.

The Rebels had two more chances to win the game, but State's Bob Hardison ended one drive with an interception, and Kent Massengale missed a drop-kick field goal from the 35. State had the 9–7 victory, only its second win in eight visits to Oxford.

1938

Sixty Superb Minutes

1938 SCHEDULES

Ole Miss 9–2

RESULT	DATE	PF	OPPONENT	PA	LOCATION
W	September 24	20	Louisiana State	7	Baton Rouge
W	October 1	27	Louisiana Tech	7	Oxford
W	October 8	14	Mississippi Teachers*	0	Oxford
L	October 15	7	Vanderbilt	13	Nashville
W	October 22	47	Centenary	14	Oxford
W	October 29	25	George Washington	0	Washington, D.C.
W	November 5	14	St. Louis	12	St. Louis
W	November 12	39	Sewanee	0	Oxford
W	November 16	20	Arkansas	14	Memphis
W	November 26	19	Mississippi State	6	Starkville
L	December 3	0	Tennessee	47	Memphis

Mississippi State 4–6

RESULT	DATE	PF	OPPONENT	PA	LOCATION
W	September 24	19	Howard**	0	Starkville
W	October 1	22	Florida	0	Starkville
W	October 8	48	Louisiana Tech	0	Starkville
L	October 14	6	Auburn	20	Montgomery
W	October 21	12	Duquesne	7	Pittsburgh
L	October 29	0	Tulane	27	New Orleans
L	November 5	7	Louisiana State	32	Baton Rouge
L	November 12	0	Centenary	19	Meridian
L	November 19	3	Southwestern***	7	Memphis
L	November 26	6	Mississippi	19	Starkville

* Now Southern Mississippi
** Now Samford
*** Now Rhodes

State had an eager young team. Ole Miss, the overwhelming favorite, had all-American Parker (Bullet) Hall, who led the nation in six offensive categories. The result was a fierce battle filled with vicious tackles "you could hear in the press box," declared the *Memphis Commercial Appeal.* "The Rebs won because they were able to show superior power in the last

A campus banner vividly expresses State students' strong feelings before the upcoming game against the Rebels. *Reveille.*

half," Walter Stewart wrote. "They were undoubtedly aided by the injury of Sonny Bruce, the great State back with the revolving hips."

Governor Hugh White was among the fifteen thousand fans who watched the kickoff under a clear blue sky in Starkville. Both teams had new head coaches, Harry Mehre in the first of seven seasons at Ole Miss after a playing career under Knute Rockne at Notre Dame and ten seasons as head coach at Georgia. Dr. Emerson (Spike) Nelson was in his only season at State. Nelson's choice of cardinal and gold uniforms did not sit well with the school's maroon and white alumni.

Both teams threatened early but could not score. In the second quarter, with Ole Miss penetrating deep in Maroon territory, Mississippi State's

November 26, 1938
Ole Miss 19, Mississippi State 6

	State	Ole Miss
First downs	7	16
Total yards	151	371
Rushing yards	116	237
Passing yards	35	134
Passes (Att-Comp)	6-1	16-10

Jack Nix stepped in front of an Erm Smith pass intended for Hall and turned toward the sideline; two key blocks opened space. Ninety-seven yards later, State had a 6–0 advantage. Nix's pick-off was the first pass interception for a touchdown in this rivalry, and the play remains tied for the series record for longest touchdown of any kind.

Ole Miss tied the game on Hall's 1-yard touchdown run and went ahead on Kent Massengale's extra-point kick. The Rebels added insurance touchdowns in the third and fourth quarters. After a State punt went out on the Maroon 28, Hall connected with Bill Schneller on the 4; Schneller, who set a rivalry record at the time with four catches, ran over two Maroons to score. When the Maroons fumbled a punt return and the Rebels recovered on the State 47, Johnny

A brilliant speedster, the Maroon's Jack Nix returned an intercepted pass 97 yards for touchdown. His steal set a rivalry record for the longest play of any kind—a mark that held for forty-six years, until tied in the 1984 game. Mississippi State University Photo.

Lenhardt went over from the 4 for the final 19–6 score. For the season, Hall led the nation in six categories, including scoring (73 points—eleven touchdowns and seven extra points), and amassed 1,558 total yards to become the first Rebel to surpass the 1,000-yard mark in a season.

1939

Mehre, McKeen, and Football Mania

1939 SCHEDULES

Ole Miss 7–2

RESULT	DATE	PF	OPPONENT	PA	LOCATION
W	September 30	14	Louisiana State	7	Baton Rouge
W	October 7	41	Southwestern*	0	Memphis
W	October 14	34	Centenary	0	Shreveport
W	October 21	42	St. Louis	0	Oxford
L	October 28	6	Tulane	18	New Orleans
W	November 4	14	Vanderbilt	7	Memphis
W	November 11	27	Mississippi Teachers**	7	Hattiesburg
W	November 18	46	West Tennessee Teachers***	7	Oxford
L	November 25	6	Mississippi State	18	Oxford

Mississippi State 8–2

RESULT	DATE	PF	OPPONENT	PA	LOCATION
W	September 23	45	Howard+	0	Starkville
W	September 30	19	Arkansas	0	Memphis
W	October 7	14	Florida	0	Gainesville
L	October 14	0	Auburn	7	Birmingham
W	October 21	37	Southwestern*	0	Starkville
L	October 28	0	Alabama	7	Tuscaloosa
W	November 4	28	Birmingham-Southern	0	Starkville
W	November 11	15	Louisiana State	12	Baton Rouge
W	November 18	40	Millsaps	0	Starkville
W	November 25	18	Mississippi	6	Oxford

* Now Rhodes
** Now Southern Mississippi
*** Now University of Memphis
\+ Now Samford

As war drums thundered across Europe, Mississippi girded for its own war: the matchup of the 7–1 Rebels and the 7–2 Maroons. Declared the Associated Press, "Mississippians—the red necks, the bustling city folks, even transplanted Yankees—are so full of football fuss and figures . . . that the largest crowd ever to see a game in the state will be on hand." Fulfilling such predictions, twenty-two thousand fans poured into Oxford for the game despite the brisk winds and a chilling forty-four-degree temperature. A midseason ranking of No. 15 gave Ole Miss its first-ever mention in the Associated Press Poll, but the Rebels soon dropped out; national attention for the Maroons was still a year away.

Harry Mehre, in his second season at Ole Miss, faced Allyn McKeen, in his first year at State—the Notre Dame system of Knute Rockne versus the Tennessee system of Bob Neyland. The Rebels were favored, but the Maroons were heavier and more experienced. The Mississippi State community was mourning the school's beloved Bulldog mascot, Bully, who was killed by a bus on campus two weeks before the game. At his funeral, attended by twenty-five hundred people and covered by *Life* magazine,

Days before the big game with Ole Miss, State's beloved mascot, Bully, was killed by a bus on a campus street. In a ceremony covered by *Life* magazine students lead the funeral procession for burial of Bully under the players' bench at Scott Field. Mississippi State University Photo.

his body lay in a glass-top coffin as the Famous Maroon Band played. After burying Bully beneath the players' bench on Scott Field, returning students chanted "Beat Ole Miss." As an additional motivation, around the clock every day during game week, freshmen took turns pounding a big bass drum on a canopy over the entrance to the Student Union. The boom, boom, boom reverberated across the campus and through students' heads.

Ole Miss leapt out to a 6–0 lead when captain Bill Schneller snatched the ball out of the hands of a Maroon receiver and dashed 32 yards with the interception for a touchdown. The Maroons followed suit in the second quarter, converting an interception into a touchdown when Billy Jefferson completed the threat by passing to Arnold Moore in the end zone to knot the game at 6.

November 25, 1939
Mississippi State 18, Ole Miss 6

	State	Ole Miss
First downs	11	11
Total plays	60	53
Total yards	256	241
Net yards rushing	147	112
Passing yards	109	129
Passes		
(Att-Comp-Int)	13-7-1	22-9-2
Punts	8	7
Penalties/yards	3/35	4/40

With Germany a threat to world peace in 1939, State students add Hitler to their lists of enemies. Mississippi State University Photo.

Fronting the Maroon and Rebel Bands were two of the South's prettiest and most famous majorettes—Bobbye Vaughn of State and Brownie Burton of Ole Miss. They were huge crowd pleasers at every appearance, and their fancy strutting was legendary. Mississippi State University Photo and University of Mississippi Archives.

Both bands delighted the crowd with their halftime performances. The Maroon Band featured the strutting of nine-year-old Bobby Schoonover; not to be outdone, the members of the Rebel Band formed an outline of the state with a phalanx of musicians led by majorette Brownie Burton tracing the route of the Mississippi River as the band played "Ol' Man River."

The Maroons squandered two scoring opportunities early in the third quarter before they finally took control in the fourth. Following a fumble recovery on the Ole Miss 10, Harvey (Boots) Johnson's 1-yard touchdown plunge gave his team the lead with thirteen minutes to play. After a short Rebel punt, Johnson added another score to ice the 18–6 win. His scores put Johnson atop the Southeastern Conference with 62 points.

1940

The J Boys and the H Boys

1940 SCHEDULES

Ole Miss 9–2

RESULT	DATE	PF	OPPONENT	PA	LOCATION
W	September 21	37	Union	0	Oxford
W	September 28	19	Louisiana State	6	Baton Rouge
W	October 5	27	Southwestern*	6	Memphis
W	October 12	28	Georgia	14	Athens
W	October 19	14	Duquesne	6	Oxford
L	October 26	20	Arkansas	21	Memphis
W	November 2	13	Vanderbilt	7	Nashville
W	November 9	34	Holy Cross	7	Worcester
W	November 16	38	West Tennessee Teachers**	7	Oxford
L	November 23	0	Mississippi State	19	Starkville
W	November 29	21	Miami	7	Miami

Mississippi State 10–0–1

RESULT	DATE	PF	OPPONENT	PA	LOCATION
W	September 28	25	Florida	7	Gainesville
W	October 5	20	Southwestern Louisiana***	0	Starkville
T	October 12	7	Auburn	7	Birmingham
W	October 19	40	Howard+	7	Starkville
W	October 26	26	North Carolina State	10	Raleigh
W	November 2	13	Southwestern*	0	Memphis
W	November 9	22	Louisiana State	7	Baton Rouge
W	November 16	46	Millsaps	13	Starkville
W	November 23	19	Mississippi	0	Starkville
W	November 30	13	Alabama	0	Tuscaloosa
W	January 1, 1941	14	Georgetown	7	Orange Bowl

* Now Rhodes
** Now University of Memphis
*** Now Louisiana-Lafayette
+ Now Samford

Toxie Tullos, with the ball in front of the official, caps the game's opening drive as the Maroons count the first of three touchdowns against Ole Miss en route to the Orange Bowl. Mississippi State University Photo.

L ed by the running of the J Boys—Harvey (Boots) Johnson and Billy Jefferson—and a powerful line, Mississippi State came into the 1940 Battle of the Golden Egg with a 7–0–1 record. Ole Miss, with only a 1-point loss marring its season, was powered by the running/passing combination of Merle Hapes and John (Junie) Hovious—the H Boys. In scoring, the two teams ranked first and second in the Southeastern Conference. The Associated Press Poll rated Mississippi No. 11 in the nation and Mississippi State No. 16. The record crowd of twenty-six thousand that packed Scott Field included the governor and lieutenant governor, two congressmen, both U.S. senators, and the commissioner of the Southeastern Conference.

The Maroons' starting team was a predominantly senior unit supported by talent so deep that second- and third-stringers had accounted for more than half of State's total points to date. Twelve players had scored the team's thirty touchdowns. To keep his players fresh, coach Allyn McKeen scrimmaged his team only once all week. Ole Miss's Harry Mehre had his squad work behind locked gates, ostensibly on the aerial game, the Rebels' ace in the hole. Captains were Ole Miss's George Kinard and State's Hunter Corhern. Maroon end Erwin (Buddy) Elrod, State's first all-American, was playing despite a broken right hand.

November 23, 1940
Mississippi State 19, Ole Miss 0

	State	Ole Miss
First downs	17	8
Total yards	381	202
Net yards rushing	293	83
Passing yards	88	119
Passes		
(Att-Comp-Int)	15-7-3	15-5-4
Yards penalized	45	55

End Buddy Elrod, State's first all-American in football, is congratulated by famous radio announcer Ted Husing during Orange Bowl Week in Miami as Maroon Head Coach Allyn McKeen shows his proud approval. A poll of SEC coaches named Elrod Player of the Year and McKeen Coach of the Year. Mississippi State University Photo.

The Maroons turned the opening kickoff into a five-play scoring drive, with Toxie Tullos bucking over from the 2 and Wilbur Dees adding the extra point to give State a 7–0 advantage. The Starkville gridders never looked back. R. N. Price intercepted a Hovious pass to set up State's second touchdown: Billy Jefferson connected with J. T. (Blondy) Black for a 4-yard pass that extended the lead to 13 before the break.

Every bounce seemed to go the Maroons' way. Tullos fumbled the second-half kickoff, but Dees snatched up the ball on State's 21 yard line and sped 73 yards to the Ole Miss 6 before John Pivarnik brought him down. Two plays later, with rain falling hard, Johnson struck right guard for the score, and his team was up, 19–0. The Maroons threatened twice more but could not add to their edge; nevertheless, they already had all the points they needed. The State defense was perfect, intercepting Hovious four times to stop Ole Miss threats.

McKeen described his team's effort as the "finest game" he had ever seen a State team play. Mehre acknowledged that the Maroons "played a great game.

. . . [W]e played a mediocre game; they were at their peak." According to the *Jackson Clarion-Ledger*, the final score was "short of the real superiority of the Bulldogs." State held an overwhelming advantage in first downs (seventeen, compared to eight for the Rebels) and in yards rushing (224 versus 106). The two teams combined for seven interceptions, still a rivalry record; Romeo Popp's 75 yards receiving for Ole Miss set another mark. Johnson set a new career scoring record at State with 98 points (sixteen touchdowns and two extra points). Ole Miss's H Boys combined to score a conference-leading 137 points during the season. Hovious also led the nation in punt returns, averaging 15.1 yards on thirty-three returns, and his seven pickoffs tied for the most in the country.

Ole Miss closed out the year with a win over Miami. State ended the regular season by whipping Alabama for the Maroons' first undefeated campaign since 1903. They had made their first-ever appearance in the Associated Press Poll in October and stood at No. 9 in the season's final rankings. The Associated Press named the entire left side of the State team to the all–Southeastern Conference team and selected McKeen as coach. The *Nashville Banner* polled SEC coaches who recognized McKeen and end Buddy Elrod as Southeastern Conference Coach and Player of the Year, respectively. In the Southeastern Conference race, State finished second to Tennessee. On New Year's Day 1941, State appeared in its second Orange Bowl and posted its first victory in the contest, beating Georgetown, 14–7. McKeen later called this squad his best ever.

1941

November 29, 1941: "The Greatest Day in Mississippi Football History"

Jackson Clarion-Ledger

1941 SCHEDULES

Ole Miss 6–2–1

RESULT	DATE	PF	OPPONENT	PA	LOCATION
L	September 26	6	Georgetown	16	Washington, D.C.
W	October 4	27	Southwestern*	0	Oxford
T	October 10	14	Georgia	14	Athens
W	October 18	21	Holy Cross	0	Worcester
W	October 25	20	Tulane	13	New Orleans
W	November 1	12	Marquette	6	Milwaukee
W	November 8	13	Louisiana State	12	Baton Rouge
W	November 22	18	Arkansas	0	Memphis
L	November 29	0	Mississippi State	6	Oxford

Mississippi State 8–1–1

RESULT	DATE	PF	OPPONENT	PA	LOCATION
W	September 27	6	Florida	0	Starkville
W	October 4	14	Alabama	0	Tuscaloosa
T	October 11	0	Louisiana State	0	Baton Rouge
W	October 25	56	Union	7	Starkville
W	November 1	20	Southwestern*	6	Memphis
W	November 8	14	Auburn	7	Birmingham
L	November 15	0	Duquesne	16	Pittsburgh
W	November 22	49	Millsaps	6	Starkville
W	November 29	6	Mississippi	0	Oxford
W	December 6	26	San Francisco	13	San Francisco

* Now Rhodes

S tate and Ole Miss had never stood higher, with both poised to reach for the championship of the Southeastern Conference. Since Harry Mehre had become coach at Ole Miss, his Rebels had amassed a 31–7–1 mark. Allyn McKeen's tenure in Starkville had included a 24–3–2 record. Both teams came into the 1941 game with 6–1–1 overall records; in conference play, State was 3–0–1, Ole Miss 2–0–1. Both rated spots in the nation's Top 20.

Headline from *Clarion-Ledger*, November 30, 1941.

The Maroons emerged from what the *Memphis Commercial Appeal*'s Walter Stewart called a "maelstrom of mayhem" with a tense 6–0 victory. The Rebels were done in by six disastrous turnovers, many of them committed deep in Maroon territory. Heartbreakingly for Ole Miss, a game-tying fourth-quarter touchdown was called back.

November 29 dawned bright and beautiful in quiet Mississippi. Tickets were scarce as hen's teeth. Twenty-eight thousand jammed into Oxford's Hemingway Stadium. None of them knew that a Japanese attack force had sailed for Pearl Harbor four days earlier.

The favored Rebels were led by cocaptains Larry Hazel (son of former Ole Miss coach Homer Hazel) and J. W. (Wobble) Davidson. State's captain was Bill Arnold. The Maroons opened the game with a drive that reached the Ole Miss 10 but could not score. The Rebels replied with two serious threats and a missed field goal. The game-winning touchdown midway through the second quarter was startling. Collins Wehner hit Kermit Davis with a 31-yard pass that moved the ball to the Ole Miss 38. Quarterback Jennings Moates took the ball, turned his back and held it. Hilliard Thorpe faked a hand-off to Billy (Spook) Murphy who hit the right side, drawing off the defense and allowing Moates to slip through the left side into the end zone. Since the quarterback in McKeen's system almost never ran with the ball, Moates's carry was completely unexpected.

Ole Miss almost scored midway through the fourth quarter when John (Junie) Hovious connected with Ray Terrell, who took off on a 65-yard jaunt

November 29, 1941
Mississippi State 6, Ole Miss 0

	State	Ole Miss
First downs	8	12
Total yards	185	283
Net yards rushing	145	175
Passing yards	40	108
Passes		
(Att-Comp-Int)	4-3-0	26-11-2
Punts/average yards	13/38	8/39.9
Penalties/yards	6/60	4/30
Fumbles/lost	2/1	4/4

An official marks the spot where Ray Terrell stepped out of bounds on a long fourth-quarter run that would have given Ole Miss the tying touchdown. Coach Mehre motions onlookers back. Mississippi State University Photo.

to pay dirt. But head linesman George Gardner ruled that Terrell stepped out of bounds at the Maroon 47, in front of the Ole Miss bench. It was not a touchdown but a 19-yard gain, and the Maroon defense held. State had the win and with it the Southeastern Conference championship, the Golden Egg, and all the bragging rights.

The Maroons' performance was "an all-time high for the men of State," wrote Stewart. "The Rebel Raiders," he continued, "played epic football—smashed into the open again and again, but the State defense was a few rough shades too bristling—the tacklers too . . . power driven." McKeen told reporters, "Either of these great ball clubs could have won. We were just lucky." Mehre declared, "Both teams played heads-up football. On one play we let up, and that one play beat us." At the end of the season, the Associated Press ranked State sixteenth in the nation, with Ole Miss just one spot lower. Despite their stellar records and State's position at the top of the Southeastern Conference, the Cotton Bowl passed over the Maroons in favor of Alabama, while the Orange Bowl took Georgia rather than Ole Miss.

1942

Rivalry Gets the Jump on Gas Rationing

1942 SCHEDULES

Ole Miss 2–7

RESULT	DATE	PF	OPPONENT	PA	LOCATION
W	September 26	39	Western Kentucky	6	Oxford
L	October 2	6	Georgetown	14	Washington, D.C.
L	October 10	13	Georgia	48	Memphis
L	October 17	7	Louisiana State	21	Baton Rouge
L	October 24	6	Arkansas	7	Memphis
W	October 31	48	Memphis State*	0	Oxford
L	November 7	0	Vanderbilt	19	Memphis
L	November 14	0	Tennessee	14	Memphis
L	November 28	13	Mississippi State	34	Starkville

Mississippi State 8–2

RESULT	DATE	PF	OPPONENT	PA	LOCATION
W	September 26	35	Union	2	Starkville
L	October 3	6	Alabama	21	Tuscaloosa
L	October 10	6	Louisiana State	16	Baton Rouge
W	October 17	33	Vanderbilt	0	Nashville
W	October 24	26	Florida	12	Gainesville
W	October 31	6	Auburn	0	Birmingham
W	November 7	7	Tulane	0	New Orleans
W	November 14	28	Duquesne	6	Starkville
W	November 28	34	Mississippi	13	Starkville
W	December 5	19	San Francisco	7	Memphis

*Now University of Memphis

World War II deeply affected daily life in Mississippi, and the annual State–Ole Miss game was no exception. Players from both schools were leaving almost weekly to enter military service—an estimated one-third of each squad already had departed—enabling players who might have been sitting on the bench to get a chance to perform on the field. The 1942 Battle of the Golden Egg was scheduled, according to custom, on the last

Saturday in November—November 28. But after the government announced in October that gas rationing would begin on November 29, officials from the two schools agreed to move the game up a week, when both the Rebels and the Bulldogs had an open date. The sixteen thousand fans who put aside wartime concerns and attended the contest in Starkville—among them U.S. Senator Jim Eastland and former Mississippi governor Mike Conner, now serving as commissioner of the Southeastern Conference—witnessed what David Bloom of the *Memphis Commercial Appeal* described as "the sort of game a football fan hopes to see and seldom does."

The Maroons entered the game in good physical shape and with a five-game winning streak. Though the underdog Rebels were banged up, Maroon coach Allyn McKeen took nothing for granted. "They are going to be hard to handle," he warned his team. As McKeen had feared, Ole Miss came out tough and scored the game's first points. A 70-yard touchdown drive that began late in the first quarter saw Harley (Duke) Greenich dive for 6 points and Oscar (Honey) Britt add the point after. 7–0.

J. T. (Blondy) Black brought the Maroons back, however, capping a 62-yard drive with a 1-yard touchdown smack. Ted Shuff kicked the first of four extra points to tie the score at the half.

A Rebel gaffe on the second-half kickoff opened the way for the Maroons to surge ahead. In the scramble after Martin Frohm's kick, two Ole Miss players booted the ball deeper into Rebel territory, and team captain Bob Patterson claimed it for State on the Rebel 24. Two plays later, Billy (Spook) Murphy reversed field twice and then flung the ball to Lamar Blount for a sensational completion on the 1-yard line. Murphy leapt over center for the score to put his team out in front, 14–7. Just before the end of the third quarter, the Maroons started a 54-yard scoring drive, with Black doing the honors again to make the score 20–7.

Ole Miss got right back in the game with a 34-yard touchdown pass from freshman John (Sonny Boy) Shelby to Leonard Stagg, but Black upped the Maroon lead to 14 points when he took the ensuing kickoff 95 yards to score. Minutes later, the Maroons' Claiborne Bishop snagged a pass for the game's

November 21, 1942
Mississippi State 34, Ole Miss 13

	State	Ole Miss
First downs	15	8
Total yards	313	185
Net yards rushing	244	57
Passing yards	108	129
Passes		
(Att-Comp-Int)	11-6-0	23-9-1
Punts/average yards	7/40.5	8/37
Penalties/yards	3/35	3/15
Fumbles/lost	4/3	3/1

only interception. State took over at the Ole Miss 45; after Lamar Blount ran two reverses, the home team had increased its total. Jerome Daly nearly duplicated Black's sensational touchdown run, taking the Bulldog kickoff on his own 5 yard line and racing 90 yards down the sideline. But State's entrenched line held, and the Maroons had their 34–13 win.

State dominated statistically as well as on the scoreboard, tallying fifteen first downs to Ole Miss's eight and outgaining the Rebels 315 to 185. The Bulldog defense set a series record by surrendering only 56 yards on the ground. The Maroons closed out the year with a victory over the University of San Francisco, and the season's final Associated Press Poll had State at No. 18.

Blondy Black's third touchdown of the day against Ole Miss was a rousing 95-yard kickoff return, a record that stood for forty-two years as the longest KO return in this rivalry. Mississippi State University Photo.

1943

No Game

B y the fall of 1943, most of the players who had participated in the 1942 Ole Miss–Mississippi State game were serving in the military. The war had decimated college athletic teams across the nation; coupled with wartime travel restrictions, this lack of players caused 189 colleges— including all of those in the Southeastern Conference except Louisiana State, Tulane, Georgia, and Georgia Tech—to drop football and all other intercollegiate sports. In Mississippi, the Board of Trustees of Institutions of Higher Learning abolished play at state-supported colleges—including, of course, Ole Miss and State. Bulldog and Rebel fans would have to wait another year.

1944

The Impossible Victory

1944 SCHEDULES

Ole Miss 2–6

RESULT	DATE	PF	OPPONENT	PA	LOCATION
L	September 23	7	Kentucky	27	Lexington
W	September 30	26	Florida	6	Jacksonville
L	October 7	7	Tennessee	20	Memphis
L	October 21	0	Tulsa	47	Memphis
L	October 28	18	Arkansas	26	Memphis
L	November 4	0	Jackson Army Air Base	10	Oxford
L	November 11	6	Alabama	34	Mobile
W	November 25	13	Mississippi State	8	Oxford

Mississippi State 6–2

RESULT	DATE	PF	OPPONENT	PA	LOCATION
W	September 30	41	Jackson Army Air Base	0	Starkville
W	October 7	56	Millsaps	0	Starkville
W	October 14	49	Arkansas A&M*	20	Starkville
W	October 21	13	Louisiana State	6	Baton Rouge
W	November 4	26	Kentucky	0	Memphis
W	November 11	26	Auburn	21	Birmingham
L	November 18	0	Alabama	19	Tuscaloosa
L	November 25	8	Mississippi	13	Oxford

* Now Arkansas State

ississippi State came into Oxford with a four-game winning streak against its in-state rivals plus an impressive 6–1 season mark and a No. 16 national ranking, while the Rebels were a mirror-image 1–6. Newsmen said it would be "impossible" for Ole Miss to win. Yet the final score read Ole Miss 13, State 8. "Ten minutes after the game," wrote David Bloom of the *Memphis Commercial Appeal*, "8,000 fans were sitting aghast . . . asking if it was just a dream."

The two captains—State's Hillery Horne, a two-year letter winner, and Ole Miss's Bob McCain—were among the very few upperclassmen on the field. Most players were seventeen- and eighteen-year-olds who were too

The Rebel defense closes in during second-quarter action while a sparse wartime crowd looks on. Dark shirts are Ole Miss's Jerry Tiblier and Boykin Boyce (13). For the Maroons are Fred Morganti (44), Sammy Carroll (12), Hal France (33), and Jay Parks (31). *Commercial Appeal*, November 26, 1944.

young for military service. After the previous year's suspension of most intercollegiate athletics, the resumption of sports had been encouraged as a civilian morale booster, and all of the Southeastern Conference schools except Vanderbilt returned to competitive play. Coaches Harry Mehre of Ole Miss and Allyn McKeen of State took teams of "fuzzless kids"—many of whom had never even seen a college game—and set out on curtailed schedules. McKeen's Maroons featured tailback Tom (Shorty) McWilliams, who had strong ties to Starkville: his father, Leon McWilliams, had played for A&M in 1920; his uncle, Kent McWilliams, had scored against Ole Miss in 1917; and another uncle, L. M. McWilliams, was a letterman. According to Coach McKeen, Shorty Mac "had no weaknesses." But McWilliams had injured his knee against Alabama a week before the Ole Miss game, and coaches feared he might not be able to play against the Rebels.

With wartime gas rationing limiting most automobiles to only four gallons a week, the game attracted the smallest crowd since 1933. The afternoon was cool and overcast, and a large number of men in military uniforms

November 25, 1944

Ole Miss 13, Mississippi State 8

	State	Ole Miss
First downs	9	9
Total yards	242	165
Net yards rushing	133	139
Passing yards	129	54
Passes		
(Att-Comp-Int)	19-7-3	6-4-0
Punting average	33.0	40.0
Yards penalized	15	35
Fumbles/lost	0/0	0/0

were sprinkled throughout the stands. Spectators saw a punting duel to start; late in the first quarter, however, Ole Miss's Rex Pearce returned a punt 20 yards to the State 38, and the Rebels were in business. As the second quarter opened, Ole Miss ran what Bloom described as a "perfect play" on third down. End Bob McCain took the ball on a handoff from quarterback John Bruce as fullback Jerry Tiblier faked beautifully. The defense bought the fake, and McCain had nothing but 23 yards of open field between him and the goal line. Though Bill Hildebrand blocked the extra-point kick by his old teammate at Memphis's Tech High, Clyde Hooker, Ole Miss had a surprising 6–0 lead.

The Maroons struck back with an 80-yard touchdown march that culminated with Owen Moore making an easy scoring grab on a pass from left halfback Doug Colston. The extra-point attempt failed. State missed a sure touchdown shortly thereafter when Rex Pearce picked off a pass near the Ole Miss goal line, and the 6–6 tie stood at the half.

Ole Miss started its second touchdown drive on the Maroon 48 late in the third quarter. On the fifth play, Bruce toted the ball over from the 1-foot line; Hooker split the uprights for the extra point, and Rebel fans were stunned to see that Ole Miss held a 13–6 edge. The Maroons stormed back to the Ole Miss 29, but Pearce recorded his second interception of the afternoon to end the threat. With the clock ticking down late in the fourth quarter, Horne tipped Bruce's punt at the Ole Miss 20. In Bloom's words, the "crazy sphere" "passed over the end zone" for a safety that brought State to within 5 points. With two minutes left, McKeen brought in McWilliams for his first action of the day. The Bulldog star led his teammates down to the Rebel 3 yard line before his injured knee buckled and he had to be carried off the field. With time for only a single play, Colston threw toward Hildebrand and Moore, but the Rebels' Tiblier got there first, gathering in the ball and running a few yards upfield as the final horn sounded. "The crowd fell back limp," Bloom wrote. "The Ole Miss players stood around dazed."

In celebration, the Rebel Band paraded across campus to play in the lobby of the Student Union Building. An Ole Miss freshman secured an ink pawprint of Bully, the State bulldog mascot, to send to his brother, a State alumnus serving in the military. At season's end, McWilliams was selected a second-team all-America (a rare achievement for a freshman) and finished tenth in the Heisman Trophy voting. The *Nashville Banner* named him Southeastern Conference Player of the Year. His 84 points for the season ranked him second in the nation, trailing only Army great Glenn Davis, and put him in fourth place on the Southeastern Conference's career scoring list.

1945

Lightning Strikes Twice

1945 SCHEDULES

Ole Miss 4–5

RESULT	DATE	PF	OPPONENT	PA	LOCATION
W	September 21	21	Kentucky	7	Memphis
L	September 29	13	Florida	26	Jacksonville
W	October 6	14	Vanderbilt	7	Nashville
W	October 13	26	Louisiana Tech	21	Oxford
L	October 27	0	Arkansas	19	Memphis
L	November 3	13	Louisiana State	32	Baton Rouge
L	November 10	0	Tennessee	34	Memphis
W	November 24	7	Mississippi State	6	Starkville
L	November 29	6	Chattanooga	31	Chattanooga

Mississippi State 6–3

RESULT	DATE	PF	OPPONENT	PA	LOCATION
W	September 29	31	Southwestern Louisiana*	0	Starkville
W	October 6	20	Auburn	0	Birmingham
W	October 13	41	Detroit	6	Memphis
W	October 20	16	Maxwell Field	6	Starkville
L	November 3	13	Tulane	14	New Orleans
W	November 10	27	Louisiana State	20	Baton Rouge
W	November 17	54	Northwestern State	0	Starkville
L	November 24	6	Mississippi	7	Starkville
L	December 1	13	Alabama	55	Tuscaloosa

*Now Louisiana-Lafayette

For the second year in a row, State came into the game with an impressive 6–1 record and a high national ranking—this year, fifteenth in the Associated Press Poll. And for the second straight year, the Rebels were a thin, injury-riddled team with little more than determination. Game day in Starkville was bright and beautiful with temperatures in the fifties. World War II had ended just three months earlier, and rationing of meats, canned fish, and oils would end at midnight.

As in 1944, the Rebels jumped out to an early lead. Just two plays after a short

Rebel Mehrecle Defeats State 7 To 6
Late Maroon Score Fails To Tie Ole Miss' Early Lead

The *Clarion-Ledger*, November 25, 1945, made a clever headline of Coach Harry Mehre's name to emphasize Ole Miss's stunning upset in 1945.

Maroon punt, Frank Davis retreated almost to midfield to throw deep and high over the secondary, where Jack Warner, alone on the left, pulled in the ball and raced across the goal. Don Kauerz's extra point put Ole Miss up 7–0. State had three good second-period chances, but the Rebel defense stopped the Maroons in the shadow of the goal each time, and the score remained unchanged at the half.

Both teams saw scoring chances undone by third-quarter miscues: a fumble halted Ole Miss, and an interception stopped State. The final period began with the Rebels clinging to their 7-point lead. Midway through the quarter, State's Bennie Ray Nobles reeled off a 40-yard breakaway for the longest run of the day. But Grady Brewer tripped up Nobles at the Ole Miss 31, and another drive fizzled. However, Ole Miss fumbled deep in its own territory, and W. D. (Dub) Garrett covered on the Ole Miss 15. Three times the Maroons pounded before State ran a double reverse on fourth down: Graham Bramlett faked left and handed off to George McIngvale; McIngvale then handed off to Harper Davis, who ran to the right and scored standing to bring the Maroons within 1 point. But the extra-point attempt flew low and to the left, and Ole Miss held on for the 7–6 win.

State dominated the game everywhere but on the scoreboard, outgaining the Rebels 323 yards to 140 and recording eleven first downs to Ole Miss's four. But the Maroons had committed five turnovers, and the Rebel defense had denied the Bulldogs on four of their five deep thrusts into Ole Miss territory.

Echoing his story about the 1944 game, the *Memphis Commercial Appeal's* David Bloom wrote, "Five minutes after the game, 18,000 people were standing around in incredulous disbelief." "It had happened last year," Bloom continued, "and simply could not happen again. But it did. Who said football lightning doesn't strike twice?"

November 24, 1945

Ole Miss 7, Mississippi State 6

	State	Ole Miss
First downs	11	4
Total plays	76	47
Total yards	223	125
Rushes/net yards	56/217	34/86
Passing yards	49	65
Passes		
(Att-Comp-Int)	20-5-2	13-3-1
Punts/average yards	8/29.5	10/32.1
Penalties/yards	2/10	5/45
Fumbles/lost	6/3	4/2

1946

Helling and Damning

1946 SCHEDULES

Ole Miss 2–7

RESULT	DATE	PF	OPPONENT	PA	LOCATION
L	September 21	6	Kentucky	20	Lexington
W	September 28	13	Florida	7	Jacksonville
L	October 5	0	Vanderbilt	7	Memphis
L	October 12	7	Georgia Tech	24	Atlanta
L	October 19	6	Louisiana Tech	7	Oxford
W	October 26	9	Arkansas	7	Memphis
L	November 2	21	Louisiana State	34	Baton Rouge
L	November 9	14	Tennessee	18	Memphis
L	November 23	0	Mississippi State	20	Oxford

Mississippi State 8–2

RESULT	DATE	PF	OPPONENT	PA	LOCATION
W	September 28	41	Chattanooga	7	Starkville
L	October 5	6	Louisiana State	13	Baton Rouge
W	October 12	6	Michigan State	0	East Lansing
W	October 19	48	San Francisco	20	Memphis
W	October 26	14	Tulane	7	New Orleans
W	November 2	69	Murray State	0	Starkville
W	November 9	33	Auburn	0	Birmingham
W	November 16	27	Northwestern State	0	Starkville
W	November 23	20	Mississippi	0	Oxford
L	November 30	7	Alabama	24	Tuscaloosa

C hock full of veteran players, the State squad was in the midst of its seventh consecutive winning season and for the third straight year was meeting the Rebels with only one loss. Ole Miss, under new coach Harold (Red) Drew, had only a 2–6 record. But the Rebs had played so well in recent weeks, edging Southwest Conference cochamp Arkansas and holding their own in close losses to Louisiana State and Southeastern Conference champion Tennessee, that writers pounced on the potential of a cataclysmic collision. They issued "storm warnings" and cautioned the "weak of heart."

"Miss Cow College" visits Ole Miss's freshman pajama parade and bonfire pep rally the night before the Big Game. In reality it is Brett Jackson, one of the Ole Miss drum majors, with cheerleader Robert (Mooch) Marcus and former cheerleader Shine Morgan. *Ole Miss.*

To absorb the impact, they visualized "extra piling" driven beneath the sod of Hemingway Stadium. The burning question: "Can a red-hot Ole Miss eleven take a cool, calculating State machine?" The Mississippi State players, however, vowed that Rebel upsets of the previous two years would not be repeated. And they were right. "Mississippi State's pent-up fury of two years of football frustration," summarized David Bloom of the *Commercial Appeal*, "burst in a fiery flood and consumed Ole Miss 20 to 0."

November 23, 1946
Mississippi State 20, Ole Miss 0

	State	Ole Miss
First downs	11	5
Total plays	63	49
Total yards	178	153
Rushes/net yards	47/146	25/102
Passing yards	42	51
Passes		
(Att-Comp-Int)	16-5-2	24-9-2
Punts/average yards	7/41.6	9/41.0
Penalties/yards	2/25	3/35
Fumbles/lost	4/3	3/2

Game week featured the usual shenanigans by students of both schools. Ole Miss students reportedly conducted a raid on the State campus but were captured and had their hair and automobiles painted. An airplane from Ole Miss allegedly dropped "Surrender!" leaflets on the Starkville campus. A daredevil bunch of Maroons supposedly burned a large S on Hemingway Stadium grass. Pep rallies at both schools kept enthusiasm sky-high. At State, the Maroon

State's versatile cheerleaders had plenty to cheer as the Maroons sought—and got—sweet revenge for two previous losses to Ole Miss by easily rolling over the Rebels in Oxford. Mississippi State University Photo.

Band marched smartly in front of supper-bound students each evening as cheerleaders asked, "Hey, what's the good word?" The resounding reply: "Go to Hell, Ole Miss!"

It was a beautiful, cool, cloudless day, and twenty-six thousand fans were primed. Mississippi State did not take long to assert itself: "Employing their canine fangs in a manner which would have wrung a testimonial from a thrashing machine," analyzed Walter Stewart of the *Commercial Appeal*, "Mississippi State's Bulldogs affixed themselves to the rear of a Rebel's trousers . . . and tore that humble garment to an embarrassing extent." Three and a half minutes into the game, the Maroons had a 7–0 advantage. Tom (Shorty) McWilliams, who had spent the previous year at Army, returned a short punt to the Ole Miss 30, and in four plays, it was touchdown, State. Bill Hildebrand leaped high for a pass on the 6 and easily scored. Teddy Shuff notched the first of two conversions. Shorty Mac then capped a 42-yard drive with a sweep into a corner of the end zone for State's 100th touchdown in this rivalry.

A breakaway run took Ole Miss deep into State territory, but a fumble on the 18 turned the Rebels back. State's third touchdown was spectacular. Wallace (Eagle) Matulich picked off Charlie Conerly's pass and, as Bloom wrote, "whirled . . . dipped . . . dodged [and] evaded" until he crossed the goal all alone 68 yards later. "Go to Hell, Ole Miss!" boomed the Maroon fans.

With a dominating 20–0 lead at halftime and the Rebels apparently no real threat, coach Allyn McKeen cautioned his celebrating Maroons against overconfidence. He needn't have worried. Although State could not score, neither could Ole Miss. Turnovers hurt both squads: Ole Miss lost two fumbles and surrendered two interceptions, while State lost three fumbles and had the ball picked off twice.

When Mississippi State president Fred Mitchell held the Golden Egg aloft for the student section, up went the loudest roar of all. After two frustrating losses, revenge was sweet indeed. Fans on both sides agreed that it had been one hell of a game—literally. From the start, State students had yelled, "Go to Hell, Ole Miss," while Ole Miss supporters had snapped back with "Go to Hell, Cow College." "I never heard so much 'helling and damning' in all my life," chuckled the mother of an Ole Miss freshman coed.

GAME 44

Scott Field, Starkville

1947

Conerly-to-Poole Meets McWilliams, Davis, and Matulich

1947 SCHEDULES

Ole Miss 9–2

RESULT	DATE	PF	OPPONENT	PA	LOCATION
W	September 20	14	Kentucky	7	Oxford
W	September 27	14	Florida	6	Jacksonville
W	October 4	33	South Carolina	0	Memphis
L	October 11	6	Vanderbilt	10	Nashville
W	October 18	27	Tulane	14	New Orleans
L	October 25	14	Arkansas	19	Memphis
W	November 1	20	Louisiana State	18	Baton Rouge
W	November 8	43	Tennessee	13	Memphis
W	November 15	52	Chattanooga	0	Oxford
W	November 29	33	Mississippi State	14	Starkville
W	January 1, 1948	13	Texas Christian	9	Delta Bowl

Mississippi State 7–3

RESULT	DATE	PF	OPPONENT	PA	LOCATION
W	September 26	19	Chattanooga	0	Chattanooga
L	October 4	0	Michigan State	7	East Lansing
W	October 11	21	San Francisco	14	San Francisco
W	October 18	34	Duquesne	0	Starkville
W	October 25	27	Hardin-Simmons	7	Starkville
W	November 1	20	Tulane	0	New Orleans
W	November 8	14	Auburn	0	Birmingham
L	November 15	6	Louisiana State	21	Baton Rouge
W	November 22	14	Mississippi Southern*	7	Starkville
L	November 29	14	Mississippi	33	Starkville

* Now Southern Mississippi

Both teams returned practically the same players as the previous year. So there was no real surprise in the fact that the running of Tom (Shorty) McWilliams (all–Southeastern Conference for the third time) and the passing of Harper Davis had led State to a 7–2 record. The real surprise was that Ole Miss owned the same mark. New coach John Vaught had turned his first Rebel team into a solid winner, only 9 points away from an undefeated season courtesy of national passing records set by the aerial duo of Charlie Conerly and Barney Poole, an all-American at Army the year before who had followed two older brothers, Jim (Buster) and Ray, as Ole Miss footballers.

Twenty-five thousand nearly filled Scott Field on a warm cloudless day. Excitement came quickly. State surged to the Rebel 33. Ole Miss recovered a fumble and reached the Maroon 3, aided by the passing of Conerly, who would hit his first eleven tosses of the day. Quarterback Buddy Bowen then sneaked for the touchdown. Bobby Oswalt kicked the first of three extra points, and the Rebels led 7–0.

A short Rebel punt set the stage for a tying score. An injured McWilliams reached the 1, Wallace (Eagle) Matulich got the short touchdown, and Max Stainbrook kicked the extra point. The score stood at 7–7 with just over eight minutes to go in the half. The Rebels immediately struck for two more touchdowns. Will Glover returned the Maroon kickoff 39 yards to midfield, and on the first play from scrimmage, Conerly connected with Joe Johnson, who caught the ball at the 15 and raced into the end zone, leaving a shoe in the hands of a would-be tackler. On the next series, Bobby Wilson intercepted McWilliams's pass and returned the ball to the State 40. Jerry Tiblier covered 19 yards on the next play; Conerly passed to Everette (Hairline) Harper for another 10 and then took the ball into the end zone to put the Rebels up 20–7 at the break.

The Rebels' fourth touchdown was unexpected, as Bobby Wilson burst 77 yards over tackle. Next, an 8-yard toss from Conerly to Farley Salmon followed a blocked Maroon punt. The Maroons stormed 90 yards drive in the fourth quarter, with Davis scoring on a 27-yard pass from quarterback Don

In his first year as head coach Johnny Vaught's special revisions of the Rebels' passing attack won SEC Coach of the Year honors and brought Ole Miss its first of six SEC championships. In his twenty-five seasons Vaught teams posted an impressive record of 190–61–12 (.745), won three national championships, and appeared in eighteen postseason bowl games. University of Mississippi Photo.

November 29, 1947
Ole Miss 33, Mississippi State 14

	State	Ole Miss
First downs	10	10
Total plays	60	50
Total yards	242	337
Rushes/net yards	44/115	32/157
Passing yards	127	180
Passes		
(Att-Comp-Int)	16-10-1	18-13-0
Punts/average yards	9/32	8/39.4
Penalties/yards	7/55	6/50
Fumbles/lost	3/2	2/1

In a gag photo that mimics Ole Miss's famous Conerly-to-Poole aerial combination, Charlie Conerly passes while Barney Poole catches a pretty flight attendant for Chicago and Southern Air Lines, which later merged with Delta. Both Conerly and Poole set national passing records in 1947 and were named all-America. University of Mississippi Photo.

Robinson and Stainbrook adding another extra point. Only seven seconds remained to play, and the Rebels had the 33–14 victory. Wrote Walter Stewart of the *Memphis Commercial Appeal*, the Maroons "were faced by a team which was too shrewd and powerful, too thirsty for triumph—equipped with too much Conerly."

Both Conerly and his favorite target, Poole, were named to at least eight all-America teams. Conerly finished fourth in the Heisman Trophy voting, and the Helms Athletic Foundation named him national Player of the Year. He also collected the Atlanta Touchdown Club's award for Southeastern Conference Back of the Year and the *Nashville Banner*'s Southeastern Conference Player of the Year honor. Conerly led the nation with 133 completions on 232 attempts (57.4 percent), and his total of 1,367 yards ranked second. His achievements are now honored with the Cellular South Conerly Trophy, awarded each year to the most outstanding football player in Mississippi. Poole set a national mark with fifty-two catches, forty-four of them on throws from

Conerly. Eight members of the Poole family—including sons, nephews, cousins, and in-laws—carried on the family tradition of playing football for Ole Miss. Bowen received the Jacobs Trophy as the Southeastern Conference's top blocking back. The Rebels took their first Southeastern Conference championship and finished the season ranked thirteenth in the Associated Press Poll. Vaught became only the second coach to take the conference title in his first season at the helm, and both the Associated Press and the *Nashville Banner* named him Coach of the Year.

The Rebels closed out the season with an appearance in the inaugural Delta Bowl in Memphis, an early-summer commitment that forced them to turn down overtures from the Sugar Bowl. On a frigid, wind-blasted New Year's Day, Texas Christian University, Vaught's alma mater, grabbed a 9-point lead before the Rebels roared back for a 13–9 win, with Conerly connecting with Earl (Dixie) Howell and Joe Johnson for the touchdowns.

GAME 45

1948

T for Two

1948 SCHEDULES

Ole Miss 8–1

RESULT	DATE	PF	OPPONENT	PA	LOCATION
W	September 25	14	Florida	0	Gainesville
W	October 2	20	Kentucky	7	Lexington
W	October 9	20	Vanderbilt	7	Oxford
L	October 16	7	Tulane	20	New Orleans
W	October 23	32	Boston College	13	Memphis
W	October 30	49	Louisiana State	19	Baton Rouge
W	November 6	34	Chattanooga	7	Chattanooga
W	November 13	16	Tennessee	13	Memphis
W	November 27	34	Mississippi State	7	Oxford

Mississippi State 4–4–1

RESULT	DATE	PF	OPPONENT	PA	LOCATION
W	September 25	21	Tennessee	6	Knoxville
T	October 2	7	Baylor	7	Memphis
L	October 9	7	Clemson	21	Starkville
W	October 16	27	Cincinnati	0	Starkville
L	October 23	7	Alabama	10	Starkville
L	October 30	0	Tulane	9	New Orleans
W	November 6	20	Auburn	0	Birmingham
W	November 13	7	Louisiana State	0	Baton Rouge
L	November 27	7	Mississippi	34	Oxford

ohnny Vaught, the mastermind who redesigned the Rebel backfield in 1947 to give Ole Miss its first Southeastern Conference championship, rebuilt the entire program in 1948, resulting in the school's most successful season in thirty-eight years. The Maroons, in their ninth season under coach Allyn McKeen, had shown early season promise, leading fans to take up the cry, "State in '48." But a series of injuries and a lack of depth left State with a .500 record.

The Rebels were rated sixteenth in the nation by the Associated Press, high on the Orange Bowl's list of prospective teams, and a 13-point favor-

All-America end Barney Poole grabs a pass from quarterback Farley Salmon before smashing over three Maroon defenders for Ole Miss's third touchdown, just twenty seconds before the end of the first half while the bands wait to perform. *Commercial Appeal*, November 28, 1948.

ite over the Maroons. Some twenty-six thousand fans, including Governor Fielding Wright, nevertheless anticipated a close game on a cloudy, damp day. Team captains were Ole Miss tackle Doug Hamley and Mississippi State guard Bob Patterson.

Ole Miss jumped ahead early, first on a 53-yard punt return by Billy Mustin, then on Oscar (Buck) Buchanan's 28-yard interception return. 14–o. Bobby Oswalt did the extra-point kicking. The Rebels' third touchdown drive—officially 80 yards—was so disrupted by penalties and setbacks that it covered 127 yards in all. With just twenty seconds remaining in the half, Farley Salmon connected with all-America end Barney Poole, who bowled over three defenders to give the Rebels a 20–o lead.

After a scoreless third period, the Maroons punted out to only their 34, and Poole scored again for the Rebels, this time on a pass from Bobby Wilson.

November 27, 1948

Ole Miss 34, Mississippi State 7

	State	Ole Miss
First downs	11	20
Total plays	55	67
Total yards	188	398
Rushes/net yards	39/88	53/305
Passing yards	100	93
Passes		
(Att-Comp-Int)	16-6-1	14-7-1
Punts/average yards	12/35.5	7/34.3
Penalties/yards	5/45	11/115
Fumbles/lost	4/1	2/0

The Maroons' Shorty McWilliams turns the corner on an end run as Murry Alexander (84) blocks Dixie Howell and Barney Poole (89) closes in. *Commercial Appeal*, November 28, 1948.

The Maroons got on the board with a long drive that began on their own 32. Tom (Shorty) McWilliams threw a 26-yard pass to Crosby Simmons, who outleaped two defenders, and Max Stainbrook added the extra point to cut the margin to 27–7. The Rebels added another touchdown in the final four minutes when Salmon connected with Earl (Dixie) Howell, making the final score 34–7.

Statistics bore out the Rebels' dominance. Ole Miss amassed 386 total yards to State's 188 and had twenty first downs to State's eleven. The contest also set rivalry records for number of penalties (sixteen by the two teams combined) and for penalty yards (160).

Despite the Rebels' convincing win, their 8–1 record, and their end-of-season ranking at No. 15 in the Associated Press Poll, the Orange Bowl passed over Ole Miss in favor of Southeastern Conference champion Georgia; the Cotton Bowl had already picked Oregon to face Southwest Conference champion Southern Methodist University. Because Southeastern Conference policy "suggested" that conference schools play only in the big four bowls (Orange, Cotton, Sugar, and Rose), Ole Miss rejected feelers from San Diego's Harbor Bowl and spent New Year's Day at home.

1949

Record-Breaking Forty-niners

1949 SCHEDULES

Ole Miss 4–5–1

RESULT	DATE	PF	OPPONENT	PA	LOCATION
W	September 16	40	Memphis State*	7	Memphis
W	September 23	40	Auburn	7	Montgomery
L	October 1	0	Kentucky	47	Oxford
L	October 8	27	Vanderbilt	28	Nashville
T	October 14	25	Boston College	25	Chestnut Hill
L	October 22	27	Texas Christian	33	Fort Worth
L	October 29	7	Louisiana State	34	Baton Rouge
W	November 5	47	Chattanooga	27	Oxford
L	November 12	7	Tennessee	35	Memphis
W	November 26	26	Mississippi State	0	Starkville

Mississippi State 0–8–1

RESULT	DATE	PF	OPPONENT	PA	LOCATION
L	September 24	0	Tennessee	10	Knoxville
L	October 1	6	Baylor	14	Starkville
T	October 8	7	Clemson	7	Clemson
L	October 15	0	Cincinnati	19	Cincinnati
L	October 22	6	Alabama	35	Tuscaloosa
L	October 29	6	Tulane	54	New Orleans
L	November 5	6	Auburn	25	Auburn
L	November 12	7	Louisiana State	34	Baton Rouge
L	November 26	0	Mississippi	26	Starkville

* Now University of Memphis

When the final horn sounded, the scoreboard showed a one-sided 26–0 Ole Miss victory. On the field, however, the game was far from dull, as the two teams combined to set a variety of new marks for series, conference, and even national competition. As the *Memphis Commercial Appeal*'s Walter Stewart explained, "It was vicious football—solidly contested, and no one asked for money back."

Kayo Dottley's forty carries for the day were a national record in 1949. He also led the nation in rushing with 1,312 yards and scored twice against State. University of Mississippi Photo.

Despite disappointing seasons in both Starkville and Oxford, Scott Field was nearly filled with thirty-two thousand loyal fans, the largest crowd ever to see a football game in Mississippi to date. The emergence of two-platoon football and its emphasis on specialists had significantly affected State and Ole Miss, and turnovers had plagued both teams all season. The Maroons were in the first of three years under coach Arthur W. (Slick) Morton, who had replaced Allyn McKeen, forced out by alumni after ten seasons. The coaching change had not helped, however, and State was winless. The Rebels, despite an offense that stood atop the Southeastern Conference in three categories, ranked just tenth in defense and were on their way to the only losing season in Vaught's twenty-five years at the helm.

Ole Miss set the tone by scoring on its first possession. Eulas (Red) Jenkins got the points for the Rebels with a two-yard run, and Don Blanchard added the extra point for a 7–0 lead with just 5:50 gone. Ole Miss needed just two plays to score its next touchdown. Bobby Jabour intercepted a Maroon pass at the Mississippi 46, and on the first play from scrimmage, John (Kayo) Dottley charged to midfield; on the next play, Billy Mustin took a quick handoff, hit the middle, charged left, and evaded the last man. Touchdown, Rebels.

The Rebels penetrated deep into Maroon territory twice more before the half and again early in the third quarter but could not add to their lead. On their next possession, however, Ole Miss took over on the State 43 after a weak punt. On the fifth play, Dottley's 6-yard touchdown run put the Rebels up by 19.

Early in the fourth quarter, the Maroons reached the Rebel 20, but a

November 26, 1949
Ole Miss 26, Mississippi State 0

	State	Ole Miss
First downs	11	21
Total plays	50	90
Total yards	163	558
Rushes/net yards	28/120	80/404
Passing yards	43	154
Passes		
(Att-Comp-Int)	22-6-3	10-6-1
Punts/average yards	8/38.0	4/39.5
Penalties/yards	3/22	12/90
Fumbles/lost	2/2	2/2

fumble halted the drive. The game's most sensational action followed two plays later when Ronald (Rocky) Byrd and Jack Stribling combined for a 74-yard catch and run, the longest pass play in the rivalry's history at the time. Max Stainbrook caught Stribling at the 2 but only delayed the inevitable. On his second try, Dottley crossed the goal line for his Southeastern Conference–high fourteenth touchdown of the year.

Dottley's forty carries for the day set a national record, while the Rebels' eighty rushing plays and ninety total plays set Southeastern Conference marks. The two teams set a slew of rivalry records for the time:

- most yards rushing—404, Ole Miss
- most yards total offense, one team—558, Ole Miss
- most yards total offense, both teams—721
- most pass attempts, one team—twenty-two, Mississippi State's Don Robinson
- most yards rushing—216, Dottley
- most first downs, one team—Ole Miss, twenty-one
- most first downs, both teams—thirty-two

Dottley's 1,312 yards rushing for the season led the nation and was the second-highest total ever recorded in college football.

The Rebels finished the year No. 1 in the Southeastern Conference in total offense (386.4 yards per game) as well as in rushing and passing. State's fiftieth football season marked the school's first winless campaign since 1896, and the defense had surrendered a school record 224 points.

GAME 47

Hemingway Stadium,
Oxford

1950

27–20

It was a barn burner from the start. As the *Meridian Star* headlined, the winner was not determined until the final whistle. Twenty-eight thousand fans came to Oxford on a gray, damp December day for the first meeting between Ole Miss and State in sixteen years outside November, and those caught in a traffic jam east of Oxford missed not only the first quarter but the first three touchdowns.

Rebel Majorettes (left to right): Frances Hilton of Laurel, Betty Gail Thomas of Greenville, Maxine Massey of Greenwood, Billie Jean Little of Greenwood, Bettye Hidgon of Belzoni, Billie Jean Hickman of McComb, and Ella May Fulmer of Jackson. Drum major is Bobby Kingsberry of Hattiesburg. University of Mississippi Photo.

The Rebels took a 7–0 lead with just over four and a half minutes gone. Wilson Dillard had returned the Maroons' second punt 45 yards to reach the State 5. On the first play from scrimmage, Dottley swept left for the touchdown, and Jimmy Lear kicked the extra point. The Rebels doubled the lead on their next possession when Granville (Scrappy) Hart took a pitchout and hit Laverne (Showboat) Boykin with a 13-yard touchdown pass and Lear added another point after.

The Maroons took the ensuing kickoff at their 30. A 26-yard run by Tom (Dutch) Rushing for the Maroon's initial first down and a 31-yard burst by Wally Beech set up the threat, before a handoff from Frank (Twig) Branch to Beech clicked from the one. Max Stainbrook's kick brought State within 7.

December 2, 1950

Ole Miss 27, Mississippi State 20

	State	Ole Miss
First downs	13	15
Total plays	61	58
Total yards	252	359
Rushes/net yards	48/195	47/219
Passing yards	57	140
Passes		
(Att-Comp-Int)	13-4-1	11-8-0
Punts/average yards	6/39.2	5/35
Penalties/yards	4/30	7/58
Fumbles/lost	0/0	1/0

OLE MISS
★
MISSISSIPPI STATE

35c

Game program.

The score remained at 14–7 through the second and third quarters, as the teams seesawed back and forth. In the final period, however, the Maroons ran off a 12-play, 63-yard drive capped by a short touchdown run by the aptly named Rushing. With just over ten minutes to play, the score was knotted at 14. Ole Miss needed just five plays to retake the lead with a 57-yard touchdown pass from quarterback Ronald (Rocky) Byrd to end Bill Stribling, who spun away from defenders to score on the Rebels' only pass of the second half. The extra point kick was no good. Not to be outdone, State unleashed its own five-play drive. Rushing returned the kickoff 48 yards to the Ole Miss 27. From the 1, Beech was stopped twice before Rushing bucked over.

Happy Rebel players give Captain Ken Farragut and Coach John Vaught college football's traditional victory ride in celebration of Ole Miss's upset win over State. University of Mississippi Photo.

The extra point was no good, and the game was knotted at 20. Five and a half minutes remained.

In his only appearance of the day, Ole Miss's Dick Westerman took the kickoff 56 yards to the Maroon 24. Another five-play drive resulted, with Byrd sneaking for the winning score. Lear's extra point put Ole Miss up 27–20 with 2:25 showing on the clock. State tried to put together one final drive, but the Rebel defense held on. "The Rebels played the game of their lives," Jack Hairston declared in the *Greenwood Morning Star*. Ole Miss's coach, Johnny Vaught, believed that his "boys won because they wanted to." In a players-only meeting that week the team had pledged "60 minutes of football." Maroon coach Arthur W. (Slick) Morton also praised the efforts of his players, who had fought back to tie the game not once but twice.

1951

Here Comes Showboat

1951 SCHEDULES

Ole Miss 6–3–1

RESULT	DATE	PF	OPPONENT	PA	LOCATION
W	September 21	32	Memphis State*	0	Memphis
W	September 29	21	Kentucky	17	Oxford
W	October 5	34	Boston College	7	Memphis
L	October 13	20	Vanderbilt	34	Memphis
W	October 20	25	Tulane	6	Oxford
L	October 26	7	Miami	20	Miami
T	November 3	6	Louisiana State	6	Baton Rouge
W	November 10	39	Auburn	14	Mobile
L	November 17	21	Tennessee	46	Oxford
W	December 1	49	Mississippi State	7	Starkville

Mississippi State 4–5

RESULT	DATE	PF	OPPONENT	PA	LOCATION
W	September 22	32	Arkansas State	0	Starkville
L	September 29	0	Tennessee	14	Knoxville
W	October 6	6	Georgia	0	Starkville
L	October 13	0	Kentucky	27	Lexington
L	October 27	0	Alabama	7	Starkville
W	November 3	10	Tulane	7	New Orleans
W	November 10	27	Memphis State*	20	Memphis
L	November 17	0	Louisiana State	3	Baton Rouge
L	December 1	7	Mississippi	49	Starkville

* Now University of Memphis

The story of the 1951 Battle of the Golden Egg begins and ends with the Rebels' Arnold Laverne (Showboat) Boykin. Living up to his nickname, Boykin scored a record-setting seven touchdowns to lead Ole Miss to a 49–7 victory. Boykin's touchdown runs alone covered 152 yards; seven other runs netted an additional 35 yards, giving him an impressive 187 yards on

Headline from *Commercial Appeal*, December 2, 1951.

the day. All of Boykin's scoring runs came on the same play, a handoff from quarterback Jimmy Lear.

The twenty-eight thousand fans at Scott Field on that bright December 1 had little inkling of what was to come. After a good freshman season in 1948, Boykin had been hampered by injuries over the next two years. And in this, his senior season, he had scored only three touchdowns prior to the big game. Boykin's first score came on the game's first drive. On the fifth play from scrimmage, Boykin took the ball at the State 21 and went "sidewheeling through the line," in the words of the *Memphis Commercial Appeal*'s David Bloom. Lear added the first of his seven extra point kicks on the day, and the Rebels were up 7–0 with just 2:02 gone. The Maroons' first possession of the day ended with a pickoff by James Kelly. After one pass play, Boykin ran 14 yards to pay dirt for his second touchdown. A fumble recovery led to Boykin's third on a 12-yard run. With two minutes to go in the first period, Ole Miss was already up by 21.

The Maroons responded with their only scoring drive of the day. Norm Duplain returned the kickoff 39 yards to the State 49, halfback Zerk Wilson carried four consecutive times for a first down on the Ole Miss 40, and fullback Joe Fortunato reached the 37 as the first

December 1, 1951
Ole Miss 49, Mississippi State 7

	State	Ole Miss
First downs	11	15
Total plays	58	72
Total yards	229	449
Rushes/net yards	45/163	58/355
Passing yards	66	94
Passes		
(Att-Comp-Int)	13-6-3	14-4-1
Punts/average yards	6/35.0	7/36.4
Penalties/yards	1/5	10/80
Fumbles/lost	7/4	2/0

period ended. Bill Stewart went 32 yards on the first play of the second quarter and followed with a 5-yard touchdown run. Stewart lost his life in the Korean War. It is in his memory that the state high school all-star game presents the Bill Stewart Trophy to the outstanding player. Pete Polovina's extra point made the score 21–7. Ole Miss closed the half on a 75-yard scoring drive, with Boykin going the final 14 yards to make the margin 28–7.

The Maroons' first possession of the second half ended with a punt that pinned the Rebels on their own 9 yard line. On third and 4, Boykin reeled off his longest run of the day, racing 85 yards down the sideline for his fifth touchdown. Until 1979, the play remained the rivalry's longest run from scrimmage.

Midway through the fourth quarter, Boykin broke the Southeastern Conference record with touchdown No. 6, a 1-yard scamper. In the game's closing minutes, he added another scoring run—this one for 5 yards—that gave him 42 points and set one-game National Collegiate Athletic Association records for most touchdowns, most points, and most rushing touchdowns. Not surprisingly, the Associated Press named Boykin national Back of the Week.

The Maroon defense, tenth-best in the nation, entered the game riddled with injuries. Yet as Bloom wrote, "They didn't quit." Bloom, who had covered the Ole Miss–State football rivalry since the 1920s, added, "Ole Miss waited a long time for its Showboat to come in, but when he did the spectacle was super colossal." In contrast, Boykin's stunning performance generated little special attention among his teammates and his coach. When Boykin entered the dressing room after the game, Johnny Vaught told him, "Nice game." Replied the quiet Boykin, "Thanks, Coach."

1952

Hemingway Stadium,
Oxford

Unbeaten Can Be a Dangerous Perch

1952 SCHEDULES

Ole Miss 8–1–2

RESULT	DATE	PF	OPPONENT	PA	LOCATION
W	September 19	54	Memphis State*	6	Memphis
T	September 27	13	Kentucky	13	Lexington
W	October 4	20	Auburn	7	Memphis
T	October 11	21	Vanderbilt	21	Nashville
W	October 18	20	Tulane	14	New Orleans
W	October 25	34	Arkansas	7	Little Rock
W	November 1	28	Louisiana State	0	Oxford
W	November 8	6	Houston	0	Houston
W	November 15	21	Maryland	14	Oxford
W	November 29	20	Mississippi State	14	Oxford
L	January 1, 1953	7	Georgia Tech	24	Sugar Bowl

Mississippi State 5–4

RESULT	DATE	PF	OPPONENT	PA	LOCATION
L	September 27	7	Tennessee	14	Memphis
W	October 4	41	Arkansas State	14	Starkville
W	October 11	14	North Texas	0	Starkville
W	October 18	27	Kentucky	14	Starkville
L	October 25	19	Alabama	42	Tuscaloosa
L	November 1	21	Tulane	34	New Orleans
W	November 8	49	Auburn	34	Auburn
W	November 15	33	Louisiana State	14	Baton Rouge
L	November 29	14	Mississippi	20	Oxford

* Now University of Memphis

Ole Miss was undefeated at 7–0–2, including an inspiring win over previously undefeated and third-ranked Maryland, a feat the Associated Press named the National Upset of the Year. State, in its first season under coach Murray Warmath, was 5–3. Warmath had been hired the preceding December in the wake of Arthur W. (Slick) Morton's

Harol Lofton's 77-yard breakaway scoring run in the third quarter gave the Rebels the necessary points to ensure victory and cap Ole Miss's first unbeaten regular season. University of Mississippi Photo.

resignation and had brought impressive credentials to Starkville, having worked under Maroon coach Allyn McKeen as well as under Bob Neyland at Tennessee and Earl Blaik at Army. Despite the contrast in records, the Maroons kept the game close before winding up on the short end of a 20–14 count. On a field made slick by morning rain, wrote the *Commercial Appeal*'s David Bloom, "the game unfolded like a melodrama, hitting its hectic peak in the last act." For the first two quarters, the Maroons played as most of the twenty-eight thousand spectators expected, fumbling the ball twice and allowing Ole Miss to take a two-touchdown lead. Jim Mask recovered a fumble at the State 4, and quarterback Jimmy Lear smashed over left tackle for the first touchdown. The Rebels inaugurated a 13-play touchdown drive after Jimmy Patton outleaped a Maroon receiver on the Ole Miss 13. Allen Muirhead capped the drive on an 8-yard pitchout from Lear, who kicked both extra points.

After the half, according to Bloom, "few games have changed complexion as this one did." State marched 70 yards on the opening drive of the third quarter to close the gap to 13–7. Jackie Parker ended a six-minute drive with a 1-yard touchdown run and kicked the extra point for good measure. The Rebels needed just one play after the kickoff to restore the margin to 13, however. Fullback Harol Lofton shook off several would-be tacklers as he thundered 77 yards to score, and Ole Miss appeared to have the game well in hand.

But appearances can be deceiving. The Maroons came right back with a scoring drive of 67 yards, with Parker accounting for 49 of them, including

November 29, 1952
Ole Miss 20, Mississippi State 14

	State	Ole Miss
First downs	17	21
Total plays	55	64
Total yards	272	425
Rushes/net yards	49/231	58/352
Passing yards	41	73
Passes		
(Att-Comp-Int)	6-4-2	6-4-0
Punts/average yards	3/44	2/22
Penalties/yards	4/50	6/100
Fumbles/lost	5/2	1/0

Maroon backfield stars. For two years Jackie Parker (12) was directly responsible for all State's points against Ole Miss. Parker was selected most valuable in the SEC for two consecutive years and in 1953 was named all-America. Other Maroon standouts are Joe Robertson (20), Joe Fortunato (31, all-America at linebacker in 1951), and Zerk Wilson (44). Mississippi State University Photo.

the final 15. His second extra point of the afternoon reduced the deficit to just 6 with an entire quarter to play. Both teams mounted threats but could not score, and Ole Miss escaped with its record unblemished.

Parker's 120 points on the season led the nation: he scored sixteen touchdowns (tying a Southeastern Conference mark) and kicked twenty-four of twenty-nine extra points. He also passed for eight touchdowns. The *Nashville Banner* named Parker the Southeastern Conference's Most Valuable Player. The Maroons scored more points than they had in six years and turned in their first winning season since 1947. They rushed for an average of 248 yards a game, second in the Southeastern Conference.

The Rebels led the conference in offense at 383 yards a game. At season's end, both the Associated Press and United Press International Polls ranked undefeated Ole Miss No. 7, the school's first-ever Top 10 finish. Lear and tackle Kline Gilbert were named all-America.

The Rebels' first visit to the Sugar Bowl, where they faced undefeated and second-ranked Georgia Tech, was frustrating. Ole Miss scored first and threatened twice more before falling, 24–7.

1953

All Dressed Up and No Place to Go

1953 SCHEDULES

Ole Miss 7–2–1

RESULT	DATE	PF	OPPONENT	PA	LOCATION
W	September 19	39	Chattanooga	6	Jackson
W	September 26	22	Kentucky	6	Oxford
L	October 3	0	Auburn	13	Auburn
W	October 10	28	Vanderbilt	6	Oxford
W	October 17	45	Tulane	14	New Orleans
W	October 24	28	Arkansas	0	Memphis
W	October 31	27	Louisiana State	16	Baton Rouge
W	November 7	40	North Texas	7	Oxford
L	November 14	0	Maryland	38	College Park
T	November 28	7	Mississippi State	7	Starkville

Mississippi State 5–2–3

RESULT	DATE	PF	OPPONENT	PA	LOCATION
W	September 19	34	Memphis State*	6	Memphis
W	September 26	26	Tennessee	0	Knoxville
W	October 3	21	North Texas	6	Starkville
T	October 10	21	Auburn	21	Starkville
L	October 17	13	Kentucky	32	Lexington
T	October 24	7	Alabama	7	Tuscaloosa
L	October 31	20	Texas Tech	27	Jackson
W	November 7	21	Tulane	0	New Orleans
W	November 14	26	Louisiana State	13	Baton Rouge
T	November 28	7	Mississippi	7	Starkville

* Now University of Memphis

The fiftieth meeting between State and Ole Miss saw the usual pre-game buildup. Most of the thirty-five thousand at Scott Field—the largest crowd to date for a sporting event in Mississippi—expected the 7–2 Rebels to down the 5–2–2 Maroons. With State and Ole Miss among the Southeastern Conference's passing leaders, fans also expected an air show. However, the game hardly conformed to expectations, as the two teams combined for only fifteen attempted passes and the ground game dominated instead, with the most notable statistic fumbles: the teams combined to drop the ball eleven times and lose eight—both rivalry records at the time. The Rebels lost five of seven bobbles, and the Maroons lost three of four.

The Rebels penetrated the Maroon 25 yard line six times in the first half yet cashed in just once—on a short touchdown drive late in the second quarter. The Maroons' attack was just as futile—they escaped their own territory just once in the first half before managing a long scoring drive after the second-half kickoff. And that's where the game ended, with a 7–7 tie.

A fumble recovery by all-America guard Crawford Mims on the State 17 set up the Rebel score. Earl Blair hit left tackle for the touchdown on the fifth play, and Lea Pasley's kick made it 7–0. The Maroons initiated a 68-yard scoring drive on their first possession of the second half. Seven ground plays got State to the Ole Miss 4, where, on fourth down, Jackie Parker lobbed a pass to Art Davis, all alone in the end zone. The extra-point kick gave the all-America quarterback a hand in all of State's points against the Rebels for two straight years. Parker played the game wearing a plastic mask over much of his face as protection for the crushed cheekbone he had suffered two weeks earlier against Louisiana State. "Any time I was in on a tackle or ran the ball it hurt," Parker said later. Nevertheless, he completed all of his nine passing attempts for 96 yards and rushed for 13 yards. At season's end, the Atlanta Touchdown Club and the Birmingham Quarterback Club named Parker Southeastern Conference Back of the Year, and for the second consecutive year, the *Nashville Banner* named him the conference's Most Valuable Player. In 1970 Alf Van Hoose of the *Birmingham News* declared that prior to Archie Manning, Parker and Alabama's Ken Stabler had been the best quarterbacks in the history of the Southeastern Conference. Parker, said Van Hoose, excelled at "getting a team over the goal line, mostly by remembering he could do the job best himself."

The tie—the first in this rivalry since 1929—ultimately did more harm to the Rebels, costing them the Southeastern Conference championship title and a bid to the Cotton Bowl. It also brought to an end Ole Miss's six-game winning streak in the annual contest against Mississippi State.

November 28, 1953
Mississippi State 7, Ole Miss 7

	State	Ole Miss
First downs	12	13
Total yards	308	261
Net yards rushing	212	254
Passing yards	96	7
Passes		
(Att-Comp-Int)	9-9-0	6-1-0
Punts/yards	7/39.7	4/51.5
Yards penalized	25	40
Fumbles/lost	4/3	7/5

GAME 51

Hemingway Stadium,
Oxford

1954

What Counts Is What's Up Front

1954 SCHEDULES

Ole Miss 9–2

RESULT	DATE	PF	OPPONENT	PA	LOCATION
W	September 17	35	North Texas	12	Memphis
W	September 25	28	Kentucky	9	Memphis
W	October 2	52	Villanova	0	Philadelphia
W	October 9	22	Vanderbilt	7	Nashville
W	October 16	34	Tulane	7	Oxford
L	October 23	0	Arkansas	6	Little Rock
W	October 30	21	Louisiana State	6	Baton Rouge
W	November 6	51	Memphis State*	0	Memphis
W	November 13	26	Houston	0	Houston
W	November 27	14	Mississippi State	0	Oxford
L	January 1, 1955	0	Navy	21	Sugar Bowl

Mississippi State 6–4

RESULT	DATE	PF	OPPONENT	PA	LOCATION
W	September 18	27	Memphis State*	7	Starkville
L	September 25	7	Tennessee	19	Memphis
W	October 2	46	Arkansas State	13	Starkville
W	October 9	14	Tulane	0	New Orleans
L	October 15	13	Miami	27	Miami
W	October 23	12	Alabama	7	Tuscaloosa
L	October 30	0	Florida	7	Gainesville
W	November 6	48	North Texas	26	Starkville
W	November 13	25	Louisiana State	0	Baton Rouge
L	November 27	0	Mississippi	14	Oxford

* Now University of Memphis

It's hard to argue with the nation's No. 1 defense. Yet the Maroons tried. Ultimately, however, as new Mississippi State coach Darrell Royal said matter-of-factly, "They out-defensed us." The Rebel defense pitched a shutout, stopping the Maroons six times in Ole Miss territory and collecting five turnovers on the way to a 14–0 win. The Maroon defense played well,

Halfback Allen Muirhead, one of the keys in the Rebels' first touchdown drive, gives an unidentified Maroon a free ride before falling to the determined defender's tackle. University of Mississippi Photo.

too, twice stopping the Rebels in the shadow of the end zone and forcing the Rebel offense to commit five turnovers of its own. But it was not enough.

Royal had taken over in Starkville early in 1954, when Murray Warmath surprised State players and officials by taking the head coaching job at Minnesota, where he would win the national championship in 1960. As his successor, athletic director C. R. (Dudy) Noble selected twenty-nine-year-old Darrell Royal, an enthusiastic tactician who had served under Warmath at State before becoming an assistant at Edmonton in the Canadian Football League. Royal inherited a squad with some excellent players, including all-America center Hal Easterwood; Charles (Dinky) Evans, who at the end of the season won the Jacobs Trophy as best blocking back in the Southeastern Conference; and Arthur Davis, whom

November 27, 1954

Ole Miss 14, Mississippi State 0

	State	Ole Miss
First downs	9	13
Total plays	60	54
Total yards	194	271
Rushes/net yards	55/136	43/169
Passing yards	38	102
Passes		
(Att-Comp-Int)	5-2-1	11-5-2
Yards penalized	35	55
Fumbles/lost	7/4	6/4

the *Nashville Banner* named the conference's Most Valuable Player. To begin 1954, highly regarded *Collier's* magazine had picked Ole Miss to become the national champion, while Southeastern Conference coaches selected the Rebels to finish third in the conference. Vaught's squad swept through the season with only a single loss, a 6–0 defeat at the hands of Southwest Conference champ Arkansas. The Rebels' eight victories had included three shutouts, and they had surrendered only 47 points in nine games. State was 6–3 and had given up just 53 points.

Thirty-six thousand, the most ever to see Ole Miss and State, came to Oxford under leaden skies. A morning rain had stopped. The Maroons kicked off, and the defense stopped the Rebels with George Suda's interception on the State 28. The Maroons reached the Ole Miss 33 but were forced to punt; the Rebs countered with a fumble on their own 18. Three plays later, Ole Miss's George Harris intercepted a pitchout and returned the ball to the 39 before quarterback Bobby Collins brought him down. The next 3:01 saw both Rebel touchdowns: first, Houston Patton capped Ole Miss's 61-yard drive with a 2-yard sweep around right end; then, after the Maroons lost a fumble on their own 23 on the first play of the second quarter, Earl Blair smacked the left side to score from the 1-foot line. For the rest of the day, both teams threatened but failed to score, undone by poor field conditions and sloppy play. The teams combined to fumble a record thirteen times (seven by State), with each team losing four. State intercepted two Ole Miss passes, while the Rebels snared a single pickoff.

Ole Miss finished the season with a 9–1 record, the school's second Southeastern Conference championship, and its second Sugar Bowl invitation. The three major newspaper polls—Associated Press, United Press International, and the International News Service—rated Ole Miss No. 6. On New Year's Day, the fifth-ranked U.S. Naval Academy, making its first postseason appearance since the 1924 Rose Bowl, stopped the Rebels cold and shredded the vaunted Ole Miss defense, administering a 21–0 whipping.

1955

A Clash of Titans? Just Call It a Clash

1955 SCHEDULES

Ole Miss 10–1

RESULT	DATE	PF	OPPONENT	PA	LOCATION
W	September 17	26	Georgia	13	Atlanta
L	September 24	14	Kentucky	21	Lexington
W	October 1	33	North Texas	0	Oxford
W	October 8	13	Vanderbilt	0	Memphis
W	October 15	27	Tulane	13	New Orleans
W	October 22	17	Arkansas	7	Oxford
W	October 29	29	Louisiana State	26	Baton Rouge
W	November 5	39	Memphis State*	6	Memphis
W	November 12	27	Houston	11	Jackson
W	November 26	26	Mississippi State	0	Starkville
W	January 2, 1956	14	Texas Christian	13	Cotton Bowl

Mississippi State 6–4

RESULT	DATE	PF	OPPONENT	PA	LOCATION
L	September 17	14	Florida	20	Gainesville
W	September 24	13	Tennessee	7	Knoxville
W	October 1	33	Memphis State*	0	Starkville
W	October 8	14	Tulane	0	Starkville
W	October 15	20	Kentucky	14	Lexington
W	October 22	26	Alabama	7	Tuscaloosa
W	October 29	20	North Texas	7	Starkville
L	November 5	26	Auburn	27	Auburn
L	November 12	7	Louisiana State	34	Baton Rouge
L	November 26	0	Mississippi	26	Starkville

* Now University of Memphis

The two top offensive teams in the Southeastern Conference: No. 1 Ole Miss versus No. 2 Mississippi State. It was supposed to be a clash of titans. Unfortunately for the Maroons, however, a rash of injuries badly weakened the State offense. Those who did not play or played only briefly included all-America halfback Arthur Davis, chosen player of the year by *Look* magazine—Football Writers of America; all-America guard Scott Suber; and fullback Frank Sabbatini. The result was a 26–0 pasting, the Rebels' second straight shutout in what many newspapers were still calling the Magnolia Classic.

Ole Miss came into Starkville favored by 7 on a bright, chilly day. The Rebels needed little time to get on the scoreboard, turning their second drive of the day into a 51-yard touchdown march. Aided by a key block by fullback Paige Cothren, who received the Jacobs Trophy as the Southeastern Conference's best blocker, halfback Earl Blair went the final 9 yards to put Ole Miss up by 6. Cothren added the extra point. The Maroons responded with their deepest penetration of the day, reaching the Ole Miss 28 before the Rebel defense defused the threat.

Ole Miss extended its lead when the Maroons fumbled a punt return to give the Rebels the ball at the 21. Blair got his second touchdown of the afternoon and Cothren again kicked the extra point. The margin grew to 17 with a rare field goal—the first in the series since 1934. Cothren split the uprights with a 41-yard kick for his Southeastern Conference–record sixth field goal of the year (and only the thirtieth field goal in the twenty-three years of conference history).

The Rebels' third touchdown followed another fumble recovery. Quarterback John Wallace Blalack hurled a 30-yard touchdown pass to end Don Williams, and Eddie Crawford kicked the point after. With 2:25 left to play, Ole Miss closed the scoring with a safety—Bill Yelverton and Bill Hurst tackled Bill Stanton in the end zone on a punt attempt. The safety was the Rebels' first ever against the Maroons and the third in the series.

The victory over State vaulted Ole Miss to tenth in the Associated Press and International News Service Polls, ninth in the United Press International Poll. As Southeastern Conference champions, the Rebels went on to the Cotton Bowl, where they fell behind by 13 against Texas Christian University before launching a comeback to take a 14–13 victory, their first in a major bowl.

November 26, 1955
Ole Miss 26, Mississippi State 0

	State	Ole Miss
First downs	9	20
Total yards	177	431
Net yards rushing	137	311
Passing yards	40	120
Passes		
(Att-Comp)	8-3	17-7
Yards penalized	55	40
Lost fumbles	5	0

1956

GAME 53

"One Mistake. Just One Mistake"

State's Wade Walker

1956 SCHEDULES

Ole Miss 7–3

RESULT	DATE	PF	OPPONENT	PA	LOCATION
W	September 22	45	North Texas	0	Oxford
W	September 29	37	Kentucky	7	Memphis
W	October 6	14	Houston	0	Jackson
W	October 13	16	Vanderbilt	0	Oxford
L	October 20	3	Tulane	10	Jackson
L	October 27	0	Arkansas	14	Little Rock
W	November 3	46	Louisiana State	17	Baton Rouge
W	November 10	26	Memphis State*	0	Memphis
L	November 17	7	Tennessee	27	Knoxville
W	December 1	13	Mississippi State	7	Oxford

Mississippi State 4–6

RESULT	DATE	PF	OPPONENT	PA	LOCATION
L	September 22	0	Florida	26	Starkville
L	September 29	7	Houston	18	Houston
W	October 6	19	Georgia	7	Athens
W	October 13	18	Trinity	6	Starkville
W	October 20	19	Arkansas State	9	Starkville
L	October 27	12	Alabama	13	Tuscaloosa
L	November 3	14	Tulane	20	New Orleans
L	November 10	20	Auburn	27	Auburn
W	November 17	32	Louisiana State	13	Baton Rouge
L	December 1	7	Mississippi	13	Oxford

* Now University of Memphis

I n his postgame press conference, new Maroon coach Wade Walker repeated himself over and over: his team's "one mistake" early in the game had allowed Ole Miss, trailing at the time, to score an important touchdown. Though the Rebels had scored again to ice the game, that "one mistake" had led to State's defeat.

Fullback Paige Cothren (40) follows Gene Hickerson's block on a short scoring run for Ole Miss's first touchdown in the close 1956 game. *Ole Miss*.

Game day, December 1, was bright and sunny in Oxford. Walker, formerly State's line coach, had moved up to the head slot when Darrell Royal left for the University of Washington. About four minutes into the second quarter, Maroon center Jimmy Dodd stole a pass from Rebel quarterback Raymond Brown at midfield and raced untouched into the end zone. When Bobby Tribble kicked the extra point, State was ahead, 7–0, for its first lead against Ole Miss in ten years.

Shortly thereafter came that "one mistake." With the ball on the State 16, Maroon quarterback Billy Stacy went back to punt. The snap was low and to the right, and after a scramble, Ole Miss had the ball at the 2. On second down, fullback Paige Cothren scored, although the usually reliable Cothren missed the extra-point kick.

The score remained 7–6 until the waning minutes of the fourth quarter, keeping thirty-four thousand fans on the edge of their seats. Led by Stacy, the

December 1, 1956

Ole Miss 13, Mississippi State 7

	State	Ole Miss
First downs	13	14
Total yards	263	230
Net yards rushing	136	213
Passing yards	127	17
Passes		
(Att-Comp-Int)	16-9-2	13-4-1

team's offensive leader, the Maroons reached the Ole Miss 27 but were held on the 2, while the Rebels got to the State 33 and missed two field goals. A good runback on a State punt opened the door for the Rebels' winning drive from the Maroon 34. Brown scored with a quarterback keeper from the 4, Cothren kicked the extra point, and Ole Miss had the victory, 13–7. The loss marked the fourth time during the 1956 season that State had gone down to defeat in the final three minutes of a game.

1957

No Cheers, No Tears. Nobody Won, Nobody Lost

1957 SCHEDULES

Ole Miss 9–1–1

RESULT	DATE	PF	OPPONENT	PA	LOCATION
W	September 21	44	Trinity	0	San Antonio
W	September 28	15	Kentucky	0	Lexington
W	October 5	34	Hardin-Simmons	7	Oxford
W	October 12	28	Vanderbilt	0	Nashville
W	October 18	50	Tulane	0	New Orleans
L	October 26	6	Arkansas	12	Memphis
W	November 2	20	Houston	7	Jackson
W	November 9	14	Louisiana State	12	Oxford
W	November 16	14	Tennessee	7	Memphis
T	November 30	7	Mississippi State	7	Starkville
W	January 1, 1958	39	Texas	7	Sugar Bowl

Mississippi State 6–2–1

RESULT	DATE	PF	OPPONENT	PA	LOCATION
W	September 28	10	Memphis State*	6	Starkville
L	October 5	9	Tennessee	14	Knoxville
W	October 12	47	Arkansas State	13	Starkville
W	October 19	29	Florida	20	Gainesville
W	October 26	25	Alabama	13	Tuscaloosa
W	November 2	27	Tulane	6	Jackson
L	November 9	7	Auburn	15	Birmingham
W	November 16	14	Louisiana State	6	Baton Rouge
T	November 30	7	Mississippi	7	Starkville

* Now University of Memphis

Game day in Starkville was sunny, windy, and cold—thirty-five degrees at kickoff. Ole Miss, favored by three, was rated sixth in the nation in one poll, seventh in another. State was thirteenth. Thirty-five thousand fans came to see which school would climb higher.

The Maroons had the ball first. They came out strong, putting together a 64-yard, eleven-play drive that ended with Bubber Trammel's 18-yard touch-

Leading 7–0 with just over four minutes remaining in the first quarter, the Maroons are literally working their way out of the shadows of the goalpost. At quarterback is Billy Stacy, and at fullback is Bill Schoenrock. Mississippi State University Photo.

down run with Charles Weatherly as escort. Bobby Tribble kicked for a 7–0 lead. The score was the Maroons' first on the ground against Ole Miss in four years. The Rebels tied the score on a 35-yard drive in the second quarter when J. L. (Cowboy) Woodruff took the ball the final 6 yards. Bob Khayat, later chancellor of the university, evened the count with 9:35 to go in the half.

After that, both teams found only frustration and futility. The Rebels threatened when quarterback/defensive back Raymond Brown intercepted at midfield and returned to the 21, but a fumble gave the ball back to the Maroons. Two Maroon bobbles led to two missed field goals by the Rebels; State, not to be outdone, also had two unsuccessful field goal attempts. With just under two minutes remaining, Milton Crain intercepted Tom Miller, and the Rebels made one last effort. Brown was stopped at the Maroon 36, and the contest ended in a 7–7 standoff.

Wrote veteran sportswriter Carl Walters in the *Jackson Clarion-Ledger*, "It was a case of two fine teams tangling under adverse weather conditions, with neither . . . able to gain the upper hand. . . . [B]oth clubs were a smidgen too 'tight' tension-wise." For guiding State to a 6–2–1 record and a third-place conference finish in only his second year at the helm, Walker received the *Nashville Banner*'s award as Southeastern Conference Coach of the Year.

The tie gave Ole Miss an 8–1–1 mark on the year and denied the Rebels a share of the Southeastern Conference

November 30, 1957
Mississippi State 7, Ole Miss 7

	State	Ole Miss
First downs	11	6
Total yards	159	196
Net yards rushing	151	154
Passing yards	8	42
Passes		
(Att-Comp-Int)	8-1-3	7-4-0

crown. Auburn not only won the conference but was voted national champion by the Associated Press. However, the Tigers had violated National Collegiate Athletic Association rules and consequently were ineligible to play in a bowl game. Ole Miss went to New Orleans in their stead, trouncing Darrell Royal's Texas Longhorns 39–7 in the Sugar Bowl. Brown was unanimously named winner of the Miller-Digby Trophy as the game's Most Outstanding Player, intercepting two passes, throwing for one touchdown, and rushing for two more, including one on a Sugar Bowl–record 92-yard run.

1958

The Billy and Bobby Show

1958 SCHEDULES

Ole Miss 9–2

RESULT	DATE	PF	OPPONENT	PA	LOCATION
W	September 20	17	Memphis State*	0	Memphis
W	September 27	27	Kentucky	6	Memphis
W	October 4	21	Trinity	0	San Antonio
W	October 11	19	Tulane	8	New Orleans
W	October 18	24	Hardin-Simmons	0	Oxford
W	October 25	14	Arkansas	12	Little Rock
L	November 1	0	Louisiana State	14	Baton Rouge
W	November 8	56	Houston	7	Oxford
L	November 15	16	Tennessee	18	Knoxville
W	November 29	21	Mississippi State	0	Oxford
W	December 27	7	Florida	3	Gator Bowl

Mississippi State 3–6

RESULT	DATE	PF	OPPONENT	PA	LOCATION
W	September 27	14	Florida	7	Gainesville
L	October 4	8	Tennessee	13	Memphis
W	October 11	28	Memphis State*	6	Starkville
W	October 18	38	Arkansas State	0	Starkville
L	October 25	7	Alabama	9	Starkville
L	November 1	12	Kentucky	33	Lexington
L	November 8	14	Auburn	33	Auburn
L	November 15	6	Louisiana State	7	Jackson
L	November 29	0	Mississippi	21	Oxford

* Now University of Memphis

S tate had Billy Stacy. Ole Miss had Bobby Franklin. Two big-play quarterbacks, top playmakers. Together they put on a show that kept all 33,500 spectators entertained. In one eight-minute span of the second quarter, Franklin ran for one touchdown, passed for two others, and kicked an extra point, earning himself honors as the Associated Press's National Back of the Week. On defense, Stacy tied a rivalry record with three interceptions;

OLE MISS
MISS. STATE

Official Program

50¢

STADIUM
1958

Game program.

on offense, he single-handedly accounted for 129 yards—two-thirds of State's total yardage. Though the scoreboard ultimately showed a one-sided 21–0 Ole Miss victory, no one could say it hadn't been exciting.

It was a cold, sunny day in Oxford, the fifty-fifth battle between the home team and the visitors from Starkville, and the first for State as Mississippi State University after the legislature had changed the school's name. The first quarter saw Ole Miss mount three scoring threats, but the Maroon defense turned each aside, aided by a fumble and Stacy's first interception. In the second quarter, however, the Rebels broke through. The first score came with just under twelve and a half minutes left: after a 20 yard punt return, Franklin kept the ball and raced 12 yards into the end zone. Robert Khayat kicked the first of two extra points to make the score 7–0. Less than four minutes later, the Rebel lead had doubled as Franklin passed 11 yards to Kent Lovelace, who dived over from the 2. On Ole Miss's next possession, Franklin did it again, connecting with Larry Grantham for the touchdown and kicking the extra point for good measure. It was now 21–0 with nearly four and a half minutes until intermission.

Neither team scored again, although both came close. One Maroon drive stalled at the Ole Miss 24 as the first half ended, and another reached the Ole Miss 2 after the break. Stacy added two more interceptions in the second half to short-circuit the Rebel offense. But the second quarter had done in Mississippi State.

Ole Miss finished the season ranked eleventh by the Associated Press and twelfth by United Press International. In postseason play, Ole Miss beat Florida 7–3 in the Gator Bowl, with Franklin named Most Valuable Player.

November 29, 1958
Ole Miss 21, Mississippi State 0

	State	Ole Miss
First downs	8	21
Total plays	51	80
Total yards	189	441
Rushes/net yards	40/138	57/282
Passing yards	51	159
Passes		
(Att-Comp-Int)	11-2-1	23-10-3
Punting average	42.6	38.8
Yards penalized	80	115
Fumbles/lost	4/3	3/2

1959

Vaught's "Best Team" Proves Too Powerful

1959 SCHEDULES

Ole Miss 10–1

RESULT	DATE	PF	OPPONENT	PA	LOCATION
W	September 19	16	Houston	0	Houston
W	September 26	16	Kentucky	0	Lexington
W	October 3	43	Memphis State*	0	Oxford
W	October 10	33	Vanderbilt	0	Nashville
W	October 17	53	Tulane	7	Oxford
W	October 24	28	Arkansas	0	Memphis
L	October 31	3	Louisiana State	7	Baton Rouge
W	November 7	58	Chattanooga	0	Oxford
W	November 14	37	Tennessee	7	Memphis
W	November 28	42	Mississippi State	0	Starkville
W	January 1, 1960	21	Louisiana State	0	Sugar Bowl

Mississippi State 2–7

RESULT	DATE	PF	OPPONENT	PA	LOCATION
L	September 26	13	Florida	14	Gainesville
L	October 3	6	Tennessee	22	Knoxville
W	October 10	49	Arkansas State	14	Starkville
L	October 17	0	Georgia	15	Atlanta
W	October 24	28	Memphis State*	23	Starkville
L	October 31	0	Alabama	10	Tuscaloosa
L	November 7	0	Auburn	31	Birmingham
L	November 14	0	Louisiana State	27	Baton Rouge
L	November 28	0	Mississippi	42	Starkville

* Now University of Memphis

State faced an awesome task. Both the Associated Press and United Press International ranked 8–1 Ole Miss No. 2 in the country. The Rebels had all the necessary ingredients—speed, power, depth, and confidence. With three or four good players at every position, Ole Miss coach John Vaught had more good players on the bench, one rival coach conceded, than many teams had on the field. All-America fullback Charlie Flowers finished third in Heisman Trophy voting. Marvin Terrell was all-America at guard, and Southeastern Conference coaches had named him Lineman of the Year. The Rebels had given up only 21 points all year.

While thirty-five thousand fans at Scott Field saw the Rebels throttle the home team in a 42–0 victory, the Maroons fought the Rebels every step with what coach Wade Walker called "our fire and keen edge." Ole Miss started the scoring early as quarterback Jake Gibbs completed a perfectly aimed touchdown pass to J. L. (Cowboy) Woodruff with one minute remaining in the first quarter. Bob Khayat kicked the first of four extra points. The Maroons fumbled the ensuing kickoff, and Ole Miss had another touchdown before the period ended when Gibbs capped the short drive with a 7-yard run. 13–0. By halftime, the margin had grown to 27–0 on Flowers's 4-yard touchdown run and a scoring pass from Gibbs to Larry Grantham.

The second half saw more of the same. Gibbs turned in a 38-yard jaunt for the next Rebel touchdown. State's farthest penetration—to the Ole Miss 15—followed, but an interception blunted the drive.

Eager now to put up points, the Maroons filled the air with passes, but Woodruff added 6 more points when he ran back an interception 42 yards with thirty-five seconds remaining. Doug Elmore added the 2-point conversion to close out the scoring.

The Rebels totaled 432 yards of offense, nearly half of that by Gibbs, who rushed for 62 yards and passed for 160. "We couldn't contain him," said Walker. The Maroons had accumulated just 115 yards and had thrown three interceptions. The Rebels held onto their No. 2 ranking in both wire-service polls at season's end. Vaught told *Jackson Clarion-Ledger* sportswriter Carl Walters that the 1959 club was "the best team I have ever coached."

The Rebels received a bid to the Sugar Bowl, where they would have an unusual postseason rematch against Louisiana State, the only school that had beaten them all year. An inspired Ole Miss squad exacted revenge for that narrow 7–3 defeat with a 21–0 whipping of the Tigers. The Rebels racked up 363 yards of offense while limiting Louisiana State to -15 yards rushing.

November 28, 1959
Ole Miss 42, Mississippi State 0

	State	Ole Miss
First downs	6	23
Total plays	--	88
Total yards	115	422
Rushes/net yards	--/52	64/248
Passing yards	63	174
Passes		
(Att-Comp-Int)	20-8-3	24-9-0
Punts/average yards	9/29.3	4/23.5
Penalties/yards	8/62	11/88
Lost fumbles	2	1

In three games with State (1957, 1959, and 1960) these Rebel backs scored eight touchdowns. From bottom are quarterback Jake Gibbs (3 TDs), half-back Cowboy Woodruff (3 TDs), fullback Charlie Flowers (1 TD), and halfback Bobby Crespino (1 TD). University of Mississippi Photo.

Quarterback Bobby Franklin, who passed for two touchdowns, was once again named the Most Outstanding Player, a repeat of the honor he had received in the Gator Bowl a year earlier.

Four rating systems—Berryman, Billingsley, Dunkel, and Jeff Sagarin—named Ole Miss national champion. The Associated Press named the 1959 Rebels Southeastern Conference Team of the Decade, and Sagarin ranked the '59 squad No. 18 among all teams over the ninety-year history of intercollegiate football.

1960

Everything's Just Jake

1960 SCHEDULES

Ole Miss 10–0–1

RESULT	DATE	PF	OPPONENT	PA	LOCATION
W	September 17	42	Houston	0	Houston
W	September 24	21	Kentucky	6	Memphis
W	October 1	31	Memphis State*	20	Memphis
W	October 8	26	Vanderbilt	0	Nashville
W	October 15	26	Tulane	13	New Orleans
W	October 22	10	Arkansas	7	Little Rock
T	October 29	6	Louisiana State	6	Oxford
W	November 5	45	Chattanooga	0	Oxford
W	November 12	24	Tennessee	3	Knoxville
W	November 26	35	Mississippi State	9	Oxford
W	January 2, 1961	14	Rice	6	Sugar Bowl

Mississippi State 2–6–1

RESULT	DATE	PF	OPPONENT	PA	LOCATION
L	September 24	10	Houston	14	Starkville
T	October 1	0	Tennessee	0	Memphis
W	October 8	29	Arkansas State	9	Starkville
L	October 15	17	Georgia	20	Athens
W	October 22	21	Memphis State*	0	Starkville
L	October 29	0	Alabama	7	Starkville
L	November 5	12	Auburn	27	Auburn
L	November 12	3	Louisiana State	7	Baton Rouge
L	November 26	9	Mississippi	35	Oxford

* Now University of Memphis

Jake ('jāk): all right, fine (slang)

For Ole Miss, the 1960 Battle of the Golden Egg was just jake. Jake Gibbs, that is. Led by their all-America quarterback, the Rebels came into the game undefeated and ranked second in the nation. State, in contrast, had managed only two wins and a scoreless tie. Against the Maroons, Gibbs scored one

Coach Johnny Vaught gives his all-America Rebel quarterback, Jake Gibbs, a review of a special pass play in a practice session. University of Mississippi Photo.

touchdown, passed for two others, and bore direct responsibility for two more, leading his team to an overwhelming 35–9 win in Oxford. At one point, he completed eight consecutive passes. Just jake, indeed.

The game began this warm sunny afternoon with an exchange of unsuccessful field goal attempts and punts. The Rebels broke through when Gibbs connected with all-America end Johnny Brewer on the goal line. Allen Green kicked the first of five extra points on the day to put Ole Miss up by 7. By halftime, the margin had grown to 14, as Gibbs and Bobby Crespino completed a 68-yard drive with a 5-yard aerial touchdown.

Undismayed, the Maroons came on like gangbusters in the third quarter. With all-American Tom Goode at center, the Maroon line began paving the way, and quarterback Billy (Tootie)

November 26, 1960
Ole Miss 35, Mississippi State 9

	State	Ole Miss
First downs	15	25
Total yards	227	444
Net yards rushing	110	304
Passing yards	117	140
Passes		
(Att-Comp-Int)	24-14-2	15-13-1
Punts/average yards	5/37.6	0
Yards penalized	26	25
Lost fumbles	0	2

Hill engineered a 78-yard, eight-play scoring drive that culminated in a short pass to end David Kelley. Sammy Dantone's kick cut the lead to 14–7 and "put Maroon rooters in a fine frenzy," wrote the *Jackson Clarion-Ledger/Daily News*.

Then the floodgates opened. Ole Miss scored three straight touchdowns before the third period was over, with the first coming on a 94-yard drive that ended with Gibbs's 8-yard touchdown gallop. The Rebels scored again when end Wes Sullivan intercepted Hill's pass on the 12 and raced in. Another interception—this one by A. J. Holloway on a pass attempt by Charlie Furlow—set up the final Rebel score. The Rebel offense took over with the ball on the Maroon 17, and three plays later, Billy Ray Adams had given Ole Miss the 35–7 advantage.

The Maroons threatened to score, reaching the Rebel 1 but failing to get the final yard. After Ole Miss took possession, Gibbs tripped in the end zone, giving State a safety. The Maroons had 9 points, the most they had scored against Ole Miss in eight years.

State coach Wade Walker gave due credit to his opponents: "Ole Miss has a great football team, and Jake Gibbs is the greatest quarterback in the United States, bar none." The Associated Press named Gibbs both Southeast and National Back of the Week. The *Nashville Banner* and Atlanta Touchdown Club named him Southeastern Conference Back of the Year. And United Press International named him Southeastern Conference Player of the Year. At the end of the season, Gibbs was named a first-team all-America by a dozen different organizations and finished third in voting for the Heisman Trophy.

With a 5–0–1 Southeastern Conference record, Ole Miss captured its fourth conference championship and a berth in the Sugar Bowl against Southwest Conference runner-up Rice. The Rebels took the game, 14–6, with Gibbs, who scored both touchdowns, winning the Miller-Digby Trophy as the Most Outstanding Player. Ole Miss finished the year with an overall 10–0–1 mark, its best record ever. The Rebels were the country's only major unbeaten team. Six rating systems, including the Football Writers Association of America, named Ole Miss national champion. However, both the Associated Press and United Press International gave the nod to Minnesota, coached by former Mississippi State coach Murray Warmath.

1961

Never Argue with a No. 1 Offense

1961 SCHEDULES

Ole Miss 9–2

RESULT	DATE	PF	OPPONENT	PA	LOCATION
W	September 23	16	Arkansas	0	Jackson
W	September 30	20	Kentucky	6	Lexington
W	October 7	33	Florida State	0	Oxford
W	October 14	47	Houston	7	Memphis
W	October 21	41	Tulane	0	Jackson
W	October 28	47	Vanderbilt	0	Oxford
L	November 4	7	Louisiana State	10	Baton Rouge
W	November 11	54	Chattanooga	0	Oxford
W	November 18	24	Tennessee	10	Memphis
W	December 2	37	Mississippi State	7	Starkville
L	January 1 1962	7	Texas	12	Cotton Bowl

Mississippi State 5–5

RESULT	DATE	PF	OPPONENT	PA	LOCATION
W	September 23	6	Texas Tech	0	Jackson
W	September 30	10	Houston	7	Houston
L	October 7	3	Tennessee	17	Knoxville
W	October 14	38	Arkansas State	0	Starkville
L	October 21	7	Georgia	10	Atlanta
W	October 28	23	Memphis State*	16	Memphis
L	November 4	0	Alabama	24	Tuscaloosa
W	November 11	11	Auburn	10	Birmingham
L	November 18	6	Louisiana State	14	Baton Rouge
L	December 2	7	Mississippi	37	Starkville

*Now University of Memphis

In 1961, Ole Miss coach John Vaught fielded yet another dominant team: the No. 5 Rebels had the nation's top-ranked offense, second-ranked passing game, and third-best defense. Only a single defeat—10–7 to Louisiana State—stood between the Rebels and a perfect season. All-America honors went to fullback Billy Ray Adams, tackle Jim Dunaway, guard Treva Bolin, and quarterback Doug Elmore.

After three straight losing seasons, things seemed to be looking up for Mississippi State. Back with the designation "Bulldogs," an honored name first used after the 1905 Ole Miss game, State started the 1961 season 3–1 before dropping a tight 10–7 contest to Georgia. Then, after alternating wins and losses and with his squad's record at 5–4, coach Wade Walker announced that he would retire at season's end.

Ole Miss was just too much for State, and the crowd of 34,500 saw the Rebels cruise to an easy 37–7 win. On its first possession, Ole Miss strung together an eight-play drive that ended with Adams's 1-yard run. Wes Sullivan missed the extra point. The Rebels' next possession saw a 73-yard drive that doubled the score to 12–0 when quarterback Doug Elmore threw a 12-yard touchdown pass to Art Doty on the first play of the second quarter. This time, Sullivan's kick was true. The Bulldogs came back with a 73-yard drive of their own that brought State within 6 points. Quarterback Billy (Tootie) Hill scored on the twelfth play of the drive with a 9-yard sprint around end, and Sammy Dantone added the extra point. 13–7.

But the Rebels immediately increased their lead when quarterback Glynn Griffing and end Ralph Smith connected for a 58-yard pass and run. And the third period saw still more Rebel scoring—an 18-yard touchdown run by Adams to highlight a 71-yard, seven-play drive, plus an 18-yard field goal by Sullivan. 30–7. Halfback Frank Halbert collected the final Ole Miss touchdown on a 1-yard run following a Bulldog fumble.

Closely watching this game was Texas coach Darrell Royal, who had been head coach at State in 1954 and 1955. Royal's Longhorns would face Ole Miss in the Cotton Bowl on New Year's Day. Adams was hurt in an automobile accident and unable to play for the Rebels, and his replacement, George (Buck) Randall, went down with a knee injury early in the game.

Texas grabbed a two-touchdown lead and hung on for a 12–7 victory. After the game, Royal told Vaught, "The loss of your fullback killed you."

For Walker's replacement, State looked within the program and promoted the team's offensive coach, Paul Davis, a football letterman at Ole Miss. Davis became only the second Mississippian to coach at State.

December 2, 1961
Ole Miss 37, Mississippi State 7

	State	Ole Miss
First downs	11	21
Total yards	134	420
Net yards rushing	67	197
Passing yards	67	223
Passes		
(Att-Comp-Int)	17-7-3	20-1-1
Punts	2	1
Yards penalized	68	80

1962

"The Goof That Laid the Golden Egg"

Memphis Commercial Appeal

1962 SCHEDULES

Ole Miss 10–0

RESULT	DATE	PF	OPPONENT	PA	LOCATION
W	September 22	21	Memphis State*	7	Memphis
W	September 29	14	Kentucky	0	Jackson
W	October 6	40	Houston	7	Jackson
W	October 20	21	Tulane	0	Jackson
W	October 27	35	Vanderbilt	0	Memphis
W	November 3	15	Louisiana State	7	Baton Rouge
W	November 10	52	Chattanooga	7	Oxford
W	November 17	19	Tennessee	6	Knoxville
W	December 1	13	Mississippi State	6	Oxford
W	January 1, 1963	17	Arkansas	13	Sugar Bowl

Mississippi State 3–6

RESULT	DATE	PF	OPPONENT	PA	LOCATION
L	September 22	9	Florida	19	Jackson
W	October 6	7	Tennessee	6	Memphis
W	October 12	35	Tulane	6	New Orleans
W	October 20	9	Houston	3	Houston
L	October 27	7	Memphis State*	28	Starkville
L	November 3	0	Alabama	20	Starkville
L	November 10	3	Auburn	9	Auburn
L	November 17	0	Louisiana State	28	Jackson
L	December 1	6	Mississippi	13	Oxford

* Now University of Memphis

Just over six minutes remained to play. The Rebels were clinging to a 1-point lead over the visiting Bulldogs. The Rebs' Louis Guy had just returned Bobby Bulloch's punt to the Ole Miss 39 yard line. Runs by quarterback Jim Weatherly and fullback George (Buck) Randall gained nice yardage, and wingback Larry Johnson's pass reception gave the Rebels a first down at the State 43. On the next play, Weatherly faked a handoff to halfback Dave Jennings but kept the ball and ran to the right. The defense was completely fooled, and forty-three yards later, Weatherly had 6 points of insurance in what would be a 13–6 win that gave the Rebels a perfect 9–0 regular season.

Was it a trick play? A busted play? Just a really good fake? In the huddle, the Rebels had called a simple handoff to Jennings, who was supposed to hit the middle. But Weatherly missed the handoff. Reacting quickly, he stuck the ball on his hip and took off. The result was, in the words of a *Memphis Commercial Appeal* headline, "The Goof That Laid the Golden Egg."

Once again, the game had pitted a highly ranked Ole Miss squad—this time led by all-Americans at quarterback (Glynn Griffing) and tackle (Jim Dunaway)—against a 3–5 Mississippi State team. First-year coach Paul Davis's Bulldogs immediately signaled that in their minds, at least, they were not 25-point underdogs, charging for a touchdown on their first possession. Halfback Ode Burrell capped a 66-yard drive with a 2-yard scoring run around right end. The extra point was blocked, but with only five minutes gone, State had a surprising 6–0 lead.

But that was it for the Bulldogs for the day. The Rebels marched 82 yards to grab the lead early in the second quarter on halfback Louis Guy's 1-yard touchdown plunge and Billy Carl Irwin's extra point. And although the Rebels had two more good scoring chances, they could not convert either, and the score remained 7–6 until Weatherly's botched play.

With a 6–0 conference record, the Rebels captured their fifth Southeastern Conference championship. United Press International named John Vaught Southeastern Conference Coach of the Year, and the Atlanta Touchdown Club named Griffing Back of the Year. The Rebels completed their first unblemished season by topping No. 6 Arkansas 17–13 in the Sugar Bowl. Griffing broke Davey O'Brien's twenty-four-year-old Sugar Bowl passing record and became the fourth Rebel to take the Miller-Digby Trophy as the game's Most Outstanding Player. At 10–0, the Rebels finished at No. 3 in both major wire-service polls, their fourth consecutive year among the Top 5. The Litkenhouse rating named Ole Miss 1962 national champion.

December 1, 1962
Ole Miss 13, Mississippi State 6

	State	Ole Miss
First downs	12	18
Total plays	56	64
Total yards	176	317
Rushes/net yards	31/47	48/211
Passing yards	179	106
Passes		
(Att-Comp-Int)	25-14-1	16-9-1
Punts/average yards	7/31.7	5/38.8

The season brought positive attention to Oxford during a semester that had started in a much more negative way. James Meredith's attempt to desegregate the University of Mississippi had resulted in a campus riot, and President John F. Kennedy had called in federal troops to protect Meredith. The soldiers remained on campus throughout the semester and were among the 31,792 spectators who watched Ole Miss and State at Hemingway Stadium.

1963

It's Not Always Like Kissing Your Sister

1963 SCHEDULES

Ole Miss 7–1–2

RESULT	DATE	PF	OPPONENT	PA	LOCATION
T	September 21	0	Memphis State*	0	Memphis
W	September 28	31	Kentucky	7	Lexington
W	October 5	20	Houston	6	Houston
W	October 19	21	Tulane	0	New Orleans
W	October 26	27	Vanderbilt	7	Oxford
W	November 2	37	Louisiana State	3	Baton Rouge
W	November 9	41	Tampa	0	Oxford
W	November 16	20	Tennessee	0	Memphis
T	November 30	10	Mississippi State	10	Starkville
L	January 1, 1964	7	Alabama	12	Sugar Bowl

Mississippi State 7–2–2

RESULT	DATE	PF	OPPONENT	PA	LOCATION
W	September 21	43	Howard**	0	Starkville
T	September 28	9	Florida	9	Gainesville
W	October 5	7	Tennessee	0	Knoxville
W	October 12	31	Tulane	10	Jackson
W	October 19	20	Houston	0	Starkville
L	October 26	10	Memphis State*	17	Memphis
L	November 2	19	Alabama	20	Tuscaloosa
W	November 9	13	Auburn	10	Jackson
W	November 16	7	Louisiana State	6	Jackson
T	November 30	10	Mississippi	10	Starkville
W	December 21	16	North Carolina State	12	Liberty Bowl

* Now University of Memphis
** Now Samford

A tie game isn't all bad. Not in this case. The standoff gave Ole Miss an undefeated season plus the Southeastern Conference championship and assured the Rebels a Sugar Bowl bid. It gave State its first winning season in six years and brought the Bulldogs their first bowl bid since

'WE SHOULD HAVE WON—'

State Squad Not
Elated Over Tie

Sugar Bowlers Back
Vaught's FG Decision

Headlines from the *Clarion-Ledger/Jackson Daily News*, December 1, 1963.

1940. Moreover, Bulldog fans, tired of a long line of losses to Ole Miss, could take pride in pointing out to their Rebel friends, "*You* tied us."

Game day, November 30, was cold and windy. The crowd of thirty-five thousand was subdued and saddened by the assassination of President John F. Kennedy just a week earlier. The No. 3–ranked visitors scored first with an 80-yard drive. Mike Dennis scored when he faked out a defender on the eleventh play, a 30-yard pass from quarterback Jim Weatherly. The Bulldogs retaliated with a field goal, a 49-yarder by Justin Canale that set a new distance record in the rivalry. At halftime, the score stood at Ole Miss 7, State 3.

The Bulldogs got on top in the third period. A poor Rebel punt gave State the ball on the Ole Miss 32, and with a bit of razzle-dazzle, the Dogs reached the end zone. Halfback Ode Burrell took a pitchout from quarterback Sonny Fisher and heaved the toss to end Tommy Inman, who raced 15 yards for a touchdown. It was the only pass Burrell threw during his college career and the Bulldogs' only completion of the day.

State's 10–7 lead held for twenty-one minutes. Taking the ball on the Ole Miss 25, the Rebels marched 72 yards in twelve plays, only to find themselves facing a big decision. Fourth and goal on the State 3 yard line. Just over three

November 30, 1963
Mississippi State 10, Ole Miss 10

	State	Ole Miss
First downs	4	14
Total yards	111	221
Rushes/net yards	--/79	--/124
Passing yards	32	97
Passes		
(Att-Comp-Int)	8-1-0	17-9-3
Punts/average yards	9/37.0	6/34.0
Yards penalized	36	37
Lost fumbles	1	1

minutes to play. Kick the easy field goal for the tie? Or gamble on the touchdown and the win? Wrote Bill Clark of the *Atlanta Journal-Constitution*, "Ole pro Johnny Vaught called for the safest, sanest route to New Orleans." Billy Carl Irwin's 20-yard boot was perfect. The two teams exchanged turnovers, and there the game ended. 10–10. A tie. After the game, Vaught silenced reporters before they could ask: "Concerning that field goal," he declared, "we're conference champions and undefeated."

The 7–0–2 Rebels had their second consecutive season without a loss. Though the tie with State dropped Ole Miss from No. 3 to No. 7 in the Associated Press and United Press International Polls, the Rebels had posted their fifth Top 10 finish in a row. Ole Miss faced No. 8 Alabama in a Sugar Bowl notable for the unprecedented four inches of snow that surrounded the field. Although the Rebel defense kept the Tide out of the end zone, Alabama converted four field goals into a 12–7 win.

The Bulldogs finished the year with a 6–2–2 mark and a No. 11 national ranking, the team's highest since 1940. The squad's dramatic turnaround earned Paul Davis the Associated Press's Southeastern Conference Coach of the Year honors as well as a bid to the Liberty Bowl. On a subfreezing December day in Philadelphia, State won its second major bowl game, 16–12 over North Carolina State. The Bulldogs' Ode Burrell was named most valuable player.

1964

Dogs Break the Drought

1964 SCHEDULES

Ole Miss 5–5–1

RESULT	DATE	PF	OPPONENT	PA	LOCATION
W	September 19	30	Memphis State*	0	Oxford
L	September 26	21	Kentucky	27	Jackson
W	October 3	31	Houston	9	Oxford
L	October 10	14	Florida	30	Gainesville
W	October 17	14	Tulane	9	New Orleans
T	October 24	7	Vanderbilt	7	Nashville
L	October 31	10	Louisiana State	11	Baton Rouge
W	November 7	36	Tampa	0	Oxford
W	November 14	30	Tennessee	0	Knoxville
L	December 5	17	Mississippi State	20	Oxford
L	December 19	7	Tulsa	14	Bluebonnet Bowl

Mississippi State 4–6

RESULT	DATE	PF	OPPONENT	PA	LOCATION
L	September 19	7	Texas Tech	21	Lubbock
L	September 26	13	Florida	16	Jackson
L	October 3	13	Tennessee	14	Memphis
W	October 10	17	Tulane	6	Starkville
W	October 17	48	Southern Mississippi	7	Starkville
W	October 24	18	Houston	13	Starkville
L	October 31	6	Alabama	23	Jackson
L	November 7	3	Auburn	12	Auburn
L	November 14	10	Louisiana State	14	Baton Rouge
W	December 5	20	Mississippi	17	Oxford

* Now University of Memphis

Bulldogs 20, Rebels 17.

For seventeen years, the Bulldog faithful had endured. Loss after loss, with only three ties to break up the losing streak. On December 5, 1964, on Ole Miss's home field, the Mississippi State drought finally ended.

Bulldogs 20, Rebels 17.

Neither team had had much success during the season. The highly touted Rebels had been a disappointment, their record only 5–3–1, the worst in fourteen years. The Bulldogs were worse, following the 1963 season's success by winning a mere three games.

Most of the thirty thousand fans this chilly, gray afternoon could not remember the last time State had beaten Ole Miss. Few if any players would have been able to recall that 1946 win. A television crew was on hand, showing the game around the country for the first time.

Bulldogs 20, Rebels 17.

The game started like many of the previous seventeen, with the Rebels taking an early lead—this time, on Billy Carl Irwin's 25-yard field goal on their first possession. Another Rebel field goal attempt failed, and the Bulldogs came back with Justin Canale's successful 28-yarder to tie the score with just forty-nine seconds gone in the second quarter. The Rebels missed another field goal from the 26, and another Rebel drive just before the half ended in the Bulldogs' second interception of the afternoon. With just four seconds remaining, Canale's second field goal—this one from 48 yards out—caught the wind and sailed over. At halftime, the Bulldogs were up, 6–3.

The third quarter saw the Bulldogs extend their lead with the day's first trip to the end zone. A 52-yard drive culminated in an easy 15-yard touchdown grab by Marcus Rhoden on Don Edwards's pass. After Canale's extra point was good, State had a 13–3 lead, their biggest edge in the rivalry since that 1946 win. The Bulldogs hadn't even scored 13 points in an entire game against Ole Miss since 1952. Maroon supporters were jumping up and down, too excited to sit.

But the Rebels would not go quietly. Starting the fourth quarter, they penetrated to State's 16, but there the Bulldogs called a halt. Undaunted, Ole Miss scored on its next possession, with Jim Heidel finding Mike Dennis in the end zone for the touchdown. Irwin's kick cut the gap to 10–13 with 5:28 remaining.

The next time Ole Miss got the ball, less than three minutes remained. The Bulldog defense came up big: Dan Bland recorded State's third interception of the day and returned the grab all the way to the Ole Miss 6 yard line. Two plays later, Hoyle Granger leaped

December 5, 1964

Mississippi State 20, Ole Miss 17

	State	Ole Miss
First downs	11	17
Total yards	189	146
Net yards rushing	127	99
Passing yards	62	147
Passes		
(Att-Comp-Int)	8-3-1	32-12-3
Punts/average yards	9/35.0	6/45.0
Penalties/yards	4/43	8/88
Lost fumbles	1	0

Hoyle Granger (33) goes for extra yardage despite a Rebel tackler's grab. Granger nailed the victory for the Bulldogs when he leaped the goal line for a touchdown with 1:40 left to play. Mississippi State University Photo.

over the goal line. Canale's extra point made the score 20–10 with just 1:40 showing on the clock.

But it was not yet time for celebrating. Ole Miss's Doug Cunningham took the ensuing kickoff at his own 19, weaved through a maze of defenders until he was clear at midfield, then hugged the right sideline the rest of the way to the end zone—81 yards. It was the first kickoff return for a touchdown in this rivalry since State's J. T. (Blondy) Black did it in 1942 and the first for Ole Miss against its archrival since Ray (Little) Hapes's 1935 runback. Irwin added another extra point, but only 1:29 was left.

Bulldogs 20, Rebels 17.

Bulldog fans stormed the field. The Maroon Band played on and on. "We were past due," said State coach Paul Davis—the same Paul Davis who had played center and been the Ole Miss cocaptain the last time there had been a Maroon victory. "State played a good, tough game and moved the ball when it needed to," Ole Miss's Johnny Vaught told Jackson sportswriter Carl Walters. The Bulldogs had capitalized on the Rebels' mistakes, turning three interceptions into 13 points; Ole Miss, in contrast, had forced two State turnovers but had failed to cash in on the miscues.

MISS. STATE 20
OLE MISS. 17

Fans quickly bought up this keepsake poster that shows Bulldog players giving Coach Paul Davis an impromptu victory ride following their drought-breaking win over Ole Miss. Players include Marcus Rhoden (43), Jim Lightsey (32), John Castleberry (77), Sherman Douglas (68), and Price Hodges (24). Mississippi State University Photo.

Back in Starkville, pandemonium reigned. Car horns blared. Amplifiers that usually played soft hymns atop the Baptist church grandly burst forth with "Hail, State." Children in one neighborhood enthusiastically rang an old farm bell long kept silent in hopes of just such a victory. The mayor went to the city limits to meet the returning Bulldogs' bus, which received a police and fire truck escort through town. At the Union Building on campus, the mayor presented the team with the key to the city. Monday classes were canceled.

Ole Miss closed the season in the Bluebonnet Bowl in Houston, where Tulsa hung a 14–7 defeat on the Rebels.

Bulldogs 20, Rebels 17.

GAME 62

1965

Scott Field, Starkville

Close—Yes and No

1965 SCHEDULES

Ole Miss 7–4

RESULT	DATE	PF	OPPONENT	PA	LOCATION
W	September 18	34	Memphis State*	14	Memphis
L	September 25	7	Kentucky	16	Lexington
L	October 2	16	Alabama	17	Birmingham
L	October 9	0	Florida	17	Oxford
W	October 16	24	Tulane	7	Jackson
W	October 23	24	Vanderbilt	7	Oxford
W	October 30	23	Louisiana State	0	Jackson
L	November 6	3	Houston	17	Houston
W	November 13	14	Tennessee	13	Memphis
W	November 27	21	Mississippi State	0	Starkville
W	December 18	13	Auburn	7	Liberty Bowl

Mississippi State 4–6

RESULT	DATE	PF	OPPONENT	PA	LOCATION
W	September 18	36	Houston	0	Houston
W	September 25	18	Florida	13	Gainesville
W	October 2	48	Tampa	7	Starkville
W	October 9	27	Southern Mississippi	9	Starkville
L	October 16	13	Memphis State*	33	Memphis
L	October 22	15	Tulane	17	New Orleans
L	October 30	7	Alabama	10	Jackson
L	November 6	18	Auburn	25	Birmingham
L	November 13	20	Louisiana State	37	Baton Rouge
L	November 27	0	Mississippi	21	Starkville

* Now University of Memphis

With their losing streak against Ole Miss finally over, the Bulldogs started the 1965 campaign riding high—undefeated after four games and ranked ninth in the polls. The Rebels, however, were slow off the mark, posting a 1–3 record, their worst start in nineteen years. But coach Johnny Vaught's team rebounded, and by the Battle of the Golden Egg,

The Rebel defense zeroes in on Bulldog back Tommy Garrison as part of a swarming attack. The Rebels took advantage of Bulldog miscues and scored two of their three touchdowns on turnovers. Mississippi State University Photo.

the Rebs had won four of their last five to improve to 5–4. Unfortunately for the Bulldogs, their season turned around, too, and they had lost five straight. Although 5–4 Ole Miss and 4–5 Mississippi State had similar records, they had taken vastly different routes to get there.

On the field, the game was close. On the scoreboard, it wasn't—Ole Miss took the 21–0 win. As in the preceding year, breaks played a big role. And like 1964, one team took advantage of those mistakes. But this time, it was Ole Miss. The first Rebel touchdown came when all-America defensive back Bill Clay intercepted a pass at midfield and sailed down the sideline untouched for 6 points. Jimmy Keyes kicked the first of three extra points for the day, and the Rebels were up 7–0 before the end of the opening quarter. The thirty-five thousand fans soon saw the lead grow to 14 after a sixteen-play, 94-yard drive—the Rebels' longest of the year—ended with quarterback Jim Heidel's 4-yard run. Up by two touchdowns, Vaught issued this order: No more passes. The Rebels threw the ball only one more time, and that pass fell incomplete. The Ole Miss special teams set up one more touchdown late in the game when the Bulldogs fumbled a fair catch of a punt and Gordon (Rocky) Fleming recovered at the State 6. Mike Dennis scored. The Bulldogs threatened twice more but were turned back at the Ole Miss 17 and 24.

Each team lost one fumble, but interceptions made the difference: the

November 27, 1965

Ole Miss 21, Mississippi State 0

	State	Ole Miss
First downs	10	11
Total plays	54	63
Total yards	176	214
Rushes/net yards	39/122	55/165
Passing yards	26	49
Passes		
(Att-Comp-Int)	15-3-3	8-4-0
Punting average	42.0	32.0
Penalties/yards	4/60	9/75
Fumbles/lost	1/1	2/1

Rebel defense picked off three passes, leading directly to 7 points and stopping two other Bulldog drives. The Rebels, keeping the ball on the ground, threw no interceptions.

Despite the victory, the Rebels did not get to take the Golden Egg back to Oxford. State students hid the trophy and refused to return it.

The Liberty Bowl was in its first year in Memphis, where it had moved from Philadelphia via Atlantic City, and the bowl chose the Rebels and the Auburn Tigers for its inaugural matchup in the new location. With the help of a magnificent goal-line stand, the Rebels emerged as the 13–7 victors. The final United Press International Poll rated Ole Miss seventeenth.

1966

GAME 63

Hemingway Stadium, Oxford

The Best Offense Is a Good . . .

1966 SCHEDULES

Ole Miss 8–3

RESULT	DATE	PF	OPPONENT	PA	LOCATION
W	September 17	13	Memphis State*	0	Memphis
W	September 24	17	Kentucky	0	Jackson
L	October 1	7	Alabama	17	Jackson
L	October 8	3	Georgia	9	Athens
W	October 15	14	Southern Mississippi	7	Oxford
W	October 22	27	Houston	6	Memphis
W	October 29	17	Louisiana State	0	Baton Rouge
W	November 12	14	Tennessee	7	Knoxville
W	November 19	34	Vanderbilt	0	Jackson
W	November 26	24	Mississippi State	0	Oxford
L	December 17	0	Texas	19	Bluebonnet Bowl

Mississippi State 2–8

RESULT	DATE	PF	OPPONENT	PA	LOCATION
L	September 17	17	Georgia	20	Jackson
L	September 24	7	Florida	28	Gainesville
W	October 1	20	Richmond	0	Starkville
W	October 8	10	Southern Mississippi	9	Starkville
L	October 15	0	Houston	28	Houston
L	October 22	0	Florida State	10	Tallahassee
L	October 29	14	Alabama	27	Tuscaloosa
L	November 5	0	Auburn	13	Jackson
L	November 12	7	Louisiana State	17	Baton Rouge
L	November 26	0	Mississippi	24	Oxford

* Now University of Memphis

A tough defense can win a tough ball game. The Rebels allowed the Bulldogs past midfield only once—to the 49 yard line. The Dogs' twenty-nine rushing attempts netted just 2 yards. They completed only nine of twenty-two pass attempts for 40 yards. No Mississippi State drive included more than one first down, and the Bulldogs had only six first

End Jerry Richardson (80) reaches for an unidentified Mississippi State ball carrier in a battle of strength. Among Bulldogs fighting the attack are guard Bubba Hampton (67) and fullback Bob Haller (31). University of Mississippi Photo.

downs for the day. Not surprisingly, the result was a one-sided 24–0 Ole Miss victory.

Under cloudy skies, just over thirty thousand came to Oxford to see the Rebels, favored by 20 points, host the Bulldogs. State's opening drive was its best of the day; after that, everything went downhill. The Rebs missed a field goal attempt before launching a 74-yard touchdown drive. Doug Cunningham went the final 13 yards and Jimmy Keyes, who was perfect on extra points all year, kicked the point after to make the score 7–0. The next Rebel possession ended just as successfully, as quarterback Bruce Newell connected with J. M. (Mac) Haik for 26 yards and a 14-point lead. Wayne (Mac) McClure recovered a Bulldog fumble at the State 13 yard line on the next possession, and

	State	Ole Miss
November 26, 1966		
Ole Miss 24, Mississippi State 0		
First downs	6	23
Total plays	51	52
Total yards	42	340
Rushes/net yards	29/2	27/165
Passing yards	40	175
Passes		
(Att-Comp)	22-9	25-14

although the Rebel offense failed to get a touchdown, Keyes's field goal upped the Ole Miss advantage to 17.

Neither team demonstrated much offense in the third period, and the fourth was a series of interceptions and fumbles. Rebel tackle Jim Urbanek snagged one of the pickoffs and galloped 15 yards for the final touchdown with about eight and a half minutes remaining.

The stifling Rebel defense finished the season ranked third in the country overall and thirteenth against the pass, with a No. 12 rating in the United Press International Poll. Coach Johnny Vaught declared that the turnaround from the disappointing early-season losses was "the finest comeback of any team I have ever had." His squad finished the year in the Bluebonnet Bowl, the Rebels' tenth consecutive postseason appearance, the nation's longest streak. In a sloppy game that featured four interceptions by each team, the sluggish Rebels went down to Darrell Royal's Texas Longhorns, 19–0.

Two weeks after the Battle of the Golden Egg, Mississippi State officials fired coach Paul Davis and athletic director Wade Walker. A few weeks later, Charley Shira, a Royal assistant at both Texas and Mississippi State, was named as the Bulldogs' twenty-sixth head coach.

1967

Mudhens 10, Ducks 3

1967 SCHEDULES

Ole Miss 6–4–1

RESULT	DATE	PF	OPPONENT	PA	LOCATION
L	September 23	17	Memphis State*	27	Memphis
W	September 30	26	Kentucky	13	Lexington
L	October 7	7	Alabama	21	Birmingham
W	October 14	29	Georgia	20	Jackson
W	October 21	23	Southern Mississippi	14	Oxford
W	October 28	14	Houston	13	Oxford
T	November 4	13	Louisiana State	13	Jackson
L	November 18	7	Tennessee	20	Memphis
W	November 25	28	Vanderbilt	7	Nashville
W	December 2	10	Mississippi State	3	Starkville
L	December 30	7	Texas–El Paso	14	Sun Bowl

Mississippi State 1–9

RESULT	DATE	PF	OPPONENT	PA	LOCATION
L	September 23	0	Georgia	30	Athens
L	September 30	7	Florida	24	Jackson
W	October 7	7	Texas Tech	3	Lubbock
L	October 14	14	Southern Mississippi	21	Starkville
L	October 21	6	Houston	43	Starkville
L	October 28	12	Florida State	24	Tallahassee
L	November 4	0	Alabama	13	Tuscaloosa
L	November 11	0	Auburn	36	Auburn
L	November 18	0	Louisiana State	55	Baton Rouge
L	December 2	3	Mississippi	10	Starkville

* Now University of Memphis

December 2, 1967. Half of Scott Field was under water. The other half was a slippery, sloppy mess. Uniforms were so muddy that Ole Miss's white shirts were almost as dark as State's maroon. Numbers were practically illegible. Field conditions were the worst coaches John Vaught and Charley Shira had ever encountered. Lightning had flashed throughout the

A few plays after the Bulldogs' Calvin Harrison blocked Julian Fagan's punt, James Neill nails a 29-yard field goal in the wet and muddy 1967 battle. *Clarion-Ledger/Jackson Daily News*, December 3, 1967.

morning. Tornado alerts were issued. The twenty-one thousand die-hards—the smallest crowd in twenty-two years—who ignored the pregame torrential rain and an afternoon of showers were treated to a battle royal.

Ole Miss converted the opening kickoff into a scoring drive. From the State 49, the Rebels marched 28 yards through the mud before Van Brown was good for a 38-yard field goal. Just five minutes were gone in the game. A few possessions later, Ole Miss extended its lead with a 47-yard drive capped by a 7-yard toss from quarterback Bruce Newell to his high school teammate, J. M. (Mac) Haik. Brown added the kick for a 10-point lead. A blocked punt

December 2, 1967
Ole Miss 10, Mississippi State 3

	State	Ole Miss
First downs	10	11
Total plays	60	58
Total yards	191	197
Rushes/net yards	44/99	42/123
Passing yards	92	74
Passes (Att-Comp-Int)	16-10-2	16-6-0
Punts/average yards	6/36.5	7/36.1
Penalties/yards	4/45	2/23
Fumbles/lost	1/0	4/0

Fourteen majorettes performing with the Famous Maroon Band are head majorette Cherie Hammond, center, and, from left, Margaret DeMoville, Carla Morris, Jane Moore, Linda Seale, Diane Dotson, Mary Louis Nickel, Nancy Luke, Judy Porter, Gayle Murphree, Dawn Miller, Barbara Jasper, Dianne Byers, and Gayle Stanley. Mississippi State University Photo.

led to a Bulldog field goal. Linebacker Calvin Harrison tipped the ball, and State took over at the Ole Miss 34. When the threat stalled, James Neill put through a 29-yard field goal.

The final two quarters of mud wrestling were highlighted only by two missed field goal attempts, one by each team. The score remained 10–3, Ole Miss, although the Bulldogs had clearly played their best game of the year. State students finally returned the Golden Egg to Ole Miss after having refused to give it up for two years. Shira called it a moral victory for the Dogs, praising the play of all-America linebacker D. D. Lewis, Tommy Corbett, Glenn Higgins, Harrison, and Don Saget. Vaught singled out the passing duo of Newell and Haik.

On the strength of their 6–3–1 record, the Rebels were invited to the Sun Bowl to play hometown University of Texas at El Paso. Ole Miss intercepted a pass for its only touchdown, but UTEP scored twice in the fourth quarter for a 14–7 win.

1968

Pharr and Manning I

1968 SCHEDULES

Ole Miss 7–3–1

RESULT	DATE	PF	OPPONENT	PA	LOCATION
W	September 21	21	Memphis State*	7	Memphis
W	September 28	30	Kentucky	14	Jackson
W	October 5	10	Alabama	8	Jackson
L	October 12	7	Georgia	21	Athens
W	October 19	21	Southern Mississippi	13	Oxford
L	October 26	7	Houston	29	Jackson
W	November 2	27	Louisiana State	24	Baton Rouge
W	November 9	38	Chattanooga	16	Oxford
L	November 16	0	Tennessee	31	Knoxville
T	November 30	17	Mississippi State	17	Oxford
W	December 14	34	Virginia Tech	17	Liberty Bowl

Mississippi State 0–8–2

RESULT	DATE	PF	OPPONENT	PA	LOCATION
L	September 21	13	Louisiana Tech	20	Starkville
L	September 28	0	Auburn	26	Jackson
L	October 5	14	Florida	31	Gainesville
L	October 12	14	Southern Mississippi	47	Starkville
T	October 19	28	Texas Tech	28	Jackson
L	October 26	17	Tampa	24	Tampa
L	November 2	13	Alabama	20	Tuscaloosa
L	November 9	14	Florida State	27	Starkville
L	November 16	16	Louisiana State	20	Baton Rouge
T	November 30	17	Mississippi	17	Oxford

* Now University of Memphis

State had not won a game all year. Ole Miss had lost only three. Yet the Bulldogs were leading 17–10 early in the fourth quarter. Would they pull off the upset?

The two quarterbacks were dominating play. The Bulldogs were led by Tommy Pharr, a highly skilled junior atop the Southeastern Conference in passing and total offense. On the receiving end of most of Pharr's passes was split end Sammy Milner, leading the conference in receptions. For Ole Miss, sophomore Archie Manning was at quarterback. Even the usually understated Ole Miss coach, Johnny Vaught, declared that Manning would be one of the best ever to play for the Rebels. Manning was right behind Pharr, second in the Southeastern Conference in both passing and total offense. Together, Pharr and Manning kept the twenty-seven thousand fans in Hemingway Stadium on the edge of their seats—when they did sit. "Two of the South's finest quarterbacks," wrote the *Atlanta Journal-Constitution*'s Frank Hyland, stating the obvious.

Game day was November 30. Ole Miss's 6–3 record included a win over Alabama for the first time in 18 games stretching back fifty-eight years. State's record included a tie with Texas Tech.

The Dogs ignored the Rebels' role as 20-point favorites and started with a bang. David Smith took the opening kickoff to the Bulldogs' 47. After a short drive, Bobby Culver's 37-yard field goal hit the goalpost's left upright and went through. 3–0 State.

State's second possession opened the way for an Ole Miss score when a Bulldog fumbled Julian Fagan's punt, and Hank Shows snapped up the ball on the Bulldog 21. On the third play from scrimmage, Steve Hindman scored on a 1-yard run, and Perry King's kick put Ole Miss up, 7–3. The Rebels added to their lead with a drive where Manning connected for seven passes in a row, including four to split end Floyd Franks, who caught a rivalry record eight catches for the day. King's 28-yard field goal made the count 10–3.

The Bulldogs came back to tie the game on a possession that began when Joe Jennings snared Manning's only interception of the day. Pharr's 4-yard touchdown toss to Lynn Zeringue knotted the score with 2:15 left in the first half.

Neither team mounted a serious threat in the third period, but the Dogs reached the Ole Miss 27 early in the fourth before Bobby Garrigues's interception halted the threat. The next Bulldog possession gave State the go-ahead score, as Pharr found his favorite target, Sammy Milner, with a 49-yard touchdown strike. Milner grabbed the pass on the 10 and ran it in. Culver's kick made it 17–10 with 13:42 left to play.

What would the Rebels do? Turn to Manning, of course. They reeled off

November 30, 1968
Ole Miss 17, Mississippi State 17

	State	Ole Miss
First downs	23	14
Total yards	317	228
Net yards rushing	169	49
Passing yards	148	179
Passes		
(Att-Comp-Int)	28-13-2	31-19-1

a 53-yard drive on which Manning accounted for 45 yards. The first play was a 21-yard completion to Franks. Three consecutive carries and a Manning sneak brought another first down on the Bulldog 23. Halfback John (Bo) Bowen's 15-yard catch put the ball on the 8. And from there Manning took it in for the touchdown. 17–16 Bulldogs. Only 4:14 remained.

Would they kick the extra point for the tie, or go for the 2-point conversion and the win? Although Rebel fans howled in protest when King stepped up to kick, Vaught later said that the decision to kick was easy: "Anything else would have been silly," he told Bill Ross, sports editor of the *Tupelo Daily Journal.* "Had we missed

Tommy Pharr, one of the SEC's total offensive leaders, staged an aerial shootout with Archie Manning in an exciting tie ball game. Pharr totaled 196 yards, while Manning collected 184 yards plus a touchdown. Mississippi State University Photo.

it, it would have been a great victory for them." King's twenty-second straight extra point of the season knotted the score at 17.

Pharr accounted for 196 of State's 317 yards—48 on the ground and 148 through the air, completing thirteen of twenty-eight attempts and throwing two interceptions. Manning matched Pharr's performance: a net 5 yards rushing plus 179 passing (nineteen of thirty-one, with one interception) gave him 184 of the Rebels' 228 yards.

Ole Miss took its 6–3–1 record to Memphis in mid-December before a record Liberty Bowl crowd. After falling behind Virginia Tech 17–0 in the first quarter, the Rebs scored 34 unanswered points for the win.

1969

Pharr and Manning II

1969 SCHEDULES

Ole Miss 8–3

RESULT	DATE	PF	OPPONENT	PA	LOCATION
W	September 20	28	Memphis State*	3	Oxford
L	September 27	9	Kentucky	10	Lexington
L	October 4	32	Alabama	33	Birmingham
W	October 11	25	Georgia	17	Jackson
W	October 18	69	Southern Mississippi	7	Oxford
L	October 25	11	Houston	25	Houston
W	November 1	26	Louisiana State	23	Jackson
W	November 8	21	Chattanooga	0	Oxford
W	November 15	38	Tennessee	0	Jackson
W	November 27	48	Mississippi State	22	Starkville
W	January 1 1970	27	Arkansas	22	Sugar Bowl

Mississippi State 3–7

RESULT	DATE	PF	OPPONENT	PA	LOCATION
W	September 20	17	Richmond	14	Starkville
L	September 27	35	Florida	47	Jackson
L	October 4	0	Houston	74	Houston
W	October 11	34	Southern Mississippi	20	Starkville
W	October 18	30	Texas Tech	26	Lubbock
L	October 25	17	Florida State	20	Tallahassee
L	November 1	19	Alabama	23	Jackson
L	November 8	13	Auburn	52	Auburn
L	November 15	6	Louisiana State	61	Baton Rouge
L	November 27	22	Mississippi	48	Starkville

* Now University of Memphis

Just like the year before, the 1969 season found State's Tommy Pharr and Ole Miss's Archie Manning atop the Southeastern Conference in offense. This year, however, Manning was No. 1 and Pharr No. 2. The rematch between these two highly regarded quarterbacks promised to be another doozy of a game.

Despite all-day rain and a slippery ball, Pharr and Manning put on a record-breaking performance for the thirty-four thousand fans: the most passes in the rivalry's history, most completions, and most yards through the air. The teams chewed up chunks of turf as they set new highs in plays, first downs, yardage, and points. All in all, eleven individual or team rivalry records were set.

This was the first Thanksgiving Day meeting between Ole Miss and State since 1937. The Rebels had toppled three Top 10 teams and would add a fourth in the postseason. Manning fans responded to taunts of "Archie Who?" with a song, "The Ballad of Archie Who?" played on Mississippi radio stations.

Manning's afternoon started off with Buddy Newsome picking off the Ole Miss quarterback's first throw.

Archie Manning, Ole Miss's star quarterback, was responsible for 315 yards of offense on a rainy afternoon, including personally scoring twice and passing for three other touchdowns. In his two career games against State the all-American Manning scored three touchdowns, passed for three, and gained 499 total yards. University of Mississippi Photo.

After an exchange of fumbles in Rebel territory, the Bulldogs headed straight for the end zone, with Lynn Zeringue leaping over tackle on a 3-yard run. Charles Jordan kicked the first of two extra points to make it 7–0, Bulldogs.

The Rebels quickly tied the score with a 66-yard, seven-play march. Manning circled left and then hit center on a 27-yard touchdown run. Fred Brister opened the way for the next Rebel score when he recovered a fumble on the State 34. Tailback Leon Felts took a pitchout from Manning on the 6 and cruised in for the score. 14–7 at the end of one.

Freddy Russell started the Bulldogs' tying drive with a fumble recovery on

November 27, 1969
Ole Miss 48, Mississippi State 22

	State	Ole Miss
First downs	19	31
Total plays	76	87
Total yards	379	571
Rushes/net yards	31/89	56/359
Passing yards	290	212
Passes		
(Att-Comp-Int)	44-24-3	31-18-3
Punts/average yards	8/38.5	3/37.3
Penalties/yards	4/28	9/84
Fumbles/lost	2/2	2/2

In the pouring rain, Archie Manning dodges the attack of Gene Wood (84). The "100" on Rebel helmets marks the centennial of college football in America. University of Mississippi Photo.

the Mississippi 37. Six plays later, David Smith evaded the Rebel defense to catch Pharr's touchdown pass, and it was a brand-new ball game—14–14 at the half.

Neither team could break the deadlock through most of the third quarter, but with 2:34 remaining, fullback John (Bo) Bowen bolted 17 yards to put the Rebels back on top, 21–14. Bowen, son of John (Buddy) Bowen, the Rebels' 1947 Jacobs Trophy winner as the best blocking back in the Southeastern Conference, was the game's leading ground gainer with 147 yards. Then, with rain still falling, "came the deluge," the *Memphis Commercial Appeal* declared. The Rebels scored 27 straight points. The first touchdown came on a long bomb—Manning to wingback Vernon Studdard on the run for 58 yards. The next drive covered 62 yards in ten plays and ended with Manning's 1-yard sneak. After Wyck Neely intercepted Pharr at the Bulldog 30, Manning and Studdard hooked up again for a score. The final Ole Miss touchdown also came on an interception, but this time Bill Jones picked the ball off on the Mississippi State 12 and ran it in himself. Perry King kicked his sixth extra point. In the blink of an eye, the Rebels had taken a 48–14 advantage.

The Bulldogs were set for a late touchdown when Bill Crick intercepted Rebel quarterback Brent (Shug) Chumbler's pass and returned the ball to the Ole Miss 44. Pharr and Sammy Milner combined for both the touchdown and the 2-point conversion (the Bulldogs' first against Ole Miss) for a 48–22 final.

"The Pharr-Milner-Smith passing combination is the best I've seen," Manning told the *Clarion-Ledger*. Milner returned the compliment: "Archie's everything they say he is." Pharr totaled 318 yards overall (290 passing, 28 rushing), while Manning racked up a nearly identical 315 (206 passing, 109 rushing).

The game set a bevy of rivalry records for the time, including

- most first downs, one team—31, Ole Miss
- most first downs, both teams combined—50
- total offense, one team—571 yards, Ole Miss
- total offense, both teams combined—950 yards
- most passing yardage, both teams combined—502 yards
- most passing attempts, both teams combined—75
- most yardage, one player—318, Pharr
- most passing attempts, one player—44, Pharr
- most passing completions, one player—24, Pharr
- most receptions, one player—14, Smith
- most passing yardage, one player—290, Pharr

Ole Miss accepted a Sugar Bowl bid for its record thirteenth postseason appearance in a row. Against No. 3 Arkansas, the Rebels rolled up an 18-point lead and won 27–22. Manning became the fifth Rebel quarterback to receive the Miller-Digby Trophy as Most Valuable Player. The final Associated Press Poll had the Rebels ranked No. 8 in the nation. Archie Manning was named Southeastern Conference Player of the Year and finished fourth in the Heisman Trophy voting. In addition, the Miami Touchdown Club named Manning the top college back, and the Washington, D.C., Touchdown Club awarded him the prestigious Walter Camp Award.

GAME 67

1970

Hemingway Stadium,
Oxford

"Something . . . You Will Never Forget"

State's Charley Shira

1970 SCHEDULES

Ole Miss 7–4

RESULT	DATE	PF	OPPONENT	PA	LOCATION
W	September 19	47	Memphis State*	13	Memphis
W	September 26	20	Kentucky	17	Jackson
W	October 3	48	Alabama	23	Jackson
W	October 10	31	Georgia	21	Athens
L	October 17	14	Southern Mississippi	30	Oxford
W	October 24	26	Vanderbilt	16	Nashville
W	November 7	24	Houston	13	Oxford
W	November 14	44	Chattanooga	7	Oxford
L	November 26	14	Mississippi State	19	Oxford
L	December 5	17	Louisiana State	61	Baton Rouge
L	January 2	28	Auburn	35	Gator Bowl

Mississippi State 6–5

RESULT	DATE	PF	OPPONENT	PA	LOCATION
W	September 12	14	Oklahoma State	13	Jackson
L	September 19	13	Florida	34	Gainesville
W	September 26	20	Vanderbilt	6	Memphis
W	October 3	7	Georgia	6	Jackson
L	October 10	14	Houston	31	Starkville
W	October 17	20	Texas Tech	16	Jackson
W	October 24	51	Southern Mississippi	15	Starkville
L	October 31	6	Alabama	35	Tuscaloosa
L	November 7	0	Auburn	56	Birmingham
L	November 14	7	Louisiana State	38	Baton Rouge
W	November 26	19	Mississippi	14	Oxford

* Now University of Memphis

While State was having just an average season, Ole Miss was riding high—undefeated, lots of national publicity, and a No. 4 ranking in the wire-service polls. The Rebel faithful were dreaming of a national championship and a Heisman Trophy for all-America quarterback Archie Manning.

QB Joe Reed fades for a pass as Bulldogs Tate Marsh (51) and Don Dudley (30) offer protection. Coming up behind is Rebel end Dennis Coleman (48). The white-coated figure in the background is Archie Manning, sidelined with a broken arm. Mississippi State University Photo.

But one by one Ole Miss's dreams were shattered. First, Ole Miss lost a game and with it any chance of a national championship. Three nights later, coach John Vaught was sidelined for the season because of a heart problem. His replacement was veteran offensive line coach Frank (Bruiser) Kinard. Then athletic director Claude M. (Tad) Smith developed a heart condition that kept him out for much of the fall. Finally, Manning, who had begun the season on the cover of *Sports Illustrated*, fractured his left arm in the Homecoming game against Houston. He would be on the sidelines for the game with State. The Rebels' string of problems continued on Thanksgiving afternoon, as they went down to the Bulldogs 19–14—State's first win over Ole Miss in six years and just its third victory since World War II.

That Thanksgiving afternoon was overcast, with winds between twelve and fifteen miles per hour. Some thirty-four thousand fans almost filled Hemingway Stadium. Despite the loss to Southern Miss, Ole Miss remained at No. 10 in the polls. But the 5–5 State team threatened early. The Bulldogs missed two field goals, but the third time was the

November 26, 1970
Mississippi State 19, Ole Miss 14

	State	Ole Miss
First downs	26	15
Total yards	453	305
Net yards rushing	284	141
Passing yards	169	164
Passes		
(Att-Comp-Int)	26-10-0	31-14-1
Punts/average yards	2/34.0	9/33.0
Yards penalized	65	125
Lost fumbles	3	1

Frank Dowsing's interception of an almost certain Rebel touchdown pass in fading minutes assured victory for the Bulldogs. One of the first African American football players at State, two years later Dowsing was named all-America. Mississippi State University Photo.

charm—Glenn Ellis's 33-yarder at the beginning of the second quarter split the uprights, and State took a 3–0 lead.

In the next eleven and a half minutes, the lead swapped hands three times. Quarterback Brent (Shug) Chumbler directed the Rebels 90 yards for their first touchdown, with tailback Bob Knight breaking away for a 49-yard touchdown run and Jim Poole adding the extra point to put Ole Miss ahead, 7–3. Twenty-seven seconds later, after a Rebel interference penalty put the ball on the Ole Miss 10, State quarterback Joe Reed hit Lewis Grubbs with a touchdown pass, and Glenn Ellis kicked to put State back on top, 10–7. With six seconds to go in the half, Chumbler completed a 63-yard drive when he took the ball in from the 4, and the Rebels had the lead again, 14–10.

Coach Charley Shira rallied his Bulldogs at halftime, reminding them, "You have something in your grasp you will never forget." His inspirational speech worked, and the second half was almost all State. About a minute before the end of the third quarter, the Bulldogs closed the gap to 1 point on Ellis's 32-yard field goal. On its next series, State put together a 71-yard scoring drive: Reed smashed over from the 1 for the touchdown on the fourteenth play. Reed's pass attempt to David Smith for the 2-point conversion was no good, but State had gone ahead, 19–14.

With 8:16 to play, the Rebels launched a drive to pull out the game. Ole Miss got as far as the State 18, but cornerback Frank Dowsing, one of the first two African American players at State and a future all-American, stepped in front of Jim Poole and took away a surefire touchdown. State's lead was safe.

The Bulldogs finished the season at 6–5, their first winning campaign in seven years. After having failed to win a conference game for the preceding four years, State had taken three during 1970, a performance that earned Shira the Associated Press's Southeastern Conference Coach of the Year award.

State's cheerleaders and team mascot would have plenty to celebrate after leading the Bulldogs on-field to upset the home-team Rebels. Mississippi State University Photo.

The Rebels went on to play in the Gator Bowl, where Manning, who had finished third in the Heisman Trophy voting, returned to the field with a cast on his arm. Ole Miss fell behind Auburn 21–0 but came back to make the game close before falling short, 35–28. The loss dropped the Rebels to twentieth in the final Associated Press Poll.

GAME 68

Scott Field, Starkville

1971

42 Points in One Quarter

1971 SCHEDULES

Ole Miss 10–2

RESULT	DATE	PF	OPPONENT	PA	LOCATION
W	September 11	29	Cal State–Long Beach	13	Jackson
W	September 18	49	Memphis State*	21	Memphis
W	September 25	34	Kentucky	20	Lexington
L	October 2	6	Alabama	40	Birmingham
L	October 9	7	Georgia	38	Jackson
W	October 16	20	Southern Mississippi	6	Oxford
W	October 23	28	Vanderbilt	7	Oxford
W	October 30	24	Louisiana State	22	Jackson
W	November 6	28	Tampa	27	Tampa
W	November 13	49	Chattanooga	10	Oxford
W	November 25	48	Mississippi State	0	Starkville
W	December 30	41	Georgia Tech	18	Peach Bowl

Mississippi State 2–9

RESULT	DATE	PF	OPPONENT	PA	LOCATION
L	September 11	7	Oklahoma State	26	Stillwater
W	September 18	13	Florida	10	Jackson
L	September 25	19	Vanderbilt	49	Starkville
L	October 2	7	Georgia	35	Athens
L	October 9	9	Florida State	27	Tallahassee
W	October 16	24	Lamar	7	Starkville
L	October 23	7	Tennessee	10	Memphis
L	October 30	10	Alabama	41	Jackson
L	November 6	21	Auburn	30	Auburn
L	November 13	3	Louisiana State	28	Jackson
L	November 25	0	Mississippi	48	Starkville

* Now University of Memphis

I n January 1971, for the first time since 1947, Ole Miss was in the market for a new head football coach. Both Johnny Vaught and athletic director Claude M. (Tad) Smith stepped down, ending their twenty-four-year partnership. The athletic committee selected Frank (Bruiser) Kinard to

The Ole Miss coaching staff congratulates quarterback Norris Weese, who passed for two touchdowns and had 148 yards for the day. From left are Dick Wood, Ken Cooper, Warner Alford, and Head Coach Billy Kinard. Cooper would be head coach between 1974 and 1977. Alford would be athletic director between 1978 and 1994. University of Mississippi Photo.

serve as the new athletic director and named his brother, Billy, an assistant at Arkansas, to succeed Vaught—the first alumnus to serve as the Rebels' head coach and one of four brothers to have played for Ole Miss.

Kinard's inaugural game against archrival Mississippi State went well—so well, in fact, that his team scored an unbelievable 42 points in the second period. The Rebels recorded six touchdowns and six extra points in 9:27 of what the *Memphis Commercial Appeal* called "football hysteria." The Rebels' 48–0 victory represented their greatest margin of victory against the Bulldogs.

At kickoff, Ole Miss was favored by no more than 10. Through the scoreless first quarter, the State offense looked good. The second quarter also started well for the Bulldogs, as they recorded an interception to end a Rebel threat. But State had to punt on that possession, and Mickey Fratesi fielded the ball

November 25, 1971
Ole Miss 48, Mississippi State 0

	State	Ole Miss
First downs	9	27
Total plays	56	88
Total yards	195	464
Rushes/net yards	26/47	60/283
Passing yards	148	181
Passes		
(Att-Comp-Int)	30-8-1	28-14-1
Lost fumbles	3	2

at the Bulldog 38 and brought it back to the 23. Five plays later, tailback Greg Ainsworth had the first of his three touchdowns for the day. Cloyce Hinton kicked the extra point (his first of four), and Ole Miss was off and running. Within fourteen seconds, the score was 14–0. Henry Walsh forced a fumble, and Reggie Dill recovered. On the first play, Ainsworth burst 19 yards through the line for his second touchdown. Two plays later, Dill recovered another fumble on a bad pitchout. On second down, quarterback Norris Weese rifled a 28-yard touchdown strike to tight end Burney (Butch) Veazey. 20–0. The next punt traveled to the Ole Miss 40, and the Rebels put together their only long drive of the day—seven plays ending with Ainsworth's 20-yard scoring jaunt and Weese's pass to Gene Allen for the 2-point conversion. Two more touchdowns quickly followed. Elmer Allen forced yet another Bulldog fumble, and Tommy Mansour recovered on the State 22. Despite a 15-yard holding penalty, the Rebels needed only three plays to score, as Weese arched a 35-yard pass to split end Riley Myers for the touchdown. Finally, Stan Moley, a defensive back, lifted State quarterback Billy Baker's pass out of the hands of a Bulldog receiver and rambled 43 yards. 42–0. Mercifully for the Bulldogs, the half ended seventy-five seconds later.

State head coach Charley Shira told the *Jackson Clarion-Ledger*, "You just don't know what to expect after 42 points have been scored on you in one quarter." His Bulldogs had not been past midfield. Many of the astounded thirty-five thousand fans who had come to see the game on a bright Thanksgiving afternoon left before the bands finished their halftime shows.

The Bulldogs threatened to score twice in the second half but could not break through, and Hinton added two field goals (from 27 and 37 yards) to account for the final margin. The Rebels had completely dominated: they led in first downs twenty-seven to nine, outgained the Bulldogs 484 yards to 195, and ran eighty-eight offensive plays, just two short of the rivalry record.

The Rebels ended the season at the Peach Bowl in Atlanta, Ole Miss's fifteenth straight appearance in a bowl game. Against Georgia Tech on a rain-flooded field, the Rebels stormed to a 38–6 halftime lead and overwhelmed the Yellow Jackets, 41–18. The Associated Press gave Ole Miss a final ranking of No. 15, while United Press International had the Rebels five spots lower.

1972

Bulldog Miscues, Rebel Points

1972 SCHEDULES

Ole Miss 5–5

RESULT	DATE	PF	OPPONENT	PA	LOCATION
W	September 16	34	Memphis State*	29	Memphis
W	September 23	21	South Carolina	0	Columbia
W	September 30	13	Southern Mississippi	9	Oxford
L	October 7	13	Auburn	19	Jackson
L	October 14	13	Georgia	14	Jackson
L	October 21	0	Florida	16	Oxford
W	October 28	31	Vanderbilt	7	Nashville
L	November 4	16	Louisiana State	17	Baton Rouge
L	November 18	0	Tennessee	17	Knoxville
W	November 25	51	Mississippi State	14	Oxford

Mississippi State 4–7

RESULT	DATE	PF	OPPONENT	PA	LOCATION
L	September 9	3	Auburn	14	Jackson
W	September 16	42	Northeast Louisiana**	7	Starkville
W	September 23	10	Vanderbilt	6	Nashville
L	September 30	13	Florida	28	Gainesville
L	October 7	13	Kentucky	17	Lexington
L	October 14	21	Florida State	25	Jackson
W	October 21	26	Southern Mississippi	7	Starkville
W	October 28	27	Houston	13	Starkville
L	November 4	14	Alabama	58	Tuscaloosa
L	November 18	14	Louisiana State	28	Baton Rouge
L	November 25	14	Mississippi	51	Oxford

* Now University of Memphis
** Now Louisiana-Monroe

oth Ole Miss and Mississippi State came into their 1972 meeting with mediocre records, but the 33,586 fans in attendance nevertheless anticipated fireworks. And that's what they got, right from the get-go: players began swinging at each other on the kickoff. After officials reestablished order and the teams settled down to business, however, things got really exciting.

Defensive tackle Robert J. Williams, nicknamed "Gentle Ben" by his Rebel teammates for his toughness, was Ole Miss's first African American football player. In 1975 Williams would be tri-captain, named all-America, and become student choice as Colonel Rebel. University of Mississippi Photo.

On a cold, dark day, the Bulldogs seemed unable to hang onto the ball. State fumbled on its first two possessions, then threw interceptions on its next two. The Rebels wasted no time in capitalizing on the mistakes, turning miscues into 17 points. Quarterback Norris Weese threw an 11-yard pass to fullback Gene Allen for the first score, and Greg Ainsworth got the second touchdown on a 1-yard run. Harry Harrison intercepted a Bulldog pass, and Steve Lavinghouze added a field goal to go with his two extra points to give the Rebels a big lead before the Bulldogs scored.

State righted the ship long enough to string together an eight-play, 77-yard touchdown drive. Quarterback Melvin Barkum rifled a 27-yard pass to the Southeastern Conference's leading pass receiver, Bill Buckley, who made a spectacular catch in the end zone. Although the 2-point conversion failed, the Bulldogs appeared to be back in the game at 17–6.

But the Rebels reeled off 21 straight points. Ainsworth scored again on the ninth play of a 66-yard drive, then notched his third touchdown of the day after Harrison collected his second interception and returned it 32 yards to the State 1. After yet another fumble—this one recovered by Richard (Stump) Russell—the Rebels drove 68 yards for their fifth touchdown. Allen got the points on a 1-yard run. The score stood at 38–6 at the half.

The Rebels took the second-half kickoff and picked up where they had left off, with Ainsworth scoring his fourth touchdown of the afternoon to

November 25, 1972
Ole Miss 51, Mississippi State, 14

	State	Ole Miss
First downs	13	26
Total plays	54	85
Total yards	287	457
Rushes/net yards	32/130	74/409
Passing yards	157	48
Passes		
(Att-Comp-Int)	22-9-5	11-4-1
Punts/average yards	10/39.7	4/33.5
Penalties/yards	5/39	5/81
Fumbles/lost	4/3	1/1

cap a 62-yard drive. The Bulldogs showed some life with a six-play scoring drive that covered 51 yards and ended with Buckley's second touchdown grab of the day and Lewis Grubbs's 2-point conversion run. 45–14. Ole Miss quarterback Bill Malouf then put the icing on the cake with a 15-yard run with 9:21 left to play. Lavinghouze, who had been perfect so far on extra points, missed the kick to make the final score 51–14.

The Bulldogs' eight turnovers had proved deadly. The Rebels, in contrast, had lost only one fumble and had allowed no interceptions. Ole Miss had rushed for a series-record 409 yards, 178 of them by Weese. The game also marked the first appearance against Mississippi State of an African American Ole Miss player: three years later, tackle Robert J. (Ben) Williams would be named all-America.

The Rebels finished the year at 5–5 overall (their worst record since 1950) and 2–4 in the Southeastern Conference (their first losing conference record since 1964). Their record streak of fifteen consecutive postseason appearances came to an end.

Three days after the game, Charley Shira gave up his post as the Bulldogs' coach to become State's athletic director. Bob Tyler, who had directed the Bulldog offense, moved up to become the squad's new head man.

1973

Vaught: One More Time

1973 SCHEDULES

Ole Miss 6–5

RESULT	DATE	PF	OPPONENT	PA	LOCATION
W	September 8	24	Villanova	6	Jackson
L	September 15	0	Missouri	17	Columbia
L	September 22	13	Memphis State*	17	Jackson
W	September 29	41	Southern Mississippi	0	Oxford
L	October 6	7	Auburn	14	Auburn
L	October 13	0	Georgia	20	Athens
W	October 20	13	Florida	10	Gainesville
W	October 27	24	Vanderbilt	14	Oxford
L	November 3	14	Louisiana State	51	Jackson
W	November 17	28	Tennessee	18	Jackson
W	November 24	38	Mississippi State	10	Jackson

Mississippi State 4–5–2

RESULT	DATE	PF	OPPONENT	PA	LOCATION
T	September 15	21	Northeast Louisiana**	21	Starkville
W	September 22	52	Vanderbilt	21	Starkville
W	September 29	33	Florida	12	Jackson
L	October 6	14	Kentucky	42	Jackson
W	October 13	37	Florida State	12	Tallahassee
W	October 20	18	Louisville	7	Louisville
T	October 27	10	Southern Mississippi	10	Starkville
L	November 3	0	Alabama	35	Jackson
L	November 10	17	Auburn	31	Auburn
L	November 17	7	Louisiana State	26	Baton Rouge
L	November 24	10	Mississippi	38	Jackson

* Now University of Memphis
** Now Louisiana-Monroe

W hen the Rebels opened the season with losses in two of their first three games, disgruntled alumni demanded the dismissal of coach Billy Kinard and his brother, athletic director Frank (Bruiser) Kinard. The athletic committee complied and invited former coach John Vaught, who had retired in January 1971 because of health problems, to return as head coach. The Rebels responded by winning four of seven prior to the game with State. Across the field, Vaught's opponent, in his first year as head coach in Starkville, was Bob Tyler, who had spent three years as an assistant to Vaught at Ole Miss. The Dogs entered the game at 4–4–2.

For the first time since 1934, the game was played not in Oxford or Starkville but in Jackson, where Mississippi Veterans Memorial Stadium had been constructed on the site of the old Hinds Memorial Stadium. Although both teams had played some "home" games at the new facility since 1961, this was their first meeting there. For the next eighteen years, the series remained in

John Vaught of Ole Miss, left, moments after coaching his twenty-fifth big rivalry game, greets State's new head coach, Bob Tyler. For three years Vaught and Tyler had coached together on the Ole Miss staff. Mississippi State University Photo.

Jackson. The schools alternated as home team, with State going first. The largest crowd ever to see Mississippi play Mississippi State—43,556—found the weather going from bright sunshine to drizzle and winds gusting up to thirty miles an hour.

As in the previous two meetings, the Bulldogs were plagued by turnovers. Five State fumbles led to four Ole Miss scores, and the Rebels cruised to a 38–10 victory. The first turnover came only three plays into the game when guard Jim Stuart covered a Bulldog fumble on the State 31. Larry Kramer ran 8 yards for the touchdown, and Steve Lavinghouze, perfect all year, kicked the first of his five points-after.

The Rebels too had trouble holding onto the football, but the Bulldogs converted only one of the three Ole Miss fumbles into touchdowns. That score, a 3-yard sweep by quarterback Melvin Barkum, plus Vic Nickels's extra point knotted the score at 7 early in the second quarter.

But another Bulldog fumble led to another Ole Miss touchdown, and the

November 24, 1973
Ole Miss 38, Mississippi State 10

	State	Ole Miss
First downs	15	23
Total plays	56	79
Total yards	285	388
Rushes/net yards	42/163	70/300
Passing yards	122	88
Passes		
(Att-Comp-Int)	14-8-0	9-5-0
Fumbles/lost	6/5	6/3

Freshman Walter Packer carries the mail against the Rebels' Pete Robertson (65) and Harry Harrison (30). Packer's career yardage would become third highest in the SEC at the time. Mississippi State University Photo.

Rebels were ahead to stay. Kramer capped the short march with his second touchdown, a 1-yard smack. Just enough time remained in the half for Nickels to kick a 42-yard field goal, and the scoreboard read 14–10 Ole Miss at intermission.

The Rebels poured it on in the second half. First Lavinghouze booted a 24-yard field goal. Then another fumble recovery started a 68-yard Ole Miss drive that Kramer topped with his third touchdown of the day. Next came James Reed, one of the first two African Americans to play for Ole Miss, who capped a 69-yard drive with a 1-yard plunge to make the score 31–10. A melee cleared both benches shortly afterward, a renewal of the bad blood that had broken out at kickoff the year before, and when the situation calmed, Ole Miss added one final easy touchdown. A botched snap on a Bulldog punt a few minutes later gave the Rebels the ball at the State 1 yard line, and fullback Doug Hamley Jr., son of the 1948 Rebel captain, hurtled into the end zone on his second attempt.

Vaught's squad finished his year at 5–3, and on December 21, Vaught announced his second retirement from coaching, although he remained as Ole Miss's athletic director for five years. Within a month, Ole Miss had a new head coach, Ken Cooper, a Georgia graduate who had been an assistant in Oxford for three seasons.

GAME 71

Mississippi Veterans
Memorial Stadium,
Jackson

1974

At Last, a Bulldog Blowout

1974 SCHEDULES

Ole Miss 3–8

RESULT	DATE	PF	OPPONENT	PA	LOCATION
W	September 14	10	Missouri	0	Jackson
L	September 21	7	Memphis State*	15	Memphis
W	September 28	20	Southern Mississippi	14	Oxford
L	October 5	21	Alabama	35	Jackson
L	October 12	0	Georgia	49	Athens
L	October 19	7	South Carolina	10	Oxford
L	October 26	14	Vanderbilt	24	Nashville
L	November 2	0	Louisiana State	24	Baton Rouge
L	November 16	17	Tennessee	29	Memphis
L	November 23	13	Mississippi State	31	Jackson
W	November 30	26	Tulane	10	New Orleans

Mississippi State 9–3

RESULT	DATE	PF	OPPONENT	PA	LOCATION
W	September 7	49	William and Mary	7	Jackson
W	September 21	38	Georgia	14	Jackson
L	September 28	13	Florida	29	Gainesville
W	October 5	21	Kansas State	16	Starkville
W	October 12	37	Lamar	21	Beaumont
W	October 19	29	Memphis	28	Memphis
W	October 26	56	Louisville	7	Starkville
L	November 2	0	Alabama	35	Tuscaloosa
L	November 9	20	Auburn	24	Jackson
W	November 16	7	Louisiana State	6	Jackson
W	November 23	31	Mississippi	13	Jackson
W	December 28	26	North Carolina	24	Sun Bowl

* Now University of Memphis

Bulldog fans had waited twenty-eight years to see this kind of game—a genuine one-sided win over Ole Miss. State's best team in nearly three decades finally administered a real, honest-to-goodness thumping, overcoming the Bulldogs' habit of turning over the ball to record an easy

31–13 win. This time, it was the Rebels who had trouble holding on, losing six fumbles to set a rivalry record. Add two interceptions, and the Rebels' eight turnovers tied the mark the Dogs had set just two years earlier. Although the Bulldogs lost three fumbles, this time those mistakes paled in comparison to those of the team from Oxford.

In his second year, coach Bob Tyler had turned the Bulldogs into a winner, taking seven of their first ten games. In the process, the Dogs established nine school records for offense and garnered State's first bowl invitation in eleven years. Ole Miss was heading in the opposite direction, with a 2–7 record in coach Ken Cooper's first season. The game remained close for three quarters, with the score tied 0–0 at the half and 7–7 at the end of the third period.

The crowd of 46,500—the largest to date—saw the Rebs break the ice with a trick play early in the second half. Starting on their own 48, the Rebels gained 6. Tailback James Reed then trotted toward the sideline as if he were leaving the field, but the Rebels snapped the ball without a huddle, and Reed streaked downfield. Freshman quarterback Tim Ellis's pass hit Reed on the State 30, and Reed outmaneuvered a defender to score untouched. The play was the same one that Maroons had used to score against Ole Miss in 1916. Steve Lavinghouze's kick put the Rebels up, 7–0.

With just under five minutes left before the end of the period, Ole Miss lost a fumble on its 24, and tailback Walter Packer needed only one play to go all the way. Vic Nickels's kick evened the score at 7. State took the lead for good on Nickels's 20-yard field goal early in the fourth quarter, then recorded three touchdowns over the remaining ten minutes to salt away the victory, aided by two Rebel miscues (an interception and a fumble) and a failed fake punt.

A Bulldog pickoff gave State the ball at the Ole Miss 9, and quarterback Rockey Felker scored on the second play from scrimmage to make it 17–7. The Rebels tried a fake punt at midfield, leading to another Bulldog score. This time it was Packer, taking the ball in from 7 yards out for a 24–7 lead. When the Rebels lost a fumble on their 25, Felker connected with Melvin Barkum for 16 before taking the ball the rest of the way. 31–7. An interception at the Bulldog 34 led to the Rebels' final touchdown, with Reed coming out of

November 23, 1974

Mississippi State 31, Ole Miss 13

	State	Ole Miss
First downs	19	18
Total plays	73	79
Total yards	300	384
Net yards rushing	237	176
Passing yards	63	208
Passes		
(Att-Comp-Int)	18-6-1	24-14-2
Fumbles/lost	4/3	7/6

Bulldogs celebrate their victory by anticipating another Mississippi State inscription on the Golden Egg. Holding the cherished trophy is all-America tackle Jimmy Webb. Mississippi State University Photo.

the backfield for his second score of the day, this one on a 3-yard toss by Ellis. But it was too little, too late.

The Bulldogs' 8–3 regular-season performance was the best since 1940's 10–0–1 record. The Atlanta Touchdown Club, the *Nashville Banner*, and the *Birmingham Post-Herald* named Felker, whose 1,593 yards led the Southeastern Conference in total offense, as the conference's Most Outstanding Player. The Bulldogs went on to the Sun Bowl, where they defeated North Carolina, 26–24, after amassing 455 yards rushing; Packer accounted for 183 of those yards. Bulldog fans loved the fact that State was playing in a bowl game and Ole Miss was not: one fan in the Sun Bowl crowd held up a sign reading, "Eat Yer Heart Out, Ole Miss." State finished the year seventeenth in the Associated Press and United Press International Polls.

1975

GAME 72

Dee-fense!

1975 SCHEDULES

Ole Miss 6–5

RESULT	DATE	PF	OPPONENT	PA	LOCATION
L	September 6	10	Baylor	20	Waco
L	September 13	0	Texas A&M	7	College Station
L	September 20	3	Tulane	14	New Orleans
W	September 27	24	Southern Mississippi	8	Oxford
L	October 4	6	Alabama	32	Birmingham
W	October 11	28	Georgia	13	Oxford
L	October 18	29	South Carolina	35	Jackson
W	October 25	17	Vanderbilt	7	Oxford
W	November 1	17	Louisiana State	13	Jackson
W	November 15	23	Tennessee	6	Memphis
W	November 22	13	Mississippi State	7	Jackson

Mississippi State 2–9

RESULT	DATE	PF	OPPONENT	PA	LOCATION
W	September 6	17	Memphis State*	7	Memphis
L	September 20	6	Georgia	28	Athens
L	September 27	10	Florida	27	Jackson
L	October 4	7	Southern Mississippi**	3	Starkville
L	October 11	28	Rice**	14	Houston
W	October 18	15	North Texas State	12	Starkville
L	October 25	28	Louisville**	14	Louisville
L	November 1	10	Alabama	21	Jackson
L	November 8	21	Auburn**	21	Auburn
L	November 15	16	Louisiana State**	6	Baton Rouge
L	November 22	7	Mississippi	13	Jackson

* Now University of Memphis
** Forfeited by order of the NCAA

A swirling wind swept Memorial Stadium to make the temperature seem even lower than the forty-seven actual degrees. Unpredictable gusts blew passes off target, limiting the two teams to a mere six completions, the longest for only 23 yards. Punts into the wind went practically

Defensive end Gary Turner's alert recovery of a bobbled Bulldog pitchout in the end zone gave the Rebels their only touchdown of the game and assured an Ole Miss victory. University of Mississippi Photo.

nowhere. Defense became the only game. But a defensive battle can be an exciting show, as 46,500 fans discovered.

The Bulldogs were in the midst of a tough season. The National Collegiate Athletic Association had imposed a two-year probation on State as punishment for recruiting violations. In addition, the Southeastern Conference banned noisemakers of all kinds, silencing State's cowbells. The situation added a new dimension to signs displayed by partisans on both sides: An Ole Miss fan's banner proclaimed, "State—Worst Team Money Can Buy," while a Mississippi State loyalist retorted, "We're on probation. We don't have a bell. But we still say—Ole Miss, go to hell." Despite the off-field problems, coach Bob Tyler's Bulldogs had won six games, including a run of four in a row at midseason. They were a slight favorite. The Rebels, on the other hand, had defied preseason predictions that they would remain near the bottom of the Southeastern Conference, had captured five of their previous seven games, and entered the Battle of the Golden Egg with a 5–5 record. One year after finishing winless in the Southeastern Conference, the team had already taken four conference foes, an achievement that earned coach Ken Cooper the nod as Southeastern Conference Coach of the Year as voted by the Associated Press, United Press International, and the conference's coaches.

November 22, 1975
Ole Miss 13, Mississippi State 7

	State	Ole Miss
First downs	10	12
Total yards	149	228
Net yards rushing	122	189
Passing yards	27	39
Passes		
(Att-Comp-Int)	15-2-1	13-4-1
Punts/average yards	9/32.4	9/35.0

The Bulldogs scored first, taking advantage of Bill Farris's punt into the wind, which traveled only 22 yards and gave State the ball on the Ole Miss 35. Halfback Walter Packer went 17 yards to set up the touchdown play from the 1, and fullback Dennis Johnson took it from there. Kinney Jordan's extra point put State up by 7. Ole Miss drove to

Though fullback Dennis Johnson is snowed under by the Rebel defense, Johnson's extra surge carried him over for the Bulldog touchdown on a handoff from Bruce Threadgill (17). *Clarion-Ledger/Jackson Daily News*. November 23, 1975.

State's 8 yard line but lost a fumble. Two plays later, however, the Rebels were back in business as State quarterback Bruce Threadgill's attempted pitchout to Packer sailed behind the halfback into the end zone, where Rebel Gary Turner pounced on the ball for a touchdown. Steve Lavinghouze, who had not missed an extra-point kick since the 1972 State–Ole Miss game, tied the score.

The teams traded interceptions before Ole Miss managed a 24-yard Lavinghouze field goal just as the half ended. Once again, the points resulted from a bad punt into the treacherous wind—this one Gerald Vaught's boot that traveled only 21 yards to the Rebel 45. The score remained 10–7 throughout the third period. The quarter's big play was another defensive effort—a stop by the Rebels when the Bulldogs tried to convert a fourth and 1 at the Rebel 34. The early fourth quarter saw a brief spurt of offense. Ole Miss secured two consecutive first downs and moved to the State 28. Lavinghouze came in again and kicked a 47-yard field goal—remarkably, into the wind. The Bulldogs had two more possessions but didn't threaten, and the final score remained Ole Miss, 13–7.

1976

Yell Like Hell

1976 SCHEDULES

Ole Miss 6–5

RESULT	DATE	PF	OPPONENT	PA	LOCATION
L	September 4	16	Memphis State*	21	Memphis
W	September 11	10	Alabama	7	Jackson
W	September 18	34	Tulane	7	Oxford
W	September 25	28	Southern Mississippi	0	Hattiesburg
L	October 2	0	Auburn	10	Jackson
W	October 9	21	Georgia	17	Oxford
L	October 16	7	South Carolina	10	Columbia
W	October 23	20	Vanderbilt	3	Nashville
L	October 30	0	Louisiana State	45	Baton Rouge
L	November 13	6	Tennessee	32	Knoxville
W	November 20	11	Mississippi State	28	Jackson

Mississippi State 0–11

RESULT	DATE	PF	OPPONENT	PA	LOCATION
L	September 4	7	North Texas**	0	Starkville
L	September 18	30	Louisville**	21	Starkville
L	September 25	30	Florida	34	Gainesville
L	October 2	38	Cal Poly–Pomona**	0	Starkville
L	October 9	14	Kentucky**	7	Jackson
L	October 16	42	Memphis State* **	33	Memphis
L	October 23	14	Southern Mississippi**	6	Hattiesburg
L	October 30	17	Alabama	34	Tuscaloosa
L	November 6	28	Auburn**	19	Jackson
L	November 13	21	Louisiana State**	13	Jackson
L	November 20	28	Mississippi**	11	Jackson

* Now University of Memphis
** Forfeited by order of the NCAA

Victory over Ole Miss meant everything to the Bulldogs. Not only had a second-half surge overwhelmed the freewheeling Rebels in a decisive 28–11 victory over the Dogs' biggest rival, but the game gave them nine wins on the year, tying the school record for most regular-season victories. Perhaps even more important, the game signaled the end of the school's two-year probation imposed by the National Collegiate Athletic Association. "For dear ole State we'll yell like Hell," indeed.

The Rebels' game plan called for a wide-open, sometimes gambling attack, and it worked. Quarterback Tim Ellis's delay passes to tight end Curtis Weathers enabled the Rebels to take the lead on their first possession, a 39-yard drive that culminated in C. E. (Hoppy) Langley's 31-yard field goal.

The 3–0 lead held up until less than three minutes remained in the half, when two Rebel turnovers led to two Bulldog field goals. Will Coltharp intercepted an Ellis pass deep in Rebel territory, and Kinney Jordan's 19-yard kick knotted the score. Moments later, Mike Lawrence fell on a Rebel fumble

Bulldog quarterback Bruce Threadgill contributed two touchdown passes to his team's four-touchdown barrage and rushed for 74 yards as State downed Ole Miss 28–11. In next year's game Threadgill would be responsible for two more touchdowns—running for one on a 42-yard breakaway and passing for another. Mississippi State University Photo.

on the Ole Miss 31, and with just five seconds remaining, Jordan came through with a 23-yard field goal to put State ahead 6–3 at the half.

Early in the third quarter, Jordan's third 3-pointer of the day—this one from 22 yards out—doubled the Bulldog lead and tied James C. Elmer's seventy-year-old mark for most field goals in an Ole Miss–State contest. After stuffing the Rebels on fourth down, the Bulldogs pounded the Rebs for three straight touchdowns to put the game out of reach. The first came on a 57-yard drive, with a 17-yard pass from quarterback Bruce Threadgill to Robert Chatman getting the 6 points. The second drive stretched 80 yards and saw Threadgill's second scoring toss of the day, a connection with Duncan McKenzie from the 4. Dennis Johnson slipped in from the 1 for the final Bulldog score with 4:44 left to play.

November 20, 1976
Mississippi State 28, Ole Miss 11

	State	Ole Miss
First downs	19	12
Total plays	71	71
Total yards	372	275
Rushes/net yards	51/265	44/148
Passing yards	107	127
Passes		
(Att-Comp-Int)	20-9-0	27-10-1
Punts/average yards	5/44.0	5/43.0
Penalties/yards	5/35	5/47
Fumbles/lost	3/2	6/2

Despite a tough—and effective—Bulldog pass defense, half the Rebel offense for the day came in the air. The attacking Bulldogs are Kenny Johnson (37), Robert Chatman (45), all-America Stan Black (36), and Larry Dixon (28). Defending for the Rebels are Freddie Williams (36) and Mark Clark (11). University of Mississippi Photo.

The Ole Miss fans in the crowd of 46,500 finally had something to cheer about when Leon Perry took the ball on the first play from scrimmage after the ensuing kickoff and zoomed 80 yards to score the lone Rebel touchdown. Quarterback Roy Coleman connected with Freddie Williams for the 2-point conversion to make the final tally 28–11.

The Bulldogs' 4–2 Southeastern Conference mark placed them in a three-way tie for third, their highest finish since 1957. At 3–4, Ole Miss was fourth. State posted its third consecutive winning season, its longest streak in twenty-one years, and was ranked No. 20 in the final Associated Press Poll.

Although the Bulldogs' NCAA-imposed probation was over, their problems with the governing body were not. A Mississippi court ruling had allowed State to use a player whom the association deemed ineligible, and the NCAA subsequently forced the school to forfeit nineteen games in which the player had appeared, including the 1976 Battle of the Golden Egg. The on-field victory was wiped away on paper.

1977

Momentum Shifts

1977 SCHEDULES

Ole Miss 6–5

RESULT	DATE	PF	OPPONENT	PA	LOCATION
W	September 3	7	Memphis State*	3	Jackson
L	September 10	13	Alabama	34	Birmingham
W	September 17	20	Notre Dame	13	Jackson
L	September 24	19	Southern Mississippi	27	Oxford
L	October 1	15	Auburn	21	Auburn
L	October 8	13	Georgia	14	Athens
W	October 15	17	South Carolina	10	Oxford
W	October 22	26	Vanderbilt	14	Oxford
L	October 29	21	Louisiana State	28	Jackson
W	November 12	43	Tennessee	14	Memphis
W	November 19	14	Mississippi State	18	Jackson

Mississippi State 0–11

RESULT	DATE	PF	OPPONENT	PA	LOCATION
L	September 3	17	North Texas**	15	Starkville
L	September 10	27	Washington**	18	Seattle
L	September 24	22	Florida	24	Jackson
L	October 1	24	Kansas State**	21	Manhattan
L	October 8	7	Kentucky	23	Lexington
L	October 15	13	Memphis State*	21	Memphis
L	October 22	7	Southern Mississippi	14	Starkville
L	October 29	7	Alabama	37	Jackson
L	November 5	27	Auburn**	13	Auburn
L	November 12	24	Louisiana State	27	Baton Rouge
L	November 19	18	Mississippi**	14	Jackson

* Now University of Memphis
** Forfeited by order of the NCAA

The Rebels started the 1977 season by setting the football world on its ear, dealing eventual national champion Notre Dame its only loss of the season, 20–13, in Jackson. Things quickly soured for Ole Miss, however, and the team bore a 5–5 record on the eve of the Mississippi State game. The Bulldogs had a similarly mediocre record—4–6—but were favored

Artist Jim Larrick agrees with the consensus that the annual clash between the Rebels and Bulldogs is all-out "war." *Clarion-Ledger/Jackson Daily News*.

against their in-state rivals. The usual intensity livened pregame antics: a Bulldog fan raced across the field clutching a wadded-up Rebel flag; a Rebel fan snatched the head off the Bulldog mascot, forcing a State cheerleader to enter the stands to retrieve the prize.

At game time, temperatures were in the fifties, with a steady drizzle and gusty winds that chilled the 47,500 spectators. On its first possession, Ole Miss went 80 yards in nearly five minutes to take a 7–0 advantage. Quarterback Tim Ellis crossed over from the 6, and C. E. (Hoppy) Langley kicked the extra point. On the Bulldogs' next series, Ole Miss safety Gary Jones intercepted Bruce Threadgill's pass, and the Rebels took over on the State 21. Ellis then racked up his second touchdown of the day and Langley booted his second point-after to shock the crowd. Ole Miss by 14. But the Rebels were not finished. Threadgill was intercepted on the first play from scrimmage, and the Rebels again marched down the field. This time, however, Langley missed the field goal, and the Rebels came away with nothing.

November 19, 1977
Mississippi State 18, Ole Miss 14

	State	Ole Miss
First downs	22	12
Total plays	79	64
Total yards	387	192
Rushes/net yards	50/230	53/169
Passing yards	157	23
Passes		
(Att-Comp-Int)	29-9-3	11-2-2
Punts/average yards	4/37.2	8/42.8
Penalties/yards	4/48	8/71
Fumbles/lost	0/0	3/2

Tim Ellis prepares a pitchout as part of a performance that saw this Rebel quarterback score two early touchdowns before the Bulldogs staged a comeback to win the golden-anniversary game of the Battle of the Golden Egg. *Clarion-Ledger/Jackson Daily News.* November 20, 1977.

Back came the Bulldogs with two 48-yard drives. The first ended with a Rebel interception, but State finally got on the scoreboard a few minutes later when Dave Marler's 44-yard field goal sailed through the uprights. Marler added another from 30 yards out just before the half to close the margin to 14–6, and the pendulum had begun to swing the other way.

The Bulldogs started the third period by stopping the Rebels on their first possession and then launching a quick 4-play touchdown drive from the State 33. Threadgill scored on a 42-yard sweep into the end zone. When the 2-point conversion failed, Ole Miss clung to a slender 2-point advantage, but State clearly had all the momentum. With just under three minutes gone in the fourth quarter, the Bulldogs seized the lead, 18–14, when Threadgill connected with Mardye McDole for a 26-yard scoring pass. Game over.

Ole Miss had not advanced beyond its own 45 during the entire second half and had picked up just two first downs. The Rebels had been unable to hold onto their first-quarter dominance and had let the game slip away. "You can tell when a team is losing control of a game," said Bulldog offensive tackle

Mark Trogdon. "When you come off the line of scrimmage on a guy he's not hitting you as hard. He doesn't stay after you as long."

The win gave the Bulldogs two in a row over Ole Miss for the first time since 1942, although both wins subsequently were forfeited because the National Collegiate Athletic Association determined that Mississippi State had used an ineligible player. Nevertheless, both games remain inscribed on the Golden Egg as State victories.

Ten days after the season ended, Ole Miss coach Ken Cooper resigned. To replace him, the school's athletic committee selected Texas Tech's Steve Sloan, a former Alabama all-American who had been with the Atlanta Falcons of the National Football League; had served as an assistant coach at Alabama, Florida State, and Georgia Tech; and had been head coach at Vanderbilt.

1978

A Rebel Surprise

1978 SCHEDULES

Ole Miss 5–6

RESULT	DATE	PF	OPPONENT	PA	LOCATION
W	September 9	14	Memphis State*	7	Jackson
L	September 23	14	Missouri	45	Columbia
W	September 30	16	Southern Mississippi	13	Jackson
L	October 7	3	Georgia	42	Athens
L	October 14	17	Kentucky	24	Oxford
L	October 21	17	South Carolina	18	Columbia
W	October 28	35	Vanderbilt	10	Nashville
L	November 4	8	Louisiana State	30	Baton Rouge
W	November 11	13	Tulane	3	Oxford
L	November 18	17	Tennessee	41	Knoxville
W	November 25	27	Mississippi State	7	Jackson

Mississippi State 6–5

RESULT	DATE	PF	OPPONENT	PA	LOCATION
W	September 2	28	West Texas A&M**	0	Jackson
W	September 9	17	North Texas	5	Irving
W	September 23	44	Memphis State*	14	Memphis
L	September 30	0	Florida	34	Gainesville
L	October 7	17	Southern Mississippi	22	Hattiesburg
W	October 14	55	Florida State	27	Starkville
W	October 28	34	Tennessee	21	Memphis
L	November 4	14	Alabama	35	Birmingham
L	November 11	0	Auburn	6	Starkville
W	November 18	16	Louisiana State	14	Jackson
L	November 25	7	Mississippi	27	Jackson

* Now University of Memphis
** Now West Texas State

Mississippi State was celebrating its centennial, and the 6–4 football team was in on the party. Against Florida State, in the school's seven hundredth game, the Dogs had rolled up a record 596 yards. Senior Dave Marler, now playing quarterback, was leading the nation in yards per attempt. And the combination of Marler and split end Mardye McDole

Linebacker Brian Moreland decks a Bulldog runner. Fierce defense held the Dogs to 86 yards on 28 rush attempts. University of Mississippi Photo.

was leading the Southeastern Conference in completions. Ole Miss, by contrast, had only four victories against six losses, and three of the losses had come after the Rebels had established 10–0 leads. Moreover, against the Bulldogs, the Rebels were going with a freshman, John Fourcade, in his first start at quarterback. Not surprisingly, therefore, the Bulldogs entered the Battle of the Golden Egg favored to win by at least a touchdown.

But the Rebels took a 3–0 lead at the beginning of the second quarter when a short punt set up Ole Miss at the Bulldog 34, and C. E. (Hoppy) Langley nailed a 24-yard field goal. Three minutes later, the surprising Rebels had another score. After end John Peel covered a Bulldog fumble, Fourcade led his team on a six-play, 26-yard drive that ended with fullback Leon Perry's 6-yard run and Langley's extra-point kick. Ole Miss by 10. About four minutes later, with the Rebels back on offense at their own 33 yard line, Fourcade spotted flanker Les Kimbrough sprinting all alone up

November 25, 1978
Ole Miss 27, Mississippi State 7

	State	Ole Miss
First downs	20	20
Total plays	74	85
Total yards	449	342
Rushes/net yards	28/86	72/234
Passing yards	363	108
Passes		
(Att-Comp-Int)	46-25-3	13-6-0
Punts/average yards	5/31	6/44
Penalties/yards	9/120	7/40
Fumbles/lost	7/4	3/2

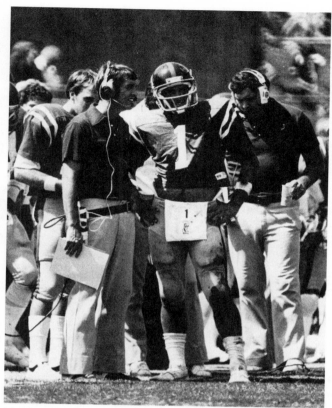

John Fourcade in his first starting role at quarterback, and Steve Sloan, left, in his first year as head coach, directed the Rebels to a surprising 27–7 upset over the Bulldogs. At right is Tom Goode, who coached at both Ole Miss and State in his career. Photo by R. D. Moore, courtesy Larry Wells.

the middle. Kimbrough took the pass on the run at the State 35 and raced into the end zone. It added up to 17 points in seven minutes of playing time. The Rebels took their 17-point lead into the locker room after forcing turnovers on the Bulldogs' final two possessions of the half.

But the Rebels were not a third-quarter team, and the Bulldogs made their big move, driving 59 yards for a touchdown. The scoring play was a 29-yard halfback option pass from James Jones to Mardye McDole. With Joey Fratesi's extra-point kick, linebacker Johnie Cooks excitedly told a reporter, "We're in the game now."

But the Bulldogs could get no closer. The Rebels added 10 fourth-quarter points—Langley's 43-yard field goal and Perry's 3-yard touchdown run following an interception—while the Bulldogs suffered three turnovers and

While team play entertained fans from the field, the Ole Miss cheerleaders' gymnastic efforts entertained fans from the sideline. University of Mississippi Photo.

surrendered the ball once on downs. When the game ended, the scoreboard showed Ole Miss 27, State 7. "Ole Miss, in the final analysis, won an egg," declared the *Memphis Commercial Appeal*, "and Mississippi State laid one." "We beat ourselves," Marler told a reporter.

Two months later, Mississippi State University president James McComas proposed separating the duties of athletic director and head football coach and suggested that Bob Tyler, who had held both posts since May 1976, be retained only as coach. In response, Tyler resigned. The school then hired Carl Maddox, athletic director emeritus at Louisiana State and formerly a highly respected high school coach in Greenwood and Greenville, as its new athletic director, and Maddox found State's new coach in Emory Bellard, who had previously coached at both Texas and Texas A&M.

1979

Mistakes Can Kill You

1979 SCHEDULES

Ole Miss 4–7

RESULT	DATE	PF	OPPONENT	PA	LOCATION
W	September 15	38	Memphis State*	34	Memphis
L	September 22	7	Missouri	33	Jackson
L	September 29	8	Southern Mississippi	38	Jackson
L	October 6	21	Georgia	24	Oxford
L	October 13	3	Kentucky	14	Lexington
L	October 20	14	South Carolina	21	Columbia
W	October 27	63	Vanderbilt	28	Oxford
L	November 3	24	Louisiana State	28	Jackson
L	November 10	15	Tulane	49	New Orleans
W	November 17	44	Tennessee	20	Jackson
W	November 24	14	Mississippi State	9	Jackson

Mississippi State 3–8

RESULT	DATE	PF	OPPONENT	PA	LOCATION
L	September 8	13	Memphis State*	14	Jackson
L	September 22	14	Maryland	35	College Park
W	September 29	24	Florida	10	Jackson
W	October 6	28	Tennessee	9	Memphis
L	October 13	6	Florida State	17	Tallahassee
W	October 20	48	Marshall	0	Starkville
L	October 27	7	Southern Mississippi	21	Starkville
L	November 3	7	Alabama	24	Tuscaloosa
L	November 10	3	Auburn	14	Auburn
L	November 17	3	Louisiana State	21	Baton Rouge
L	November 24	9	Mississippi	14	Jackson

* Now University of Memphis

The 1979 Battle of the Golden Egg was a battle of mistakes. According to Ole Miss's Steve Sloan, "We made our mistakes early. They made theirs late." State's Emory Bellard summarized, "The way we lost it was by our mistakes down near the end zone." Mistakes early proved better than mistakes late, and the Rebels won the game, 14–9.

Bully offers his warmest welcome for former State student Cheryl Prewitt after her selection as Miss America. Mississippi State University Photo.

The Bulldogs collected points on their first possession, moving the ball to the Rebel 25 before the drive stalled and Jerry Rye put through a 38-yard field goal. The Bulldogs attempted to add to their lead but missed a field goal, and the Rebels then marched deep into Bulldog territory before losing a fumble. Facing third down and 7 on the State 10 yard line, Bulldog quarterback Tony Black handed off to fullback Fred Collins, who thundered 90 yards to the Rebel end zone for the longest run from scrimmage in the history of the Ole Miss–State rivalry. Despite the missed extra point, the Bulldogs held a 9–0 lead at the half. Though the Rebels had moved the ball effectively on two drives, fumbles had kept them off the scoreboard.

The situation improved for the Rebels on their first possession of the third quarter, as they strung together a 65-yard, thirteen-play drive that

November 24, 1979

Ole Miss 14, Mississippi State 9

	State	Ole Miss
First downs	17	21
Total plays	66	66
Total yards	391	355
Rushes/net yards	59/369	49/212
Passing yards	22	143
Passes		
(Att-Comp-Int)	7-2-0	17-11-0
Fumbles/lost	3/1	2/2

culminated with a 1-yard scoring run by Leon Perry. With C. E. (Hoppy) Langley's point after, the Rebs trailed just 9–7.

The Bulldogs reached the Ole Miss 19 on their next possession but botched a pitchout to give the Rebels the ball. Eleven plays later, the Rebels had the winning touchdown on a 29-yard pass from quarterback John Fourcade to a wide-open Ken Toler. Langley's extra-point kick was good. The Bulldogs had won the first half, but the Rebels had won the second—and, most importantly, the game. In the aftermath of his Bulldogs' upset loss, State coach Emory Bellard was obviously irritated: "Mississippi State will be a damn good team next year," he predicted confidently. "And you can write that down."

1980

Bulldog Blitz

1980 SCHEDULES

Ole Miss 3–8

RESULT	DATE	PF	OPPONENT	PA	LOCATION
L	September 6	20	Texas A&M	23	Jackson
W	September 13	61	Memphis State*	7	Oxford
L	September 20	35	Alabama	59	Jackson
L	September 27	24	Tulane	26	Oxford
L	October 4	22	Southern Mississippi	28	Jackson
L	October 11	21	Georgia	28	Athens
L	October 18	3	Florida	15	Oxford
W	October 25	27	Vanderbilt	14	Nashville
L	November 1	16	Louisiana State	38	Baton Rouge
W	November 15	20	Tennessee	9	Memphis
L	November 22	14	Mississippi State	19	Jackson

Mississippi State 9–3

RESULT	DATE	PF	OPPONENT	PA	LOCATION
W	September 6	34	Memphis State*	7	Memphis
W	September 13	31	Louisiana Tech	11	Starkville
W	September 20	24	Vanderbilt	14	Nashville
L	September 27	15	Florida	21	Gainesville
W	October 4	28	Illinois	21	Champaign
L	October 11	14	Southern Mississippi	42	Starkville
W	October 18	34	Miami	31	Miami
W	October 25	24	Auburn	21	Jackson
W	November 1	6	Alabama	3	Jackson
W	November 15	55	Louisiana State	31	Jackson
W	November 22	19	Mississippi	14	Jackson
L	December 27	17	Nebraska	31	Sun Bowl

* Now University of Memphis

As coach Emory Bellard had predicted, the Bulldogs indeed had a strong team in 1980. State's eight wins prior to the Egg Bowl included a 6–3 upset of No. 1 Alabama in Jackson that ended Bama's 28-game victory streak.

PATTERSON and BORDEN, Page 2
HOOD, TURNER COLUMNS, Page 3

It was State's victory licked, sealed, Bonded

EGG BOWL

1980

The Clarion-Ledger
DAILY NEWS
·November 23, 1980·

Rebel fans cheered on their team as the Egg Bowl got underway in time a record crowd on a rainy day.

Clarion-Ledger/Jackson Daily News, November 23, 1980.

Ole Miss, conversely, was having a rough year. Though the Rebs stood atop the Southeastern Conference in offense, the defense was surrendering an average of 24 points a game. The Rebels had won only three games to date.

Just two days before the game, the final seats in the new north-end horse-shoe were bolted in place at Mississippi Veterans Memorial Stadium, enlarging its capacity so that a record crowd of 62,250—still the largest ever—could watch the game. Those who braved the rain saw the Bulldogs, ranked seventh in the nation in rushing yardage, score first on a 73-yard drive that culminated in a 24-yard field goal by Dana Moore. The Dogs needed only two plays on their next possession to up their lead to 10–0 when quarterback John Bond followed Donald Ray King's block on the way to a 57-yard touchdown run and Moore booted the extra point.

November 22, 1980
Mississippi State 19, Ole Miss 14

	State	Ole Miss
First downs	20	19
Total plays	69	77
Total yards	473	304
Rushes/net yards	55/322	44/139
Passing yards	151	165
Passes (Att-Comp-Int)	14-8-1	33-16-4
Punts/average yards	5/36.0	5/42.4
Penalties/yards	7/81	2/35
Fumbles/lost	3/2	1/0

John Bond, at quarterback, with Michael Haddix leading the way in this photo, scored a touchdown in the 1980 and 1983 games. Mississippi State University Photo.

The Rebels responded with two scoring threats, but both were undone by interceptions, a problem that had plagued Ole Miss all season. Undaunted, however, the Rebels got back into the game with 1:30 remaining in the first half as Kinny Hooper scored from the 1 and Todd Gatlin kicked the extra point.

The score remained at 10–7 through the third period. After one Bulldog possession ended on a fumble at the Rebel 33, State came back to extend its lead with a 32-yard Moore field goal early in the fourth. Back came Ole Miss with an 80-yard drive that featured a surprise pass from flanker Michael Harmon (whose older brother, Clarence, had starred at State in mid-1970s) to tight end Breck Tyler (son of former Bulldog coach Bob Tyler) that gobbled up 36 yards. With the ball on the Mississippi State 7, Rebel quarterback John Fourcade, who led the Southeastern Conference in total yardage, connected with Gino English for the touchdown. Gatlin's point-after gave Ole Miss the lead, 14–13, with 8:20 left to play.

The lead lasted just three plays. For reasons that puzzled many fans, the Rebels had Darryl Graham try an onside kick. Bulldog Charlie Brentz covered the ball on the State 36, and the Dogs quickly marched to the Ole Miss end zone. After an incomplete pass, Bond hit Glen Young for 54 yards to the Rebel 10, and Michael Haddix scored on the next play. The 2-point conversion failed, but the Bulldogs had regained the lead, 19–14. Each team had three more possessions, but neither could come through, and the Bulldogs had the victory.

The loss to State was the Rebels' eighth of the year, equaling the 1974 squad for the most losses ever by an Ole Miss team. Bond had accounted for 314 total yards (163 on the ground, 151 through the air), more than the entire Rebel team, a performance that earned him a citation as *Sports Illustrated's* national Back of the Week. The Bulldogs finished the season tied with Alabama for second place in the Southeastern Conference, missing a trip to the Sugar Bowl. In the Sun Bowl, the Nebraska defense shut down State's offense, and the Bulldogs fell to the Cornhuskers, 31–17. The final Associated Press Poll had State at No. 19.

GAME 78

1981

0:02 on the Clock

1981 SCHEDULES

Ole Miss 4–6–1

RESULT	DATE	PF	OPPONENT	PA	LOCATION
W	September 5	19	Tulane	18	New Orleans
W	September 12	20	South Carolina	13	Columbia
W	September 19	7	Memphis State*	3	Memphis
L	September 26	13	Arkansas	27	Jackson
L	October 3	7	Alabama	38	Tuscaloosa
L	October 10	7	Georgia	37	Oxford
L	October 17	3	Florida	49	Gainesville
L	October 24	23	Vanderbilt	27	Oxford
T	October 31	27	Louisiana State	27	Jackson
L	November 14	20	Tennessee	28	Knoxville
W	November 21	21	Mississippi State	17	Jackson

Mississippi State 8–4

RESULT	DATE	PF	OPPONENT	PA	LOCATION
W	September 5	20	Memphis State*	3	Jackson
W	September 19	29	Vanderbilt	9	Starkville
W	September 26	28	Florida	7	Jackson
L	October 3	3	Missouri	14	Jackson
W	October 10	37	Colorado State	27	Fort Collins
W	October 17	14	Miami	10	Starkville
W	October 24	21	Auburn	17	Auburn
L	October 31	10	Alabama	13	Tuscaloosa
L	November 7	6	Southern Mississippi	7	Jackson
W	November 14	17	Louisiana State	9	Baton Rouge
L	November 21	17	Mississippi	21	Jackson
W	December 31	10	Kansas	0	Hall of Fame Classic

*Now University of Memphis

G ame tied, 14–14, with 3:37 left to play. And then the fireworks started. Ten points in the final three and a half minutes. An interference call as time wound down. The winning score with just two seconds to go. When the smoke cleared, the Rebels had a thrilling 21–17 victory—or, depending on your point of view, the Bulldogs had had the game stolen from them by a bad call.

State had begun the season 6–1 and entered the Egg Bowl with a 7–3 record, a No. 7 national ranking (their highest ever), and a bowl bid coming up. It would be the first time that the Bulldogs appeared in back-to-back postseason contests. State had given up two touchdowns only twice in the season and had lost three games by a combined total of 15 points. Ole Miss had won its first three games by a total of just 12 points and had been winless the rest of the way. On paper, the game was a mismatch.

Game day dawned bright and sunny, and at kickoff time, the thermometer stood at fifty-nine degrees. Rebel quarterback John Fourcade came out slinging, leading his team to a touchdown in under two minutes. On third and 6 from the State 39, Fourcade hit fullback Andre Thomas, who sped untouched to pay dirt. Todd Gatlin's extra-point kick put the Rebels up 7–0.

When the Rebels punted only 25 yards on the first play of the second quarter, the Bulldogs were in business. Starting on their own 49, they needed twelve plays—eleven of them runs—to score. Donald Ray King got the touchdown on a 1-yard run, and Bob Morgan's kick knotted the game. Later in the quarter, State took the lead after Mike McEnany grabbed a fumble in Ole Miss territory. Quarterback John Bond engineered a Bulldog drive capped by Danny Knight's 5-yard touchdown run. The scoreboard read 14–7 until late in what would become the wild fourth quarter.

The Rebs' drive to tie the game began when the Dogs' Dana Moore

Breck Tyler, a son of former State coach Bob Tyler, is one of only three players to have lettered at both State and Ole Miss. Tyler played for the Bulldogs in 1977 and 1978, and for the Rebels in 1980 and 1981. University of Mississippi Photo.

November 21, 1981

Ole Miss 21, Mississippi State 17

	State	Ole Miss
First downs	22	15
Total plays	75	64
Total yards	323	314
Rushes/net yards	67/256	35/74
Passing yards	67	240
Passes		
(Att-Comp-Int)	12-6-1	29-21-0
Punts/average yards	7/39.5	7/32.1
Penalties/yards	3/50	6/69
Fumbles/lost	7/2	3/3
Time of possession	34:05	25:55

On a quarterback keeper, John Fourcade races into the end zone for the winning touchdown with only two seconds remaining. Michael Stearns (60) braces to block as the Bulldogs' Rob Fesmire (6) races in. University of Mississippi Photo.

punted to the Ole Miss 24. Fourcade marched his squad across in eleven plays, seven of them passes, including one on which Kenneth Johnson was flagged for pass interference against the Rebs' split end, Michael Harmon. Fourcade scored on a 6-yard scramble, and Gatlin's kick tied the game, setting the stage for the final 3:37.

Bond brought the Bulldogs back down the field, reaching the Rebel 10 with just thirty-five seconds to play. Bulldog coach Emory Bellard's squad had already committed seven fumbles (though only two were lost), and Bellard opted to go for the field goal. Moore nailed the kick, and State was back on top, 17–14. Thousands headed for the exits, thinking that the game was over.

Little did they know.

Morgan kicked off for State, intending to hit a low ground ball that would be hard to return. But the pigskin bounced high in the air, and Danny Jansen nabbed it and returned it 7 yards to the Ole Miss 40. "Listen," Fourcade told his teammates in the huddle, "we're going to score, go for the tie, and we've got nothing to lose." Twenty-six seconds remained. Fourcade immediately went to the air. First he found Harmon, the team's leading receiver, for 19 yards. The two connected again for another 16. First down on the State 25. Thirteen seconds left. After the Rebels used their final time-out, Fourcade again sought

Harmon, who was again up against Johnson, the Bulldog leader in intercep-tions. According to Mickey Spagnola in the *Jackson Clarion-Ledger*, "Harmon made his cut to the left sideline in the end zone. The ball was already in the air. It was underthrown. State defensive back Kenneth Johnson went for broke. Harmon sensed his perilous situation and stopped for the ball, shield-ing Johnson. [Johnson] tried to step in front. But he bumped Harmon, then stepped in front and made the interception."

As the Bulldogs screamed in protest and the Rebels cheered, a yellow flag fluttered to the ground. Pass interference. No interception. Rebel ball on the 1 yard line. The touchdown came on a fake handoff that fooled even Sloan. Thomas dived empty-handed over center into a mass of defenders, while Fourcade raced around right end into the end zone. "The only way they were going to keep me out of that end zone," Fourcade later declared, "was to shoot me." The clock showed 0:02.

So was it pass interference? Johnson told the *Clarion-Ledger* that Harmon "ran into me trying to make his path open to the corner. When he bumped me, I slipped inside him. If anything, I thought he interfered." Not surpris-ingly, Harmon believed that pass interference had indeed been the correct call: Johnson "bumped me and kind of pushed me and intercepted it. After he bumped me, I kind of leaned back into him. It was a close call, but he hit me first." Bellard sought to defuse the controversy, stating succinctly, "The official made the call, and that's that."

State ended the season sixth nationally in rushing defense (giving up only 88 yards a game) and twelfth in scoring defense (allowing 12.5 points a game). Three Bulldog defenders—linebacker Johnie Cooks, tackle Glenn Collins, and end Billy Jackson—were named to all-America teams. Despite the dispiriting loss to Ole Miss, State cheered its fans with a victory in the Hall of Fame Bowl in Birmingham. The inspired Dogs scored a touchdown on the game's first play and easily defeated Kansas, 10–0. The final United Press International Poll had State at No. 17.

1982

Year of the Bulldogs

1982 SCHEDULES

Ole Miss 4–7

RESULT	DATE	PF	OPPONENT	PA	LOCATION
W	September 4	27	Memphis State*	10	Oxford
W	September 11	28	Southern Mississippi	19	Oxford
L	September 18	14	Alabama	42	Jackson
L	September 25	12	Arkansas	14	Little Rock
L	October 9	10	Georgia	33	Athens
W	October 16	27	Texas Christian	9	Oxford
L	October 23	10	Vanderbilt	19	Nashville
L	October 30	8	Louisiana State	45	Baton Rouge
W	November 6	45	Tulane	14	Jackson
L	November 13	17	Tennessee	30	Jackson
L	November 20	10	Mississippi State	27	Jackson

Mississippi State 5–6

RESULT	DATE	PF	OPPONENT	PA	LOCATION
W	September 4	30	Tulane	21	New Orleans
W	September 11	31	Arkansas State	10	Starkville
W	September 18	41	Memphis State*	17	Memphis
L	September 25	17	Florida	27	Gainesville
L	October 2	22	Georgia	29	Starkville
L	October 9	14	Southern Mississippi	20	Jackson
L	October 16	14	Miami	31	Miami
L	October 23	17	Auburn	35	Starkville
L	October 30	12	Alabama	20	Jackson
W	November 13	27	Louisiana State	24	Starkville
W	November 20	27	Mississippi	10	Jackson

* Now University of Memphis

In Chinese lore it was the Year of the Dog. In the Egg Bowl, it was the Year of the Bulldog. Those superior Dogs, tenth in the nation in defense and eleventh in offense, convincingly downed the Rebels, 27–10. Mississippi State dominated on both sides of the ball, racking up 467 yards of total offense and holding Ole Miss without an offensive touchdown.

State had started the year at No. 13 in the United Press International Poll, winning its first three games before injuries struck. The Bulldogs lost their next six games—all to teams that were ranked in the Top 20 at some time during the season—before downing previously undefeated No. 6 Louisiana State. The National Collegiate Athletic Association rated the Bulldogs' schedule the twelfth-toughest in the country. Playing the nineteenth-most-difficult slate, the Rebels matched the Bulldogs' 4–6 record on the eve of the Egg Bowl, but State was favored by 3½ points.

The 61,286 fans were speculating not only on the outcome but also on whether either coach would be leaving. Rumors had both State's Emory Bellard and Ole Miss's Steve Sloan considering other offers. Once kickoff occurred, however, all attention focused on the field. The Rebels won the coin toss, but a confused Ole Miss captain pointed the wrong way when indicating which way his team would kick. The Bulldogs would not only have the ball first but would be driving with the twenty-mile-an-hour south wind. They took full advantage of the mistake, scoring on their opening drive. Though Glenn Young bobbled the kickoff, the error worked in his favor as the Rebel coverage team overran the play, allowing Young to race down to the Ole Miss 39. Four plays later, halfback Lamar Windham bulled over from the 4. Bob Morgan kicked the first of his three extra points on the day, and State had jumped ahead, 7–0.

Another State touchdown soon followed. The Bulldogs covered 74 yards in eight plays—all on the ground—with not a single third-down play to slow the pace. With the ball on the Rebel 26, quarterback John Bond pitched out to fullback Elmer Wilson, who dashed around left end for the score. Bulldogs 13, Rebels 0.

November 20, 1982
Mississippi State 27, Ole Miss 10

	State	Ole Miss
First downs	23	18
Total plays	71	72
Total yards	467	280
Rushes/net yards	63/357	33/105
Passing yards	110	175
Passes		
(Att-Comp-Int)	8-3-1	39-22-1
Punts/average yards	2/50.0	5/43.0
Penalties/yards	3/33	5/35
Fumbles/lost	4/3	2/0
Time of possession	33:17	26:43

Ole Miss was down by two touchdowns and had yet to make even one first down. But the Rebels responded with their longest drive of the day. Starting on the Mississippi 10 after a Bulldog fumble, quarterback Kent Austin led his team to the State 17, where the drive stalled. Todd Gatlin came in to kick the 3-pointer, and the Rebels trailed by only 10. They soon cut the lead to 3. Keith Fourcade—brother of former Rebel quarterback

John Fourcade—intercepted a Bond pass and ran the ball back 36 yards to give the Rebels their only touchdown of the day and cut the margin to 13–10 with 3:57 left in the half.

But momentum quickly swung back to the maroon and white. The Bulldogs added another touchdown before the break with a 75-yard drive highlighted by Danny Knight's spectacular 52-yard grab of a pass from Bond. Fullback Henry Koontz went the final 7 yards to increase State's cushion to 10.

The second half featured ball control, as each team had just two possessions in the first nineteen minutes. The Rebs took the kickoff and drove 63 yards to the Mississippi State 8, but linebacker Cookie Jackson blocked an attempted field goal, and the Dogs took over on their own 6. Back came State, with a 94-yard scoring drive on which the big play was another Bond-Knight collaboration, this one for 46 yards. Tailback Michael Haddix dived over for the final Bulldog score with 1:01 remaining in the third quarter. In the final period, the teams exchanged long drives but no points, and the Bulldogs had the 27–10 victory.

And what about the coaches? Well, Bellard announced that he would remain in Starkville, silencing rumors that he might go to Texas Christian. But Sloan accepted the coaching job at Duke. Coming in to lift Rebel hopes was Billy Brewer, head coach at Louisiana Tech and a former Rebel quarterback and defensive back.

1983

"The Immaculate Deflection"

Butch John, *Jackson Clarion-Ledger*

1983 SCHEDULES

Ole Miss 7–5

RESULT	DATE	PF	OPPONENT	PA	LOCATION
L	September 3	17	Memphis State*	37	Memphis
W	September 10	23	Tulane**	27	New Orleans
L	September 17	0	Alabama	40	Tuscaloosa
W	September 24	13	Arkansas	10	Jackson
L	October 1	7	Southern Mississippi	27	Oxford
L	October 8	11	Georgia	36	Oxford
W	October 15	20	Texas Christian	7	Fort Worth
W	October 22	21	Vanderbilt	14	Oxford
W	October 29	27	Louisiana State	24	Jackson
W	November 12	13	Tennessee	10	Knoxville
W	November 19	24	Mississippi State	23	Jackson
L	December 10	3	Air Force	9	Independence Bowl

Mississippi State 3–8

RESULT	DATE	PF	OPPONENT	PA	LOCATION
W	September 3	14	Tulane	9	Starkville
W	September 17	38	Navy	10	Jackson
L	September 24	12	Florida	35	Starkville
L	October 1	7	Georgia	20	Athens
L	October 8	6	Southern Mississippi	31	Jackson
L	October 15	7	Miami	31	Starkville
L	October 22	13	Auburn	28	Auburn
L	October 29	18	Alabama	35	Tuscaloosa
L	November 5	13	Memphis State*	30	Starkville
W	November 12	45	Louisiana State	26	Baton Rouge
L	November 19	23	Mississippi	24	Jackson

* Now University of Memphis
** Forfeited by order of NCAA

Twenty-four seconds to play. The scoreboard reads Ole Miss 24, State 23. The Bulldogs are knocking at the door, desperately trying to take back a game they had owned for three quarters. It's third and 5, with the ball on the Rebel 10, directly in front of the goalposts. It's do-or-die time.

In the balance hangs not only the big game but the Bulldogs' attempt to salvage a dismal season as well as the Rebels' first winning season since 1976 and their first bowl bid since 1971.

Time-out, Ole Miss.

The two teams had taken divergent paths to Jackson. The Bulldogs had started the season strong, winning their first two games in what the National Collegiate Athletic Association ranked the country's sixth-toughest schedule. But seven losses had followed, a slump broken by a victory over Louisiana State in the game preceding the Egg Bowl. The Rebels, in contrast, had started slowly at 1–5 but had gotten hot in midseason, winning four in a row prior to the Mississippi State game.

Against the Rebels, the Bulldogs followed their season-long pattern, starting off in an almost overpowering fashion before faltering. State recorded points on its first three possessions to take a 17–0 lead. Artie Cosby opened the scoring with a 19-yard field goal with about two and a half minutes remaining in the first quarter. Then a 57-yard, eleven-play drive ended with quarterback John Bond's 1-yard dive over the middle. Finally, fullback Henry Koontz capped a 60-yard drive with a 2-yard burst. Cosby added both extra points.

Ole Miss got on the scoreboard before the half when Tim Moffett returned a punt 66 yards for a touchdown—the first punt return for a touchdown in the rivalry since 1948—and Neil Teevan added the extra point. Although the Rebels trailed by only 10 at the break, the Bulldogs had completely dominated. Ole Miss had been to midfield only once, had managed just two first downs to State's fifteen, and had mustered only 48 yards of offense to the Bulldogs' 288. But Ole Miss would not go quietly: in the locker room, Rebel linebacker Lee Cole exhorted his teammates to remember the possibility of a bowl game: "We've worked too hard to get this opportunity. We're not going to let this . . . get away from us without one hell of a fight."

Going with the wind in the third quarter, the Bulldogs increased their lead with two Cosby field goals, from 25 and 51 yards out, respectively. The longer one set a new rivalry record for field-goal distance. The Dogs had what looked to be an insurmountable 23–7 lead.

November 19, 1983
Ole Miss 24, Mississippi State 23

	State	Ole Miss
First downs	22	11
Total plays	83	53
Total yards	416	163
Rushes/net yards	70/334	332/80
Passing yards	82	74
Passes		
(Att-Comp-Int)	13-5-1	21-13-0
Punts/average yards	3/38.6	8/41.2
Penalties/yards	1/15	6/51
Fumbles/lost	3/2	3/1
Time of possession	35:36	24:24

The sudden gust of wind that blew away the Bulldogs' last-minute field goal attempt is vividly illustrated by artist Henry Gentry of the *Clarion-Ledger*. Sportswriter Butch John forever dubbed the play "The Immaculate Deflection." Courtesy of the *Clarion-Ledger*, November 19, 1984.

But State began to make mistakes, and the fourth quarter belonged to Ole Miss. First the Dogs bobbled a handoff deep in their own territory, and the Rebs took over at the 12. On the first play of the final period, Rebel fullback Arthur Humphrey lost control of the ball when he charged into a mass of tacklers at the 3, but the ball bounced 2 yards backward into the hands of quarterback Kelly Powell, who trotted in for the score. Mississippi State's lead had shrunk to just 9 points, 23–14. The Bulldogs fumbled again just three plays later, and Matthew Lovelady recovered the ball, giving the Rebels possession on the State 22. Moffett then scored his second touchdown of the day on a 10-yard pass from Powell, and the score was 23–21. The next Bulldog possession

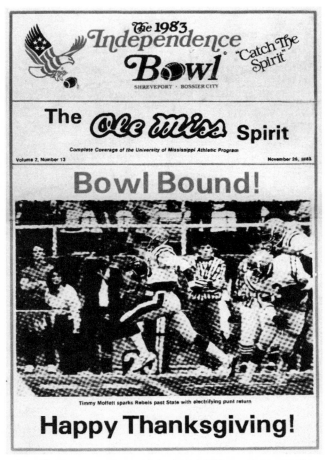

Tim Moffett returns a punt 66 yards for the Rebels' first touchdown. Moffett also scored on a fourth-quarter pass. *Ole Miss Spirit*, November 26, 1983.

went even more poorly: State ran only one play before Joe Hall intercepted a pass. Rebel ball on the State 18. Ole Miss failed to advance the ball further, but Teevan kicked a 35-yard field goal to put the Rebels up, 24–23. No team had ever before come back from a 16-point deficit in the Egg Bowl. Moreover, in five and a half minutes, the Rebels had run only thirteen plays, had covered a mere 52 yards, yet had scored 17 points. Nearly ten minutes remained to play, however, and the game was still up for grabs.

This time, Ole Miss made the miscue, fumbling the ball deep in Bulldog territory. Darrell Moore recovered at the State 20 with 4:50 to go. Over the next four and a half minutes, the Bulldogs drove toward the Ole Miss goal.

With twenty-four seconds left and the unpredictable south wind swirling around the stadium, Cosby prepared for the field goal attempt that would decide the game.

With the ball on the 10, it's a 27-yarder—a chip shot for Cosby, who has already tied the series record for field goals in a game, with three. Observers note that the wind has died down. On the Ole Miss sideline, tailback Buford McGee turns his back. Others close their eyes. The ball is snapped, and Cosby swings his leg. Up, up the ball goes, flipping end over end, straight toward the goalposts. Bulldog players raise their arms to signal that the kick is good, and Maroon fans in the opposite end zone begin to cheer. But wait—just as the ball reaches its zenith, a sudden gust of wind hits, and the ball hangs motionless, about ten feet short of the crossbar, for what seems an eternity. And then it begins to head back the way it came. The ball is not going over the crossbar. The wind has stopped it short. The Bulldog fans' roars change to cries of astonishment, then to agonizing groans of frustration. The ball falls harmlessly to the ground, and it is the Rebel fans' turn to go wild. As pointed out by Ole Miss media relations director Langston Rogers, "It is probably the only field goal ever celebrated by both teams." Said State head coach Emory Bellard, "It was like someone was standing over there saying, 'Naw, you're not going through. Mississippi State's not going to win this son-of-a-gun.'" In Monday's *Clarion-Ledger*, sportswriter Butch John forever named it the Immaculate Deflection.

State had thoroughly overwhelmed Ole Miss everywhere except on the scoreboard. The Bulldogs had generated 416 yards of offense, more than twice as much as the Rebels, and had penetrated the Rebel 25-yard line seven times, scoring on five of those occasions. The Bulldogs doubled the Rebels' eleven first downs and held the ball for 35:36, versus the Rebels' 24:24. For the second time in his career, Bond alone had outgained the entire Rebel team, recording 211 yards (129 rushing, 82 passing) compared to Ole Miss's 163.

For turning around a losing program in his first year at the helm, Ole Miss's Billy Brewer shared honors as Coach of the Year with Kentucky's Jerry Claiborne as voted by the Southeastern Conference coaches. On a rainy night in Shreveport, unranked Ole Miss took on No. 13 Air Force in the Independence Bowl but fell in a game of field goals, 9–3.

1984

The Straw That Broke the Camel's Back

1984 SCHEDULES

Ole Miss 4–6–1

RESULT	DATE	PF	OPPONENT	PA	LOCATION
W	September 8	22	Memphis State*	6	Oxford
T	September 15	14	Arkansas	14	Little Rock
W	September 22	14	Louisiana Tech	8	Oxford
W	September 29	19	Tulane	14	Oxford
L	October 6	13	Auburn	17	Oxford
L	October 13	12	Georgia	18	Athens
L	October 20	10	Southern Mississippi	13	Jackson
L	October 27	20	Vanderbilt	37	Nashville
L	November 3	29	Louisiana State	32	Baton Rouge
L	November 17	17	Tennessee	41	Jackson
W	November 24	24	Mississippi State	3	Jackson

Mississippi State 4–7

RESULT	DATE	PF	OPPONENT	PA	LOCATION
W	September 1	30	Tulane	3	New Orleans
W	September 8	14	Colorado State	9	Starkville
L	September 22	30	Missouri	47	Columbia
L	September 29	12	Florida	27	Gainesville
W	October 6	27	Southern Mississippi	18	Jackson
L	October 13	13	Kentucky	17	Starkville
L	October 20	12	Memphis State*	23	Memphis
L	October 27	21	Auburn	24	Starkville
L	November 3	20	Alabama	24	Jackson
W	November 17	16	Louisiana State	14	Starkville
L	November 24	3	Mississippi	24	Jackson

* Now University of Memphis

For nearly three quarters, the game remained tight. The Rebels established a 7–0 lead in the opening quarter with a 78-yard drive capped by Nathan Wonsley's run from the 1 and Jon Howard's extra point. For the next thirty minutes, the teams exchanged threats and the

Quarterback Kent Austin tosses to Rebel receiver Nathan Wonsley for extra yardage. Wonsley scored two of Ole Miss's three touchdowns. Photo by Stan Badz, *Clarion-Ledger/Jackson Daily News*, November 25, 1984.

Rebels missed two field goals, but the score remained unchanged. At halftime, Mississippi State coach Emory Bellard sought "to start a spark" by pulling quarterback Orlando Lundie in favor of Don Smith, who had not played since suffering a shoulder injury two weeks earlier. The change paid off with about two minutes to go in the third period, as Smith led the Bulldogs on a 62-yard march and Artie Cosby put his team on the board with a 25-yard field goal. 7–3, Rebels.

For about sixteen seconds.

Cornerback Lee Davis waited for the kickoff at the Ole Miss 3 but muffed the catch. Instead of following his instincts and falling on the ball, Davis grabbed it at the 5 and headed upfield. The fastest man on the Rebel

November 24, 1984

Ole Miss 24, Mississippi State 3

	State	Ole Miss
First downs	13	23
Total plays	62	78
Total yards	255	402
Rushes/net yards	38/131	45/175
Passing yards	124	227
Passes		
(Att-Comp-Int)	24-9-4	33-17-1
Punts/average yards	6/40.0	5/43.7
Penalties/yards	5/51	4/35
Fumbles/lost	2/0	1/0
Time of possession	25:57	34:03

squad, he followed his blockers as far as the 30 and then found himself in the clear. Seventy yards later, Ole Miss owned an 11-point lead and, in Smith's words, had "knocked everything back to kaput." The Bulldog comeback died aborning. Declared Ole Miss coach Billy Brewer, Davis's run "was the straw that broke the camel's back." The Rebs added 10 more points (on a 20-yard run by Nathan Wonsley, whose older brother, George, had been a halfback at Mississippi State, and a 21-yard field goal by Howard) and took a convincing 24–3 victory. At 97 yards, Davis's run was the longest kickoff return in rivalry records and tied Jack Nix's forty-six-year-old record for the longest play of any kind.

Sunny skies greeted the fans who got up early to get to Mississippi Veterans Memorial Stadium in time for the 11:15 kickoff. For the first time since 1964, the game was being televised nationally, and TV wanted an early game, so an early game it was. Unfortunately for those at home, satellite problems caused viewers to miss twenty-eight minutes of action. Neither team was having a good season, although in State's previous game, the Bulldogs had broken a four-game losing streak with a 16–14 upset of ninth-ranked Louisiana State for State's sole Southeastern Conference win of the season. The Rebels' season included six straight defeats, and the Egg Bowl represented their only conference victory of the year.

1985

A Point a Minute and More

1985 SCHEDULES

Ole Miss 4–6–1

RESULT	DATE	PF	OPPONENT	PA	LOCATION
T	September 7	17	Memphis State*	17	Memphis
L	September 14	19	Arkansas	24	Jackson
W	September 21	18	Arkansas State	16	Oxford
W	September 28	27	Tulane	10	New Orleans
L	October 5	0	Auburn	41	Auburn
L	October 12	21	Georgia	49	Jackson
W	October 26	35	Vanderbilt	7	Oxford
L	November 2	0	Louisiana State	14	Jackson
L	November 9	14	Notre Dame	37	South Bend
L	November 16	14	Tennessee	34	Knoxville
W	November 23	45	Mississippi State	27	Jackson

Mississippi State 5–6

RESULT	DATE	PF	OPPONENT	PA	LOCATION
W	September 7	22	Arkansas State	14	Starkville
W	September 14	30	Syracuse	3	Starkville
W	September 21	23	Southern Mississippi	20	Jackson
L	September 28	22	Florida	36	Starkville
W	October 5	31	Memphis State*	28	Starkville
L	October 12	19	Kentucky	33	Lexington
W	October 19	31	Tulane	27	Starkville
L	October 26	9	Auburn	21	Auburn
L	November 2	28	Alabama	44	Tuscaloosa
L	November 16	15	Louisiana State	17	Baton Rouge
L	November 23	27	Mississippi	45	Jackson

* Now University of Memphis

Years had passed since Ole Miss and State had engaged in a good, old-fashioned shootout. It was about time. The two teams combined to equal their previous high of ten touchdowns and totaled 72 points—more than a point a minute. Nine players marched in the touchdown parade, including six for Ole Miss.

Don Smith scored three touchdowns, passed for another, and ran for a two-point conversion while compiling 176 total yards for the Bulldogs in an aerial shoot-out. Mississippi State University Photo.

Several things about the offensive explosion were surprising: The 5–5 Bulldogs allowed the 3–6–1 Rebels to roll up 45 points. And despite having a quarterback who had amassed more total offense over the course of the season than the entire Rebel team had, the Dogs scored only 27 points. Bulldog coach Emory Bellard offered a bleak and to-the-point analysis of the game: "Their offense out-performed our defense. Their defense out-performed our offense. Their kicking game out-performed our kicking game. Their coaches out-performed our coaches."

Both teams arrived in Jackson carrying three-game losing streaks. Nevertheless, 48,705 fans paid fourteen dollars each for a ticket. If they were hoping to see an offensive show, they got their money's worth. The scoring started early, with Bulldog quarterback Don Smith doing much of the work on his team's first drive, which culminated in his 1-yard touchdown run midway through the first quarter. Artie Cosby booted the point after to put State up by 7.

November 23, 1985
Ole Miss 45, Mississippi State 27

	State	Ole Miss
First downs	16	21
Total plays	73	69
Total yards	226	269
Rushes/net yards	45/38	44/85
Passing yards	188	184
Passes		
(Att-Comp-Int)	28-13-0	25-12-1
Punts/average yards	10/39.0	5/39.2
Penalties/yards	17/116	9/80
Fumbles/lost	0/0	2/1
Time of possession	32:34	27:26

The Rebs responded with a dizzying 38 straight points. Quarterback Mark Young, subbing for the injured Kent Austin, needed just four plays to lead the Rebels 58 yards to knot the score. The key play was Young's 38-yard scoring strike to J. R. Ambrose. Bryan Owen booted the first of his six extra points. After a 55-yard punt return by Willie Goodloe and a Bulldog penalty gave Ole Miss the ball deep in Mississippi State terri-

Ole Miss players celebrate a sack, one of seven they put on the Bulldog quarterback that afternoon. The 1986 *Ole Miss.*

tory, Young opened the second quarter by connecting with Jamie Holder on a 13-yard touchdown pass. A 41-yard Owen field goal on the Rebels' next drive made the score 17–7 at the half.

In the third quarter, the Rebels picked up where they had left off, scoring touchdowns on their first three possessions. The opening drive featured three consecutive penalties that changed the game. The Rebels had driven 71 yards to the Mississippi State 11 and were facing a third and 5 when Young fumbled and linebacker Cedric Corse grabbed the loose ball. But an official ruled that Young had been down before the fumble. An angry Bulldog player then threw the ball, resulting in a penalty. The State players continued to argue, and two more penalties were stepped off. By the time the Bulldogs calmed down, the ball was on the 2½ yard line. Instead of the Bulldogs having possession of the ball or the Rebels facing fourth and 15 from the 21, it was first and goal. Nathan Wonsley took the ball into the end zone on the next play, and the Rebels had a 24–7 advantage. "Game, set, match," wrote Rusty Hampton in Sunday's *Jackson Clarion-Ledger.* "The final 25 minutes were played for statistical reasons only."

Wonsley scored his second touchdown—this one from 6 yards out—on the next series, and Willie Goodloe closed out the third period with a 4-yard run to make the score 38–7. The fourth quarter, however, belonged to the

Bulldogs. In six and a half minutes, they scored three touchdowns, including two that resulted from Rebel errors. After the Bulldogs recovered a fumble on the Ole Miss 41, Smith took his team to pay dirt, scoring the touchdown himself on a 1-yard dive, although his attempt at the 2-point conversion failed. Johnny Gussio then blocked a Rebel punt, and Mike Harper recovered on the Ole Miss 34. Smith passed 33 yards to James Bloodworth, then dived across the goal line for his third touchdown. This time, his run gave the Dogs the two-point conversion, and State had cut the gap to 38–21.

But the Bulldogs' onside kickoff failed, and the Rebels drove for their sixth touchdown when Shawn Sykes scored from the 3 with 1:16 left to play. The Bulldogs managed one final score on Smith's fifteenth touchdown pass of the year—this one to Michael Taylor—but it was not enough. Ole Miss 45, Mississippi State 27.

For a game with so many points, the total yardage was surprisingly low—269 for the Rebels, 226 for the Bulldogs. The teams managed only 123 yards rushing, fewest ever in the history of the rivalry. Perhaps the most notable statistic, however, was penalties: the teams combined for twenty-six penalties for 196 yards, the most ever in a clash between State and Ole Miss. The Bulldogs alone accumulated seventeen penalties, a series record for one team.

After the Bulldogs' fourth consecutive losing season, State terminated Bellard's contract and selected as his successor Rockey Felker, who had quarterbacked the 1974 Bulldog team and had served as an assistant at State, Texas Tech, Memphis State, and Alabama. Less than a month away from his thirty-third birthday, Felker became the youngest head coach in Division I-A.

1986

GAME 83

Mississippi Veterans
Memorial Stadium,
Jackson

Winner Take All

1986 SCHEDULES

Ole Miss 8–3–1

RESULT	DATE	PF	OPPONENT	PA	LOCATION
W	September 6	28	Memphis State*	6	Jackson
L	September 13	0	Arkansas	21	Little Rock
T	September 20	10	Arkansas State	10	Oxford
W	September 27	35	Tulane	10	Oxford
L	October 4	10	Georgia	14	Athens
W	October 11	33	Kentucky	13	Jackson
W	October 18	21	Southwestern Louisiana**	20	Oxford
W	October 25	28	Vanderbilt	12	Nashville
W	November 1	21	Louisiana State	19	Baton Rouge
L	November 15	10	Tennessee	22	Jackson
W	November 22	24	Mississippi State	3	Jackson
W	December 20	20	Texas Tech	17	Independence Bowl

Mississippi State 6–5

RESULT	DATE	PF	OPPONENT	PA	LOCATION
W	September 6	24	Syracuse	17	Syracuse
W	September 13	27	Tennessee	23	Knoxville
L	September 20	24	Southern Mississippi	28	Jackson
W	September 27	16	Florida	10	Starkville
W	October 4	34	Memphis State*	17	Memphis
W	October 11	24	Arkansas State	9	Starkville
W	October 18	34	Tulane	27	New Orleans
L	October 25	6	Auburn	35	Starkville
L	November 1	3	Alabama	38	Starkville
L	November 15	0	Louisiana State	47	Jackson
L	November 22	3	Mississippi	24	Jackson

* Now University of Memphis
** Now Louisiana-Lafayette

he 1986 Egg Bowl bore unusual similarities with the game two years earlier. Both were on national television, both kickoffs occurred before noon, and both contests resulted in 24–3 Ole Miss victories. But similarities end there. While sunny skies had hovered over the 1984 game, the

[259]

In his four-year career Bill Smith punted 21 times for the Rebels in rivalry games, averaging 45.8 yards each and earning all-America honors. Photo courtesy of University of Mississippi Media Relations.

1986 game was played in an almost steady rain that prompted more than six thousand of the fifty-one thousand ticket holders to stay home. And whereas the 1984 game had been close for most of the first three quarters, in 1986 Ole Miss sprang out to a 17-point lead before the Bulldogs even got on the board. Furthermore, the 1984 game had pitted the Southeastern Conference's two worst teams, but the 1986 contest featured stakes that reached unprecedented heights. In addition to the usual rewards on the line—the Golden Egg and a year's worth of bragging rights—the winner of the game would take home a bid to play in the Independence Bowl. The loser would just go home, season over. This year, it was winner take all.

It looked to be a fairly even match, pitting the running and passing

November 22, 1986

Ole Miss 24, Mississippi State 3

	State	Ole Miss
First downs	16	13
Total plays	72	58
Total yards	257	312
Rushes/net yards	48/205	50/219
Passing yards	52	93
Passes (Att-Comp-Int)	23-6-1	8-3-1
Punts/average yards	5/40.0	5/47.6
Penalties/yards	6/70	10/98
Fumbles/lost	5/2	2/0
Time of possession	30:56	29:04

Reid Hines evades would-be tacklers and races 35 yards for a touchdown on the first carry of his collegiate career. Photo courtesy of University of Mississippi Media Relations.

of State quarterback Don Smith versus the Ole Miss defense; Smith, the Southeastern Conference's offensive leader for the second straight year, against the Southeastern Conference's stingiest defense, at one time fourth in the nation. The teams sported nearly identical records—Ole Miss at 6–3–1, State at 6–4 playing a schedule ranked as the country's third-toughest by *Athlon* magazine.

The Rebels collected points on two of their first three possessions. Their first touchdown came on a 73-yard drive that included Shawn Sykes's 42-yard sprint to the Mississippi State 4. Willie Goodloe swept for the 6, and Bryan Owen kicked the extra point. The Rebels scored their next touchdown off a Bulldog fumble. Quarterback Mark Young connected with Ricky Myers for 34 yards, then hit wide receiver J. R. Ambrose on a swing pass, and Ambrose scored easily. Later, in the second quarter, Owen added a 34-yard field goal to put Ole Miss up 17–0.

The Bulldogs responded with their only points of the day on their longest drive—41 yards. The Dogs got as far as the Rebel 3, and Artie Cosby's 3-pointer from 20 yards out cut Mississippi's lead to 14 points at the half.

The Bulldog defense played a strong third quarter, holding the Rebels to a mere 11 yards and no first downs. The State offense charged into Rebel territory three times, reaching the 33, 28, and 30, but was turned back each time. State threatened again early in the fourth quarter, but the Rebel defense stopped the incursion at the 31, and the Ole Miss offense came back with its final touchdown of the day. On his first collegiate carry, Reid Hines scored from the Bulldog 35, and with 7:11 left to play, the Rebels had the 24–3 win.

The Rebel defense had clearly won the battle against Smith, although he still put up impressive numbers—109 yards rushing on twenty-one carries, 52 yards passing on six of twenty-three attempts. Declared Rebel defensive tackle Mike Fitzsimmons admiringly, "You knock him down. . . . He gets up . . . and comes back . . . again. You just have to keep coming at him." But the Rebels kept him out of the end zone.

Finishing the season at 7–3–1, the Rebels posted their first winning season since 1983. The team's 4–2 Southeastern Conference mark earned Billy Brewer the nod as United Press International's Southeastern Conference Coach of the Year. With a bid to the Independence Bowl, the Rebels went to Shreveport and topped Texas Tech, 20–17.

1987

GAME 84

Mississippi Veterans
Memorial Stadium,
Jackson

Top Dogs

1987 SCHEDULES

Ole Miss 3–8

RESULT	DATE	PF	OPPONENT	PA	LOCATION
L	September 5	10	Memphis State*	16	Memphis
L	September 12	10	Arkansas	31	Jackson
W	September 19	47	Arkansas State	10	Oxford
L	September 26	24	Tulane	31	New Orleans
L	October 3	14	Georgia	31	Oxford
L	October 10	6	Kentucky	35	Lexington
W	October 17	24	Southwestern Louisiana**	14	Oxford
W	October 24	42	Vanderbilt	14	Oxford
L	October 31	13	Louisiana State	42	Jackson
L	November 14	13	Tennessee	55	Knoxville
L	November 21	20	Mississippi State	30	Jackson

Mississippi State 4–7

RESULT	DATE	PF	OPPONENT	PA	LOCATION
W	September 5	31	Southwestern Louisiana**	3	Starkville
L	September 12	10	Tennessee	38	Starkville
W	September 19	14	Louisiana Tech	13	Starkville
L	September 26	3	Florida	38	Gainesville
W	October 3	9	Memphis State*	6	Starkville
L	October 17	14	Southern Mississippi	18	Jackson
L	October 24	7	Auburn	38	Auburn
L	October 31	18	Alabama	21	Birmingham
L	November 7	19	Tulane	30	Starkville
L	November 14	14	Louisiana State	34	Baton Rouge
W	November 21	30	Mississippi	20	Jackson

* Now University of Memphis
** Now Louisiana-Lafayette

Celebration time! The spontaneous victory parade that started moments after State throttled Ole Miss seemed to go on and on. One Bulldog after another proudly carried the coveted Golden Egg around the end zone as State students cheered wildly. Then the team headed for the locker room to light up victory cigars. The 30–20 win not only broke the

Dawgs' Bite

$1.00

VOLUME 11 NUMBER 15

NOVEMBER 28, 1987

In this issue

Dogs rout Rebels 30-20 in '87 season finale
See pages 4-8

Ron Polk talks fall baseball
Turn to page 9

Pre-season outlooks for men's, women's hoops
Look on pages 10-13

Going out in style...

Seniors Cedric Corse and Michael Simmons take turns parading around Memorial Stadium with the coveted Golden Egg that the Bulldogs had just captured. *Dawgs' Bite*, November 28, 1987.

November 21, 1987
Mississippi State 30, Ole Miss 20

	State	Ole Miss
First downs	17	17
Total plays	76	71
Total yards	370	298
Rushes/net yards	49/153	37/169
Passing yards	217	133
Passes (Att-Comp-Int)	27-12-1	34-14-0
Punts/average yards	7/35.3	7/39.3
Penalties/yards	13/105	9/74
Fumbles/lost	3/1	4/3
Time of possession	29:09	30:51

Bulldogs' four-game Egg Bowl losing streak but also ended their five-game season skid.

Despite the pleasant sunny weather, only 43,450 fans—the fewest in fifteen years—came out to see two 3–7 teams battle for nothing more than home-state pride. Neither team found success early, as each came up empty on its first four possessions. Ole Miss finally broke the ice with a field goal after linebacker Stevon Moore intercepted the ball on the State 44 and returned it to the 13. Three plays later, Bryan Owen's 22-yarder had the Rebels up by 3. But the lead lasted only a minute and a half. Facing third and 1 on the Bulldog 46, quarterback Eric Underwood found end Jesse Anderson just past the line of scrimmage, and Anderson raced 54 yards for the touchdown. Freshman Joel Logan kicked, and the Bulldogs had a 7–3 advantage.

Back came the Rebels. Starting with good field position on the Ole Miss 46, they needed nine plays to reach the end zone, with quarterback Mark Young and tight end Shawn Sowder combining for the score and Owen adding the extra point. The 10–7 advantage was the Rebels' last of the day, however. The fired-up Bulldogs sacked Young, who fumbled, and State took advantage of the opportunity with a 9-yard touchdown pass from Underwood to tailback Albert Williams, all alone in the flat. The next Ole Miss drive went 51 yards in twelve plays for a 42-yard Owen field goal that brought Ole Miss to within 1 at the half, 14–13.

State upped the lead with a 65-yard drive that featured ten running plays and only two passes. On fourth and 1 at the 3, Hank Phillips ran to the right for the score. Early in the fourth quarter, Bulldog tailback Orlando Wade charged 11 yards for another touchdown that gave State a 27–13 advantage.

But only fifty-nine seconds later, Ole Miss fullback Ed Thigpen reeled off a 56-yard scoring run that put the Rebels right back in the game, down only 7 with 8:42 remaining. The Bulldogs responded by adding an insurance field goal five minutes later. The drive featured two outstanding catches: on third and 18, a Rebel defender deflected Underwood's pass, but Fred Hadley retreated just enough to haul it in for a 43-yard gain; then Hadley made another spectacular grab along the sideline, barely keeping a foot inbounds on the Ole Miss 28. Hadley's first catch was "the play of the game," said State coach Rockey Felker. Logan's 32-yard field goal gave State the 30–20 victory and touched off the wild celebrations.

1988

Flingin' in the Rain

1988 SCHEDULES

Ole Miss 5–6

RESULT	DATE	PF	OPPONENT	PA	LOCATION
W	September 3	24	Memphis State*	6	Jackson
L	September 10	15	Florida	27	Jackson
L	September 17	13	Arkansas	21	Little Rock
L	October 1	12	Georgia	36	Athens
W	October 8	22	Alabama	12	Tuscaloosa
W	October 15	25	Arkansas State	22	Oxford
W	October 22	36	Vanderbilt	28	Nashville
L	October 29	20	Louisiana State	31	Baton Rouge
L	November 5	9	Tulane	14	Oxford
L	November 12	12	Tennessee	20	Oxford
W	November 26	33	Mississippi State	6	Jackson

Mississippi State 1–10

RESULT	DATE	PF	OPPONENT	PA	LOCATION
W	September 3	21	Louisiana Tech	14	Starkville
L	September 10	20	Vanderbilt	24	Nashville
L	September 17	35	Georgia	42	Starkville
L	September 24	0	Florida	17	Gainesville
L	October 1	10	Memphis State*	31	Memphis
L	October 15	21	Southern Mississippi	38	Jackson
L	October 22	0	Auburn	33	Auburn
L	October 29	34	Alabama	53	Starkville
L	November 12	3	Louisiana State	20	Starkville
L	November 19	22	Tulane	27	New Orleans
L	November 26	6	Mississippi	33	Jackson

* Now University of Memphis

A game played in a steady rain. Lots of conservative ground plays, right? Nope. Not this time. The two teams combined for eighty-six attempted passes, forty-two completions, and 585 yards through the air—all tying or bettering rivalry records. Bulldog quarterback Tony Shell's forty-five attempts bested the previous individual mark, as did Rebel quarter-

The Rebels' Wesley Walls charges through to make a tackle. On the left is the Bulldogs' Harold Rials (74). One of the few two-way players in college football in 1988, all-American Walls played tight end on offense and linebacker on defense. University of Mississippi Photo.

back Mark Young's 334 yards. The teams totaled only 48 rushing attempts. As expected, a wet ball produced fumbles (four by the Rebs, three by the Dogs), but interceptions were more significant: two pickoffs led to Ole Miss points, and one led to State points.

A crowd estimated at only twenty-eight thousand endured lightning, thunder, wind, and rain to see two teams that had combined for only five wins to date. The Bulldogs were 1–9. Though a mediocre 4–6, the Rebels had recorded a 22–12 road win over Alabama for Ole Miss's first ever victory over the Crimson Tide in that state.

The game remained close for the first two quarters. Jerry Myers (whose brother, Ricky, had played for the Rebels) intercepted an Ole Miss pass and raced back 56 yards to the Rebel 23. The Bulldogs then advanced the 8, where Joel Logan was good for a 24-yard field goal. State's 3–0 lead did

November 26, 1988
Ole Miss 33, Mississippi State 6

	State	Ole Miss
First downs	17	25
Total plays	76	78
Total yards	292	473
Rushes/net yards	31/68	37/112
Passing yards	224	361
Passes		
(Att-Comp-Int)	45-21-3	41-21-1
Punts/average yards	6/33.5	6/37.8
Penalties/yards	5/30	6/74
Fumbles/lost	3/1	4/1
Time of possession	29:46	31:14

not last long, as Ole Miss's Bryan Owen capped a 70-yard drive with a 26-yard boot.

The Rebels' Todd Sandroni then picked off the first of his two interceptions on the day, and Ole Miss needed just one play to capitalize on the mistake: Pat Coleman's 27-yard catch and run on a pass from Mark Young. The point after failed, and Logan added another field goal for State with time winding down in the second period. At halftime, Ole Miss led, 9–6.

The Rebels broke open the game early in the third quarter when Ole Miss's Dwayne Amos blocked Mike Riley's punt and the Rebs took over at the State 43. Young and Coleman combined for their second touchdown of the afternoon. Reggie Parrot picked off a pass from Shell, and the Rebels drove for another touchdown—this one on a 13-yard pass from Young to Willie Green. Early in the final period, Owen kicked his second field goal, and then backup quarterback John Darnell directed the Rebels on a short drive topped by an 11-yard scoring pass to tight end Shawn Sowder. Owen's extra-point kick ended the scoring. Rebels 33, Bulldogs 6.

1989

A Change in Tactics Works Wonders

1989 SCHEDULES

Ole Miss 8–4

RESULT	DATE	PF	OPPONENT	PA	LOCATION
W	September 2	20	Memphis State*	13	Memphis
W	September 9	24	Florida	19	Gainesville
W	September 16	34	Arkansas State	31	Oxford
L	September 23	17	Arkansas	24	Jackson
L	October 7	27	Alabama	62	Jackson
W	October 14	17	Georgia	13	Oxford
W	October 21	32	Tulane	28	New Orleans
W	October 28	24	Vanderbilt	16	Oxford
L	November 4	30	Louisiana State	35	Oxford
L	November 18	21	Tennessee	33	Knoxville
W	November 25	21	Mississippi State	11	Jackson
W	December 28	42	Air Force	29	Liberty Bowl

Mississippi State 5–6

RESULT	DATE	PF	OPPONENT	PA	LOCATION
W	September 2	42	Vanderbilt	7	Starkville
W	September 9	26	Southern Mississippi	23	Hattiesburg
L	September 23	6	Georgia	23	Athens
L	September 30	0	Florida	21	Tampa
W	October 7	28	Northeast Louisiana**	14	Starkville
W	October 21	35	Memphis State*	10	Starkville
L	October 28	0	Auburn	14	Auburn
L	November 4	10	Alabama	23	Birmingham
W	November 11	27	Tulane	7	Starkville
L	November 18	20	Louisiana State	44	Baton Rouge
L	November 25	11	Mississippi	21	Jackson

* Now University of Memphis
** Now Louisiana-Monroe

At halftime, the Rebels were clinging to a narrow 7–3 lead. But the Bulldogs had been dominant. Ole Miss had scored its touchdown on a short drive set up by a fumble recovery, but the Bulldog defense, which would finish the year ranked fifteenth in the nation, had allowed the

Trea Southerland forces a fumble as he knocks the legs from under the Bulldogs' Tony James. The recovery set up the Rebels' first touchdown. *Clarion-Ledger*, November 26, 1989.

Rebels just 71 yards of offense and three first downs, had sacked the quarterback twice, and had intercepted the ball twice. A bobbled punt led to the Rebel touchdown. Scott Swatzell recovered on the State 17, and Ed Thigpen went over from the 1 on the first play of the second period. Greg Hogue, perfect all year, kicked the point after. When the Bulldogs followed with a drive that stalled on the Ole Miss 3, Joel Logan came through with a 27-yard field goal. The 43,218 fans eagerly anticipated an exciting second half.

The Rebels had come to Jackson with a 6–4 record and had a bowl bid waiting despite the fact that they were dead last in the Southeastern

November 25, 1989

Ole Miss 21, Mississippi State 11

	State	Ole Miss
First downs	15	14
Total plays	70	64
Total yards	258	327
Rushes/net yards	37/77	39/129
Passing yards	181	198
Passes		
(Att-Comp-Int)	33-17-1	24-12-2
Punts/average yards	10/40.6	7/38.7
Penalties/yards	7/52	5/55
Fumbles/lost	2/2	1/1
Time of possession	34:01	25:59

Conference in defense. The Bulldogs were 5–5 and were favored by a point or so although they had the conference's last-place offense.

Early in the second half, the Rebs' Charles Childers got off a short punt, and Tony James returned the ball 33 yards to the Rebel 30. The Dogs moved to the Rebel 7 but fumbled a fourth-and-1 pitchout, and the Rebels took over on their 12. The Rebel drive went nowhere, and Ole Miss punted the ball back. On the next play, Bulldog quarterback Todd Jordan, State's first freshman signal-caller since 1980, threw the ball to Chauncey Godwin, who had been Jordan's high school teammate in Tupelo. Unfortunately for Jordan, however, Godwin was now a Rebel. Ole Miss took over at its own 7 and promptly stormed 93 yards to take a 14–3 lead. Ole Miss opened up its offense, and the change in tactics worked. The thirteen-play, five-and-a-half-minute-drive included five straight pass completions passes by quarterback John Darnell as well as a 1-yard scoring run by Randy Baldwin.

The Rebs counted an insurance touchdown four plays later, taking a 21–3 advantage on quarterback Russ Shows's 3-yard keeper. But the Bulldogs did not surrender, charging 83 yards for a score on their longest push of the day. Jerry Bouldin got to quarterback Tony Shell's pass a split second before Rebel defender Gerald McAllister and raced in for a 32-yard touchdown. Shell hit Jesse Anderson for a 2-point conversion pass to make the final score 21–11. Bulldog coach Rockey Felker identified his team's fumble near the Rebel goal line as the key play: "We had a chance to take the lead there. It seemed after that all the momentum swung over to the Ole Miss side."

Fans at the game were among the many supporters of both schools who donated money to help Ole Miss defensive back Roy Lee (Chucky) Mullins, who had been paralyzed during the school's Homecoming game against Vanderbilt. Roughly half a million dollars was contributed to help Mullins, who returned to school before his unexpected death in May 1991, and the remainder of the donations were used to establish a scholarship in his memory.

Ole Miss went on to the Liberty Bowl, where Rebel fans helped set a record for one-team ticket sales and another for attendance. All those Rebels went home happy, as their team whipped the Air Force Academy, 42–29.

1990

Like a Mule Hit by a Two-by-Four

1990 SCHEDULES

Ole Miss 9–3

RESULT	DATE	PF	OPPONENT	PA	LOCATION
W	September 8	23	Memphis State*	21	Oxford
L	September 15	10	Auburn	24	Jackson
W	September 22	21	Arkansas	17	Little Rock
W	September 29	31	Tulane	21	Oxford
W	October 6	35	Kentucky	29	Oxford
W	October 13	28	Georgia	12	Athens
W	October 20	42	Arkansas State	13	Oxford
W	October 27	14	Vanderbilt	13	Nashville
W	November 3	19	Louisiana State	10	Baton Rouge
L	November 17	13	Tennessee	22	Memphis
W	November 24	21	Mississippi State	9	Jackson
L	January 1, 1991	3	Michigan	35	Gator Bowl

Mississippi State 5–6

RESULT	DATE	PF	OPPONENT	PA	LOCATION
L	September 8	7	Tennessee	40	Starkville
W	September 15	27	Cal State–Fullerton	13	Starkville
W	September 22	13	Southern Mississippi	10	Starkville
L	September 29	21	Florida	34	Gainesville
L	October 13	15	Kentucky	17	Lexington
W	October 20	38	Tulane	17	New Orleans
L	October 27	16	Auburn	17	Starkville
L	November 3	0	Alabama	22	Starkville
W	November 10	27	Memphis State*	23	Memphis
W	November 17	34	Louisiana State	22	Jackson
L	November 24	9	Mississippi	21	Jackson

* Now University of Memphis

Well into the third quarter, the Bulldogs were clinging to a 3–0 lead over the favored Rebels. Ole Miss had not ventured within 40 yards of the Mississippi State goal. The current Ole Miss possession was looking no more promising: the Rebels were backed up on their own 15 yard line, where they faced third down and a daunting 11. Rebel quarterback

Tom Luke spotted Camp Roberts downfield and scrambled right, barely avoided a sack, and leaped to throw a pass across his body to the left. Although the Dogs' Frankie Luster tipped the throw, Roberts made a diving catch on his 41 for a 26-yard completion, his only reception of the day. The Rebels, declared Raad Cauthon in the *Atlanta Journal-Constitution*, were like "a mule that has to be hit by a 2-by-4 to get its attention." And the play was the two-by-four. Bulldog linebacker Reggie Stewart concurred: "That play completely shifted momentum. It just killed us." Awakened from their somnolent play, the Rebels scored three touchdowns in 6:17 playing time to capture a 21–9 victory.

Faced with sagging attendance in Jackson and threats to return the games to campus play, Jackson's Convention and Visitors Bureau sponsored a colorful minifair outside the stadium, with attractions including hot-air-balloon rides, live music, free food, and samples of Mississippi-made products. Perhaps because of the added enticements or maybe because both teams were having better seasons and the Rebels were looking at the prospect of a bowl bid, the game drew a crowd of 56,652, the largest since 1983.

The first quarter's most exciting action was a game-stopping fight between the two teams. The Rebels' Vincent Brownlee fumbled a punt, and in the scramble, newspapers said, Brownlee's helmet was pushed back. Both benches cleared, and for five minutes pent-up emotions erupted across the field before coaches could restore calm.

An interception in the second quarter paved the way for the Bulldogs' first points. Lance Aldridge picked off Rebel quarterback Russ Shows's pass on the Mississippi State 22 and returned it to the 44. State reached the Ole Miss 23 before the drive stalled, and Joel Logan was good on a 40-yard field goal. The possession constituted the Bulldogs' only first-half incursion into Rebel territory.

Gospel according to Luke
Relentless option propels Rebels 21-9

Headline from the *Clarion-Ledger*, November 25, 1990.

November 24, 1990
Ole Miss 21, Mississippi State 9

	State	Ole Miss
First downs	15	16
Total plays	69	69
Total yards	294	341
Rushes/net yards	38/149	53/254
Passing yards	145	87
Passes		
(Att-Comp-Int)	31-17-1	16-9-1
Punts/average yards	9/47.1	7/47.3
Penalties/yards	5/50	6/46
Fumbles/lost	3/1	1/1
Time of possession	29:39	30:21
Third-down conversions	2/15	3/12
Sacks by: Number/yards	0/0	3/21
Field goals attempted/made	1/1	0/0

Players strike, kick, and shove in an all-out, all-over-the-field battle in the tension-tinged first quarter and continue for five minutes before coaches can cool the heat of rivalry. *Clarion-Ledger*, November 25, 1990.

The score remained 3–0, State, until Luke's pass to Roberts opened the floodgates. A few plays later, Luke scored from the State 32 to give the Rebels a 7–3 lead. State immediately fumbled the ball back to the Rebels, and running back Marvin Courtney quickly scored on a 15-yard run that put the Rebels up 14–3 with about a minute gone in the fourth quarter.

Back came the Dogs, needing just fifty-two seconds and three plays to move 80 yards for a touchdown. Quarterback Tony Shell found split end Jerry Bouldin all alone in the end zone, and although Shell's pass for the attempted 2-point conversion fell incomplete, State had closed to within 5. But the Rebels responded with another score when Luke dodged and broke tackles for a 33-yard scamper. It was more than enough to ensure the win.

Two days later, Mississippi State coach Rockey Felker announced his resignation after five seasons in Starkville. He was succeeded by Jackie Sherrill, a high school all-American from Biloxi who had played on two national championship teams at Alabama and had been head coach at Washington State, Pittsburgh, and Texas A&M.

Ole Miss's 9–2 season mark was the school's best in nearly twenty years. The *Nashville Banner* and *Birmingham News* named Billy Brewer Southeastern Conference Coach of the Year, and the Rebels went on to the Gator Bowl, where the Michigan Wolverines trounced the Rebels, 35–3. The season ended with Ole Miss ranked No. 21 in the Associated Press Poll.

1991

Right Where We Want You

1991 SCHEDULES

Ole Miss 5–6

RESULT	DATE	PF	OPPONENT	PA	LOCATION
W	August 31	22	Tulane	3	New Orleans
W	September 7	10	Memphis State*	0	Memphis
L	September 14	13	Auburn	23	Auburn
W	September 21	38	Ohio	14	Oxford
W	September 28	24	Arkansas	17	Jackson
W	October 5	35	Kentucky	14	Lexington
L	October 12	17	Georgia	37	Oxford
L	October 26	27	Vanderbilt	30	Oxford
L	November 2	22	Louisiana State	25	Jackson
L	November 16	25	Tennessee	36	Knoxville
L	November 23	9	Mississippi State	24	Starkville

Mississippi State 7–5

RESULT	DATE	PF	OPPONENT	PA	LOCATION
W	August 31	47	Cal State–Fullerton	3	Starkville
W	September 7	13	Texas	6	Starkville
W	September 14	48	Tulane	0	Starkville
L	September 21	24	Tennessee	26	Knoxville
L	September 28	7	Florida	29	Orlando
W	October 12	31	Kentucky	6	Starkville
L	October 19	23	Memphis State*	28	Starkville
W	October 26	24	Auburn	17	Auburn
L	November 2	7	Alabama	13	Tuscaloosa
W	November 16	28	Louisiana State	19	Baton Rouge
W	November 23	24	Mississippi	9	Starkville
L	December 29	15	Air Force	38	Liberty Bowl

* Now University of Memphis

In spite of Jackson business leaders' efforts and the relatively high 1990 attendance, the Egg Bowl returned to alternating on the two campuses. It was Mississippi State's turn to host, and the school's athletic director, Larry Templeton, believed that the return to Starkville would not only

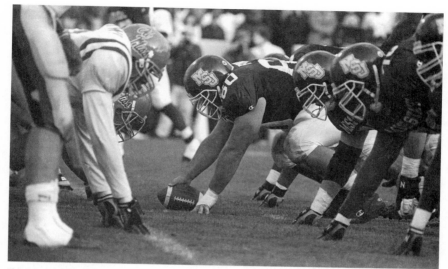

The Rebel defense, left, eyes the Bulldogs just moments before the Dogs get off another play in the '91 game. Courtesy Russ Houston/Mississippi State University.

boost season ticket sales but give the Bulldogs some needed confidence after losing to the Rebels for seven of the preceding eight years. For a change, the Bulldogs came into the game favored by 3 points as a consequence of their home-field advantage, Ole Miss's .500 season, and key injuries suffered by the Rebels. The Bulldogs had the Rebs right where they wanted them. And State did not disappoint its home crowd, keeping Ole Miss out of the end zone until late in the game on the way to an easy 24–9 win.

In the months leading up to the battle, the two coaches had feuded publicly. In February, Rebel coach Billy Brewer had accused Jackie Sherrill of interfering with the recruitment of a player. As the war of words intensified, Brewer called Sherrill a "habitual liar," while Sherrill retorted that Brewer did not know the meaning of *habitual*. Conference officials issued a public reprimand of Brewer and put an end to the overt sniping, but the bad blood remained. Then, on the Monday before the two teams were to meet, the Liberty Bowl invited State to play in that year's contest, dashing

November 23, 1991

Mississippi State 24, Ole Miss 9

	State	Ole Miss
First downs	19	14
Total plays	69	60
Total yards	395	160
Rushes/net yards	61/258	29/33
Passing yards	137	127
Passes		
(Att-Comp-Int)	8-6-1	31-11-2
Punts/average yards	4/35.0	5/31.0
Penalties/yards	10/77	1/5
Fumbles/lost	3/1	2/1
Time of possession	36:02	23:58

Sleepy Robinson scored once, threw for another, and got the Bulldogs downfield for every score and every threat. Mississippi State University Photo.

Ole Miss's hopes of receiving the bid. With the Rebels at 5–5, they could only dream that with a victory over State, another bowl would come a-calling.

More than forty-one thousand fans—the third-largest crowd in the stadium's history—entered Scott Field for the teams' first meeting there in twenty years, while others watched at home on pay-per-view television. State's pregame prayer, a long-standing tradition, was omitted because no matter the opponent, students ended the prayer with a resounding, "Go to hell, Ole Miss!" The Bulldogs came into the game virtually injury-free. In contrast, both Ole Miss quarterbacks, Tom Luke and Russ Shows, were injured, and Luke suffered a concussion on the game's third play that put him out for the rest of the contest.

An early Rebel mistake set the tone for the game. A muffed snap on a punt gave the Bulldogs the ball on the Ole Miss 24, and State quickly drew first blood with a pass from quarterback William (Sleepy) Robinson to Willie Harris in a corner of the end zone The extra-point kick, one of Chris Gardner's three for the day, put the Bulldogs up 7–0. The Dogs recorded another touchdown on their next possession when their strong ground game moved 64 yards in 10 plays. Tay Galloway scored, and State had a 14-point lead before the Rebels even had a first down.

The Bulldogs benefited from a 41-yard return on the second-half kickoff, starting on the Rebel 48 and scoring their third touchdown on a 4-yard bootleg by Robinson. The third quarter was not quite two and a half minutes old, and State was up 21–0.

The Rebels responded with a good kickoff return, a 29-yarder by Tyrone Ashley that enabled the Rebel offense to start on the Ole Miss 46. The Rebels reached the State 28, only to settle for Brian Lee's 45-yard field goal. The Dogs promptly replied with a field goal of their own, this one a 46-yarder by Gardner that put the score at 24–3, Dogs. Ole Miss closed the scoring with an

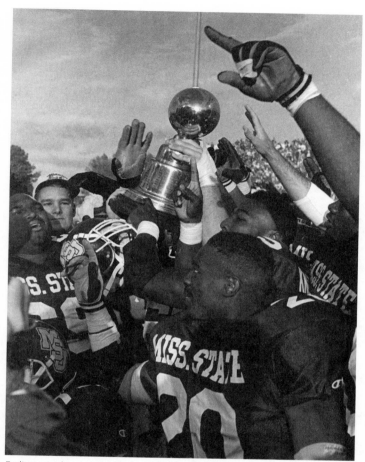

Excitement reigns as celebrating Bulldogs hold high the Golden Egg after their home-field victory over Ole Miss, the first game at Starkville in the rivalry in twenty years. Courtesy Russ Houston/Mississippi State University.

88-yard drive late in the fourth when Shows connected with Darrick Owens for the touchdown, but Lee missed his only extra point of the year. It just was not the Rebels' day. Robinson alone accounted for 216 yards, 56 more than the entire Rebel output.

The happy home team carried Sherrill onto the field and paraded around with the Golden Egg. Sherrill and Brewer engaged in a quick postgame handshake, with no hint of their previous animosity.

State's 7–4 season mark was the school's best in ten years. Fans snapped up more than 26,600 tickets to the Liberty Bowl to help set a new attendance record, but Air Force surprised the favored Bulldogs and took a 38–15 victory.

1992

Eleven Times within the 11

1992 SCHEDULES

Ole Miss 9–3

RESULT	DATE	PF	OPPONENT	PA	LOCATION
W	September 5	45	Auburn	21	Oxford
W	September 12	35	Tulane	9	Oxford
L	September 19	9	Vanderbilt	31	Nashville
L	September 26	11	Georgia	37	Athens
W	October 3	24	Kentucky	14	Oxford
W	October 17	17	Arkansas	3	Little Rock
L	October 24	10	Alabama	31	Tuscaloosa
W	October 31	32	Louisiana State	0	Jackson
W	November 7	17	Memphis State*	12	Oxford
W	November 14	13	Louisiana Tech	6	Oxford
W	November 28	17	Mississippi State	10	Oxford
W	December 31	13	Air Force	0	Liberty Bowl

Mississippi State 7–5

RESULT	DATE	PF	OPPONENT	PA	LOCATION
W	September 5	28	Texas	10	Austin
L	September 12	3	Louisiana State	24	Baton Rouge
W	September 19	20	Memphis State*	16	Memphis
W	October 1	30	Florida	6	Starkville
W	October 10	14	Auburn	7	Starkville
L	October 17	6	South Carolina	21	Columbia
W	October 24	56	Arkansas State	6	Starkville
W	October 31	37	Kentucky	36	Lexington
W	November 7	10	Arkansas	3	Starkville
L	November 14	21	Alabama	30	Starkville
L	November 28	10	Mississippi	17	Oxford
L	January 2 1993	17	North Carolina	21	Peach Bowl

* Now University of Memphis

Rarely have two teams in this rivalry battled so ferociously or have goal-line stands been so fierce. Eleven times in the final three and a half minutes the Bulldogs hammered inside the Ole Miss 11 yard line, and eleven times the frustrated Dogs came away empty-handed. "The Stand,"

Fullback Marvin Courtney scores Ole Miss's first touchdown on a 20-yard pass receipt from quarterback Russ Shows. Courtesy of University of Mississippi Media Relations.

as the *Ole Miss Spirit* dubbed it, made all the difference, enabling Ole Miss to hang on for a 17–10 victory.

The teams were back in Oxford for the first time in twenty years, and for only the fourth time, the game was being televised—this time, regionally, across twelve southern states. The 11:40 A.M. kickoff found 41,200 fans under cloudy skies with temperatures in the low thirties and a mild wind. Both teams had compiled 7–3 records, and for the first time in twenty-nine years, both were bowl-bound. The Associated Press had State at No. 16, with Ole Miss eight spots lower, although the Rebels were a 1½-point favorite.

The Dogs recorded all 10 of their points in just three minutes of the second quarter. After a Rebel fumble and a failed field goal attempt, the Dogs gained new life with another fumble recovery and a personal foul against the Rebels. Fullback Michael Davis powered over from the 7, and Chris Gardner added the extra point. One play

November 28, 1992
Ole Miss 17, Mississippi State 10

	State	Ole Miss
First downs	14	13
Total plays	72	63
Total yards	209	239
Rushes/net yards	41/39	40/166
Passing yards	170	73
Passes		
(Att-Comp-Int)	31-12-1	23-12-2
Punts/average yards	8/39.8	6/34.3
Penalties/yards	5/24	5/31
Fumbles/lost	3/3	5/5
Time of possession	32:21	27:39
Third-down conversions	4/14	6/13
Sacks by: Number/yards	0/0	4/21
Field goals attempted/made	1/1	1/1

Chad Brown throws halfback Randy Brown for a three-yard loss in Play No. 9 of the Rebels' "11 plays within the 11" in closing moments. At right is quarterback Greg Plump. Courtesy of University of Mississippi Media Relations.

later, Charlie Davidson intercepted a pass to set the stage for the Bulldog field goal, a 22-yarder by Gardner.

Just five minutes remained in the half when the Bulldogs fumbled a punt and Danny Boyd recovered the ball at the State 36. The Rebels took only three plays to reach pay dirt, with quarterback Russ Shows connecting with fullback Marvin Courtney for the score and Brian Lee's kick cutting the lead to 10–7. All three first-half scores—two by the Bulldogs and one by the Rebels—had resulted from turnovers. By halftime, the two teams had committed a total of nine, including seven fumbles.

The Rebels took a 14–10 edge with two minutes left in the third period on Cory Philpot's 7-yard scoring jaunt and Lee's extra point. Tony James returned the ensuing kickoff 44 yards, but the Bulldogs could not score, and

Enthusiastic Ole Miss fans attack the north goalpost at Vaught-Hemingway Stadium in celebration of their team's victory. Courtesy Russ Houston/Mississippi State University.

the Rebels tacked on another 3 on their next possession when Lee sent the ball just inside the left upright from 22 yards out. The ensuing 44-yard kick-off return gave the Bulldogs' Tony James a national record for career yardage on punt/kickoff returns. His 199 returns (also a National Collegiate Athletic Association record) had amassed 3,194 yards.

So two possessions later, State had the ball on the Ole Miss 8. In the game now was the Bulldogs' substitute signal-caller, Todd Jordan, in for injured starter Greg Plump, who in turn had replaced William (Sleepy) Robinson, hurt in the season's fourth game.

On Play No. 1, Davis charged the middle for 2 yards. Play No. 2 saw Chad Brown and Cassius Ware bring Jordan down for a loss of 4. Time-out, Bulldogs. 2:35 left to play. Michael Lowery intercepted Jordan's third-down pass in the end zone and returned the ball to the 3-yard line. Two plays later, Philpot fumbled, Frankie Luster recovered, and the Bulldogs had the ball again on the 8. Two incomplete passes and a loss of 3 brought up Play No. 7, where interference on a fourth-down pass put the ball on the Rebel 2. With first down, the Bulldog attack had new life. Could the Rebels hold on again?

With Plump back in at quarterback, Randy Brown picked up a yard, then lost three on Plays No. 8 and 9. With forty-seven seconds left, the Dogs called their last time-out. Plump's third-down naked bootleg lost 2. Fourth down; twenty-four seconds remaining. Plump faded and threw under pressure. Willie Harris was open in the end zone, but the pass was wide and Harris could get only one hand on the elusive ball. Game, Rebels. Enthusiastic fans attacked the goalposts.

The win garnered Ole Miss an invitation to face Air Force in the Liberty Bowl. The result was a 13–0 Rebel victory, the first time the Falcons had been shut out in 150 games. State went to the Peach Bowl, played for the first time inside the new Georgia Dome, where the Bulldogs built a two-touchdown lead against North Carolina. However, State failed to hold the advantage, and the Tar Heels came back to win, 21–17. Ole Miss finished the season at No. 10 in the *New York Times* Poll, while the Associated Press had Ole Miss at No. 16 and State at No. 23, the first time since 1965 that both schools closed the season in the Top 25.

1993

Davis Has a Blast

1993 SCHEDULES

Ole Miss 6–5

RESULT	DATE	PF	OPPONENT	PA	LOCATION
L	September 2	12	Auburn	16	Auburn
W	September 11	40	Tennessee-Chattanooga	7	Oxford
W	September 18	49	Vanderbilt	7	Oxford
W	September 25	31	Georgia	14	Oxford
L	October 2	0	Kentucky	21	Lexington
W	October 16	19	Arkansas	0	Jackson
W	October 23	14	Alabama*	19	Oxford
L	October 30	17	Louisiana State	19	Baton Rouge
L	November 6	3	Memphis State**	19	Memphis
W	November 13	44	Northern Illinois	0	Oxford
L	November 27	13	Mississippi State	20	Starkville

Mississippi State 4–5–2

RESULT	DATE	PF	OPPONENT	PA	LOCATION
L	September 4	35	Memphis State**	45	Starkville
L	September 11	16	Louisiana State	18	Starkville
W	September 25	36	Tulane	10	New Orleans
L	October 2	24	Florida	38	Gainesville
L	October 9	17	Auburn	31	Auburn
W	October 16	23	South Carolina	0	Starkville
T	October 23	15	Arkansas State	15	Starkville
L	October 30	17	Kentucky	26	Starkville
T	November 6	13	Arkansas	13	Little Rock
W	November 13	25	Alabama*	36	Tuscaloosa
W	November 27	20	Mississippi	13	Starkville

* Forfeited by order of NCAA
** Now University of Memphis

A t the end of the 1993 season, the Rebel defense was ranked No. 1 in the country. But they couldn't stop Michael Davis. Against Ole Miss, the Bulldog tailback carried forty times for 154 yards and a touchdown to lead his team to a 20–13 victory before a hometown crowd of 40,328 on a cool November afternoon.

Bulldogs' Davis rules

Despite threats such as Dewayne Dotson (33), Michael Davis's 40 carries for the Bulldogs tied a 44-year-old rivalry record and gained 154 yards. *Clarion-Ledger*, November 28, 1993.

Davis staked his team to a 7–0 lead, carrying the ball on eight of the possession's nine plays, including the 1-yard score. Juan Long set up the drive with a 45-yard interception return, and Tom Burke kicked the extra point. The Rebels immediately narrowed the margin to 4 with a 42-yard field goal by Tim Montz.

The Bulldogs' Eric Moulds returned the kickoff to the Mississippi State 43, and Davis carried the ball across midfield to the Ole Miss 49. With almost three minutes remaining in the first quarter, Davis already had nearly 50 yards. State took advantage of the situation with a flea-flicker that fooled the Rebels: Davis took

November 27, 1993
Mississippi State 20, Ole Miss 13

	State	Ole Miss
First downs	18	14
Total plays	65	66
Total yards	279	227
Rushes/net yards	46/143	43/135
Passing yards	136	92
Passes		
(Att-Comp-Int)	19-7-0	23-11-1
Punts/average yards	6/43.7	8/37.9
Penalties/yards	9/65	8/80
Fumbles/lost	3/3	1/0
Time of possession	29:09	30:51
Third-down conversions	3/13	5/16
Sacks by: Number/yards	2/18	1/8
Field goals attempted/made	2/2	2/2

Receiver Eric Moulds celebrates his 49-yard catch that gives the Bulldogs their second touchdown. *Clarion-Ledger*, November 28, 1993.

the handoff, but instead of running behind the fullback, his specialty play, he flipped the ball back to quarterback Todd Jordan, who threw a perfect pass to Moulds for 6 more points. Another Burke kick put the Dogs up 14–3.

The Rebs got right back in the game with a touchdown at the beginning of the second quarter. The Bulldogs fumbled a punt return, and Kyle Wicker recovered the ball for the Rebels on the State 13. Quarterback Lawrence Adams found wide receiver Roell Preston on the 5, and Preston spun just inside the right pylon for the touchdown. Montz kicked to make the score State 14, Ole Miss 10. The Bulldogs committed another error, fumbling a handoff, and the Rebels took advantage to add a 20-yard Montz field goal to get within a point of their archrivals. But with about six minutes to go before the half, State extended its lead back to 4 with a 49-yard field goal by Burke. At halftime, the scoreboard showed State up, 17–13. For the fourth straight year, the Bulldogs had a lead midway through the Egg Bowl, but so far, only one of those leads had lasted through the fourth quarter.

This one held up, as the Bulldog defense, ranked just tenth in the Southeastern Conference, came up big, holding the Rebels without a first down during the third quarter. The Bulldog offense padded the lead with another Burke field goal—this time, from 37 yards out—and the teams went to the fourth quarter with State ahead, 20–13.

The Rebels' last chance to score included their own trick play. Renard Brown lined up behind the left guard as an extra fullback, Adams slipped Brown the ball, and the fullback faked a block for a count of three before heading around left end. By the time the Bulldogs sorted through the confusion and strong safety Frankie Luster tackled Brown, he had gained 18 yards. Even with the trickery, the Rebels could not reach the end zone, however, and the Bulldogs had the win.

1994

Ten Minutes, 38 Points

1994 SCHEDULES

Ole Miss 4–7

RESULT	DATE	PF	OPPONENT	PA	LOCATION
L	September 3	17	Auburn	22	Oxford
W	September 10	59	Southern Illinois	3	Oxford
W	September 17	20	Vanderbilt	14	Nashville
L	September 24	14	Georgia	17	Athens
L	October 1	14	Florida	38	Oxford
L	October 15	7	Arkansas	31	Fayetteville
L	October 22	10	Alabama	21	Tuscaloosa
W	October 29	34	Louisiana State	21	Oxford
L	November 5	16	Memphis	17	Oxford
W	November 12	38	Tulane	0	New Orleans
L	November 26	17	Mississippi State	21	Oxford

Mississippi State 8–4

RESULT	DATE	PF	OPPONENT	PA	LOCATION
W	September 3	17	Memphis	6	Memphis
L	September 10	24	Louisiana State	44	Baton Rouge
W	September 24	24	Tennessee	21	Starkville
W	October 1	49	Arkansas State	3	Starkville
L	October 8	18	Auburn	42	Starkville
W	October 15	41	South Carolina	36	Columbia
W	October 22	66	Tulane	22	Starkville
W	October 29	47	Kentucky	7	Lexington
W	November 5	17	Arkansas	7	Starkville
L	November 12	25	Alabama	29	Starkville
W	November 26	21	Mississippi	17	Oxford
L	January 1, 1995	24	North Carolina State	28	Peach Bowl

If you missed the second quarter, you missed the scoring. All of the Bulldogs' 21 points and all of the Rebels' 17 came in one ten-minute span. Five touchdowns. Two field goals. Seven lead changes.

The rest of the game kept fans fascinated, too—three missed field goal attempts, a fumble in the shadow of the goal, a touchdown-saving tackle, and

Receiver Roell Preston scores Ole Miss's first touchdown on a 30-yard catch from quarterback Josh Nelson. Photo by J. D. Schwalm for the *Clarion-Ledger*, November 27, 1994.

two interceptions. It all added up to the second-most yardage ever accumulated in an Ole Miss–State contest.

The Bulldogs were 7–3 for the season, ranked nineteenth in the Associated Press Poll and headed for a postseason bowl. In Oxford, however, the news was worse. Head football coach Billy Brewer had been fired over the summer after the National Collegiate Athletic Association began investigating the school's recruiting practices and found rules violations that led to sanctions against Ole Miss: a reduction in football scholarships and bans on TV and bowl appearances. The Rebels' interim coach, defensive coordinator Joe Lee Dunn, had guided the team to only four wins. The odds favored the Bulldogs.

More than 36,500 fans turned out on a mild afternoon with temperatures in the fifties. They saw an exchange of threats during the first fifteen minutes, but neither side could score until that wild second quarter. The Bulldogs went first, recording a field goal on a 27-yard kick by Tim Davis to cap a 74-yard drive. 3–0, State. The Rebels surged ahead on the third play from scrimmage on the following drive, a pass from quarterback Josh Nelson to split end Roell Preston. The drive ate up just thirty-six seconds on the clock, and Tim Montz's first extra point kick of the day gave Mississippi the 7–3 edge.

The Dogs came right back with a three-play drive of their own that consumed only fifty-four seconds. Quarterback Derrick Taite completed two passes for 70 yards to take the ball to the Ole Miss 1, and Kevin Bouie smashed over on the next play. After the extra-point kick failed, Mississippi State was back on top, 9–7.

Yet another three-play drive followed, with this one highlighted by an 83-yard scoring pass from Nelson to flanker LeMay Thomas. In just sixty seconds, the Rebels had seized back the lead. Montz nailed the extra point to make the score Ole Miss 14, State 9.

On the kick off, the Rebels attempted to boot the ball away from Eric Moulds, who led the nation in kickoff returns. But Moulds fielded the ball anyway and raced 52 yards to the Rebel 41. From there, the Dogs needed a relatively long 2:25 and six plays to reach the end zone, with Michael Davis contributing the 4-yard scoring run. After the 2-point conversion failed, the scoreboard showed State 15, Ole Miss 14.

Next, Thomas nearly matched Moulds, returning the kickoff 47 yards to the State 45. After three straight touchdown drives, the Rebels broke the pattern, managing only a Montz field goal on this possession. Still, the 3-pointer gave the lead back to Ole Miss, 17–14. The Dogs closed out the dizzying second-quarter scoring with a nine-play, 67-yard drive. Bouie notched his second touchdown of the game, and despite the unsuccessful 2-point conversion, State had a 21–17 lead.

November 26, 1994
Mississippi State 21, Ole Miss 17

	State	Ole Miss
First downs	27	16
Total plays	82	72
Total yards	471	394
Rushes/net yards	62/304	33/101
Passing yards	167	293
Passes		
(Att-Comp-Int)	20-9-2	39-17-0
Punts/average yards	2/43.0	6/31.3
Penalties/yards	3/25	7/65
Fumbles/lost	2/2	1/0
Time of possession	35:44	24:16
Third-down conversions	8/15	7/19
Sacks by: Number/yards	1/10	0/0
Field goals attempted/made	2/1	3/1

On this foggy day Kevin Bouie finds extra running room as part of the game-high 141 yards this Bulldog compiled. Rebel co-captain Abdul Jackson is No. 53. *Northeast Mississippi Daily Journal,* November 27, 1994.

Both defenses tightened in the second half, and both teams failed to capitalize on opportunities. Nursing a badly bruised hand, Nelson connected on only four of sixteen second-half passes, and the Rebels missed a 31-yard field goal. For their part, the Dogs squandered four scoring chances by four different means: an interception, a fumble, a miss on a 47-yard field goal attempt, and a stalled drive. Final score, State 21, Ole Miss 17.

The Bulldogs and Rebels combined for 865 yards on the afternoon, the second-highest total in rivalry records. Nearly half of that yardage (401) had come in the second quarter. The win gave State eight victories for the first time since 1976, and the Associated Press had the Bulldogs at No. 16. In the Peach Bowl, State recorded a touchdown, five field goals, and a safety against North Carolina State but fell, 28–24. In the final Associated Press Poll of the year, State came in at No. 24, while CNN had the Bulldogs twenty-fifth.

In December, Ole Miss officials announced the selection of forty-year-old Tommy Tuberville as the school's new head coach. Tuberville, a graduate of Southern Arkansas, had most recently served as defensive coordinator at Texas A&M and had previously held that position at Miami and been assistant head coach at Arkansas State.

1995

Dooooouuu!

1995 SCHEDULES

Ole Miss 6–5

RESULT	DATE	PF	OPPONENT	PA	LOCATION
L	September 2	13	Auburn	46	Auburn
W	September 9	56	Indiana State	10	Oxford
W	September 23	18	Georgia	10	Oxford
L	September 30	10	Florida	28	Gainesville
W	October 7	20	Tulane	17	Oxford
L	October 14	6	Arkansas	13	Memphis
L	October 21	9	Alabama	23	Oxford
W	October 28	21	Vanderbilt	10	Oxford
W	November 4	34	Memphis	3	Memphis
L	November 11	9	Louisiana State	38	Baton Rouge
W	November 25	13	Mississippi State	10	Starkville

Mississippi State 3–8

RESULT	DATE	PF	OPPONENT	PA	LOCATION
W	September 2	28	Memphis	18	Starkville
L	September 9	16	Louisiana State	34	Starkville
W	September 16	30	Baylor	21	Waco
L	September 23	14	Tennessee	52	Knoxville
L	September 30	32	Louisiana-Monroe	34	Starkville
L	October 7	20	Auburn	48	Auburn
L	October 14	39	South Carolina	65	Starkville
W	October 28	42	Kentucky	32	Starkville
L	November 4	21	Arkansas	26	Little Rock
L	November 11	9	Alabama	14	Tuscaloosa
L	November 25	10	Mississippi	13	Starkville

The day started perfectly for Mississippi State. The school was celebrating the football program's one hundredth anniversary. Not only were the Bulldogs playing at home under clear skies with the temperature in the mid-fifties and a light breeze, but they had scored on their first two possessions to take a 10–0 lead halfway through the first quarter. The touchdown had come on a 17-yard pass from quarterback Derrick Taite to tight end John

Dou Innocent (22) bursts through a big hole that Greg Favors (56) and Izell McGill (23) rush to close. *Ole Miss Spirit*, December 2, 1995.

Jennings, and Tim Rogers had booted the extra point. A field goal followed, with Brian Hazelwood kicking from 49 yards out. The defense had held the Rebels to just one three-and-out possession where they gained only a single yard. When the Dogs intercepted a pass on the Rebels' next possession and the State offense took over at the Ole Miss 43, the lead looked like it was about to grow even larger. But this time, the Rebel defense held. On came the Ole Miss offense, led by Dou (pronounced *Doo*) Innocent. Marching 95 yards over the next five and a half minutes, the Rebels got back in the game on Innocent's 6-yard touchdown blast, prompting the Ole Miss fans in the crowd to chant "Doooouuu!" Tim Montz's point after cut the Bulldog lead to just 3 with about half of the second quarter remaining.

After the Bulldogs' next offensive series, the Rebs got the ball back on their 6 yard line with only 1:54 to go in the first half. Inspired by a Bulldog penalty and Innocent's carries, the Rebels reached the State 29 with the clock showing one second. Montz easily drilled a field goal from 46 yards away, and the score was knotted 10 all at the half.

November 25, 1995

Ole Miss 13, Mississippi State 10

	State	Ole Miss
First downs	14	20
Total plays	58	67
Total yards	242	351
Rushes/net yards	28/63	47/243
Passing yards	179	108
Passes		
(Att-Comp-Int)	30-13-1	20-9-1
Punts/average yards	6/42.0	5/39.0
Penalties/yards	12/127	5/69
Fumbles/lost	1/0	1/0
Time of possession	27:46	32:14

Rebs Dou it to 'Dogs 13-10

Rebels out-Dou Bulldogs, 13-10

Headlines from *Northeast Mississippi Daily Journal*, November 26, 1995, and *Dawgs' Bite*, November 27, 1995.

Neither team could add points in the third quarter, and the Rebels' winning drive began with 11:49 left to play in the game. Innocent carried six times on the eight-play, 55-yard effort, reaching the 12 on a 28-yard scamper. Montz came in and kicked, this time from 29 yards away, and with 7:25 left, Ole Miss had a 3-point advantage. The Bulldogs could not mount scoring drives on their final two possessions, and the Rebels held on for the win, 13–10.

Newspaper headlines had a field day with the name of the Rebels' leading rusher: "Innocent no bystander as Ole Miss kicks Miss. State"; "Rebels out-Dou Bulldogs, 13–10." With 242 yards on the ground, Innocent broke the Ole Miss–State rushing record held by John (Kayo) Dottley. And Innocent's thirty-nine carries brought him within one of the rivalry record set by Dottley (1949) and tied by Mississippi State's Michael Davis (1993). Innocent also topped all Bulldog carriers combined.

Doooouuu!

1996

Defense Dogs the Rebels

1996 SCHEDULES

Ole Miss 5–6

RESULT	DATE	PF	OPPONENT	PA	LOCATION
W	August 31	38	Idaho State	14	Oxford
W	September 7	31	Virginia Military Institute	7	Jackson
L	September 14	28	Auburn	45	Oxford
W	September 21	20	Vanderbilt	9	Nashville
L	October 3	3	Tennessee	41	Memphis
L	October 19	0	Alabama	37	Tuscaloosa
W	October 26	38	Arkansas State	21	Oxford
L	November 9	7	Arkansas	13	Fayetteville
L	November 16	7	Louisiana State	39	Oxford
W	November 23	31	Georgia	27	Athens
L	November 30	0	Mississippi State	17	Oxford

Mississippi State 5–6

RESULT	DATE	PF	OPPONENT	PA	LOCATION
W	September 7	31	Memphis	10	Memphis
L	September 21	23	Louisiana Tech	38	Starkville
W	September 28	14	South Carolina	10	Columbia
L	October 5	19	Georgia	38	Starkville
L	October 12	15	Auburn	49	Starkville
L	October 26	20	Louisiana State	28	Baton Rouge
W	November 2	59	Louisiana-Monroe	0	Starkville
L	November 9	21	Kentucky	24	Lexington
W	November 16	17	Alabama	16	Starkville
L	November 23	13	Arkansas	16	Starkville
W	November 30	17	Mississippi	0	Oxford

They might as well have left the offense back in Starkville. It wasn't needed. The Mississippi State defense turned in a magnificent performance on a slippery, rain-flooded field, holding the Rebels scoreless and recording both interception and fumble returns for touchdowns as well as a safety in a 17–0 pasting. It represented State's first shutout of Ole Miss in fifty years.

State's Tim Nelson breaks up a sure touchdown pass as Ole Miss's Ta'Boris Fisher reaches for the elusive ball. *Northeast Mississippi Daily Journal*, December 1, 1996.

The heavier Bulldogs entered the game favored by 2½ points, and the wet conditions only added to their advantage against the Rebels' finesse attack. Injuries had dogged the Dogs all year—forty-nine different players had started for State—but quarterback Derrick Taite had anchored the team on his way to eleven school passing records. Nearing the end of their two-year National Collegiate Athletic Association probation, the Rebel team had only forty-nine scholarship players and twelve walk-ons, leaving Ole Miss with a decided personnel disadvantage.

The game was telecast regionally, resulting in another morning kick-off. Well over 36,000 tickets had

November 30, 1996
Mississippi State 17, Ole Miss 0

	State	Ole Miss
First downs	10	15
Total plays	66	68
Total yards	255	208
Rushes/net yards	40/161	41/145
Passing yards	109	156
Passes		
(Att-Comp-Int)	26-10-1	27-10-1
Punts/average yards	8/37.5	7/33.6
Penalties/yards	10/108	4/35
Fumbles/lost	1/1	4/3
Time of possession	31:58	28:02
Third-down conversions	6/18	6/19
Sacks by: Number/yards	9/80	1/8
Field goals attempted/made	2/0	2/0

Greg Favors (56) and Paul LaCoste (20) bring down a scrambling John Avery in the end zone to register two points for the Bulldogs. It was the first safety in this rivalry in thirty-six years. *Clarion-Ledger,* December 1, 1996.

been sold, but the weather situation reduced attendance to 23,678, the smallest since 1967.

The Rebel offense had early success in moving the ball, entering Mississippi State territory on three occasions but coming away empty-handed each time. The Bulldog offense managed just one early foray onto the Ole Miss side but got as far as the 8 before an end-zone interception halted the threat. Midway through the second quarter, however, with the ball on the Ole Miss 6, Rebel quarterback Stewart Patridge threw a short pass to his right. Bulldog safety Eric Brown batted the ball, juggled it once, and hauled it in. Thirteen yards later, he was in the end zone. Brian Hazelwood's extra-point kick put State up by 7. Late in the half, the Rebels drove 70 yards to the Mississippi State 20, where Tim Montz's field goal attempt was wide, and State retained its one-touchdown lead at the half.

The rain slackened after the break, but the Bulldog defense did not. The Rebels were struggling on their own 4 yard line on their opening possession when the Bulldogs' Greg Favors tackled John Avery in the end zone for a safety—the first in this rivalry in thirty-six years. 9–0. With under a minute to go in the game and the line of scrimmage the Mississippi State 28, Brown forced Patridge to fumble. Bulldog tackle Kevin Sluder scooped up the pig-

A watery splash typical of the day finds Chris Rainey holding onto the slippery ball despite the attack of Rebel tacklers. *Northeast Mississippi Daily Journal*, December 1, 1996.

skin and sprinted 60 yards for the final touchdown. Matt Wyatt got 2 points on a keeper, and the Bulldogs had their 17–0 shellacking.

The Bulldog defenders had recovered four fumbles to go with their interception. They had sacked the Ole Miss quarterback nine times and had dropped Rebel runners for a loss fourteen times, costing Ole Miss 93 yards. For good measure, State also blocked a field goal attempt. The architect of this dominant performance was State's defensive coordinator, Joe Lee Dunn, who had previously held that position at Ole Miss and had served as the school's interim head coach in 1994. He found his new team's performance against the old "gratifying," he grinned after the game.

1997

Go for Two

1997 SCHEDULES

Ole Miss 8–4

RESULT	DATE	PF	OPPONENT	PA	LOCATION
W	August 30	24	Central Florida	23	Oxford
W	September 6	23	Southern Methodist	15	Oxford
L	September 13	9	Auburn	19	Auburn
W	September 27	15	Vanderbilt	3	Oxford
L	October 4	17	Tennessee	31	Knoxville
W	October 18	36	Louisiana State	21	Baton Rouge
L	October 25	20	Alabama	29	Oxford
W	November 6	19	Arkansas	9	Oxford
W	November 15	41	Tulane	24	New Orleans
L	November 22	14	Georgia	21	Oxford
W	November 29	15	Mississippi State	14	Starkville
W	December 26	34	Marshall	31	Motor City Bowl

Mississippi State 7–4

RESULT	DATE	PF	OPPONENT	PA	LOCATION
W	August 30	13	Memphis	10	Starkville
W	September 6	35	Kentucky	27	Starkville
L	September 13	9	Louisiana State	24	Starkville
W	September 27	37	South Carolina	17	Starkville
L	October 4	0	Georgia	47	Athens
W	October 11	24	Louisiana-Monroe	10	Starkville
W	October 25	35	Central Florida	28	Starkville
W	November 1	20	Auburn	0	Auburn
W	November 15	32	Alabama	20	Tuscaloosa
L	November 22	7	Arkansas	17	Fayetteville
L	November 29	14	Mississippi	15	Starkville

Twenty-five seconds to play. The Rebels have just scored a touchdown to make the score Ole Miss 13, State 14. Coach Tommy Tuberville has a big decision to make: attempt an extra-point kick for a tie and over-time, or go for the 2-point conversion and a win? The Rebs may be faster than

Andre Rone scored both Ole Miss touchdowns on pass receipts. For the day Rone averaged 15 yards per catch on five receipts. *Northeast Mississippi Daily Journal*, November 30, 1997.

the Dogs, but they're smaller. And they're playing on the Dogs' home field. Worse, the Rebels are about spent.

Tough call? Tuberville quickly opted to go for 2. And when quarterback Stewart Patridge found Cory Peterson in the end zone, Ole Miss went home 15–14 winners as darkness fell on 33,200 stunned fans.

With State at 7–3 and ranked No. 22 and Ole Miss at 6–4, both were assured of winning records and were hoping for bowl bids. The Bulldogs' season had peaked with a No. 15 ranking after victories over Auburn (ranked eleventh at

November 29, 1997
Ole Miss 15, Mississippi State 14

	State	Ole Miss
First downs	18	17
Total plays	65	67
Total yards	295	359
Rushes/net yards	45/209	33/125
Passing yards	86	234
Passes		
(Att-Comp-Int)	20-10-2	34-20-2
Punts/average yards	6/45.0	7/39.6
Penalties/yards	1/15	9/72
Fumbles/lost	0/0	0/0
Time of possession	29:51	30:09
Third-down conversions	4/14	5/15
Sacks by: Number/yards	1/6	0/0

A barrage of tacklers brings down J. J. Johnson on one of 21 carries. Johnson rushed for 119 yards for the Bulldogs and scored once. *Northeast Mississippi Daily Journal*, November 30, 1997.

the time) and Alabama; coming off a .500 season and a National Collegiate Athletic Association–imposed probation, the Rebels felt that they were headed in the right direction.

The ninety-fourth meeting between the two Mississippi rivals got off on the wrong foot, with a fight between players warming up about forty minutes before kickoff. Coaches, game officials, and officers from the Mississippi Highway Patrol calmed things down, but officials required the teams to enter and leave their adjoining dressing rooms separately for the rest of the day.

With light rain falling, the Rebs took the opening kickoff 71 yards for a touchdown. Quarterback Stewart Patridge frequently ended practice sessions by tossing a wet ball, a habit that paid off early in this game. From the Mississippi

State 35, Patridge had no trouble hitting halfback Andre Rone, open on the 13. Touchdown, Rebels. After Steve Lindsey's kick, the scoreboard read 7–0.

Three possessions later, the Bulldogs tied the game with a five-play, 34-yard drive set up by Robert Isaac's 25-yard punt return. With the ball on the 5, quarterback Rob Morgan found John Jennings in the end zone, and Brian Hazelwood knotted the score with less than five minutes remaining in the half.

The third quarter was nearly two-thirds gone when the Bulldog defense opened the way for the second Mississippi State touchdown. Izell McGill's interception on the Ole Miss 47 set the Dogs up, and they needed just eight plays to get the go-ahead score on James (J. J.) Johnson's 1-yard run. Hazelwood's kick upped the advantage to 14–7.

The teams exchanged missed field goal attempts, and the Bulldogs held onto their 7-point lead until just 2:12 remained in the fourth quarter. Ole Miss had the ball on its own 36. Patridge would be fighting not only the Bulldog defense but also the clock. Over the next 1:47, Patridge, whose father, Jim Patridge, had played for State in 1969–71, completed six of nine passes, moving his team relentlessly downfield. Rone caught his second scoring pass of the day—this one from 10 yards out—and Tuberville had his decision to make.

The Dogs still had one last chance. After the Rebel kickoff, State had the ball on its own 36 with twenty-two seconds to go. A penalty against the Rebels moved the ball to midfield with thirteen seconds to play. Fifteen more yards, and the Bulldogs would be in position to have Hazelwood attempt the game-winning field goal. But Tim Strickland came out of nowhere to intercept Matt Wyatt's throw with the clock showing 0:03, and the Rebels had their victory.

Although both squads finished the year at 7–4, season-ending consecutive losses marred the Bulldog record, and only the Rebels received an invitation to go bowling. Ole Miss faced Marshall in the first Motor City Bowl, held in Pontiac, Michigan, and came away with a 34–31 win. Postseason polls rated Ole Miss No. 22.

1998

Under the Lights

1998 SCHEDULES

Ole Miss 7–5

RESULT	DATE	PF	OPPONENT	PA	LOCATION
W	September 5	30	Memphis	10	Oxford
L	September 12	0	Auburn	17	Oxford
W	September 19	30	Vanderbilt	6	Nashville
W	September 26	48	Southern Methodist	41	Dallas
W	October 3	30	South Carolina	28	Oxford
L	October 10	17	Alabama	20	Tuscaloosa
W	October 24	30	Arkansas State	17	Oxford
W	October 31	37	Louisiana State	31	Oxford
L	November 7	0	Arkansas	34	Fayetteville
L	November 21	17	Georgia	24	Athens
L	November 26	6	Mississippi State	28	Oxford
W	December 31	35	Texas Tech	18	Independence Bowl

Mississippi State 8–5

RESULT	DATE	PF	OPPONENT	PA	LOCATION
W	September 5	42	Vanderbilt	0	Starkville
W	September 12	14	Memphis	6	Memphis
L	September 19	23	Oklahoma State	42	Stillwater
W	September 26	38	South Carolina	0	Columbia
W	October 10	38	Auburn	21	Starkville
W	October 17	53	East Tennessee State	6	Starkville
L	October 24	6	Louisiana State	41	Baton Rouge
L	November 7	35	Kentucky	37	Lexington
W	November 14	26	Alabama	14	Starkville
W	November 21	22	Arkansas	21	Starkville
W	November 26	28	Mississippi	6	Oxford
L	December 5	14	Tennessee	24	Atlanta
L	January 1	11	Texas	38	Cotton Bowl

Although the Bulldogs and Rebels had squared off at ten different locations in seven cities, they had never played each other at night. Until now. With the game scheduled for Thanksgiving Day for the first time in twenty-seven years, a national television audience would get to witness the South's fiercest football rivalry in its first incarnation under the lights.

Twin acts! Ole Miss's Sheldon Morris and State's Robert Bean perform a duel grab at a Rebel pass in the first quarter before the elusive ball falls to the ground. *Northeast Mississippi Daily Journal*, November 27, 1998.

A win would give the twenty-fifth-ranked Bulldogs the championship of the Southeastern Conference's Western Division. That prize proved to be a powerful motivator. State scored in every quarter, kept the Rebels out of the end zone, and thrashed Ole Miss 28–6.

November 28, 1998
Mississippi State 28, Ole Miss 6

	State	Ole Miss
First downs	14	16
Total plays	60	73
Total yards	287	265
Rushes/net yards	40/123	49/190
Passing yards	164	75
Passes		
(Att-Comp-Int)	20-7-1	24-8-3
Punts/average yards	6/35.8	5/39.6
Penalties/yards	5/55	6/37
Fumbles/lost	0/0	1/0
Time of possession	25:25	34:35

Vaught-Hemingway Stadium had just been expanded with club seating, and even the new seats were nearly filled by the 50,412 in attendance. To prevent a recurrence of the previous year's pregame fisticuffs, assistant coaches formed a cordon to prevent contact between the two teams during warm-ups.

The Rebels were in bad physical shape. Starting quarterback Romaro Miller had suffered a broken col-

The Bulldogs' J. J. Johnson hits the end zone for the first of his two touchdowns as Eddie Strong leaps to avoid an illegal hit. *Clarion-Ledger*, November 27, 1998.

larbone on the last play of the previous week's game, and freshman David Morris, a walk-on who had generaled exactly five plays all season, was called on to take command. Nevertheless, the Rebs scored first, taking the opening kickoff and driving for a 40-yard Carlisle McGee field goal. The 3–0 lead was short-lived, however: after Ole Miss punted on its next possession, the Bulldogs needed only five plays to go 44 yards for a touchdown. Quarterback Wayne Madkin connected with flanker Kevin Prentiss for a 39-yard gain, and James (J. J.) Johnson took the ball over from the 2 for the touchdown. Brian Hazelwood kicked the first of his four extra points on the night, and State was ahead 7–3.

The Bulldogs' notched their second touchdown with a fifteen-play, 98-yard drive capped by another Johnson scoring plunge, this one on fourth down. Johnson separated his shoulder on the play, however, and did not return to the game. With less than two minutes to go in the first half, Ole Miss cut the margin to 14–6 with a 72-yard drive that culminated in McGee's 22-yard field goal. But the Rebels never got any closer. The second half belonged entirely to the Bulldogs.

The third Bulldog touchdown came on a 28-yard pass from Madkin to Dicenzo Miller—Miller's only catch of the year. A gift touchdown with about two and a half minutes to play rounded out the scoring. Rebel quarterback David Morris threw a ball that bounced off receiver Grant Heard's knee and into the arms of the Bulldogs' Tim Nelson, who cruised into the end zone.

Pregame publicity had focused on No. 22 for both teams—State's Johnson and his Ole Miss counterpart at running back, D. J. (Deuce) McAllister. With Johnson's running room hampered by the absence of three State offensive linemen and his day cut short by injury, he accumulated only 34 yards on nine carries, although he did score twice. McAllister tied an Egg Bowl record with forty carries and racked up an impressive 177 yards. Johnson finished the year with 1,383 yards, McAllister 1,082.

In addition to the Western Division championship, the victory of course brought the Bulldogs the Golden Egg. "There's no better way to finish the regular season," pointed out Prentiss. "It was a packed house, Thursday night on ESPN, on their home field."

As the final seconds ticked down, Bulldog fans chanted not only "S-E-C, S-E-C" but also "Goodbye, Tommy" in response to rumors that Coach Tuberville was considering leaving Ole Miss. The next day, he was at Auburn, negotiating the head coach's job. As his replacement, Ole Miss officials chose David Cutcliffe, an assistant head coach at Tennessee who had just won the Broyles Award as the nation's top assistant.

State had two more games left on its season slate. First came the Southeastern Conference championship game in Atlanta, where the Bulldogs went up against Tennessee—and David Cutcliffe, who was finishing out the season with the Vols before coming to Oxford. No. 1–ranked Tennessee defeated Mississippi State 26–14 and went on to the national championship after a victory over No. 2 Florida State in the Fiesta Bowl.

The No. 23–ranked Bulldogs closed out the season on New Year's Day with their first appearance in the Cotton Bowl. Despite Johnson's return and his 112 yards rushing, the Texas Longhorns and Heisman Trophy winner Ricky Williams were too much for State, and Texas won, 38–11. The night before, the Rebels had made their third appearance in the Independence Bowl, where a 35–18 win over Texas Tech gave Cutcliffe his first victory at Ole Miss.

1999

An Unbelievable Comeback

1999 SCHEDULES

Ole Miss 8–4

RESULT	DATE	PF	OPPONENT	PA	LOCATION
W	September 4	3	Memphis	0	Memphis
W	September 11	38	Arkansas State	14	Oxford
L	September 18	34	Vanderbilt	37	Oxford
W	September 25	24	Auburn	17	Auburn
W	October 2	36	South Carolina	10	Columbia
W	October 9	20	Tulane	13	Oxford
L	October 16	24	Alabama	30	Oxford
W	October 30	42	Louisiana State	23	Baton Rouge
W	November 6	38	Arkansas	16	Oxford
L	November 20	17	Georgia	20	Oxford
L	November 25	20	Mississippi State	23	Starkville
W	December 31	27	Oklahoma	25	Independence Bowl

Mississippi State 10–2

RESULT	DATE	PF	OPPONENT	PA	LOCATION
W	September 4	40	Middle Tennessee State	7	Starkville
W	September 11	13	Memphis	10	Starkville
W	September 18	29	Oklahoma State	11	Starkville
W	September 25	17	South Carolina	0	Starkville
W	October 2	42	Vanderbilt	14	Nashville
W	October 9	18	Auburn	16	Auburn
W	October 23	17	Louisiana State	16	Starkville
W	November 4	23	Kentucky	22	Starkville
L	November 13	7	Alabama	19	Tuscaloosa
L	November 20	9	Arkansas	14	Little Rock
W	November 25	23	Mississippi	20	Starkville
W	December 30	17	Clemson	7	Peach Bowl

D own by two touchdowns at the end of three quarters, the Bulldogs scored 17 unanswered points, staging one of the most amazing comebacks in this rivalry to take a 23–20 victory. The explosive ending ignited a wild celebration at Scott Field, but it should not have surprised Mississippi State fans. It was the Bulldogs' fourth late come-from-behind rally

Unbelievable

Scott Westerfield's 44-yard field goal gives State another zany come-from-behind victory

Headline from *Northeast Mississippi Daily Journal*, November 26, 1999.

of the season, following consecutive narrow victories over Auburn, Louisiana State, and Kentucky, all of whom had led State with under two minutes to go.

The weather was chilly and misty for the second consecutive Thanksgiving night meeting on national television between Mississippi State and Ole Miss. Both the No. 18–ranked Bulldogs and the No. 23–ranked Rebels remained very much in the bowl picture. For three quarters, the Bulldogs played sloppy football, committing four fumbles and throwing two interceptions. Three of those miscues led to Ole Miss points, while a fourth almost certainly deprived State of points.

The Rebels jumped into the lead on their first possession of the second quarter when quarterback Romaro Miller zeroed on wide receiver Maurice Flournoy for an easy 30-yard touchdown strike. Les Binkley, 100 percent accurate all year, kicked the first of two extra points, and the Rebels were in front, 7–0.

Eddie Strong then intercepted Bulldog quarterback Wayne Madkin's pass to give the Rebels the ball on the Bulldog 35, and Binkley's 32-yard kick upped the lead to 10–0 with 4:19 remaining in the half. That was plenty of time for the Bulldogs to drive 68 yards in eight plays for a touchdown on Dicenzo Miller's 29-yard run. When a poor snap doomed the extra point, the score stood at 10–6.

November 25, 1999

Mississippi State 23, Ole Miss 20

	State	Ole Miss
First downs	17	16
Total plays	59	72
Total yards	345	281
Rushes/net yards	25/112	45/131
Passing yards	233	150
Passes		
(Att-Comp-Int)	34-20-2	27-13-2
Punts/average yards	5/39.8	6/35.7
Penalties/yards	5/48	13/95
Fumbles/lost	4/4	2/2
Time of possession	23:23	36:37
Third-down conversions	4/12	3/13
Sacks by: Number/yards	1/8	1/13
Field goals attempted/made	1/1	2/2

Scott Westerfield kicked the winning field goal in 1999. Rob Morgan held. Mississippi State University Photo.

But the half was not yet over. After an Ole Miss possession went nowhere, the Bulldogs fumbled a punt, and Strong recovered at the State 32. The Rebels failed to move the chains and had to settle for a 49-yard field goal—Binkley's second of the night—that made the score 13–6. The Bulldogs still had time for a 60-yard drive, but it came up short when Rebel linebacker Ronnie Heard (brother of Ole Miss wide receiver Grant Heard) intercepted on the Mississippi 3 just seconds before the half ended.

Things continued to go poorly for the Bulldogs at the beginning of the second half. Ole Miss safety Tim Strickland recovered a fumble on the Bulldog 18, and three plays later, the Rebels had another touchdown on a 6-yard pass from Romaro Miller to tight end Adam Bettis.

Trailing 20–6 with time winding down in the third period and the ball on the Bulldog 29, State began its remarkable resurgence. A 38-yard strike to Justin Griffith set the stage for Madkin's 5-yard pass to tight end Donald Lee for 6 points. Scott Westerfield added 1 more, and the Bulldogs trailed just 20–13.

It appeared as though the Rebels had the game salted away after the Bulldogs fumbled a punt and Ole Miss recovered on the State 36. But the determined Bulldog defense held, forcing a punt. With only 2:10 left, the Dogs regained possession on their own 12. Eighty-eight yards to the tying score? No problem. Madkin attempted seven straight passes, completing five. The last one was the key: on third down with the ball on the Mississippi 38, Madkin spotted C. J. Sirmones on the 15, far behind the Rebel safety. The wide-open Sirmones collected Madkin's throw and dashed into the end zone. When Westerfield's kick sailed through the uprights, the game was knotted at 20 with twenty-seven seconds to go.

After the kickoff, Ole Miss coach David Cutcliffe declined to settle for a tie that would send the game into overtime. Instead, Cutcliffe opted to go for the win. Miller aimed a pass toward Jamie Armstrong at midfield, but the Bulldogs' Robert Bean deflected the throw. The ball spun wildly through the air and directly into the hands of Bulldog Eugene Clinton, who took the prize to the Ole Miss 26. Eight seconds left.

First State took a time-out; then Ole Miss called one. In front of more than forty thousand standing and screaming spectators, Westerfield split the uprights with a 43-yard field goal. The clock showed just 00:04. After scoring 10 points in 23 seconds, the Bulldogs had the incredible 23–20 win.

According to Ole Miss running back D. J. (Deuce) McAllister, Cutcliffe's decision not to play for overtime had been the right call. The Rebels were physically whipped. Miller was playing with a severe ankle injury. With

Robert Bean tipped the pass that was intercepted and led to Westerfield's kick. Mississippi State University Photo.

Joe Gunn injured early, McAllister had carried the ball thirty-six times for 134 yards and had gained 71 more on three punt returns.

On New Year's Eve, Ole Miss ended the century with a squeaker over Oklahoma in the Independence Bowl. Taking a page from the Bulldog game, Binkley kicked a 39-yard field goal as time expired to give the Rebels a 27–25 win and secure a No. 22 ranking in the final polls.

The Bulldogs ended the season with a visit to the Peach Bowl. They led all the way to take an easy 17–7 victory over Clemson and finish the year ranked twelfth and thirteenth in the two major polls. For the first time in fifty-nine years, a Bulldog team had compiled ten wins in a season, including four heart-stopping turnarounds like the one they staged on Thanksgiving night.

2000

Rebels with a Cause

2000 SCHEDULES

Ole Miss 7–5

RESULT	DATE	PF	OPPONENT	PA	LOCATION
W	September 2	49	Tulane	20	Oxford
L	September 9	27	Auburn	35	Oxford
W	September 16	12	Vanderbilt	7	Nashville
W	September 30	35	Kentucky	17	Oxford
W	October 7	35	Arkansas State	10	Oxford
L	October 14	7	Alabama	45	Tuscaloosa
W	October 28	43	Nevada–Las Vegas	40	Oxford
W	November 4	38	Arkansas	24	Fayetteville
L	November 11	9	Louisiana State	20	Oxford
L	November 18	14	Georgia	32	Athens
W	November 23	45	Mississippi State	30	Oxford
L	December 28	38	West Virginia	49	Music City Bowl

Mississippi State 8–4

RESULT	DATE	PF	OPPONENT	PA	LOCATION
W	September 2	17	Memphis	3	Memphis
W	September 14	44	Brigham Young	28	Provo
L	September 23	19	South Carolina	23	Columbia
W	September 30	47	Florida	35	Starkville
W	October 7	17	Auburn	10	Starkville
L	October 21	38	Louisiana State	45	Baton Rouge
W	October 28	61	Middle Tennessee State	35	Starkville
W	November 4	35	Kentucky	17	Lexington
W	November 11	29	Alabama	7	Starkville
L	November 18	10	Arkansas	17	Starkville
L	November 23	30	Mississippi	45	Oxford
W	December 31	43	Texas A&M	41	Independence Bowl

A s cheering Mississippi State fans stormed Scott Field in celebration of their team's stunning comeback victory in the 1999 Egg Bowl, Ole Miss coach David Cutcliffe and running back D. J. (Deuce) McAllister watched grimly, committing the scene to memory, they said, "so we will never forget."

Rivals on-field, friends off-field, the Bulldogs' Kevin Fant, left, and the Rebels' Romaro Miller are in close conversation after the high-scoring 2000 meeting. The topic most certainly is their passing game. University of Mississippi Photo.

They didn't.

When the two teams met again on Thanksgiving night 2000, the Rebels took their revenge with a relentless 45–30 defeat of the Bulldogs. The game was close through three quarters, but Ole Miss poured it on in the fourth, recording 17 unanswered points to seal the win. When it was all over, the two teams had combined for a rivalry record 75 points. The ten touchdowns scored equaled three other battles between State and Ole Miss.

In the week before the game, student and administrative leaders from the two schools conferred to work out a plan to defuse the tensions and bitterness that were again becoming a problem when Ole Miss and State met. They agreed that the bands would jointly play

November 23, 2000
Ole Miss 45, Mississippi State 30

	State	Ole Miss
First downs	18	17
Total plays	67	67
Total yards	368	377
Rushes/net yards	40/184	44/230
Passing yards	184	147
Passes (Att-Comp-Int)	27-13-1	23-11-1
Punts/average yards	5/38.2	7/43.4
Penalties/yards	10/81	4/42
Fumbles/lost	4/1	2/0
Time of possession	31:18	28:42
Third-down conversions	7/16	6/14
Sacks by: Number/yards	0/0	7/45
Field goals attempted/made	1/1	1/1

Deuce McAllister, in one of his patent parallel leaps, counts one of three touchdowns he scored for the Rebels. McAllister also passed for another touchdown and had 121 yards rushing. Photo by J. D. Schwalm for the *Clarion-Ledger*, November 24, 2000.

Dicenzo Miller rounds end as part of his contribution to the Bulldog cause. Miller scored for State in the '98, '99, and '01 Egg Bowls. *Northeast Mississippi Daily Journal*, November 24, 2000.

the national anthem before the game, and they reinstated the original, dignified Golden Egg presentation involving the presidents of both universities. The governor would present the trophy to the winning school's student president.

The 48,811 fans who braved the pouring rain saw the Bulldogs score their first points on their second possession. Playing despite a high fever, State quarterback Wayne Madkin completed three passes on the drive, including the scoring toss to Terrell Grindle. When Scott Westerfield's extra-point try failed, State had a 6–0 advantage. Madkin then had to leave the game, but his replacement, Kevin Fant, quarterbacked the Bulldogs to another touchdown on their next series, which started on the Ole Miss 35 and required only four plays. Dontae Walker picked up the 6, Westerfield added the extra point, and before the first quarter was even half over, State was up 13–0. Three more Bulldog points followed when Westerfield kicked a 39-yard field goal with two minutes gone in the second period.

The Rebel revival started with an 80-yard drive that included only two passes—a 20-yarder from quarterback Romaro Miller to Omar Rayford, and Grant Heard's 8-yard catch for the touchdown. Les Binkley's extra point gave Ole Miss 7 on the scoreboard. Five minutes remained in the half, but that was plenty of time for more Rebel damage via the air, even though Ole Miss's main offensive weapon was the ground game. With the ball on his 49, Miller unexpectedly rolled out of the pocket, burst through the line, and raced 50 yards before all-American Fred Smoot pushed him out on the 1. McAllister dived over and Binkley kicked to bring the Rebels up to 14–16. The Bulldogs immediately fumbled the wet ball, giving the Rebels possession at the State 23. When Miller and Heard combined for their second aerial touchdown of the night and Binkley booted yet another extra point, the Rebels suddenly found themselves with a 21–16 lead.

Just twenty-six seconds into the third quarter, Ole Miss scored again. McAllister took the second-half kickoff at the goal line and returned the ball 28 yards. On the next play, he burst over left guard and went the rest of the way to put the Rebs ahead by 12.

But the Dogs were undaunted. After all, they too remembered the 1999 game. Kendall Roberson intercepted on the first play of the Rebels' next possession, and the Dogs had just 28 yards to go. Walker scored his second touchdown, and the scoreboard read Ole Miss 28, Mississippi State 23. Walker's third touchdown quickly followed, when he powered through the middle for a 73-yard run that put the Dogs back on top by 2.

Rebel defensive end Derrick Burgess rallied his teammates with a sideline pep talk, and they responded with 17 points over the final twenty-two minutes. First came a 67-yard drive that culminated in a flea-flicker. Miller took the snap and lateraled the ball to McAllister, who then lofted the ball downfield to an unnoticed Miller. Rebels 35, Bulldogs 30. 0:44 left in the third.

The Rebs' sixth and seventh scores came gift wrapped. State's botched punt snap gave Ole Miss the ball at the Bulldog 8, and McAllister recorded his third touchdown of the game on a 1-yard dive over the line. The Bulldogs then fumbled a punt return, Lanier Goethie recovered at the Mississippi State 9, and Binkley iced the game with a 34-yard field goal.

McAllister and Walker recorded almost identical statistics. Each gained 121 yards and scored three touchdowns. McAllister's longest touchdown run was 72 yards, Walker's was 73.

Mississippi State went on to the Independence Bowl, played in heavy snow. The Bulldogs, fittingly dressed all in white, down to their helmets, edged Texas A&M 43–41 in overtime. State finished twenty-second in the ESPN/*USA Today* Poll, twenty-fourth in the Associated Press rankings. Ole Miss appeared in the Music City Bowl but fell to West Virginia, 49–38.

2001

Dogs Salvage a Season

2001 SCHEDULES

Ole Miss 7–4

RESULT	DATE	PF	OPPONENT	PA	LOCATION
W	September 1	49	Murray State	14	Oxford
L	September 8	21	Auburn	27	Auburn
W	September 29	42	Kentucky	31	Lexington
W	October 6	35	Arkansas State	17	Jonesboro
W	October 13	27	Alabama	24	Oxford
W	October 20	45	Middle Tennessee State	17	Oxford
W	October 27	35	Louisiana State	24	Baton Rouge
L	November 3	56	Arkansas (Overtime)	58	Oxford
L	November 17	15	Georgia	35	Oxford
L	November 22	28	Mississippi State	36	Starkville
W	December 1	38	Vanderbilt	27	Oxford

Mississippi State 3–8

RESULT	DATE	PF	OPPONENT	PA	LOCATION
W	September 3	30	Memphis	10	Starkville
L	September 20	14	South Carolina	16	Starkville
L	September 29	0	Florida	52	Gainesville
L	October 6	14	Auburn	16	Auburn
L	October 13	9	Troy State	21	Starkville
L	October 20	0	Louisiana State	42	Starkville
W	November 3	17	Kentucky	14	Starkville
L	November 10	17	Alabama	24	Tuscaloosa
L	November 17	21	Arkansas	24	Fayetteville
W	November 22	36	Mississippi	28	Starkville
L	December 1	38	Brigham Young	41	Starkville

O ne hundred years after the first game between Mississippi A&M and the University of Mississippi, things were right back where they started, more or less. Not far from the site of the first game—a makeshift gridiron at the old fairgrounds—Ole Miss and Mississippi State (then known as Mississippi A&M) faced off for the ninety-eighth time, with the

Kevin Fant and Coach Sherrill with the Golden Egg, 2001. Courtesy Russ Houston/Mississippi State University.

6–3 Rebels trying to salvage their bowl hopes and the 2–7 Bulldogs trying to salvage respect.

For the fourth consecutive Thanksgiving night, ESPN was beaming the Egg Bowl nationwide. State was opening its grand new east-side addition that enabled 51,112 fans to see the game, the most ever to watch the two schools play on campus. In the wake of the September 11 terrorist attacks, the pregame activities included the Famous Maroon Band and the Pride of the South Band jointly performing "God Bless America" and the "Star Spangled Banner."

The Rebels established dominance early in the game with a 70-yard touchdown drive led by quarterback Eli Manning, son of Rebel hero Archie Manning. Joe Gunn capped the drive with a 1-yard run, and Jonathan Nichols, who did all the kicking, easily got the point after.

The Bulldogs countered with an eleven-play, 86-yard drive that culminated in Dontae Walker's first touchdown of the game. Although State missed on the attempted 2-point conversion, the Dogs now trailed by only a point. But not for long. The Rebels raised the margin to 14–6 with an eight-snap march that ended with a 6-yard scoring toss from Manning to fullback Charles Stackhouse.

Each team squeezed in another touchdown before halftime. The Rebels failed on a fourth-down flea-flicker, turning the ball over to the Bulldogs on downs. The Bulldogs added 6 when Dicenzo Miller grabbed an 11-yard scoring toss from quarterback Kevin Fant.

November 22, 2001
Mississippi State 36, Ole Miss 28

	State	Ole Miss
First downs	21	22
Total plays	66	78
Total yards	462	348
Rushes/net yards	45/199	41/137
Passing yards	263	211
Passes (Att-Comp-Int)	21-14-0	37-17-3
Punts/average yards	2/36.5	3/43.2
Penalties/yards	11/113	4/45
Fumbles/lost	0/0	0/0
Time of possession	28:30	31:30
Third-down conversions	5/11	8/17
Sacks by: Number/yards	1/0	1/6
Field goals attempted/made	2/1	1/0

Eli Manning proved he could run as well as pass before two Bulldogs, including Demetric Wright (24), brought the Rebel quarterback down. *Northeast Mississippi Daily Journal*, November 23, 2001.

Another 2-point conversion pass fell to the ground, and the score stood at 14–12. The Bulldogs then deliberately attempted a high boot on the kickoff, hoping to prevent Jason Armstead from returning the ball. Instead, Armstead reversed field and dashed 23 yards to the Bulldog 46. The Rebels needed only five plays—including a key catch by none other than Armstead—before Gunn recorded his second 6 points. With 0:31 left in the half, the Rebels were up, 21–12.

The first score of the second half was a 70-yard Bulldog drive with a 50-yard pass from Fant to Miller paving the way for John Michael Marlin's 32-yard field goal. Five minutes later, State took the lead on Walker's second touchdown run of the night, this one from 7 yards out. When Marlin sent the ball squarely through the uprights, State was on top, 22–21.

Less than a minute into the fourth quarter, the Rebs missed a 31-yard field goal. Then Manning, who had thrown only three interceptions all season, sent

Dontae Walker tries to evade Justin Coleman's grab. Still, Walker scored three touchdowns for State. With the three he counted in the 2000 Egg Bowl, Walker's six touchdowns are the most ever by a Bulldog against Ole Miss. *Northeast Mississippi Daily Journal*, November 23, 2001.

three into Bulldog hands. The first pickoff, by Korey Banks, gave State possession at the Rebel 20. Walker needed five plays to cover those 20 yards and give his team an 8-point edge. Three plays later, Banks had another interception, this time returning the ball to the 6. The Dogs added another touchdown on a trick play: Fant lined up wide left, while split end Ray Ray Bivines moved directly behind center to take the ball on a shotgun snap, confusing the Rebels enough that Bivines burst over. After scoring 24 unanswered points, State held a 36–21 lead and seemed firmly in charge.

Ole Miss made two desperate efforts to catch up, starting with a 75-yard drive that covered two minutes. When Manning found Ross Barkley alone in the end zone for a 19-yard score, the Bulldog advantage was down to 36–28. The Rebels tried an onside kickoff and recovered the ball on the Mississippi State 48, but Demetric Wright snatched the Dogs' third interception of the night to seal the game for State. For the second time in three years, State had won the Golden Egg with a dramatic comeback.

As a result of the events of 9/11, which had forced the postponement of a week's worth of college football games as well as numerous other sporting events, both teams had one more game before the end of the season. Undefeated and No. 10–ranked Brigham Young edged the Bulldogs in Starkville by a comeback score of 41–38, while the Rebels scored five touchdowns over an eighteen-minute span to record a 38–27 comeback victory at home over Vanderbilt. For the first time in five seasons, however, neither Ole Miss nor Mississippi State received a postseason bowl bid.

2002

Fant and Manning Battle It Out

2002 SCHEDULES

Ole Miss 7–6

RESULT	DATE	PF	OPPONENT	PA	LOCATION
W	August 31	31	Louisiana-Monroe	3	Oxford
W	September 7	38	Memphis	16	Oxford
L	September 14	28	Texas Tech	42	Lubbock
W	September 21	45	Vanderbilt	38	Oxford
W	October 5	17	Florida	14	Oxford
W	October 12	52	Arkansas State	17	Oxford
L	October 19	7	Alabama	42	Tuscaloosa
L	October 26	28	Arkansas	48	Fayetteville
L	November 2	24	Auburn	31	Oxford
L	November 9	17	Georgia	31	Athens
L	November 23	13	Louisiana State	14	Baton Rouge
W	November 28	24	Mississippi State	12	Oxford
W	December 27	27	Nebraska	23	Independence Bowl

Mississippi State 3–9

RESULT	DATE	PF	OPPONENT	PA	LOCATION
L	August 31	13	Oregon	36	Eugene
W	September 14	51	Jacksonville State	13	Starkville
L	September 19	14	Auburn	42	Starkville
L	September 28	13	Louisiana State	31	Baton Rouge
L	October 5	10	South Carolina	34	Columbia
W	October 12	11	Troy State	8	Starkville
W	October 19	29	Memphis	17	Memphis
L	November 2	24	Kentucky	45	Starkville
L	November 9	14	Alabama	28	Tuscaloosa
L	November 16	17	Tennessee	35	Starkville
L	November 23	19	Arkansas	26	Starkville
L	November 28	12	Mississippi	24	Oxford

Not since 1996 had both the Rebels (5–6) and the Bulldogs (3–8) come into the Egg Bowl with subpar records. But disappointing seasons did not mean that nothing was riding on the game: a win would make the Rebels eligible for a bowl game, a situation motivating both teams. The game also featured a rematch between two quarterbacks slowed by injury but nevertheless stellar—Ole Miss's Eli Manning, the Southeastern Conference's leading passer, and Mississippi State's Kevin Fant. With both teams near the bottom of the conference in rushing, the game promised to be an aerial duel between Manning and Fant, on-field competitors but off-field friends who had begun their acquaintance while serving as instructors at football camps.

Completion of Vaught-Hemingway Stadium's south end-zone horseshoe gave the rivalry a new on-campus record for attendance, 60,245, despite the night's chilly thirty-four degrees. Ole Miss was favored by 8, but the Bulldogs dominated first-quarter play, controlling the ball for twelve minutes to the Rebels' three and leading in first downs eight to two, plays twenty-seven to seven, and yardage 107 to 32. Yet State led only 3–0 after kicker Brent Smith's 35-yard field goal on the Bulldogs' second possession.

The Rebels got on the board early in the second quarter after a drive that started on their 45 yard line courtesy of a 30-yard punt return by Jason Armstead, whose three punt runbacks and two kickoff returns gave the Rebels good field position all night. Seven plays later, Manning hit split end Chris Collins on a third-and-15 screen pass. Collins raced 28 yards untouched into the end zone, and after Jonathan Nichols booted his forty-third consecutive extra point, Ole Miss led 7–3.

After the break, the two teams swapped interceptions, with Manning's pickoff occurring at midfield and Fant's at the Ole Miss 14. The Bulldog error was costly. Three plays later, Manning and Collins connected again, this time for a 77-yard touchdown pass that gave the Rebels a 14–3 edge.

Still in the third, Fant led his team 70 yards in only four plays, reaching the Ole Miss 5. When the Bulldogs couldn't go the final handful of yards, Smith booted a 22-yard kick, and the Dogs had narrowed the gap. But the Rebels took advantage of 40 yards in Bulldog penalties on the next drive, matching the field goal with a 27-yarder by Nichols to restore the 11-point lead.

The Dogs opened the fourth with a 57-yard drive that ended in a 22-yard touchdown pass from Fant to Ray Ray Bivines. Although the 2-point conversion failed, State was back in the game, down only 17–12. With just under five minutes left,

November 28, 2002
Ole Miss 24, Mississippi State 12

	State	Ole Miss
First downs	23	16
Total plays	77	56
Total yards	419	297
Rushes/net yards	35/79	27/90
Passing yards	340	207
Passes		
(Att-Comp-Int)	42-23-3	29-16-2
Punts/average yards	5/37.8	5/34.8
Penalties/yards	8/80	6/39
Fumbles/lost	0/0	1/0
Time of possession	32:59	27:01
Third-down conversions	8/17	4/12
Sacks by: Number/yards	0/0	4/30
Field goals attempted/made	2/2	2/1

For three years it was a true passing duel between the quarterbacks Eli Manning, Ole Miss, top, and Kevin Fant, State. In 2002 Manning completed 16 of 29 for 207 yards, counted one touchdown, and threw for two other scores. Fant passed for a touchdown and completed 22 of 42 in setting a new rivalry passing record of 340 yards. *Northeast Mississippi Daily Journal*, November 29, 2002.

Mississippi State fans brave the elements to show school spirit. *Northeast Mississippi Daily Journal*, November 29, 2002.

Chris Collins takes a 28-yard pass from Eli Manning and outraces Bulldog pursuers for Ole Miss's first touchdown as escort Doug Buckles cheers him on. *Northeast Mississippi Daily Journal*, November 29, 2002.

however, the Rebels hiked their lead on a Manning keeper to secure the 24–12 win. Travis Johnson had set up the touchdown with an interception at the State 25 and a 21-yard return.

Manning completed sixteen of twenty-nine passes with two interceptions for 207 yards. Fant connected on twenty-three of forty-two with three interceptions for 340 yards passing, a new rivalry record. With his -22 yards on the ground, Fant tied Tommy Pharr's thirty-three-year-old record for most yardage in a State–Ole Miss contest.

The win made the Rebs bowl-eligible, and they happily accepted a bid to face Nebraska in the Independence Bowl, where they twice erased 10-point deficits to capture a 27–23 victory.

2003

GAME 100

Davis Wade Stadium at
Scott Field, Starkville

One Hundred and Going Strong

2003 SCHEDULES

Ole Miss 10–3

RESULT	DATE	PF	OPPONENT	PA	LOCATION
W	August 30	24	Vanderbilt	21	Nashville
L	September 6	34	Memphis	44	Memphis
W	September 13	59	Louisiana-Monroe	14	Oxford
L	September 27	45	Texas Tech	49	Oxford
W	October 4	20	Florida	17	Gainesville
W	October 11	55	Arkansas State	0	Oxford
W	October 18	43	Alabama	28	Oxford
W	October 25	19	Arkansas	7	Oxford
W	November 1	43	South Carolina	40	Oxford
W	November 8	24	Auburn	20	Auburn
L	November 22	14	Louisiana State	17	Oxford
W	November 27	31	Mississippi State	0	Starkville
W	January 2, 2004	31	Oklahoma State	28	Cotton Bowl

Mississippi State 2–10

RESULT	DATE	PF	OPPONENT	PA	LOCATION
L	August 30	34	Oregon	42	Starkville
L	September 13	28	Tulane	31	New Orleans
L	September 20	35	Houston	42	Houston
L	September 27	6	Louisiana State	41	Starkville
W	October 4	30	Vanderbilt	21	Starkville
W	October 11	35	Memphis	27	Starkville
L	October 18	13	Auburn	45	Auburn
L	October 25	17	Kentucky	42	Lexington
L	November 8	0	Alabama	38	Starkville
L	November 15	21	Tennessee	59	Knoxville
L	November 22	6	Arkansas	52	Fayetteville
L	November 27	0	Mississippi	31	Starkville

O n an evening when even the chill of falling rain couldn't cool the heat generated by the rivalry between the Rebels and the Bulldogs, ESPN-TV allowed the entire nation to witness the one hundredth meeting between the schools. The more than fifty-three thousand spectators

Tremaine Turner is pursued heavily by Slovakia Griffith (25) and Jeramie Johnson (34), but still Turner rushed for 70 yards and scored Ole Miss's first touchdown on a 25-yard pass from Eli Manning. Photo by Rick Guy for the *Clarion-Ledger*, November 28, 2003.

plus millions more at home watched as Ole Miss jumped out to a first-half lead and then used a stifling defense to cruise to a 31–0 shutout.

November 27, 2003

Ole Miss 31, Mississippi State 0

	State	Ole Miss
First downs	7	20
Total plays	56	66
Total yards	192	359
Rushes/net yards	101	99
Passing yards	91	260
Passes		
(Att-Comp-Int)	31-14-1	27-19-0
Punts/average yards	9/38.2	6/42.0
Penalties/yards	3/44	2/17
Fumbles/lost	1/1	4/2
Time of possession	26:40	33:20
Third-down conversions	2/14	5/14
Sacks by: Number/yards	0/0	3/13
Field goals attempted/made	0/0	2/1

For the third straight year, the game promised to be a battle between Bulldog quarterback Kevin Fant and Rebel signal-caller Eli Manning, who were rewriting their schools' passing records. And with State and Ole Miss standing at the bottom of the Southeastern Conference in pass defense, observers expected a high-scoring offensive show.

They were right—sort of. Rain, heavy at times, during the second and third quarters forced both

Wide receiver Mike Espy had two receptions and returned four punts in the rainy 2003 game. University of Mississippi Photo.

teams to abandon the long pass. Nevertheless, Manning completed nineteen of twenty-seven passes for 260 yards and no interceptions. Fant was good on fourteen of twenty-eight for 91 yards, and he threw one pickoff. Most importantly, of course, Manning's Rebels bested their archrivals for the second time in the three Manning-Fant face-offs.

The Rebels recorded their first points of the game on their third possession, on which they took the ball 73 yards on only four snaps for their longest drive of the night. The touchdown came when Manning spotted Tremaine Turner in the end zone. Turner reached high for Manning's 25-yard throw and fell backward out of the end zone, barely keeping both feet in. All-American Jonathan Nichols continued his two seasons of point-after perfection to put Ole Miss up by 7 with about three and a half minutes remaining in the first period.

The Rebs put 17 points on the board in the second quarter. After the Bulldogs failed on a fourth-and-1 sneak on their own 37, Ole Miss strung

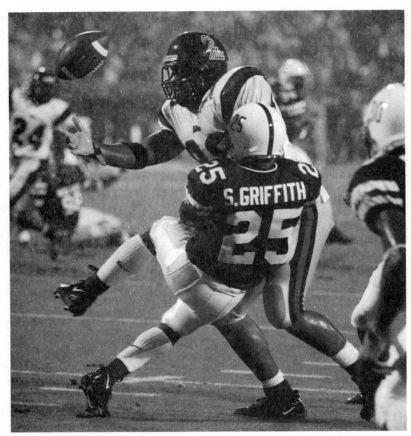

The most unusual touchdown of the night was this 17-yard catch by the Rebels' Lawrence Lilly. When the ball bounced off defender Slovakia Griffith's shoulder, Lilly plucked the spinning ball out of the air and fell across the goal line. *Northeast Mississippi Daily Journal*, November 28, 2003.

together another four-play drive. From the 17, Manning threw toward tight end Lawrence Lilly. The throw bounced off the shoulder of defender Slovakia Griffith before Lilly snatched the ball out of the air and fell across the goal line. Three plays later, Charlie Anderson struck Fant's arm as he went back to pass, and Rob Robertson picked off the errant throw on the Mississippi State 32 and returned the ball to the 18. Once again, the Rebels needed only four plays to score, although this time the points came when Nichols split the uprights with a 32-yard field goal.

With just fifteen seconds to go before the half, the Rebels finished a 55-yard drive with their third touchdown. Brandon Jacobs bucked across from the 3, and Ole Miss took a 24–0 lead into the locker room.

Ole Miss added one more touchdown near the end of the third quarter after the Dogs mishandled a punt return. Taye Biddle recovered the ball on State's 23. The first play went nowhere. On second and 10, however, Manning tossed a short pass to his favorite target, wide receiver Chris Collins, who raced untouched for 6 more points. Another successful extra point made the final score 31–0.

With 12:39 remaining in the fourth quarter, the Dogs mounted their first genuine drive of the game. They got as close as the Ole Miss 9 before the Rebel defense clamped down. With 1:23 left to play, State made one final bid for points, moving 47 yards to the Ole Miss 29 before two incomplete passes ended the threat. The shutout was the Rebels' first against State since 1971 and represented a point of pride for the defense: explained end Charlie Anderson, "We wanted the Golden Egg and the goose egg."

The Rebels finished the regular season at 8–3, their best record in thirteen years, and shared the Southeastern Conference Western Division championship with Louisiana State. The Tigers had defeated the Rebels, however, and thus went on to the conference championship game. Ole Miss nonetheless received a bid to the Cotton Bowl, where the Rebels defeated Oklahoma State 31–28 for their tenth win of the season, the first time they had reached that milestone since 1971. The two major polls subsequently had the Rebels at thirteenth and fourteenth. Coach David Cutcliffe was honored by his peers as Southeastern Conference Coach of the Year.

Following in his father's footsteps, Manning received a slew of honors while at Ole Miss. He was named all-America; he received the Maxwell Award as the nation's top collegiate player; he won the Johnny Unitas Award as the nation's top senior quarterback; and he twice received the Cellular South Conerly Trophy as the state's most outstanding collegiate player. After his senior season, the conference's coaches named him Southeastern Conference Player of the Year, and he finished third in the 2003 Heisman Trophy voting.

Mississippi State coach Jackie Sherrill had already announced his intention to retire at season's end, and four days after the Egg Bowl, school officials announced the selection of Sylvester Croom as Sherrill's replacement. Croom became not only the first African American to serve as head coach of a Mississippi college football team but also the first African American to hold such a position in the Southeastern Conference. Croom had played at Alabama (where he would have known a student assistant named David Cutcliffe) and had served as an assistant at his alma mater for ten years before going on to similar positions with five National Football League teams.

GAME 101

Vaught-Hemingway
Stadium/Hollingsworth
Field, Oxford

2004

Throw Away the Book

2004 SCHEDULES

Ole Miss 4–7

RESULT	DATE	PF	OPPONENT	PA	LOCATION
L	September 4	13	Memphis	20	Oxford
L	September 11	7	Alabama	28	Tuscaloosa
W	September 18	26	Vanderbilt	23	Oxford
L	September 25	32	Wyoming	37	Laramie
W	October 2	28	Arkansas State	21	Oxford
W	October 9	31	South Carolina	28	Columbia
L	October 16	17	Tennessee	21	Oxford
L	October 30	14	Auburn	35	Oxford
L	November 13	3	Arkansas	35	Fayetteville
L	November 20	24	Louisiana State	27	Baton Rouge
W	November 27	20	Mississippi State	3	Oxford

Mississippi State 3–8

RESULT	DATE	PF	OPPONENT	PA	LOCATION
W	September 4	28	Tulane	7	Starkville
L	September 11	14	Auburn	43	Starkville
L	September 18	7	Maine	9	Starkville
L	September 25	0	Louisiana State	51	Baton Rouge
L	October 2	13	Vanderbilt	31	Nashville
L	October 9	13	Alabama-Birmingham	27	Starkville
W	October 23	38	Florida	31	Starkville
W	October 30	22	Kentucky	7	Starkville
L	November 6	14	Alabama	30	Tuscaloosa
L	November 20	21	Arkansas	24	Starkville
L	November 27	3	Mississippi	20	Oxford

"The book" said that the Bulldogs would literally run over the Rebels. The Mississippi State offense was averaging 167 yards rushing per game, while the Ole Miss defense was surrendering an average of 30 yards more than that per game—and had given up 287 rushing yards per outing over the past three games. Moreover, Bulldog run-

Quarterback Robert Lane dashes past the Bulldog bench in a long sprint that boosted his total yardage for the day to 97 on 16 carries. Lane also scored one touchdown and passed for another. University of Mississippi Photo.

ning back Jerious Norwood had gone over the 100-yard mark in four of State's past five games.

But when Ole Miss and State meet, you can throw away the book. The Rebels limited the Bulldogs to just 70 yards on the ground, with Norwood accounting for only 24 of those yards. The Rebel defense recorded four sacks plus six tackles for a loss against Bulldog ball carriers. On the other side of the ball, the Rebel offense called sixty-two rushing plays for a season-high 283 yards. Ole Miss retained possession of the ball for more than thirty-seven minutes, allowing the Dogs just fifty-four total plays. By keeping the Bulldog offense off the field, the Rebels took a relatively easy 20–3 win.

November 27, 2004
Ole Miss 20, Mississippi State 3

	State	Ole Miss
First downs	6	24
Total yards	220	421
Rushes/net yards	26/70	62/283
Passing yards	150	138
Passes		
(Att-Comp-Int)	28-8-1	26-13-3
Punts/average yards	7/40.9	3/40.3
Penalties/yards	5/55	4/41
Fumbles/lost	5/2	2/1
Time of possession	22:32	37:28
Third-down conversions	1/12	10/18
Sacks by: Number/yards	1/5	4/35
Field goals attempted/made	2/1	3/2

Running back Jamal Pittman rounds end as lineman Tre' Stallings blocks the way against an onrushing Bulldog. University of Mississippi Photo.

After six years of airing the Egg Bowl on national television, ESPN decided that a contest between two 3–7 squads did not merit watching. The nearly fifty-six thousand fans disagreed, however, cheering on their respective teams as if a championship was on the line—which, in their eyes, was indeed the case.

The Rebels scored on a 78-yard drive on their second possession of the afternoon. Quarterback Robert Lane—one of three men who had started at that position for Ole Miss over the course of the season—got the ball rolling with a 4-yard touchdown strike to tight end Lawrence Lilly. Jonathan Nichols's extra-point kick was good. Nichols added a 39-yard field goal midway through the second quarter to put the Rebels up by 10.

State recorded its first points after Darren Williams intercepted a pass on the Mississippi State 35 and brought the ball back 9 yards. On the second play from scrimmage, Bulldog running back Fred Reid gobbled up 46 yards before being pulled down by linebacker Patrick Willis on the 9. The Ole Miss defense held State to just 3 more yards, however, and the Bulldogs came away with Keith Andrews's 23-yard field goal.

The score remained at 10–7 through the third quarter, but the Rebels took command on the first play of the fourth when Lane scored from the 2. The touchdown capped a 98-yard scoring drive and came after a bit of deception: Lane faked a handoff to running back Vashon Pearson but kept the ball, reversed field, and dashed untouched into the end zone. Even Pearson was in the dark on the play—only Lane and Ole Miss coach David Cutcliffe knew that a quarterback keeper had been called. Nichols made his 118th consecutive extra-point kick, and the Rebels were ahead by 14. A few minutes later, Nichols closed out the scoring with his second field goal of the day, this one from 22 yards away.

LOOKING FOR AN OASIS

The victory-starved Rebels and Bulldogs—with identical 3-7 records—are perceived as crawling with high hopes toward the oasis represented by the Golden Egg that will quench their thirst for victory. Chuck McIntosh/*Northeast Mississippi Daily Journal*, November 26, 2004.

Ole Miss outgained State by 201 yards (421–220) and kept the football fifteen minutes longer—equal to a full quarter of play. Declared Cutcliffe, "We set the tone early, especially defensively." Admitted Bulldog coach Sylvester Croom, "Mainly we just got whipped up front, one on one. In the first half we didn't even show up."

Ole Miss terminated Cutcliffe's contract after the season as a result of disagreements between him and Rebel athletic director Pete Boone and chancellor Robert C. Khayat concerning the future of the football program. To take Cutcliffe's place, university officials named Southern California assistant coach Ed Orgeron, who had been an assistant at five other schools and had helped to win national titles at Miami and Southern Cal.

2005

Jerious Norwood

2005 SCHEDULES

Ole Miss 3–8

RESULT	DATE	PF	OPPONENT	PA	LOCATION
W	September 5	10	Memphis	6	Memphis
L	September 17	23	Vanderbilt	31	Nashville
L	September 24	14	Wyoming	24	Oxford
L	October 1	10	Tennessee	27	Knoxville
W	October 8	27	The Citadel	7	Oxford
L	October 15	10	Alabama	13	Oxford
W	October 22	13	Kentucky	7	Oxford
L	October 29	3	Auburn	27	Auburn
L	November 12	17	Arkansas	28	Oxford
L	November 19	7	Louisiana State	40	Oxford
L	November 26	14	Mississippi State	35	Starkville

Mississippi State 3–8

RESULT	DATE	PF	OPPONENT	PA	LOCATION
W	September 3	38	Murray State	6	Starkville
L	September 10	0	Auburn	28	Auburn
W	September 17	21	Tulane	14	Shreveport
L	September 24	10	Georgia	23	Starkville
L	October 1	7	Louisiana State	37	Starkville
L	October 8	9	Florida	35	Gainesville
L	October 22	16	Houston	28	Starkville
L	October 29	7	Kentucky	13	Lexington
L	November 5	0	Alabama	17	Starkville
L	November 19	10	Arkansas	44	Little Rock
W	November 26	35	Mississippi	14	Starkville

A senior halfback with impressive speed and a special knack for breaking tackles rushed for 204 yards and matched a 97-year-old Maroon
record in this rivalry by scoring four touchdowns in State's one-
sided 35–14 win. Without Jerious Norwood, Bulldog coach Sylvester Croom
declared unequivocally, "we wouldn't have won." The win broke the Bulldogs'
seven-game season losing streak, their string of three straight losses to Ole

Jerious Norwood stiff-arms a charging Rebel on the way to a 204-yard day. Norwood scored three touch-downs rushing for the Bulldogs, then caught a pass for a fourth, giving him more points in one game against Ole Miss than any Bulldog. Mississippi State University Photo.

Miss, and their four-year, nineteen-game skid in the Southeastern Conference Western Division.

Outside the stadium stood four large trucks collecting coats and blankets for the needy, particularly those who had lost their homes and possessions when Hurricane Katrina slammed ashore on the Gulf Coast just three months earlier. Inside the stadium, those in the crowd of 53,655 had barely settled into their seats on this cloudy afternoon when the Rebels reeled off a flashy five-play touchdown drive that took just ninety seconds on the clock. After two quick runs and two short passes, quarterback Ethan Flatt faked a reverse and uncorked a perfect 41-yard scoring bomb to wide receiver Taye Biddle. Matt Hinkle kicked the first of two extra points on the afternoon, and the Rebels had a 7–0 advantage.

The Dogs tied the score at the start of the second quarter. Clarence McDougal blocked a punt to give State the ball on the Ole Miss 33,

November 26, 2005
Mississippi State 35, Ole Miss 14

	State	Ole Miss
First downs	23	12
Total plays	76	49
Total yards	409	189
Rushes/net yards	56/304	25/31
Passing yards	105	158
Passes		
(Att-Comp-Int)	20-11-1	24-15-4
Punts/average yards	4/39.8	5/38.0
Penalties/yards	6/52	3/11
Fumbles/lost	0/0	1/0
Time of possession	34:47	25:13
Third-down conversions	8/15	3/10
Sacks by: Number/yards	4/41	0/0
Field goals attempted/made	1/0	0/0

The head coach's traditional icy bath goes to Sylvester Croom as happy Bulldogs celebrate their victory over Ole Miss. *Northeast Mississippi Daily Journal*, November 27, 2005.

Defensive back Kevin Dockery makes a spectacular leap to break up a pass. Dockery had two pass break-ups against the Rebels. *Northeast Mississippi Daily Journal*, November 27, 2005.

and Norwood needed only one play to charge for his first touchdown of the day. Adam Carlson kicked five extra points during the game, including this one. Six plays later, another turnover opened the door for State to take the lead. Cornerback Jeramie Johnson snared an interception—the first of his three on the day, tying another rivalry record—on the State 49 and raced to the Ole Miss 11. Norwood powered over from the 2, and State was up 14–7.

Back came the Rebels. Micheal Spurlock, now at quarterback, completed a 7-yard touchdown pass to fullback Robert Lane, and the game was knotted at 14. An 80-yard drive put State on top to stay. Norwood

Bully and Bully. Mississippi State University Photo.

carried seven times for 40 yards, including a 1-yard scoring plunge that gave his team the 21–14 halftime lead.

In the second half, the Dogs restricted Ole Miss to just four possessions—two in each quarter—and did not allow the Rebels past their own 46 yard line. Two fourth-quarter touchdowns salted away the game for the Bulldogs. The first came on a 73-yard drive that featured eleven rushing plays and only one pass—quarterback Michael Henig's 1-yarder to Bryson Davis for 6 points. Two plays later, Johnson grabbed his second interception, and the Dogs took over at the Ole Miss 44. Norwood capped his day with his fourth touchdown, this one on a 5-yard pass from Henig. Three plays into Ole Miss's next possession, Johnson pulled down his third interception, and the game ended four minutes later.

Norwood had accumulated two-thirds of the Bulldogs' rushing yardage on the day on his way to his second 1,000-yard campaign. He was named Southeastern Conference Player of the Week and received the Cellular South Conerly Trophy as the most outstanding football player in Mississippi. Not since 1908, when Harry (Little) Furman did it, had a Bulldog scored four touchdowns in one game with Ole Miss. Norwood's performance set a new mark for points by a Bulldog against Ole Miss: each of Furman's scores had counted for only five points according to the rules of the day.

GAME 103

2006

Right Down to the Wire

2006 SCHEDULES

Ole Miss 4–8

RESULT	DATE	PF	OPPONENT	PA	LOCATION
W	September 3	28	Memphis	25	Oxford
L	September 9	7	Missouri	34	Columbia
L	September 16	14	Kentucky	31	Lexington
L	September 23	3	Wake Forest	27	Oxford
L	September 30	9	Georgia	14	Oxford
W	October 7	17	Vanderbilt	10	Oxford
L	October 14	23	Alabama (Overtime)	26	Tuscaloosa
L	October 21	3	Arkansas	38	Fayetteville
L	October 28	17	Auburn	23	Oxford
W	November 4	27	Northwestern State	7	Oxford
L	November 18	20	Louisiana State (Overtime)	23	Baton Rouge
W	November 25	20	Mississippi State	17	Oxford

Mississippi State 3–9

RESULT	DATE	PF	OPPONENT	PA	LOCATION
L	August 31	0	South Carolina	15	Starkville
L	September 9	0	Auburn	34	Starkville
L	September 16	29	Tulane	32	Starkville
W	September 23	16	Alabama-Birmingham	10	Birmingham
L	September 30	17	Louisiana State	48	Baton Rouge
L	October 7	14	West Virginia	42	Starkville
W	October 14	35	Jacksonville State	3	Starkville
L	October 21	24	Georgia	27	Athens
L	October 28	31	Kentucky	34	Starkville
W	November 4	24	Alabama	16	Tuscaloosa
L	November 18	14	Arkansas	28	Starkville
L	November 25	17	Mississippi	20	Oxford

Not until the last play was the seventy-ninth Battle of the Golden Egg decided: a 51-yard Bulldog field goal attempt that sailed wide left as the final horn sounded.

The Rebels, favored by 3, never trailed. The Bulldogs came into Oxford on a beautiful, sunny afternoon with a 3–8 record that included three 3-point losses.

Patrick Willis (49), going against wide receiver Tony Burks (4), led all tacklers with 13 and was named the SEC Defensive Player of the Year. He won both the Butkus and the Jack Lambert Awards as the nation's most outstanding linebacker and won all-America honors. Leading the Bulldogs was Quinton Culberson who was a consensus all-SEC linebacker. University of Mississippi Photo.

The Rebels, also 3–8, had dropped four games by 6 points or less. Though both teams had had disappointing seasons, pride, as always, was primary.

The crowd of 57,685 watched as Ole Miss turned the opening kickoff into a 56-yard, six-play touchdown drive. With the ball on the State 23, freshman defensive end Greg Hardy, making an unusual offensive appearance, outleaped a defender in the end zone to take a pass from quarterback Brent Schaeffer, and Joshua Shene's kick made it 7–0.

Though the Bulldogs answered with a 76-yard drive that ended with a missed field goal attempt, they got the ball right back on the Ole Miss 39 after a short Rebel punt and quickly got on the scoreboard. Adam Carlson's 41-yard field goal cut the deficit to 7–3 with just two minutes gone in the second quarter.

November 25, 2006
Ole Miss 20, Mississippi State 17

	State	Ole Miss
First downs	19	10
Total plays	69	50
Total yards	314	200
Rushes/net yards	35/152	27/58
Passing yards	162	142
Passes		
(Att-Comp-Int)	34-16-1	23-10-0
Punts/average yards	5/37.6	6/39.7
Penalties/yards	4/25	7/60
Fumbles/lost	0/0	0/0
Time of possession	33:15	26:45
Third-down conversions	5/13	4/13
Sacks by: Number/yards	2/6	1/10
Field goals attempted/made	3/1	2/2

Rebel freshman Marshay Green races 47 yards for the winning touchdown with a punt that he was told to field but chose to return instead. Green's was the first punt return for score in Egg Bowl play in twenty-three years and only the fifth ever in this rivalry. University of Mississippi Photo.

The Rebels answered with a field goal of their own. With Schaeffer running or passing on eight of eleven plays, the Rebs went 56 yards, and Shene's 22-yard kick upped the Rebel margin back to 7.

The Bulldogs' next possession included four carries by freshman running back Anthony Dixon and three pass completions by quarterback Omarr Conner, subbing for Michael Henig, suffering his second collarbone break of the season. On his fifth carry, Dixon blasted into the end zone from the 2, and Carlson's kick tied the score at 10 with 2:55 remaining in the first half. At the break, Dixon already had 97 yards on sixteen carries.

Ole Miss opened the second-half scoring with an eight-play drive that ended with Shene's 20-yard field goal to put the Rebels back in the lead, 13–10, with just under three minutes left in the third. Nearly a full quarter passed before either team added to its total.

Pinned back on their goal, the Bulldogs got off a short punt that Rebel return man Marshay Green fielded at the State 47 despite instructions to let the ball go. Green charged upfield, turned left, and, following a block by Peria Jerry that crushed a defender, raced untouched along the sideline for 6 points. Shene's extra point put the Rebels up by 10.

The Bulldogs moved 73 yards for a touchdown, with the score coming on Conner's 8-yard flip to tight end Jason Hubbard. After Carlson's kick was true, the Bulldogs were within 3 points of the Rebels, 20–17, with 2:20 left on the clock.

That was enough time for each team to mount one last drive. The Rebels grabbed the onside kick and moved to the State 37, but Seth Adams's fourth-and-1 quarterback sneak failed, and a personal foul against the Rebels gave State the ball at the Ole Miss 48 with thirty-seven seconds to go. After Conner's 10-yard completion to Will Prosser and 4-yarder to Dixon, in came Carlson, hoping to send the game into overtime. Ole Miss had already lost two overtime games during the

Loyal fans give their best Rebel yell when the cheerleaders run this red and blue flag around the stadium. University of Mississippi Photo.

season, so Rebel fans' loudest cheer of the day came when the kick sailed wide left by a yard. Rebel players raced onto the field in celebration.

Both defenses had played a stellar game. Led by consensus all-American Patrick Willis, the Rebels held Dixon to just 28 yards in the second half. Willis finished the day with thirteen tackles and received both the Butkus and Jack Lambert Awards as the nation's most outstanding linebacker as well as the Cellular South Conerly Trophy as the most outstanding college player in Mississippi. The State defense held Ole Miss to 200 yards, including just 58 on the ground. Ole Miss's BenJarvus Green-Ellis, who had 1,000 yards for the season, managed just 37 on the day. State linebacker Quinton Culberson, averaging 8.5 tackles per game for the season, made all–Southeastern Conference.

But as State coach Sylvester Croom observed, special teams had made the difference. "It really came down to the kicking game, and we didn't make plays." Ole Miss coach Ed Orgeron praised his defense's second-half effort: "We've been so close [all season] and haven't found a way to win. Today we hung in there and finally won the game."

Earlier in the year John Vaught, whose coaching innovations are nationally recognized and whose 25-year career spanned more Egg Bowl rivalry games than any other, died in Oxford at the age of ninety-six. His record in Egg Bowl play was 19-2-4.

2007

The Value of a Single Play

2007 SCHEDULES

Ole Miss 3–9

RESULT	DATE	PF	OPPONENT	PA	LOCATION
W	September 1	23	Memphis	21	Memphis
L	September 8	25	Missouri	38	Oxford
L	September 15	17	Vanderbilt	31	Nashville
L	September 22	17	Georgia	45	Athens
W	October 6	24	Louisiana Tech	0	Oxford
L	October 13	24	Alabama	27	Oxford
L	October 20	8	Arkansas	44	Oxford
L	October 27	3	Auburn	17	Auburn
W	November 3	38	Northwestern State	31	Oxford
L	November 17	24	Louisiana State	41	Oxford
L	November 23	14	Mississippi State	17	Starkville

Mississippi State 8–5

RESULT	DATE	PF	OPPONENT	PA	LOCATION
L	August 30	0	Louisiana State	45	Starkville
W	September 8	38	Tulane	17	New Orleans
W	September 15	19	Auburn	14	Auburn
W	September 22	31	Gardner-Webb	15	Starkville
L	September 29	21	South Carolina	31	Columbia
W	October 6	30	Alabama-Birmingham	13	Starkville
L	October 13	21	Tennessee	33	Starkville
L	October 20	13	West Virginia	38	Morgantown
W	October 27	31	Kentucky	14	Lexington
W	November 10	17	Alabama	12	Starkville
L	November 17	31	Arkansas	45	Little Rock
W	November 23	17	Mississippi	14	Starkville
W	December 29	10	Central Florida	7	Liberty Bowl

I t could be argued that never in the 104-year-old series has one solitary play meant so much to so many—on both sides of the field. For one team it meant an improbable comeback and a postseason bowl game; for the other . . . well, a winless season in the Southeastern Conference and a new head coach.

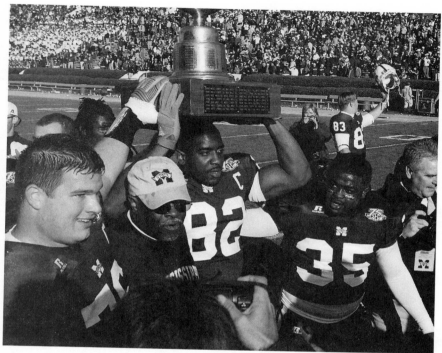

Mississippi State coach Sylvester Croom celebrates with his players after the Bulldogs' come-from-behind win that secured them a spot in the 2007 Liberty Bowl. © Mansel Guerry, Photographer.

Adam Carlson blasted a bloody-foot 48-yard field goal with only twelve seconds remaining to give Mississippi State a 17–14 victory in the 104th renewal of this storied rivalry. Carlson's field goal—the longest of his career—capped a 17-point rally for the Bulldogs in the game's final seven minutes and fifty-one seconds.

"I knew all along this was going to be a great day for Mississippi State football," said Bulldogs head coach Sylvester Croom, "but I never thought it would come down to that."

What it came down to was a stubborn MSU defense that buried an Ole Miss fourth-down gamble with ten minutes left in the ballgame.

November 23, 2007
Mississippi State 17, Ole Miss 14

	State	Ole Miss
First downs	10	21
Total plays	61	80
Total yards	273	319
Rushes/net yards	25/81	50/204
Passing yards	192	115
Passes		
(Att-Comp-Int)	36-15-1	30-10-1
Punts/average yards	8/41.2	7/36.6
Penalties/yards	9/80	6/42
Fumbles/lost	1/1	3/1
Time of possession	23:43	36:17
Third-down conversions	2/12	6/17
Sacks by: Number/yards	1/4	2/15
Field goals attempted/made	1/1	0/1

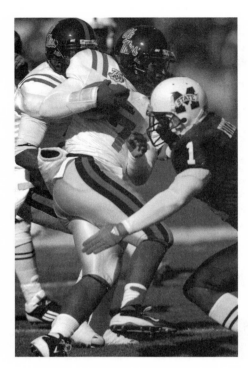

Mississippi State defensive back Keith Fitzhugh (1) stops Ole Miss quarterback Brent Schaeffer for no gain in the fourth quarter. Mississippi State University Photo.

Mississippi State safety Derek Pegues scores on a 75-yard punt return with 2:38 remaining to tie the 2007 Egg Bowl at 14–14. The Bulldogs would go on to win on a field goal by Adam Carlson with twelve seconds left. Mississippi State University Photo.

The Rebels took a 7–0 lead on the game's opening series when tailback BenJarvus Green-Ellis scored from 14 yards out. The touchdown capped a methodical 75-yard, twelve-play drive with Rebels quarterback Brent Schaeffer effectively mixing up the running and passing games.

Both defenses slugged it out for most of the next two-plus quarters before Ole Miss took a 14–0 lead when Shay Hodge hauled in a 13-yard pass from Schaeffer with 7:26 left in the third quarter.

Neither offense could gain any momentum and Mississippi State even benched starter Wesley Carroll for Michael Henig for a couple of series. Carroll returned to open the fourth quarter but his three incomplete passes and Blake McAdams punt gave Ole Miss the ball on its 40-yard line with 12:42 remaining. With good field position and a 14–0 lead, the Rebels appeared to be in control. The Bulldogs, however, had different ideas.

Three Ole Miss running plays gained only 9 yards, and on fourth-and-one Rebels head coach Ed Orgeron decided to gamble. Tailback Green-Ellis, who would finish the game with 117 rushing yards, took the handoff and was promptly smothered for a 3-yard loss by Bulldog defenders Jasper O'Quinn, Keith Fitzhugh, and Dominique Douglas.

"If I had to do it all over again, I probably would not make the same call," Orgeron said following the game. "I understand that was a bad call and that it probably cost us the game."

It was indeed the spark State needed. Carroll came back in with 10:05 left to play and a little over two minutes later hit tailback Anthony Dixon from 4 yards out for the score that capped a six-play, 46-yard drive. Carroll hit three of four passes in the drive the pulled the Bulldogs to within 14–7.

On its next possession, Carroll drove MSU to the Ole Miss 12-yard line but Rebel defender Ashlee Palmer came up with an interception with 3:51 left to seemingly seal the deal for Ole Miss.

Bulldogs safety Derek Pegues changed all that in less than two minutes when he took a Justin Sparks punt and returned it 75 yards to make it 14–14 with 2:38 left to play.

While the Rebels were held in check by the stingy State defense after the ensuing kickoff, they did manage to kill nearly two minutes. But it wasn't enough, and with only forty-three seconds left the Bulldogs got the ball back on their own 35-yard line.

Carroll took over and found Dixon for 6 yards, then scrambled for 11 yards and a first down. Two plays later he connected with Tony Burks for 17 yards to the Ole Miss 31, then threw an incompletion to kill the clock with twelve seconds left.

Enter Carlson, whose kicking foot had been stepped on earlier in the game. His kick from 48 yards out was never in doubt and Mississippi State had a 17–14 victory.

"I knew my foot hurt," Carlson said, "and when I got back to the locker room and took my shoe off, my sock was soaking wet."

If Carlson felt no pain, neither did the Bulldogs, who finished the regular season 7–5 overall and 4–4 in the SEC, and would go on to defeat Central Florida in the Liberty Bowl—their first bowl trip since 2000. And MSU coach Croom would be named SEC Coach of the Year.

Ole Miss (3–9, 0–8) finished the season winless in the SEC for the first time since 1982; the following day Orgeron was fired as coach.

2008

"Total Domination" on Both Sides of the Ball

2008 SCHEDULES

Ole Miss 9–4

RESULT	DATE	PF	OPPONENT	PA	LOCATION
W	August 30	41	Memphis	24	Oxford
L	September 6	28	Wake Forest	30	Winston-Salem
W	September 13	34	Samford	10	Oxford
L	September 20	17	Vanderbilt	23	Oxford
W	September 27	31	Florida	30	Gainesville
L	October 4	24	South Carolina	31	Oxford
L	October 18	20	Alabama	24	Tuscaloosa
W	October 25	23	Arkansas	21	Fayetteville
W	November 1	17	Auburn	7	Oxford
W	November 15	59	Louisiana-Monroe	0	Oxford
W	November 22	31	Louisiana State	13	Baton Rouge
W	November 28	45	Mississippi State	0	Oxford
W	January 2	47	Texas Tech	34	Cotton Bowl

Mississippi State 4–8

RESULT	DATE	PF	OPPONENT	PA	LOCATION
L	August 30	14	Louisiana Tech	22	Ruston
W	September 6	34	Southeastern Louisiana	10	Starkville
L	September 13	2	Auburn	3	Starkville
L	September 20	7	Georgia Tech	38	Atlanta
L	September 27	24	Louisiana State	34	Baton Rouge
W	October 11	17	Vanderbilt	14	Starkville
L	October 18	3	Tennessee	34	Knoxville
W	October 25	31	Middle Tennessee	22	Starkville
L	November 1	13	Kentucky	14	Starkville
L	November 15	7	Alabama	32	Tuscaloosa
W	November 22	31	Arkansas	28	Starkville
L	November 28	0	Mississippi	45	Oxford

Ole Miss made Houston Nutt's first Egg Bowl a game to remember—and Sylvester Croom's final one a game he'd rather forget. The Rebels scored on their first four offensive drives and their defense decimated Mississippi State to give Nutt, their first-year coach, a 45–0 victory in a rare Friday afternoon contest.

Ole Miss defensive end Greg Hardy (86) brushes off a block by Mississippi State running back Anthony Dixon (24) in the 2008 Egg Bowl. University of Mississippi Photo.

Jevan Snead, a sophomore quarterback, threw four touchdown passes, and the Ole Miss defense held the Bulldogs to 37 total yards and a minus-51 yards rushing. "Total domination," was Nutt's description, "and it starts with our defense."

Technically, this one started with the offense—with Snead hooking up with Shay Hodge for a 20-yard gain on the Rebels' first play from scrimmage. Four plays later, Dexter McCluster scampered in from 36 yards out to give Ole Miss a 7–0 lead, and the Rebels never looked back in chalking up their fifth consecutive win of the season and improving their record to 8–4 (5–3 in the Southeastern Conference.)

November 28, 2008
Ole Miss 45, Mississippi State 0

	State	Ole Miss
First downs	8	22
Total plays	56	68
Total yards	37	461
Rushes/net yards	26/(-51)	44/220
Passing yards	88	241
Passes		
(Att-Comp-Int)	30-10-2	24-14-1
Punts/average yards	12/37.0	3/29.3
Penalties/yards	6/52	3/40
Fumbles/lost	4/0	1/1
Time of possession	27:10	32:50
Third-down conversions	2/15	5/12
Sacks by: Number/yards	1/5	11/110
Field goals attempted/made	0-0	1–2

Ole Miss running back Dexter McCluster sets sail on a 36-yard touchdown run on the fifth play of the 2008 Egg Bowl. University of Mississippi Photo.

Ole Miss coach Houston Nutt and his players celebrate with the 2008 Egg Bowl trophy moments after their 45–0 win to clinch a berth in the Cotton Bowl. University of Mississippi Photo.

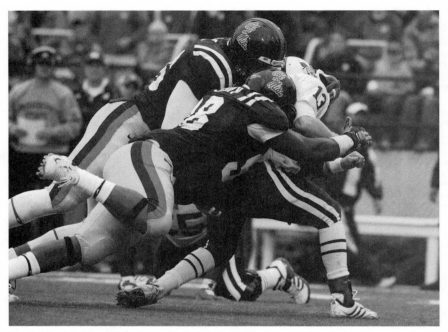

The Ole Miss defense smothered any and all Mississippi State efforts on offense in the 2008 Egg Bowl. The Rebels held the Bulldogs to 37 yards of total offense and minus-51 rushing yards. University of Mississippi Photo.

And as Nutt said, the Ole Miss defense was indeed dominant. The Rebels sacked Mississippi State quarterbacks a school-record eleven times for 97 yards in losses and had another fourteen tackles behind the line of scrimmage.

Ole Miss defensive end Greg Hardy had three quarterback sacks and tackle Peria Jerry had four tackles for loss, including two sacks. Freshman tackle Jerrell Powe had one and one-half sacks, two tackles for loss, and a pass interception.

"We had planned for them all week because we knew this was our biggest rivalry game all year," Jerry said. "We just tried to come out and make this the best game of the season defensively. I think we came up with a school record for sacks and it was a lot of fun."

Bulldogs tailback Anthony Dixon, coming off a career-high 179-yard game against Arkansas a week earlier, was held to only 14 yards. Croom could only shake his head later and say, "I didn't see that one coming."

Neither did the MSU quarterbacks. Tyson Lee and Wesley Carroll were hit by Ole Miss defenders nine times in their first ten pass attempts, and were intercepted twice in their first five throws.

Ole Miss defensive tackle Peria Jerry (98) spent most of the afternoon in the Mississippi State backfield. Jerry had four tackles for losses, including two quarterback sacks. University of Mississippi Photo.

The Rebels' Snead, however, completed his first nine passes for 117 yards and two touchdowns—to Hodge (10 yards) and to Mike Wallace (17 yards). The scoreboard read 24–0 after only one quarter.

"We wanted to send a message," said Snead, who on the day completed fourteen of nineteen passes for 213 yards and four touchdowns. "We knew (State) would come out with intensity and we knew we had to top that."

Top it they did. The Rebels finished the game with 461 yards of total offense—a balanced 241 passing yards and 220 rushing yards. Mississippi State got only 88 yards passing and a minus-51 rushing for a net offense of 37 yards. While Ole Miss averaged 6.8 yards per offensive play, the Bulldogs averaged 0.7.

The Rebels made it 31–0 at halftime when Snead completed a 72-yard bomb to Wallace with forty-two seconds remaining. There was nothing scientific about the play, Snead explained: "I just knew I had to get out there as far as I could. I let it go and fortunately Mike has a lot of speed, so he was able to get to it."

Snead also completed a 1-yard touchdown pass to tight end Bradley Sowell in the third quarter, and in the fourth quarter running back Brandon

Bolded finished off the scoring with a 24-yard touchdown romp. Placekicker Joshua Shene made all six of his extra-point kicks and booted a 42-yard field goal.

It was the final game of a remarkable regular season for the Rebels. Their victory earned them a spot in the Cotton Bowl where they beat No. 7 Texas Tech 47–30 and wound up 14th in the final Associated Press ratings. Nutt shared the SEC Coach of the Year honors with Vanderbilt's Bobby Johnson and Alabama's Nick Saban, and Jerry and offensive tackle Michael Oher earned first team All-American honors.

The Bulldogs finished the season with a 4–8 record (2–6 in the SEC), and Croom, who a year earlier signed a contract extension, resigned under pressure the following day.

2009

Dixon and Relf Too Hard to Handle

2009 SCHEDULES

Ole Miss 9–4

RESULT	DATE	PF	OPPONENT	PA	LOCATION
W	September 6	45	Memphis	14	Memphis
W	September 19	52	Southeastern Louisiana	6	Oxford
L	September 24	10	South Carolina	16	Columbia
W	October 3	23	Vanderbilt	7	Nashville
L	October 10	3	Alabama	22	Oxford
W	October 17	48	Alabama-Birmingham	13	Oxford
W	October 24	30	Arkansas	17	Oxford
L	October 31	20	Auburn	33	Auburn
W	November 7	38	Northern Arizona	14	Oxford
W	November 14	42	Tennessee	17	Oxford
W	November 21	25	Louisiana State	23	Oxford
L	November 28	27	Mississippi State	41	Starkville
W	January 2	21	Oklahoma State	7	Cotton Bowl

Mississippi State 5–7

RESULT	DATE	PF	OPPONENT	PA	LOCATION
W	September 5	48	Jackson State	7	Starkville
L	September 12	24	Auburn	49	Auburn
W	September 19	15	Vanderbilt	3	Nashville
L	September 26	26	Louisiana State	30	Starkville
L	October 3	31	Georgia Tech	42	Starkville
L	October 10	24	Houston	31	Starkville
W	October 17	27	Middle Tennessee	6	Murfreesboro
L	October 24	19	Florida	29	Starkville
W	October 31	31	Kentucky	24	Lexington
L	November 14	3	Alabama	31	Starkville
L	November 21	21	Arkansas	42	Little Rock
W	November 28	41	Mississippi	27	Starkville

Another first-year coach, another dominating win. This time it was Mississippi State pounding, giving their new leader Dan Mullen a 41–27 victory over Ole Miss in his first Egg Bowl, before a sellout crowd of 55,365 at Davis Wade Stadium.

Mississippi State running back Anthony Dixon dives for a 2-yard touchdown in the first half to give the Bulldogs a 10–6 lead over Ole Miss in the 2009 Egg Bowl. *Northeast Mississippi Daily Journal* Photo.

While the Bulldogs' defense limited the Rebels' running game to only 90 yards, their offense pile-drived to 412 total yards, including 317 on the ground. The one-two punch of tailback Anthony Dixon and quarterback Chris Relf proved too much for the Rebels. Dixon rushed for 133 yards and became State's single-season rushing leader with 1,391 yards. Relf came off the bench early in the game to replace quarterback Tyson Lee and gained 131 yards on the ground. He didn't pass much but when he did Relf made it count. He completed just three of five passes but two were for touchdowns.

"Chris got it rolling and got a feel for what was going on, and we were able to run the football," Mullen said of his sophomore quarterback. "I think they had eleven guys on the line of scrimmage and we were able to run the football."

There weren't many style points early-on, with Ole Miss getting two field goals from Joshua

November 28, 2009
Mississippi State 41, Ole Miss 27

	State	Ole Miss
First downs	24	15
Total plays	73	53
Total yards	412	385
Rushes/net yards	59/317	23/90
Passing yards	95	295
Passes		
(Att-Comp-Int)	14-8-1	30-18-3
Punts/average yards	1/48.0	2/39/5
Penalties/yards	2/15	5/25
Fumbles/lost	1/1	1/1
Time of possession	37:02	22:58
Third-down conversions	9/13	4/11
Sacks by: Number/yards	1/7	2/9
Field goals attempted/made	2/2	2/2

Mississippi State senior running back Anthony Dixon is all smiles after his Bulldogs walloped Ole Miss in the 2009 Egg Bowl. Dixon rushed for 133 yards against the Rebels and set a single-season Mississippi State rushing record with 1,391 yards. *Northeast Mississippi Daily Journal* Photo.

Shene (26 and 28 yards) and State getting a 28-yard three-pointer from Derek DePasquale. The Bulldogs offered a glimpse of things to come, however, when they drove 81 yards in nine plays, including seven running plays, to go ahead 10–6 on Dixon's 2-yard touchdown with 3:22 left in the half.

Ole Miss responded with its own 73-yard, six-play drive to take a 13–10 halftime lead. Rebels' quarterback Jevan Snead completed three of three passes on the drive, hooking up with Shay Hodge from 20 yards out for the go-ahead score.

The Bulldogs Bash began as soon as the second half began. State tied the game on a 48-yard field goal from DePasquale. The MSU defense stuffed the Ole Miss offense, and the Bulldogs mounted a thirteen-play, 70-yard drive for a lead they would not relinquish. Relf, who completed only two passes in the drive, hit Marcus Green on a 2-yard throw for a 20–13 lead with 4:07 left in the third quarter.

MSU made it 27–13 (17–0 in the third quarter alone) when Relf connected with Chad Bumphis on a 34-yard aerial touchdown set up by Chris Mitchell's pass interception.

Mississippi State's first-year head coach Dan Mullen celebrates the Bulldogs' 41–27 ambush of Ole Miss in the 2009 Egg Bowl. *Northeast Mississippi Daily Journal* Photo.

And when Ole Miss struck back on a 48-yard pass from Snead to Markeith Summers to open the fourth quarter, the Bulldogs responded with another eight-play (all rushes) drive that Relf capped off with a 10-yard run for a 34–20 lead. Freshman defensive back Corey Broomfield made it 41–20 when he picked off Snead for the second time and returned it 64 yards for the score.

Ole Miss got one more touchdown—a 52-yard pass from Snead to Dexter McCluster with just under five minutes remaining—but the Dixon-led ground game ate up the rest of the clock and the Golden Egg returned to Starkville.

Rebels coach Houston Nutt summed it up best: "It is not what we planned, but give Mississippi State credit. They did a good job. Did we do a good job of running the ball or not turning the ball over? I do not think so. You absolutely cannot turn the ball over, especially in a rivalry game like this. . . . Mississippi State just did a great job of running the football."

The Bulldogs finished their first season under Mullen with a 5–7 record (3–5 in the SEC). Ole Miss wound up with its second straight 8–4 season (4–4 in the SEC) and its second straight trip to the Cotton Bowl where it would defeat Oklahoma State, 21–7.

2010

A Second Straight for State

2010 SCHEDULES

Ole Miss 4-8

RESULT	DATE	PF	OPPONENT	PA	LOCATION
L	September 4	48	Jacksonville State (Overtime)	49	Oxford
W	September 11	27	Tulane	13	New Orleans
L	September 18	28	Vanderbilt	14	Oxford
W	September 25	55	Fresno State	38	Oxford
W	October 2	42	Kentucky	35	Oxford
L	October 16	10	Alabama	23	Tuscaloosa
L	October 23	24	Arkansas	38	Fayetteville
L	October 30	31	Auburn	51	Oxford
W	November 6	43	Louisiana	21	Oxford
L	November 13	14	Tennessee	52	Knoxville
L	November 20	36	Louisiana State	43	Baton Rouge
L	November 27	23	Mississippi State	31	Oxford

Mississippi State 9-4

RESULT	DATE	PF	OPPONENT	PA	LOCATION
W	September 4	49	Memphis	7	Starkville
L	September 9	14	Auburn	17	Starkville
L	September 18	7	Lousiana State	29	Baton Rouge
W	September 25	24	Georgia	12	Starkville
W	October 2	49	Alcorn State	16	Starkville
W	October 9	47	Houston	24	Houston
W	October 16	10	Florida	7	Gainesville
W	October 23	29	Alabama-Birmingham	24	Starkville
W	October 30	24	Kentucky	17	Starkville
L	November 13	10	Alabama	30	Tuscaloosa
L	November 20	31	Arkansas (Overtime)	38	Starkville
W	November 27	31	Mississippi	23	Oxford
W	November 1	52	Michigan	14	Jacksonville

The 2010 season had not gone well for the Ole Miss Rebels. They entered the Battle for the Golden Egg on a two-game losing streak with back-to-back losses to Tennessee and LSU and an overall record of only 4-7.

Ole Miss hosted the Egg Bowl that season on November 27, two days after Thanksgiving. It was the third year of the Houston Nutt era for the Rebels, and likely very few in the preseason could have foreseen the unraveling and dismal outcomes ahead. That would be especially true since Ole Miss had just posted back-to-back nine-win seasons with Cotton Bowl victories.

The 2010 season started in a shocking manner. A loss that would prove difficult to overcome kicked off the season on September 4 in Oxford. Ole Miss lost 49-48 in two overtimes to Jacksonville (Ala.) State after building what appeared to be a comfortable 31-10 advantage at halftime. Games against Tulane, Fresno State, Kentucky, and Louisiana-Lafayette on Homecoming were the only ones Ole Miss managed to win entering the season finale against the Bulldogs.

Mississippi State, meanwhile, arrived for the game on a roll in its second season under Dan Mullen. The Bulldogs appeared to be building something special in Starkville. MSU would finish the season ranked among the nation's top 20 teams. In the Associated Press poll, Mississippi State was No. 15 after a 52-14 Gator Bowl rout of Michigan.

The Bulldogs' record entering the Egg Bowl was 7-4. Key victories had been over Georgia, Florida, and Kentucky. The 10-7 win over the No. 22 Gators was especially noteworthy since Mullen had been an assistant coach in Gainesville before coming to Starkville.

On that November Saturday night in Oxford for the finale, MSU trailed 6-0 at the end of the first quarter but claimed the second quarter handily to take a 21-9 lead into the locker room at intermission.

Ole Miss's first-quarter touchdown came after a Bulldog fumble was recovered by the Rebels' Jeremy McGee deep in MSU territory. On the very next play, the Rebels' Jeff Scott carried the football into the end zone from 16 yards out. The extra point kick was blocked.

In the second quarter, the Bulldogs gained control. MSU took a 7-6 lead on a 15-yard touchdown pass from quarterback Chris Relf to Chris Smith. The extra point kick

November 27, 2010
Mississippi State 31, Ole Miss 23

	State	Ole Miss
First downs	18	19
Total plays	70	79
Total yards	498	326
Rushes/net yards	50/210	35/65
Passing yards	288	261
Passes		
(Att-Comp-Int)	20-13-1	44-24-1
Punts/yards	6/257	8/378
Penalties/yards	3-25	5/45
Fumbles/lost		2/2 1/1
Time of possession	31:31	28:29
Third-down conversions	5/16	3/17
Sacks by: Number/yards	3/19	2/13
Field goals attempted/made	2/1	1/1

Bulldog quarterback Chris Relf (No. 14) in the 2010 Egg Bowl. Courtesy of Mississippi State University Athletics.

by Derek DePasquale was good. After Ole Miss retook the lead on a 34-yard Bryson Rose field goal, the Bulldogs would score twice more before halftime.

Both MSU scoring drives before the half were brief. In only three plays Relf led State downfield 82 yards, with the touchdown a pass play from Relf to LaDarius Perkins for 33 yards. DePasquale was again good on his kick for a 14-9 lead for the visiting team.

Ole Miss couldn't produce anything on its next three possessions. On MSU's third possession after its most recent score, the Bulldogs did. As halftime was nearing, MSU took just two plays to score on a drive covering 53 yards. The touchdown was another pass from Relf to Perkins, this time for 36 yards. DePasquale's kick made it 21-9 in favor of State.

In the third quarter MSU expanded its lead to 24-9 on a DePasquale field goal of 42 yards. The Bulldogs scored again late in the third period on a Vick

MSU running back LaDarius Perkins in the Egg Bowl of 2010. Courtesy of Mississippi State University Athletics.

Ballard rush for 8 yards that capped a 79-yard, six play drive. DePasquale's point after kick gave his team a 31-9 lead, and all appeared comfortable for Mississippi State heading into the fourth quarter.

But the Rebels put up a fight to the end, scoring two touchdowns before the final horn. A 10-yard rush by Brandon Bolden ended a ten-play drive for Ole Miss. With Rose's extra point, the home team was back in it, trailing just 31-16. If the Rebels could score again before State scored, anything was possible. And that is exactly what happened.

Another ten-play drive, with quarterback Jeremiah Masoli connecting with Ja-Mes Logan for 24 yards and a touchdown, made the Bulldog faithful anxious and gave Rebel fans hope. The extra point by Rose pulled Ole Miss to within 8 points at 31-23 with 4:21 to go in the contest. This was now anybody's game to win.

After Heath Hutchins punted for MSU with 2:30 to go in the game, Ole Miss started a drive on its own 11-yard line. But the Rebels were only able to move the football as far as their own 23 before Mississippi State's defense stopped them.

For the second straight season, the Golden Egg would reside in Starkville, and the following year MSU would go for three wins in a row in the series. That was something that had not happened since the 1939–42 seasons when State claimed four consecutive victories.

Relf had thrown for a career-high 288 yards and three touchdowns in the contest on 13-of-20 passing with one interception but three touchdowns.

Masoli had a statistically good night as well, completing 24-of-44 passes for one touchdown and one interception. But it was on the ground that the Bulldogs dominated.

State rushed for 210 yards on fifty carries, while the Bulldog defenders held Ole Miss to only 65 yards on thirty-five attempts. Total offense was 498 yards for MSU and 326 yards for the Rebels.

Mississippi State had not won in Oxford since 1998. But the Bulldogs headed to Starkville victorious and bowl bound with their 8-4 record for the regular season.

"In the end, we made one more play when we needed to," said Mullen, with his second Egg Bowl win in as many seasons. "We are going to go home and celebrate this win."

"It's been a tough season," Nutt said, falling to 1-2 in Egg Bowls. "I really hate it for the seniors. We got off to a bad start back in September, and it has been an uphill struggle since the first game."

MSU's 4-4 Southeastern Conference record was good for only fifth place in the six-team SEC West. The Rebels were a distant last at 1-7, with their lone conference win against Kentucky in early October. Later, Ole Miss was forced to vacate its four 2010 wins due to an NCAA ruling.

2011

Wrapped Again in Maroon and White

2011 SCHEDULES

Ole Miss 2-10

RESULT	DATE	PF	OPPONENT	PA	LOCATION
L	September 3	13	Brigham Young	14	Oxford
W	September 10	42	Southern Illinois	24	Oxford
L	September 17	7	Vanderbilt	30	Nashville
L	September 17	13	Georgia	27	Oxford
W	October 1	38	Fresno State	28	Fresno
L	October 15	7	Alabama	52	Oxford
L	October 22	24	Arkansas	29	Oxford
L	October 29	23	Auburn	41	Auburn
L	November 5	13	Kentucky	30	Lexington
L	November 12	7	Louisiana Tech	27	Oxford
L	November 19	3	Louisiana State	52	Oxford
L	November 26	3	Mississippi State	31	Starkville

Mississippi State 7-6

RESULT	DATE	PF	OPPONENT	PA	LOCATION
W	September 1	59	Memphis	14	Memphis
L	September 10	34	Auburn	41	Auburn
L	September 15	6	Louisiana State	19	Starkville
W	September 24	26	Louisiana Tech (Overtime)	20	Starkville
L	October 1	10	Georgia	24	Athens
W	October 8	21	Alabama-Birmingham	3	Birmingham
L	October 15	12	South Carolina	14	Starkville
W	October 29	28	Kentucky	16	Lexington
W	November 5	55	Tennessee Martin	17	Starkville
L	November 12	7	Alabama	24	Starkville
L	November 19	17	Arkansas	44	Little Rock
W	November 26	31	Mississippi	3	Starkville
W	December 30	23	Wake Forest	17	Nashville

Entering the 2011 Battle for the Golden Egg, Mississippi State had claimed two straight Egg Bowl wins. The game that season would give the Bulldogs an opportunity for something that hadn't happened in decades—a third straight win over Ole Miss in football.

Defensive tackle Fletcher Cox (No. 94) of MSU in the 2011 Battle for the Golden Egg. Courtesy of Mississippi State University Athletics.

Not since the 1939–42 State squads claimed four wins in a row over the Rebels had the Bulldogs had as much sustained success in the rivalry game. This one was in Starkville, and Dan Mullen and company intended to win it and make history.

As this game unfolded, the outcome was really never in doubt. Mississippi State rolled to a 31-3 victory to finish 6-6 overall and 2-6 in the Southeastern Conference. The Bulldogs would advance to the Music City Bowl and defeat Wake Forest of the Atlantic Coast Conference.

The Rebels, meanwhile, finished 2-10 overall and 0-8 in the SEC. It was the first time since 1946 that an Ole Miss football team had won as few as two games in a season. It would also mean a change in leadership for the Rebel program as Houston Nutt coached his last game for Ole Miss in the 2011 Egg Bowl. A new direction for the program had actually been announced earlier in November. Nutt knew several weeks before the finale that his tenure in Oxford was ending. Later, Ole Miss was forced to vacate its two 2011 wins due to an NCAA ruling.

At the end of the 2008 regular season, Ole Miss had won 45-0 over State in Oxford. The programs had now basically exchanged places. A new coaching staff, led by Hugh Freeze, would be in place in Oxford just a few days following the Bulldogs' win over the Rebels.

November 26, 2011
Mississippi State 31, Ole Miss 3

	State	Ole Miss
First downs	17	10
Total plays	61	64
Total yards	317	202
Rushes/net yards	48/247	42/92
Passing yards	70	110
Passes (Att-Comp-Int)	13-8-1	22-12-0
Punts/yards	6/273	6/287
Penalties/yards	8/80	4/45
Fumbles/lost	0/0	0/2
Time of possession	29:33	30:27
Third-down conversions	4/13	5/18
Sacks by: Number/yards	2/17	0/0
Field goals attempted/made	1/1	1/1

MSU's Vick Ballard races downfield in the 2011 Egg Bowl. Courtesy of Mississippi State University Athletics.

On November 26, 2011, Mississippi State jumped out to a 14-0 lead at the end of the first quarter, and made it 21-0 by halftime. The Rebels, down 28-0 before finally getting points on a 28-yard field goal by Bryson Rose midway through the third quarter, were never really a threat to stop the Bulldogs' run to their third win in a row in the series.

Ole Miss won the game's opening toss but deferred to the second half. MSU took the kickoff from Andrew Ritter and began a drive at its own 32. In eleven plays, the Bulldogs led 7-0 on a quarterback Chris Relf–to–Vick Ballard

18-yard pass play and a point-after-kick by Derek DePasquale. Momentum, already on the side of the home team, would continue to build.

Late in the first period, MSU got on the scoreboard again, this time an impressive nine-play drive of 98 yards that began following a Tyler Campbell punt of 59 yards for the Rebels down to the 2-yard line. The Bulldogs methodically moved the length of the football field, and the result was a 36-yard touchdown rush for LaDarius Perkins. The extra point by DePasquale was good, and MSU led 14-0.

In the second quarter, with the MSU crowd already sensing a possible overwhelming margin of victory, Relf connected with Perkins on a touchdown pass of 20 yards. The point after touchdown by DePasquale made the score 21-0 in favor of the Bulldogs. Ole Miss was clearly in trouble in this one.

The third quarter was no better for the Rebels, and MSU was on the board again quickly for a four-score advantage. After an Ole Miss fumble deep in Mississippi State territory, the Bulldogs scored on two runs by Vick Ballard. The first was a 2-yard rush from the 27-yard line, and the scoring run was the very next play from 25 yards out. DePasquale was again good on his kick, and MSU was in total command, up 28-0 early in the third quarter.

Later in the third period, Ole Miss began a drive at its own 43-yard line after a State punt. The Rebels took a lot of time off the clock in driving twelve plays for a score but only managed to get 3 points. With 4:59 to go in the third, Ole Miss chose a field goal by Bryson Rose, and the kick was good from 28 yards out.

The Rebels trailed 28-3, and that's the way things stood heading into the fourth quarter. A drive that had begun for State late in the third quarter continued into the fourth, which added to MSU's point total. With 12:03 remaining, DePasquale kicked a 35-yard field goal, and the Bulldogs led 31-3.

All that remained was to see if either team would score again. Neither did, and MSU claimed another victory in the series.

Mississippi State dominated the statistics, as would be expected in such a lop-sided game. The Bulldogs had 317 yards of offense and 17 first downs to 202 offensive yards and 10 first downs for the Rebels. Ballard had 144 yards rushing on twenty-three carries and one touchdown to lead the way for MSU. Ole Miss's six fumbles, with two of them recovered by Mississippi State, contributed to the outcome on this day.

"This is definitely not how we wanted to go out," said senior Rebel defensive player Kentrell Lockett, "but this game was a reflection of the entire season."

Nutt was reflective but steadfast after his fourteenth season as an SEC head coach ended, ten of them as head coach at Arkansas and four at Ole Miss.

"This is not the way I wanted to go out," Nutt said. "But I wouldn't have changed a thing I did."

In the winning locker room, there was a celebration with a trophy that had found a home in Starkville for an extended period of time. The 28-point margin was the largest for MSU in a victory over Ole Miss since a 33-0 win in 1919.

"It's definitely a blessing to be able to get this third straight win in the Egg Bowl," said MSU defensive player Brandon Wilson.

"Obviously, it was a great win," Mullen said. "Three straight Egg Bowl championships is something special. I'm really proud of our guys. They know how important [the Egg Bowl] is for us, and how important it is for our fans."

2012

A New Era Begins with an Ole Miss Win

2012 SCHEDULES

Ole Miss 7-6

RESULT	DATE	PF	OPPONENT	PA	LOCATION
W	September 1	49	Central Arkansas	27	Oxford
W	September 8	28	Texas-El Paso	10	Oxford
L	September 15	31	Texas	66	Oxford
W	September 22	39	Tulane	0	New Orleans
L	September 29	14	Alabama	33	Tuscaloosa
L	October 6	27	Texas A&M	30	Oxford
W	October 13	41	Auburn	20	Oxford
W	October 27	30	Arkansas	27	Little Rock
L	November 3	10	Georgia	37	Athens
L	November 10	26	Vanderbilt	27	Oxford
L	November 17	35	Louisiana State	41	Baton Rouge
W	November 24	41	Mississippi State	24	Oxford
W	January 5	38	Pittsburgh	17	Birmingham

Mississippi State 8-5

RESULT	DATE	PF	OPPONENT	PA	LOCATION
W	September 1	56	Jackson State	9	Starkville
W	September 8	28	Auburn	10	Starkville
W	September 15	30	Troy State	24	Troy
W	September 22	30	South Alabama	10	Starkville
W	September 29	27	Kentucky	14	Lexington
W	October 6	41	Tennessee	31	Starkville
W	October 13	45	Middle Tennessee State	3	Starkville
L	October 27	7	Alabama	38	Tuscaloosa
L	November 3	13	Texas A&M	38	Starkville
L	November 10	17	Louisiana State	37	Baton Rouge
W	November 17	45	Arkansas	14	Starkville
L	November 24	24	Mississippi	41	Oxford
L	January 1	20	Northwestern	34	Jacksonville

O le Miss had lost three games in a row to Mississippi State entering the 2012 Battle for the Golden Egg, which was being played in Oxford. It was the Bulldogs' most successful run against their archrivals since the late 1930s and early 1940s.

Young Ole Miss fan at the 2012 Egg Bowl. Courtesy of Ole Miss Athletics.

Most Ole Miss–Mississippi State football games through the years have been played on the two campuses. There is a large segment of fans from both institutions, however, who grew up as children through college age, some of them even into young adulthood, that knew nothing but Egg Bowl games in the capital city of Jackson. From 1973 through 1990, Mississippi Veterans Memorial Stadium, near the University of Mississippi Medical School campus, played host to the regular season finale.

By 2012, those games at the neutral site were a distant memory. As the 109th edition of the game approached, twenty-fourth-ranked MSU was favored, entering the game at 8-3 overall and 4-3 in Southeastern Conference play. Ole Miss, meanwhile, was 5-6 on the season and 2-5 in the SEC.

But the Rebels were in the first season of a new era. Although their record wasn't stellar entering the Egg Bowl, new head coach Hugh Freeze brought a mentality of reclaiming the Golden Egg as one of his program's immediate goals. The teams were tied 17-17 at halftime, but it was Ole Miss that totally dominated the second half for a 41-24 victory.

Until MSU scored a touchdown with seven seconds to go in the game, the Rebels had built a 41-17

November 24, 2012
Ole Miss 41, Mississippi State 24

	State	Ole Miss
First downs	28	17
Total plays	64	78
Total yards	333	527
Rushes/net yards	25/30	56/233
Passing yards	303	294
Passes		
(Att-Comp-Int	39-21-2	22-15-2
Punts/yards	6/233	3/94
Penalties/yards	5/66	4/35
Fumbles/lost	0/0	1/1
Time of Possession	28:19	31:41
Third-down conversions	1/13	6/14
Sacks by: Number/yards	¼	3/22
Field goals attempted/made	2/1	3/2

Rebels receiver Donte Moncrief had a big night against MSU in the 2012 Egg Bowl. Courtesy of Ole Miss Athletics.

lead since halftime and were on their way to ending the Mississippi State winning streak at three games.

"Feed Moncrief" became the battle cry for the Rebels in this victory on November 24, 2012. Rebel quarterback Bo Wallace found a favorite target on this night as Donte Moncrief caught three touchdown passes to lead the Ole Miss attack.

The sophomore wide receiver was on the scoring end of a 77-yard touchdown pass play from Wallace with 5:19 to go in the second quarter which, along with a Bryson Rose extra point, gave Ole Miss a 17-14 lead.

Moncrief, who finished the game with seven receptions for 173 yards, also scored on touchdown catches of 21 yards and 16 yards, which, with Rose's successful point after kicks, helped give the Rebels a 34-17 lead late in the third quarter.

MSU won the game's opening toss but deferred to the second half. Ole Miss got the football first and scored quickly. In only four plays, the Rebels put together a scoring drive covering 71 yards, including a 42-yard pass from Wallace to Moncrief. The touchdown was a 25-yard pass from Wallace to tight end Jamal Mosley. Rose's kick made it 7-0 Ole Miss with less than two minutes gone in the first quarter. Some fans were still settling into their seats by the time the first drive ended.

But MSU responded to score without ever snapping the football as Jameon Lewis returned Rose's kickoff 100 yards for a Bulldog touchdown. With Devon Bell's successful extra point kick, the score was 7-7 and less than two minutes had been played in the game. If the early going was any indication, this contest would be a thriller.

It was indeed that throughout the first half. The visiting Bulldogs went ahead 14-7 with 2:46 to go in the opening period.

In the 2012 Egg Bowl in Oxford, Mississippi, State quarterback Tyler Russell. Courtesy of Mississippi State University Athletics.

Quarterback Tyler Russell connected with wide receiver Chad Bumphis on a 42-yard pass for the touchdown, and Bell's point after gave State a 7-point lead and the momentum.

Ole Miss cut into the MSU advantage with a Rose field goal of 43 yards to make the score 14-10 with 13:36 to go in the second quarter after a Rebel drive of nine plays stalled at the MSU 26-yard line. Ole Miss retook the lead late in the second quarter on Moncrief's 77-yard catch as the Rebels scored in only two plays when an MSU drive ended at the Rebels' 18 after an unsuccessful fourth-down play. Rose's extra point made it 17-14 with the home team ahead.

State tied things up at 17-17 with 3:21 to go before halftime on a Bell field goal of 23 yards. That's the way things stood at intermission, but it would be mostly Ole Miss the rest of the way.

An eleven-play drive in the third quarter ended for Ole Miss with a successful 41-yard field goal by Rose and the Rebels led 20-17. Then came the two Wallace to Moncrief touchdown passes of 21 yards and 16 yards to give Ole Miss huge momentum and a 34-17 lead heading into the fourth quarter. When Wallace connected with wide receiver Vincent Sanders on a 16-yard scoring

The Rebels celebrate the 2012 Egg Bowl victory after having lost to MSU the three previous seasons, the first time State had beaten Ole Miss three straight times in football since World War II. Courtesy of Ole Miss Athletics.

pass, along with a Rose kick, to finish an eleven-play, 87-yard drive with 11:44 to go, the only aspect to be determined was the final score. Ole Miss led 41-17.

State added a touchdown with only seven seconds remaining in the contest as Bumphis caught an 8-yard pass from quarterback Dak Prescott. Bell connected on his extra point kick for the final 17-point margin. Later, Ole Miss was forced to vacate the 2012 victory due to an NCAA ruling.

Freeze and the Rebels, at 6-6 overall and 3-5 in the SEC, moved on to play in Birmingham's BBVA Compass Bowl against the Pittsburgh Panthers. The rookie Rebel head coach said he was happy for his players.

"These kids have had some difficult times, and now they can hear the good side of it, so I'm thrilled," Freeze said in the postgame of the Egg Bowl. "To send them out to a bowl game will be really nice."

"Give them credit," MSU head coach Dan Mullen said of the Rebels. "Their kids played hard and made a lot of plays when they needed to make big plays. This is such a big game for us, and we take this game extremely serious."

MSU was 8-4 on the season and 4-4 in the SEC. The Bulldogs would play Northwestern of the Big Ten in the Gator Bowl in Jacksonville.

Although he did not score, running back Jeff Scott had 111 yards on twenty-eight carries for Ole Miss. Wallace ended the game 15-of-22 for 294 yards and five touchdowns with two interceptions.

For State, Russell was 18-of-33 for 268 yards and one touchdown with two interceptions. Bumphis had six receptions for 146 yards and two scores.

Ole Miss had 28 first downs and MSU had 17. The Rebels had 527 yards of offense. Ole Miss had 233 rushing yards on fifty-six carries. The Bulldogs had 333 yards, but only 30 of those were rushing yards on twenty-five carries.

The Rebels also had possession of the Golden Egg for the first time since winning the 2008 Egg Bowl 45-0 in Oxford.

2013

A Close Encounter and an Overtime Ending

2013 SCHEDULES

Ole Miss 8-5

RESULT	DATE	PF	OPPONENT	PA	LOCATION
W	August 29	39	Vanderbilt	35	Nashville
W	September 7	31	SEMO	13	Oxford
W	September 14	44	Texas	23	Austin
L	September 28	0	Alabama	25	Tuscaloosa
L	October 5	22	Auburn	30	Auburn
L	October 12	38	Texas A&M	41	Oxford
W	October 19	27	Louisiana State	24	Oxford
W	October 26	59	Idaho	14	Oxford
W	November 9	34	Arkansas	24	Oxford
W	November 16	51	Troy State	21	Oxford
L	November 23	10	Missouri	24	Oxford
L	November 28	10	Mississippi State (Overtime)	17	Starkville
W	December 30	25	Georgia Tech	17	Nashville

Mississippi State 7-6

RESULT	DATE	PF	OPPONENT	PA	LOCATION
L	August 31	3	Oklahoma State	21	Houston
W	September 7	51	Alcorn State	7	Starkville
L	September 14	20	Auburn	24	Auburn
W	September 21	62	Troy State	7	Starkville
L	October 5	26	Louisiana State	59	Starkville
W	October 12	21	Bowling Green	20	Starkville
W	October 24	28	Kentucky	22	Starkville
L	November 2	16	South Carolina	34	Columbia
L	November 9	41	Texas A&M	51	College Station
L	November 16	7	Alabama	20	Starkville
W	November 23	24	Arkansas (Overtime)	17	Little Rock
W	November 28	17	Mississippi (Overtime)	10	Starkville
W	December 31	44	Rice	7	Memphis

Hugh Freeze vs. Dan Mullen, edition two, would play out in Starkville, on Scott Field at Davis-Wade Stadium. And it would have a dramatic ending, as Egg Bowls often do.

Mississippi State defensive lineman Chris Jones in the 2013 Egg Bowl in Starkville. Courtesy of Mississippi State University Athletics.

There wasn't much scoring in this game, and it would conclude with an overtime finish. Mississippi State won 17-10, the Bulldogs' fourth Egg Bowl victory in the past five seasons.

The game's regulation play ended when MSU field goal kicker Evan Sobiesk wasn't successful on what would have been a game-winner from 39 yards as the kick sailed wide right. The hearts of a crowd of 55,000 predominantly State fans collectively sank as the field goal that would have won it missed.

However, Sobiesk only minutes earlier had been the reason the Bulldogs were able to get the game into overtime in the first place. With MSU trailing Ole Miss 10-7, which was the score at the end of the third quarter, Sobiesk connected on a 36-yard field goal that knotted the score at 10-10 with only 2:21 to go in the game—at least the regulation part of it.

After getting the football back following Devon Bell's kickoff for

November 28, 2013
Mississippi State 17, Ole Miss 10

	State	Ole Miss
First downs	23	17
Total plays	82	78
Total yards	296	318
Rushes/net yards	43/99	35/117
Passing yards	197	201
Passes (Att-Comp-Int)	19-39-1	28-43-3
Punts/yards	9/334	8/338
Penalties/yards	5/39	7/50
Fumbles/lost	2/1	1/1
Time of possession	32:48/	27:12/
Third-down conversions	5/17	8/20
Sacks by: Number/yards	2/12	2/17
Field goals attempted/made	2/1	2/1

Bulldog quarterback Dak Prescott follows his blockers in the 2013 Egg Bowl. Courtesy of Mississippi State University Athletics.

MSU, the Rebels had the ball at their own 12-yard line. It would have been at the 22 but a holding call on Ole Miss on the return brought it back 10 yards. Three plays only netted 7 yards for the Rebels up to their own 19-yard line, and Tyler Campbell was sent in to punt with 1:14 to go.

That's when the Bulldogs, behind the passing of quarterback Dak Prescott, moved from their own 34 to the Rebels' 21 before stalling out. And that's when Sobiesk came in for the field goal, which missed from 39 yards as time expired.

In the extra period, MSU got the football first and began its quest for points. From the Ole Miss 25-yard line, State moved methodically in six plays for a touchdown. Prescott kept the football from the 3-yard line and took it in for the go-ahead score. Sobiesk was good on his extra point attempt, and MSU led 17–10. But Ole Miss would now have its turn to attempt to score in the overtime period.

At the Bulldogs' 25-yard line, Ole Miss quarterback Bo Wallace passed to Jaylen Walton on first down for 5 yards. After an incomplete pass attempt by Wallace for Vincent Sanders, Wallace connected with Donte Moncrief for 9 yards to the MSU 11. The dramatic end to this game, unbeknownst to the crowd, was moments away.

Wallace kept the football from the 11-yard line and appeared to be headed for the goal line. But at the 3-yard line, State's Nickoe Whitley forced a fumble, and the football found its way into the end zone. Had an Ole Miss player

Bulldog defensive back Nickoe Whitley (No. 1) pressures Ole Miss quarterback Bo Wallace in the 2013 Egg Bowl in Starkville. Courtesy of Mississippi State University Athletics.

recovered the ball, it would have meant a touchdown, and only a successful extra point kick by the Rebels' Andrew Ritter would have remained for the overtime to continue.

But it was Mississippi State that recovered the football, much to the delight of the home crowd, and the game was over at that point. The Bulldogs' Jamerson Love was the player who came up with the football in the end zone, and Mississippi State had claimed another Battle for the Golden Egg, this one on Thanksgiving night, November 28, 2013.

For the first time in the history of the series, MSU had won five straight games at home against Ole Miss. The Rebels had their chances for two wins in a row against the archrival, but they fell just short of at least continuing the game into a second overtime period.

Much like the final outcome, the game was relatively close throughout. The final statistics made that clear.

MSU had 23 first downs, while Ole Miss had 17. State rushed the football 43 times for 99 yards, and Ole Miss had thirty-five carries for 117 yards on the ground.

In the passing department, Wallace for the Rebels was 26-for-40 for 182 yards but with three interceptions and no touchdowns. The Ole Miss starting signal-caller was also sacked two times by the MSU defense. For the Rebels, Barry Brunetti also passed the football in the contest, going 1-for-2 on his throws. Receiver Laquon Treadwell also threw one pass that was completed for 19 yards.

Bulldog quarterback Prescott eliminated the interceptions that haunted Wallace in this one, although the MSU signal-caller didn't throw a touchdown pass either. He was 11-for-20 for 115 yards. Damien Williams was also 8-for-18 for 82 yards with one interception for the Bulldogs.

Total offense looked like this: For Mississippi State 296 yards, and for Ole Miss 318 yards.

The Rebels had five players with multiple catches: Treadwell with nine for 57 yards, Walton with six for 15 yards, Ja-Mes Logan with four for 51 yards, Sanders with four for 33 yards, and Moncrief with three for 24 yards.

State had the same number with multiple receptions: Jameon Lewis with six for 68 yards, De'Runnya Wilson with four for 45 yards, Malcolm Johnson with three for 37 yards, Robert Johnson with two for 18 yards, and LaDarius Perkins with two for 10 yards.

On the ground, MSU was led by Williams with thirteen carries for 29 yards. Perkins had 5 yards on twelve carries. Prescott had nine carries for 29 yards and a touchdown. Josh Robinson scored one touchdown and had 38 yards on seven rushes.

Walton led Ole Miss rushers with ten carries for 37 yards, while Wallace kept the football 12 times for 31 yards. I'Tavius Mathers had seven carries for 10 yards, Robert Nkemdiche four for 21, and Brunetti two for 18.

Defensive leaders for each team were Taveze Calhoun for the Bulldogs with 11 total tackles, nine of them solos, while Mike Hilton paced the Rebel defenders with five solo stops and seven total tackles.

Ole Miss, with its regular season final mark of 7-5 overall and 3-5 in the Southeastern Conference, moved on to defeat Georgia Tech 25-17 in Nashville's Music City Bowl for its eighth win of the season. Mississippi State was bowl eligible with the victory and at 6-6 overall and 3-5 in the SEC played Rice in the Liberty Bowl in Memphis, defeating the Owls 44-7, for its seventh victory.

2014

Two Stellar Seasons and National Headlines for Mississippi

2014 SCHEDULES

Ole Miss 9-4

RESULT	DATE	PF	OPPONENT	PA	LOCATION
W	August 28	35	Boise State	13	Atlanta
W	September 6	41	Vanderbilt	3	Nashville
W	September 13	56	Louisiana	15	Oxford
W	September 27	24	Memphis	3	Oxford
W	October 4	23	Alabama	17	Oxford
W	October 11	35	Texas A&M	20	College Station
W	October 18	34	Tennessee	3	Oxford
L	October 25	7	Louisiana State	10	Baton Rouge
L	November 1	31	Auburn	35	Oxford
W	November 8	48	Presbyterian	0	Oxford
L	November 22	0	Arkansas	30	Fayetteville
W	November 29	31	Mississippi State	17	Oxford
L	December 31	3	Texas Christian	42	Atlanta

Mississippi State 10-3

RESULT	DATE	PF	OPPONENT	PA	LOCATION
W	August 30	49	Southern Miss	0	Starkville
W	September 6	47	Alabama-Birmingham	34	Starkville
W	September 13	35	South Alabama	3	Mobile
W	September 20	34	Louisiana State	29	Baton Rouge
W	October 4	48	Texas A&M	31	Starkville
W	October 11	38	Auburn	23	Starkville
W	October 25	45	Kentucky	31	Lexington
W	November 1	17	Arkansas	10	Starkville
W	November 8	45	Tennessee Martin	16	Starkville
L	November 15	20	Alabama	25	Tuscaloosa
W	November 22	51	Vanderbilt	0	Starkville
L	November 29	17	Mississippi	31	Oxford
L	December 31	34	Georgia Tech	49	Miami Gardens

O le Miss hosted the 2014 Battle for the Golden Egg in Oxford in what had already been a golden season for both the Rebels and their Southeastern Conference rival Bulldogs in Starkville.

By November both teams had risen as high in the polls as they'd been in years. Mississippi State ascended to the top spot and Ole Miss made it to No. 3 in the polls. Then came the first-ever College Football Playoff poll of the new era in college football, which allowed for four teams to meet at the end of the bowl season to determine a national champion.

Although neither MSU nor UM qualified for the playoffs a few weeks later, when that first official poll came out in late October, the Bulldogs were indeed No. 1 and the Rebels were No. 4.

When the two teams entered Hollingsworth Field at Vaught-Hemingway Stadium for the regular season finale, MSU had a 10-1 record and a CFP ranking of No. 4. Ole Miss, meanwhile, had slipped to No. 19 with its record now standing at 8-3.

The home team doesn't always win games in college football, and the Egg Bowl is no exception. But on this night in the friendly confines of the house that was draped in red and blue, it was the Rebels who clawed their way to a 31-17 victory. Later, Ole Miss was forced to vacate the victory due to an NCAA ruling.

Mississippi State would take its 10-2 record to the Orange Bowl to play Georgia Tech. Ole Miss at 9-3 wound up in another New Year's Six bowl—the Peach vs. TCU.

Ole Miss quarterback Bo Wallace was playing for the third and final time against Mississippi State. Both schools had recruited him. He chose Ole Miss. He and his Rebel teammates, just two years earlier, had won the Egg Bowl in Oxford. But Wallace had not forgotten the dramatic overtime loss in Starkville just one year earlier, and it was on his mind as play began in the latest edition of the rivalry on November 29, 2014.

"I felt like how last year ended pushed me the whole offseason," Wallace said after the game, "and there wasn't a day that went by that I didn't think about it. This one feels great. I can't even put into words how it feels."

Wallace was 13-of-30 for 296 yards passing with one interception in the game. Jordan Wilkins, a running back by trade, threw one pass in

November 29, 2014
Ole Miss 31, Mississippi State 17

	State	Ole Miss
First downs	21	15
Total plays	84	62
Total yards	445	532
Rushes/net yards	47/163	3½05
Passing yards	282	327
Passes		
(Att-Comp-Int)	22-37-0	14-31-1
Punts/yards	8/365	8/318
Penalties/yards	4/25	2/25
Fumbles/lost	0/0	1/0
Time of possession	35:45	24:15
Third-down conversions	8/21	4/14
Sacks by: Number/yards	1/5	3/21
Field goals attempted/made	2/1	1/1

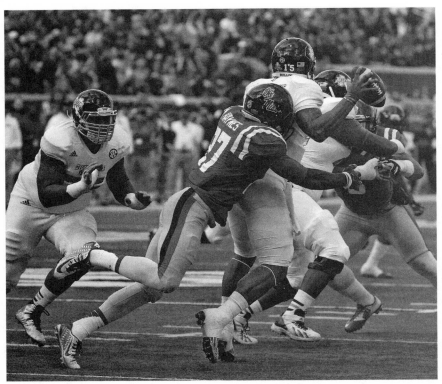

In the 2014 Egg Bowl, Rebels defensive end Marquis Haynes (No. 27) sacks Mississippi State quarterback Dak Prescott (No. 15). Courtesy of Ole Miss Athletics.

the game and completed it for 31 yards to Cody Core for a touchdown. Along with the extra point by placekicker Gary Wunderlich, those were the last points of the contest that all but put it out of reach for MSU as the Rebels led 31-17 with just over nine minutes to go. There was still plenty of time for MSU, but Ole Miss was playing well.

The Rebels were also strong on the ground, accumulating 205 net yards with nine different players carrying the football at some point in the game. Jaylen Walton led the way with 148 yards and one touchdown, while Jeremy Liggins and Wallace accounted for a touchdown each.

State trailed just 17-10 late in the third quarter. Quarterback Dak Prescott led his offense but wasn't able to move the Bulldogs past their own 30-yard line. Punter Devon Bell launched one 61 yards to the Rebel 9-yard line. MSU had Ole Miss right where it wanted the Rebels—backed up near their own goal inside the 10-yard line and down by only a touchdown.

Dak Prescott (No. 15), MSU quarterback, is pressured by Ole Miss defenders in the 2014 Egg Bowl. Courtesy of Ole Miss Athletics.

But the Rebels' Walton managed to give his team a huge lift in just one play. The speedster took a handoff from Wallace and raced 91 yards for a touchdown, running down the visiting sideline directly in front of the Mississippi State bench. It was the third longest touchdown run in Ole Miss football history.

Wunderlich made the extra point to give the home team a 24-10 lead with 2:13 to go in the third period. But Mississippi State wasn't nearly done, not by a long shot.

A Prescott touchdown pass of 32 yards to De'Runnya Wilson one minute and two seconds into the fourth quarter, along with an Evan Sobiesk extra point, pulled the visitors to within one touchdown yet again. The Bulldogs needed a stop and got one before Ole Miss could muster anything offensively to answer.

But after getting the football again, State wasn't able to move it and punted back to Ole Miss. That's when Wilkins assisted his team in scoring in two

Ole Miss tight end Evan Engram signals for a first down in the 2014 Egg Bowl.
Courtesy of Ole Miss Athletics.

plays—a 41-yard rush, followed by the 31-yard pass from Wilkins to Core. Wunderlich's kick was good, and Ole Miss had stretched the lead back to 14 points.

In the game's final moments, MSU drove deep into Ole Miss territory to the 4-yard line. But three straight incompletions by Prescott gave the ball back to Ole Miss. The Rebels ran out the clock for the victory.

Prescott was a solid 22-of-37 in the game for 282 yards and with one touchdown pass. He also had 48 yards rushing and one touchdown on twenty-four carries, second only to his teammate Ashton Shumpert in rushing yards. Shumpert had 68 yards on ten carries.

State had 21 first downs to Ole Miss's 15. But the Rebels outgained the Bulldogs 532 yards to 445 yards, even though MSU had 84 offensive snaps to Ole Miss's 62.

"There is plenty of blame to go around," said MSU head coach Dan Mullen. "To give up as many big plays as we gave up today is unacceptable. That is pathetic. That is just an awful job by our defense. Not a great job on offense."

Ole Miss cornerbacks Mike Hilton (No. 28) and Tony Conner (No. 12) chase Bulldog De'Runnya Wilson in the 2014 Egg Bowl. Courtesy of Mississippi State University Athletics.

Prescott said his team had some miscues, but he also gave Ole Miss's defense credit.

"We had a lot of self-mistakes," Prescott said, likely knowing the Bulldogs, at 10-2 overall and 6-2 in the SEC, were headed to a major bowl game. "We just have to come back out to practice and get better.

"They are good," Prescott continued as he talked about the Rebel defenders. "They are very fast and did some things up front to cause us some problems."

Ole Miss finished the regular season 9-3 overall and 5-3 in the SEC. Hugh Freeze was happy to have the Golden Egg back in Oxford.

"It's obviously good to win a rivalry game," said Freeze, in his third year as the Ole Miss head coach. "It's a priority we have every year. We played with great resolve for 60 minutes."

Ole Miss linebacker Deterrian Shackelford said the Rebels were ready and had to be, considering the level of opponent they were facing.

"We worked hard all week and prepared ourselves," he said. "Hats off to Mississippi State. You don't only lose two games in this league by not being good."

GAME 112

Davis Wade Stadium at
Scott Field, Starkville

2015

The Rebel Road to New Orleans Goes through Starkville

2015 SCHEDULES

Ole Miss 10-3

RESULT	DATE	PF	OPPONENT	PA	LOCATION
W	September 5	76	Tennessee Martin	3	Oxford
W	September 12	73	Fresno State	21	Oxford
W	September 19	43	Alabama	37	Tuscaloosa
W	September 26	27	Vanderbilt	16	Oxford
L	October 3	10	Florida	38	Gainesville
W	October 10	52	New Mexico State	3	Oxford
L	October 17	24	Memphis	37	Memphis
W	October 24	23	Texas A&M	3	Oxford
W	October 31	27	Auburn	19	Auburn
L	November 7	52	Arkansas (Overtime)	53	Oxford
W	November 21	38	Louisiana State	17	Oxford
W	November 28	38	Mississippi State	27	Starkville
W	January 1	48	Oklahoma State	20	New Orleans

Mississippi State 9-4

RESULT	DATE	PF	OPPONENT	PA	LOCATION
W	September 5	34	Southern Miss	16	Hattiesburg
L	September 12	19	Louisiana State	21	Starkville
W	September 19	62	Northwestern State	13	Starkville
W	September 26	17	Auburn	9	Auburn
L	October 3	17	Texas A&M	30	College Station
W	October 10	45	Troy State	17	Starkville
W	October 17	45	Louisiana Tech	20	Starkville
W	October 24	42	Kentucky	16	Starkville
W	November 5	31	Missouri	13	Columbia
L	November 14	6	Alabama	31	Starkville
W	November 21	51	Arkansas	50	Fayetteville
L	November 28	27	Mississippi	38	Starkville
W	December 30	51	North Carolina State	28	Charlotte

Mississippi State hosted the Egg Bowl on November 28, 2015. A lot was on the line for both Ole Miss, ranked No. 18 in the Associated Press poll that week, and for MSU, at No. 21 in the AP ranking.

MSU quarterback Dak Prescott (No. 15) races down the sideline in the Egg Bowl of 2015. Courtesy of Mississippi State University Athletics.

The Bulldogs entered the annual season-ending contest 8-3 overall and 4-3 in Southeastern Conference play. Ole Miss was also 8-3 overall but had a record of 5-2 in the SEC.

While neither team was likely headed to Atlanta for the SEC Championship game, even with a victory in the Battle for the Golden Egg, both were having outstanding seasons. Ole Miss had been ranked as high as third in the country in some earlier polls before a few setbacks derailed the Rebels. The most significant one was on November 7 in Oxford when Arkansas played the role of spoiler in a dramatic overtime game, beating Ole Miss 53-52.

The Rebels, with a win over Alabama earlier in the season and over LSU the week before the Egg Bowl, looked like they might be

November 28, 2015
Ole Miss 38, Mississippi State 27

	State	Ole Miss
First downs	21	26
Total plays	76	67
Total yards	402	479
Rushes/net yards	34/148	37/243
Passing yards	254	236
Passes		
(Att-Comp-Int)	31-42-1	21-30-0
Punts/yards	3/148	3/68
Penalties/yards	6/50	3/11
Fumbles/lost	1/0	1/1
Time of possession	29:34	30:26
Third-down conversions	7/16	6/12
Sacks by: Number/yards	0/0	7/41
Field goals attempted/made	3/1	2/2

MSU cornerback Cedric Jiles (No. 5) defends an Ole Miss wide receiver in the 2015 Egg Bowl. Courtesy of Ole Miss Athletics.

headed for victory that afternoon against Arkansas. But the Razorbacks came up with a win that eventually cost the Rebels a real shot at a trip to Atlanta in early December as the SEC West's representative.

The Bulldogs had lost conference games to LSU, Texas A&M, and Alabama along the way. Still, the Ole Miss game meant something more than just bragging rights. A major bowl, actually for both teams, was on the line.

As it turned out, Ole Miss dominated the Egg Bowl game and won 38-27, a contest that actually wasn't as close as the final score.

Ole Miss led 21-0 after one quarter and 28-3 at halftime. Considering the game was on the road and in the archrival's home stadium, those were remarkable statements that proved just how well the Rebels were playing.

Only two late MSU touchdown passes from quarterback Dak Prescott to receiver Malik Dear narrowed the gap from a 38-13 Rebel lead early in the fourth quarter to the 11-point final margin at the game's end.

The Rebels were rewarded in several ways following the victory. Besides keeping the Golden Egg in Oxford, Ole Miss, at 9-3 on the season, was headed to its ninth Sugar Bowl appearance, but its first in 46 years. Not since Ole Miss beat Arkansas 27-22 on January 1, 1970, with the game's Most Outstanding Player, quarterback Archie Manning, leading the troops, had a Rebel football team played in the New Year's Classic in New Orleans.

After the win at MSU in 2015, Ole Miss accepted an invitation to the Sugar Bowl and defeated Oklahoma State 48-20 on January 1, 2016. Rebel quarterback Chad Kelly was named the bowl's Most Outstanding Player.

The Bulldogs still finished with an 8-4 record and traveled to Charlotte, North Carolina, for the Belk Bowl. On December 30, 2015, Mississippi State defeated North Carolina State 51-28.

But back on November 28, few could have predicted the one-sided score of the Egg Bowl. Kelly, the Rebels' outstanding quarterback, threw for 236 yards and two touchdowns and ran for another touchdown to lead his team to the win. In the first quarter alone, the tone was set, and the score was all but out of reach for State.

Ole Miss scored three opening-quarter touchdowns. After the Rebel defense stopped MSU on its first possession with Chief Brown recovering a Dak Prescott fumble caused by DeMarquis Gates, Kelly took the Rebels downfield and ran for 27 yards himself for the first score of the game. Gary Wunderlich's extra point gave Ole Miss an early lead of 7-0 with less than four minutes gone in the first period.

After another defensive stop for Ole Miss, the Rebels had the football on offense again. In nine plays, Kelly and company had again found the end zone, this time a 2-yard pass to Damore'ea Stringfellow. There was still 5:10 to play in the opening quarter, and with another Wunderlich point after, Ole Miss led 14-0.

The Rebel defenders stepped up yet again on MSU's next possession. On the drive's fifth play, Bulldog quarterback Prescott was picked off by Ole Miss's Tony Bridges, as his fellow teammate Gates was credited with a quarterback hurry. Bridges raced 45 yards for the third Ole Miss touchdown of the night. Wunderlich made it 21-0 with his kick, and the game clock still had 3:05 remaining in the first quarter. The partisan Bulldog crowd at Scott Field and Davis Wade Stadium sat in stunned silence. Few on either side could have foretold such a dominant first quarter by either team.

The Ole Miss defense once again stood tall as the second quarter began, this time holding MSU to only a field goal of 22 yards by placekicker Westin Graves in the first minute of the period. But the Rebels, ahead 21-3, would soon add more points to their side of the ledger.

MSU's Fred Ross avoids Ole Miss defenders in the Battle for the Golden Egg in 2015. Courtesy of Mississippi State University Athletics.

Kelly found Stringfellow again for a touchdown, this time a 36-yard reception that capped an eight-play, 75-yard drive. Wunderlich's extra point made it 28-3 Ole Miss with 10:45 to go before halftime.

Mississippi State began an attempt at a comeback in the third quarter, still trailing 28-3. First was a touchdown, this one a Prescott rush of 1 yard. Graves made the extra point. It was 28-10. After Wunderlich missed on a 33-yard field goal attempt, MSU moved downfield and got a 27-yard field goal by Graves to make it 28-13 and put his team within striking distance. But Ole Miss then stretched it out to 31-13 as Wunderlich made a 48-yard field goal before the end of the third quarter.

The Rebels added a touchdown on their first possession of the fourth quarter on a beautiful 38-yard rush up the middle by Jordan Wilkins. Wunderlich added the point after, and with 13:22 to go in the game, the Rebels led by the impressive score of 38-13.

But MSU didn't fold. The Bulldogs scored all the points the rest of the way, beginning with a Prescott pass of 13 yards to Malik Dear and an extra point by Graves. It was 38-20 with the Rebels leading.

Ole Miss wide receivers Laquon Treadwell (No. 1) and Quincy Adeboyejo (No. 8) celebrate in the 2015 Egg Bowl. Courtesy of Ole Miss Athletics.

Then after an Ole Miss punt, State drove down again for a touchdown, with the same combination of Prescott to Dear, this time for 7 yards. Graves was successful and the score was 38-27.

Graves then attempted an onsides kickoff, but it was recovered by the Rebels' Jaylen Walton with 1:12 left in the game. The Rebels were able to run out the clock and take the Golden Egg back to Oxford where it had resided for the past year.

"It's huge to get a win in this game," said Kelly, as his team celebrated the Egg Bowl victory, then set its sights on the Sugar Bowl. "I am just excited to be a part of this great team."

"I'm proud of our guys' effort," said MSU head coach Dan Mullen. "They played hard for four quarters, and that is always something we stress."

2016

The Bulldogs Roll on Enemy Turf

2016 SCHEDULES

Ole Miss 5-7

RESULT	DATE	PF	OPPONENT	PA	LOCATION
L	September 5	34	Florida State	45	Orlando
W	September 10	38	Wofford	13	Oxford
L	September 17	43	Alabama	48	Oxford
W	September 24	45	Georgia	14	Oxford
W	October 1	48	Memphis	28	Oxford
L	October 15	30	Arkansas	34	Fayetteville
L	October 22	21	Louisiana	38	Baton Rouge
L	October 29	29	Auburn	40	Oxford
W	November 5	37	Georgia Southern	27	Oxford
W	November 12	29	Texas A&M	28	College Station
L	November 19	17	Vanderbilt	38	Nashville
L	November 26	20	Mississippi State	55	Oxford

Mississippi State 6-7

RESULT	DATE	PF	OPPONENT	PA	LOCATION
L	September 3	20	South Alabama	21	Starkville
W	September 10	27	South Carolina	14	Starkville
L	September 17	20	Louisiana State	23	Baton Rouge
W	September 24	47	UMass	35	Foxborough
L	October 8	14	Auburn	38	Starkville
L	October 14	21	Brigham Young (Overtime)	28	Provo
L	October 22	38	Kentucky	40	Lexington
W	October 29	56	Samford	41	Starkville
W	November 5	35	Texas A&M	28	Starkville
L	November 12	3	Alabama	51	Tuscaloosa
L	November 19	42	Arkansas	58	Starkville
W	November 26	55	Mississippi	20	Oxford
W	December 26	17	Miami (OH)	16	St. Petersburg

Heading into the 2016 season, Ole Miss was coming off a win against Mississippi State in Starkville and a Sugar Bowl win against Oklahoma State in New Orleans as a successful 2015 season with 10 vic-

Ole Miss wide receiver Damore'ea Stringfellow (No. 3) goes up for a contest catch in the Battle for the Golden Egg in 2016. Courtesy of Ole Miss Athletics.

tories was in the record books. All appeared to be going well for the Rebels, but the 2016 season would prove to be difficult for head coach Hugh Freeze and his squad.

Mississippi State continued to field winning teams under head coach Dan Mullen, play in bowl games, and compete at a high level. However, in 2016 MSU went only 5-7 but kept its bowl streak alive at 7 straight, despite the first losing season since 2009. Mississippi State qualified for a bowl due to its high APR academic score, which allows a team with less than 6 wins to be eligible for an NCAA postseason bowl, if there is a bowl game that hasn't been filled by teams with winning records. The Bulldogs defeated the Miami (Ohio) Redhawks 17-16 in the St. Petersburg Bowl to finish the season.

Both teams had found winning games difficult as the Egg Bowl

November 26, 2016
Mississippi State 55, Ole Miss 20

	State	Ole Miss
First downs	23	31
Total plays	64	86
Total yards	566	528
Rushes/net yards	47/457	38/208
Passing yards	109	320
Passes		
(Att-Comp-Int)	8-17-0	27-48-2
Punts/yards	3/140	4/182
Penalties/yards	6/55	3/20
Fumbles/lost	2/1	0/0
Time of possession	28:37	31:23
Third-down conversions	8/13	5/15
Sacks by: Number/yards	1/3	3/16
Field goals attempted/made	0/0	2/2

of 2016 approached. State arrived in Oxford 4-7, while host Ole Miss was only slightly better at 5-6. On November 26, 2016, on Hollingsworth Field in Vaught-Hemingway Stadium, Mississippi State owned the day, defeating Ole Miss 55-20. The 35-point margin of victory was State's fourth-largest ever in this rivalry game, which was first played in 1901.

The Bulldogs amassed 457 rushing yards in the game as the Rebel defenders could not stop the MSU offense. It was the third-most-rushing yardage in a single game for a State team in its football history. Through the air, MSU quarterback Nick Fitzgerald was 8-for-17 for 109 yards and three touchdowns.

Ole Miss led 10-6 in the first quarter when State took a 13-10 lead on a Fitzgerald 8-yard pass to Donald Gray, which was followed by a successful extra point kick by Westin Graves. There was 2:33 to go in the opening period. The Rebels would not lead again in the contest.

"What an unbelievable feeling to come in and get that win and bring that trophy back to Starkville," a jubilant Mullen said. "I know this game means so much to all of the fans, everyone in Mississippi. I am so happy to get that win for the Bulldog fans. They believed in us and believed in what we try to do and what we try to build. We raised expectations here pretty high, and I am just really excited to bring that trophy back."

In the home team's postgame, Freeze was obviously disappointed with the outcome but felt his team had some chances to stay in it early.

"Unfortunately, it felt like it was going to be a score fest," he said. "We obviously couldn't stop them all night, so we had to score with them and we failed to do that. It is disappointing. I hate it for our fans, university, seniors, and for everyone involved in our program. It's not the way you want to end the season."

It was early in the second quarter that MSU began to pull away. Aeris Williams raced 13 yards for a touchdown, and with Graves's point after, the Bulldogs led by 10 points at 20-10 with 12:55 to go before halftime.

Ole Miss drove the football deep into Mississippi State territory on its next possession. But a Shea Patterson pass on first down at the 17-yard line was intercepted in the end zone by Jamal Peters, and State was in business again.

The Bulldogs then drove 80 yards in six plays, a Fitzgerald pass of 24 yards to Malik Dear completing the drive. Graves connected on the point after, and MSU was in command, up 27-10 with 9:13 to go in the second quarter.

The Rebels did score next, however, to trim the MSU lead to 27-17. Patterson hit Damore'ea Stringfellow on a 25-yard scoring pass, and with Gary Wunderlich's extra point, Ole Miss was within 10 points with 4:47 to go in the first

Bulldog quarterback Nick Fitzgerald (No. 7) runs out of bounds with the Rebels' DeMarquis Gates in pursuit. Courtesy of Mississippi State University Athletics.

half. After Wunderlich connected on a 38-yard field goal just before halftime, the Rebels actually carried momentum into the locker room, trailing just 27-20.

But the rest of the scoring in this Egg Bowl would be all MSU. Two touchdowns in the third quarter and two more in the fourth quarter gave the Bulldogs an impressive win against the rivals on the road.

A Fitzgerald pass to Fred Ross for 38 yards, and a Graves extra point, made it 34-20. A Fitzgerald run of 61 yards, along with Graves's point after, made it 41-20 as the third quarter came to a close.

In the fourth period, Mississippi State scored on another Fitzgerald rush, this time of 30 yards. Graves's kick made it 48-20. While maroon-clad faithful celebrated, some red and blue fans began to make their way out of the stadium. There had been 66,038 announced as the attendance for the game, the second-largest crowd in Vaught-Hemingway Stadium history for any game.

Later in the fourth quarter, when a Patterson pass was intercepted by State's Cedric Jiles and returned 74 yards for a touchdown, all that remained for a final tally of 55 points on the MSU side was Graves's successful extra point.

Fitzgerald ended the contest with 258 rushing yards on fourteen carries, the most rushing yards in a single game for any player at any position in MSU

Mississippi State celebrates an Egg Bowl victory in Oxford in 2016 as A. J. Jefferson (No. 47) carries the prize for his teammates. Courtesy of Mississippi StateUniversity Athletics.

football history. Included in that total were his two rushing touchdowns. It was his seventh 100-yard rushing game of the season, a new MSU record for a single player in a single season, surpassing Don Smith's five in 1986.

Williams had 191 yards and two touchdowns on twenty-five carries for the Bulldogs. Akeem Judd led the Ole Miss ground game with 107 yards on nineteen carries. Also for the Rebels, Stringfellow had six catches for 97 yards, two of them for touchdowns. Ole Miss's Patterson was 27-for-48 for 320 yards, with two touchdowns and two interceptions.

"The offensive line was blocking their butts off," MSU's Fitzgerald said after the game. "We were running extremely hard. It really goes to our offensive line. To end on something so high, a big-time Egg Bowl win, it's phenomenal to see where we started and where we ended up."

2017

Luke's Troops Bring the Egg Back to Oxford

2017 SCHEDULES

Ole Miss 6-6

RESULT	DATE	PF	OPPONENT	PA	LOCATION
W	September 2	47	South Alabama	27	Oxford
W	September 9	45	Tennessee Martin	23	Oxford
L	September 16	16	California	27	Berkeley
L	September 30	3	Alabama	66	Tuscaloosa
L	October 7	23	Auburn	44	Auburn
W	October 14	57	Vanderbilt	35	Oxford
L	October 21	24	Louisiana State	40	Oxford
L	October 28	37	Arkansas	38	Oxford
W	November 4	37	Kentucky	34	Lexington
W	November 11	50	Louisiana	22	Oxford
L	November 18	24	Texas A&M	31	Oxford
W	November 23	31	Mississippi State	28	Starkville

Mississippi State 9-4

RESULT	DATE	PF	OPPONENT	PA	LOCATION
W	September 2	49	Charleston Southern	0	Starkville
W	September 9	57	Louisiana Tech	21	Ruston
W	September 16	37	Louisiana State	7	Starkville
L	September 23	3	Georgia	31	Athens
L	September 30	10	Auburn	49	Auburn
W	October 14	35	Brigham Young	10	Starkville
W	October 21	45	Kentucky	7	Starkville
W	October 28	35	Texas A&M	14	College Station
W	November 4	34	UMass	23	Starkville
L	November 11	24	Alabama	31	Starkville
W	November 18	28	Arkansas	21	Fayetteville
L	November 23	28	Mississippi	31	Starkville
W	December 30	31	Louisville	27	Jacksonville

The Ole Miss football program was under new leadership for the 2017 season as head coach Matt Luke, a former player and assistant coach for the Rebels, was in charge. Luke was in an interim position. Former head coach Hugh Freeze had been relieved of his duties by the university prior to the 2017 season.

Mississippi State's successful run under head coach Dan Mullen was continuing in Starkville. The Bulldogs hosted Ole Miss inside Davis Wade Stadium at Scott Field for the Egg Bowl in the season finale as the favorites. MSU had records of 8-3 overall and 4-3 in Southeastern Conference play heading into the November 23, 2017, rivalry matchup. Ole Miss had departed Oxford for the contest with a 5-6 mark for the season and a 2-5 record inside the SEC.

In what turned out to be a significant case of "throw the records out" football, it was Ole Miss that would be on the winning side of a 31-28 score as the final horn sounded, perhaps to the surprise of many. But one never knows what will unfold in rivalry games such as the Rebels and the Bulldogs play at the end of each football season in the Battle for the Golden Egg.

Early in the game, veteran MSU quarterback Nick Fitzgerald, so dominant in the Egg Bowl the year before, went down with an ankle injury. It occurred on State's second offensive possession, and Ole Miss was already leading 7-0, having scored in the contest's first minute of play on a running back Jordan Wilkins 22-yard run and a Gary Wunderlich extra point kick. After Fitzgerald's injury, Bulldog freshman quarterback Keytaon Thompson took over the MSU offense.

Fast forward, and by midway through the fourth quarter, the Rebels appeared to be in total control, leading the Bulldogs 31-13. Even with the score as one-sided as it was at that point, this game was still far from over.

An impressive run of 46 yards by Wilkins, along with another Wunderlich kick, had given Ole Miss that commanding 18-point lead with 8:23 to go in the game. But the Bulldogs would make things highly interesting before this edition of the Egg Bowl was in the record book.

State scored a touchdown on a Kylin Hill rush of 30 yards with 4:58 remaining in the contest. A successful 2-point conversion on a keeper by quarterback Thompson closed the gap to 10 points with Ole Miss leading 31-21.

After a Logan Cooke onside kick for the Bulldogs was recovered by the Rebels' Breeland Speaks, Ole Miss was not able to advance for

November 23, 2017

Ole Miss 31, Mississippi State 28

	State	Ole Miss
First downs	27	11
Total plays	94	54
Total yards	501	355
Rushes/net yards	62/294	32/108
Passing yards	207	247
Passes		
(Att-Comp-Int)	14-32-2	10-22-1
Punts/yards	4/149	8/269
Penalties/yards	9/88	13/121
Fumbles/lost	3/3	1/1
Time of possession	37:30	22:30
Third-down conversions	7/19	2/12
Sacks by: Number/yards	4.0/36	3.0/22
Field goals attempted/made	2/2	1/1

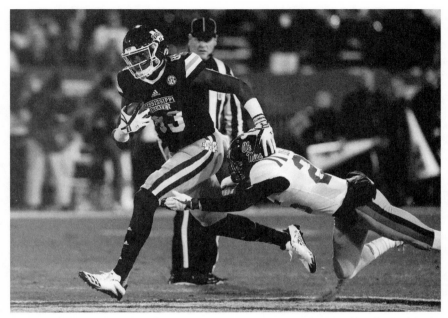

MSU tight end Jordan Thomas (No. 83) churns his way downfield and out of the grasp of the Ole Miss defender in the 2017 Egg Bowl. Courtesy of Mississippi State University Athletics.

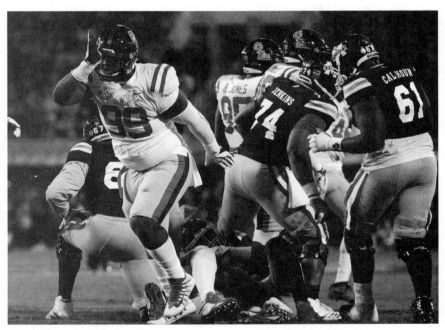

Rebel defender Herbert Moore (No. 99) throws up a landshark sign after stopping MSU in Egg Bowl 2017. Courtesy of Ole Miss Athletics.

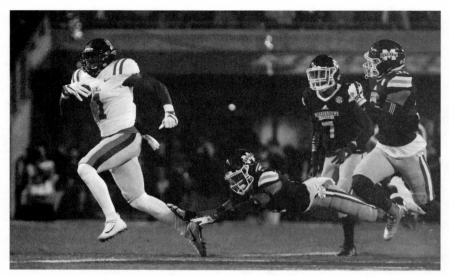

Ole Miss wide receiver A. J. Brown (No. 1) runs out of reach of MSU defenders in the Egg Bowl of 2017. Courtesy of Ole Miss Athletics.

even one first down. A Will Gleeson punt followed, and MSU had the football at its own 38-yard line, still trailing by 10, but with another opportunity to close the gap as 2:58 remained on the clock.

That is indeed what happened. In eight plays State covered 62 yards with Thompson scoring a touchdown from the 1-yard line. Jace Christmann made the extra point kick, and what at one time appeared to be an almost insurmountable Ole Miss lead was down to 3 points at 31-28 with 1:05 to go. The MSU team and its fans still had hope as this one had turned into a thriller.

Cooke again tried an onside kick, but Ole Miss again recovered the football, this time by Wilkins at the MSU 45-yard line. The Rebels were able to run out the clock with two snaps of the football. The Golden Egg was headed back to Oxford following the upset victory.

It had arguably been a tale of two games, as Ole Miss dominated for more than three quarters, and Mississippi State continued to battle, almost coming all the way back to win. But Matt Luke's Rebels had not only won the game but evened their record at 6-6 and improved to 3-5 in SEC games.

"To the people of the state of Mississippi, this is the most important game of the year," said Luke, whose father, Tommy, and brother, Tom, also played football for Ole Miss. "I am so happy for our players and our fans. This means so much to them. These seniors went 3-1 against Mississippi State. Four for the last six (wins for Ole Miss) against those guys, so we are really proud."

Mississippi State finished the season with a record of 8-4 overall and 4-4 in the conference. It was not the way the Bulldogs wanted to complete the regular season.

"Obviously frustrating," Mullen said. "It was a big game, and you always want to go find a way to win that game. Our guys battled; they continued to battle for four quarters. Unfortunately, I think in the end, we just ran out of time."

Mullen thought his freshman quarterback Thompson, who was 13-for-27 passing for 195 yards with one touchdown and one interception, showed promise.

"I thought as the game went on, he continued to play, continued to relax. I think as everybody sees, he has a really bright future."

Thompson agreed with Mullen's assessment.

"I learned a lot throughout the game," he said. "I felt like I got better as the game went on."

Mullen also said not taking care of the football was a factor for his team.

"We turned it over five times," he said. "You're not going to win many games when you turn the ball over five times as a team."

MSU dominated much of the team stats, with 27 first downs to the Rebels' 11, and 294 yards rushing to Ole Miss's 108. In the passing department, Ole Miss quarterback Jordan Ta'amu threw for 247 yards and two touchdowns, while State's combined total through the air for Fitzgerald and Thompson was 207 yards.

The Rebel players were overjoyed with the outcome.

"We're really excited about this win," said Starkville native and Ole Miss wide receiver A. J. Brown, with six receptions and one touchdown to lead his team. "We had to get the Egg Bowl back."

D. K. Metcalf caught two passes, one of them for a touchdown. Wilkins, who ran for 110 yards on fourteen carries with two touchdowns, moved past the 1,000-yard mark for rushing on the season. He said statistics are nice, but victory is even better.

"The 'W' is most important, so that is the big thing," he said. "But 1,000 yards is definitely a plus. It feels great. Last year I was telling people 'I'm going to run for 1,000. I am working my tail off to run for 1,000. My O-line did a great job. It wasn't just me."

Indeed, this team victory belonged to the Ole Miss Rebels, and the Golden Egg would reside in Oxford for at least the next twelve months.

2018

A One-Sided Game Goes State's Way

2018 SCHEDULES

Ole Miss 5-7

RESULT	DATE	PF	OPPONENT	PA	LOCATION
W	September 1	47	Texas Tech	27	Houston
W	September 8	76	Southern Illinois	41	Oxford
L	September 15	7	Alabama	62	Oxford
W	September 22	38	Kent State	17	Oxford
L	September 29	16	Louisiana State	45	Baton Rouge
W	October 6	70	Louisiana-Monroe	21	Oxford
W	October 13	37	Arkansas	33	Little Rock
L	October 20	16	Auburn	31	Oxford
L	November 3	44	South Carolina	48	Oxford
L	November 10	24	Texas A&M	38	College Station
L	November 17	29	Vanderbilt	36	Nashville
L	November 22	3	Mississippi State	35	Oxford

Mississippi State 8-5

RESULT	DATE	PF	OPPONENT	PA	LOCATION
W	September 1	63	Stephen F. Austin	6	Starkville
W	September 8	31	Kansas State	10	Manhattan
W	September 15	56	Louisiana	10	Starkville
L	September 22	7	Kentucky	28	Lexington
L	September 29	6	Florida	13	Starkville
W	October 6	23	Auburn	9	Starkville
L	October 20	3	Louisiana State	19	Baton Rouge
W	October 27	28	Texas A&M	13	Starkville
W	November 3	45	Louisiana Tech	3	Starkville
L	November 10	0	Alabama	24	Tuscaloosa
W	November 17	52	Arkansas	6	Starkville
W	November 22	35	Mississippi	3	Oxford
L	January 1	22	Iowa	27	Tampa

Dan Mullen left Mississippi State to become the head coach at Florida following the 2017 season. Joe Moorhead was hired to replace Mullen, who won more games as head coach at MSU than any coach prior with the exception of Jackie Sherrill, who had served from 1991 to 2003.

MSU defensive end Montez Sweat applies pressure on Ole Miss quarterback Jordan Ta'amu in the Battle for the Golden Egg 2018. Courtesy of Mississippi State University Athletics.

The mission of Moorhead, a former head coach at Fordham University in New York and the offensive coordinator and quarterbacks coach at Penn State prior to his arrival in Starkville, was to continue winning on the foundation built under Mullen and staff the previous nine seasons.

The Bulldogs were 7-4 overall and 3-4 in Southeastern Conference action when they arrived in Oxford for the 2018 Egg Bowl. Ole Miss was 5-6 heading into the game and 1-6 in the SEC.

The Battle for the Golden Egg, in the Rebels' possession since the game in Starkville a year earlier, wasn't close. Given the two teams' records, the outcome on November

November 22, 2018
Mississippi State 35, Ole Miss 3

	State	Ole Miss
First downs	23	13
Total plays	69	54
Total yards	420	189
Rushes/net yards	51/309	29/37
Passing yards	111	152
Passes		
(Att-Comp-Int)	11-18-0	13-25-2
Punts/yards	6/231	6/262
Penalties/yards	3/35	3/24
Fumbles/lost	1/0	1/1
Time of possession	36:14	23:46
Third-down conversions	6/13	0/10
Sacks by: Number/yards	4/34	1/6
Field goals attempted/made	0/0	1/1

Bulldog quarterback Nick Fitzgerald finds a big opening in the Rebels' defense and surges up field in the 2018 Egg Bowl. Courtesy of Mississippi State University Athletics.

22, 2018, might not have been a surprise. But the final score being so one-sided likely was to many.

MSU dominated from start to finish and won 35-3.

Two seasons prior, the Bulldogs had also taken the Golden Egg back to Starkville after a 55-20 win. That made it two victories in a row for the visiting team at Vaught-Hemingway Stadium/Hollingsworth Field, and neither game was close.

The Bulldogs rolled into Oxford playing what appeared to be their best football of the season. They'd won three of their last four games, with victories over Texas A&M, Louisiana Tech, and Arkansas, the only loss in that span a 24-0 setback at Alabama.

Some veteran names dotted the MSU lineup, players who had been in prior Egg Bowls and knew about the game and what it means—players like Kylin Hill, Aeris Williams, Jeffery Simmons, Nick Fitzgerald, and Gerri Green, the latter two serving as State's team captains for the contest.

Ole Miss was in its second full season under head coach Matt Luke but the first after the interim tag had been removed following the 2017 Egg Bowl. A 47-27 win in Houston against Texas Tech to open the season showed promise. A 37-33 win against Arkansas in the capital city of Little Rock proved to be the Rebels' lone SEC victory.

Fitzgerald certainly had something to prove following his early departure from the game the year before, a contest Ole Miss won 31-28.

State built an early lead in the 2018 battle, holding a 21-3 advantage at halftime. Two more touchdowns were added in the second half, and MSU was simply the better team on this night, winning in methodical fashion.

After early drives for each team produced no points, State took a 7-0 lead with 5:02 to go in the opening stanza. The scoring drive began for the Bulldogs when Ole Miss veteran quarterback Jordan Ta'amu fumbled as a result of a hit by State's Simmons. The football was recovered by the Bulldogs' Willie Gay Jr. After a 15-yard unsportsmanlike conduct penalty against State, MSU was still in business at the Rebels' 45-yard line. In seven plays the Bulldogs had taken the lead. With the successful extra point kick by Jace Christmann, the visitors were up a touchdown. They would not trail in the contest.

Mississippi State's defense stopped Ole Miss in three plays on the possession that followed, and Mac Brown punted. MSU had first down and 10 at its own 14-yard line and began another drive for points. It took eight rushing plays. Not a pass was thrown. The Bulldogs found they could simply run the football with authority, and Fitzgerald took it in from the 8-yard line with less than a minute gone in the second period. Christmann's kick made it 14-0 Bulldogs, and this game was beginning to look like what it ultimately turned out to be, even though almost three full quarters remained.

Ole Miss got its only points of the game on a Luke Logan 32-yard field goal with 6:46 to go before halftime. The score was 14-3, but it wouldn't be long before MSU scored again. After Brown boomed a 65-yard punt, State began a drive at its own 8-yard line.

Ten plays later, Fitzgerald connected with Deddrick Thomas on a touchdown pass play of 9 yards. Christmann's successful point after touchdown gave MSU a 21-3 lead with just 25 seconds to go before halftime.

The Bulldogs continued to add to their lead, a 9-yard run by Fitzgerald and a Christmann extra point kick in the third, and a Williams 1-yard run and Christmann kick in the fourth. That would be all the scoring in this one. Later, MSU was forced to vacate the 2018 victory due to an NCAA academic ruling.

At one point in the second half, the "rivalry" truly showed up. As the third quarter came to a close, a bench-clearing brawl erupted. Players on both teams were given unsportsmanlike conduct penalties before play resumed. Rivalry games can bring out those moments in players.

In the postgame, the Rebels were disappointed, and the Bulldogs were jubilant.

In the trenches of the 2018 Egg Bowl in Oxford. Courtesy of Ole Miss Athletics.

"It felt great honestly," said Fitzgerald. "It really did. It feels great knowing that we won the Egg Bowl and finished out the season strong."

"Obviously we are very proud of our football program, both players and coaches," said Moorhead, who became the first MSU head coach to win at least eight games in his first season since Allyn McKeen in 1938. "We talked about showing our emotions without being emotional, but at the end of the day, how hard we played and how well we executed would determine the outcome of the game."

Luke said it was tough to lose a second home game in a row to the Bulldogs.

"I am really disappointed for the seniors," he said. "They've been through a lot, and I hate for them to go out this way."

Ole Miss tight end Dawson Knox said it was a difficult game for the Rebel offense, and too many things went wrong.

"We have a good scheme going into every game," he said. "It's a combination of us not executing and a bunch of different things."

Statistically, MSU dominated, just as it did the final score—23 first downs to 13 for Ole Miss, 420 yards to 189 for the Rebels, and 36:14 time of possession to 23:46 for Ole Miss.

Mississippi State played in the Outback Bowl in Tampa, Florida, to end its season, but lost to Iowa 27-22. After the Battle for the Golden Egg, the Ole Miss football season was over.

2019

A Hike, a Miss, and a Most Unusual Finish

2019 SCHEDULES

Ole Miss 4-8

RESULT	DATE	PF	OPPONENT	PA	LOCATION
L	August 31	10	Memphis	15	Memphis
W	September 7	31	Arkansas	17	Oxford
W	September 14	40	Southern Louisiana	29	Oxford
L	September 21	20	California	28	Oxford
L	September 28	31	Alabama	59	Tuscaloosa
W	October 5	31	Vanderbilt	6	Oxford
L	October 12	27	Missouri	38	Columbia
L	October 19	17	Texas A&M	24	Oxford
L	November 2	14	Auburn	20	Auburn
W	November 9	41	New Mexico State	3	Oxford
L	November 16	37	Louisiana State	58	Oxford
L	November 28	20	Mississippi State	21	Starkville

Mississippi State 6-7

RESULT	DATE	PF	OPPONENT	PA	LOCATION
W	August 31	38	Louisiana	28	New Orleans
W	September 7	38	Southern Miss	15	Starkville
L	September 14	24	Kansas State	31	Starkville
W	September 21	28	Kentucky	13	Starkville
L	September 28	23	Auburn	56	Auburn
L	October 12	10	Tennessee	20	Knoxville
L	October 19	13	Louisiana State	36	Starkville
L	October 26	30	Texas A&M	49	College Station
W	November 2	54	Arkansas	24	Fayetteville
L	November 16	7	Alabama	38	Starkville
W	November 23	45	Abilene Christian	7	Starkville
W	November 28	21	Mississippi	20	Starkville
L	December 30	28	Louisville	38	Nashville

Coach Joe Moorhead won his first Battle for the Golden Egg when his Mississippi State Bulldogs defeated Ole Miss 35-3 in Oxford in 2018. Now he was coaching in his second battle, the game set for the Mississippi State campus on Thanksgiving night, November 28, 2019.

Matt Luke was coaching his third Egg Bowl as the head coach of his alma mater, Ole Miss, and his teams were 1-1 so far. Two seasons earlier, when the Rebels won 31-28, Luke still wore the label of interim head coach, having taken over the program that summer from Hugh Freeze.

Every Egg Bowl is unique. The 2019 edition certainly was, especially the way it ended.

The two teams weren't having stellar seasons. Both had more losses than wins heading into the game at Davis Wade Stadium at Scott Field. The Rebels were 4-7 and only had wins against Arkansas, Southeastern Louisiana, Vanderbilt, and New Mexico State, with all of those games having been played in Oxford.

MSU, meanwhile, still had visions of a bowl game and would play in one if it could beat Ole Miss at home. Entering the contest at 5-6, the Bulldogs had wins over Louisiana-Lafayette, Southern Mississippi, Kentucky, Arkansas, and Abilene Christian. A win over the Rebels would mean that State's impressive bowl streak would extend to ten years.

Obviously, the stakes weren't as high for this game as they had been in some seasons. But there is no Egg Bowl that doesn't mean something if nothing more than bragging rights. However, many felt Luke needed a victory to continue in his role as head coach at Ole Miss. Few could have predicted that Moorhead might also be gone before the 2020 matchup in Oxford. But that's exactly what happened.

Whether the 2019 version of the instate rivalry had a little or a lot to do with either of the coaching situations may always be up for debate. But in the last Egg Bowl between Luke and Moorhead, the final score was Mississippi State 21, Ole Miss 20.

Here's how an interesting game with a strange ending unfolded.

In the first quarter, the teams exchanged possessions twice before State scored a touchdown the third time it had the football on offense. After a Mac Brown punt of 47 yards for the Rebels, MSU started at its own 28-yard line and moved quickly for a score. On the drive's fourth play,

November 28, 2019
Mississippi State 21, Ole Miss 20

	State	Ole Miss
First downs	15	23
Total plays	58	73
Total yards	318	384
Rushes/net yards	44/210	47/139
Passing yards	108	245
Passes (Att-Comp-Int)	10-14-0	15-26-1
Punts/yards	5/218	5/222
Penalties/yards	5/41	5/34
Fumbles/lost	2/1	3/2
Time of possession	31:19	28:41
Third-down conversions	4/12	5/14
Sacks by: Number/yards	4/22	3/12
Field goals attempted/made	0/0	0/0

MSU's Nick Gibson (No. 21) celebrates following a touchdown in the 2019 Egg Bowl. Courtesy of Mississippi State University Athletics.

Nick Gibson raced 27 yards for a touchdown, and the extra point kick by Jace Christmann made it 7-0 for the home team.

Early in the second quarter, MSU stretched its lead to two touchdowns as quarterback Garrett Shrader scored from the 1-yard line, and Christmann converted the point after. It was 14-0 with 11:22 to go in the second quarter, and the Bulldogs looked to be in control.

But the Rebels answered before halftime. After State's second score of the game, Ole Miss moved 81 yards in ten plays, with quarterback John Rhys Plumlee scoring on a 2-yard rush. Luke Logan's extra point kick was good, and the Rebels had cut the MSU lead to 14-7 with 6:15 to go in the second period.

After an MSU drive stalled at midfield, the Rebels got the ball back and moved in for more points. Jerrion Ealy scored from the 5-yard line with 34 seconds to go in the first half. After Logan's kick was good again, the score was 14-14, and that's the way things stood at intermission.

The second half remained close, and there obviously wasn't much scoring. The Bulldogs went back out in front in the third quarter with 3:24 to go by a 21-14 margin when Shrader took it in from the 5-yard line. Christmann made the extra point, and things remained that way until very late in the game.

Rebel quarterback John Rhys Plumlee (No. 10) tries to hurdle two Mississippi State defenders in the 2019 Egg Bowl. Courtesy of Ole Miss Athletics.

MSU had the football at its own 39, still leading by 7 points, when Tucker Day punted 51 yards to the Rebels' 10. Elijah Moore returned it 8 yards to the 18, and with 2:06 to go in the game, Ole Miss had a long way to go and not much time to get there.

The Rebels were going with quarterback Matt Corral at this point, and he drove his team downfield in twelve plays for a touchdown, executing play after play, and passing to Moore on a short 2-yard scoring play to pull his team to within a single point.

Only four seconds remained in the game, and that's when something happened that likely affected the outcome of this close affair. After Moore scored, he was called for unsportsmanlike conduct following the touchdown for hiking one leg from a prone position on his hands and knees. That meant the extra point attempt was moved from the 3-yard line to the 18.

Matt Corral (No. 2), Ole Miss quarterback, drops back for a pass in Egg Bowl 2019. Courtesy of Ole Miss Athletics.

The continuation of the game would hinge on an extra point kick, 15 yards longer now, by Logan and into the direction of the MSU student section. The kick missed wide right, and all MSU had to do was recover an onside kickoff.

Then, after an unsportsmanlike penalty on each team prior to the kickoff for extracurricular activity, Logan's short kick was recovered by MSU's JaVonta Payton. One Bulldog offensive snap later and the Golden Egg remained in Starkville for the second straight year.

"Especially disappointed for our seniors," said Luke, who within days would be relieved of his duties with the Rebels' football program. "It's a disappointing loss."

As for Moore's penalty that cost Ole Miss an easier shot at the tie and potential overtime because it moved the extra point attempt back 15 yards, Luke said it was an unfortunate moment for his team.

"It's not who we are," Luke said. "We've been a disciplined team all year. I'm just disappointed that it happened."

Meanwhile, the other locker room full of Bulldogs celebrated victory, like the winning team always does in an Egg Bowl.

But Moorhead had also coached his last Egg Bowl, as fans would find out not too many days after the 2019 version of this rivalry game was in the record book.

"I'm incredibly proud of this team, particularly the twenty-six seniors," Moorhead said. "For them to fight the way that they did today in all three phases . . . until the very end of the game and until the last second ticked off the clock."

GAME 117

2020

Vaught-Hemingway
Stadium/Hollingsworth
Field, Oxford

Two Coaches, a New Era, and the Pandemic

2020 SCHEDULES

Ole Miss 5-5

RESULT	DATE	PF	OPPONENT	PA	LOCATION
L	September 26	35	Florida	51	Oxford
W	October 3	42	Kentucky (Overtime)	41	Lexington
L	October 10	48	Alabama	63	Oxford
L	October 17	21	Arkansas	33	Fayetteville
L	October 24	28	Auburn	35	Oxford
W	October 31	54	Vanderbilt	21	Nashville
W	November 14	59	South Carolina	42	Oxford
W	November 28	31	Mississippi State	24	Oxford
Canceled	December 12	0	Texas A&M	0	College Station
L	December 19	48	Louisiana State	53	Baton Rouge
W	January 2	26	Indiana	20	Tampa

Mississippi State 4-7

RESULT	DATE	PF	OPPONENT	PA	LOCATION
W	September 26	44	Louisiana State	34	Baton Rouge
L	October 3	14	Arkansas	21	Starkville
L	October 10	2	Kentucky	24	Lexington
L	October 17	14	Texas A&M	28	Starkville
L	October 31	0	Alabama	41	Tuscaloosa
W	November 7	24	Vanderbilt	17	Starkville
L	November 21	24	Georgia	31	Athens
L	November 28	24	Mississippi	31	Starkville
L	December 12	10	Auburn	24	Starkville
W	December 19	51	Missouri	32	Starkville
W	December 31	28	Tulsa	26	Fort Worth

For the 2020 football season, Mississippi's two Southeastern Conference universities welcomed new head coaches but old friends to their respective football programs. The Battle for the Golden Egg would be played later that season. Like always, all eyes would be on the big game.

Less of those eyes would be watching from the actual game site, however. Only a limited number of fans were allowed into Vaught-Hemingway Stadium/

Head coach Lane Kiffin (left) of Ole Miss and head coach Mike Leach of Mississippi State greet each other prior to the regular season finale in 2020, the first time either had coached in the Battle for the Golden Egg. Courtesy of Mississippi State University Athletics.

Hollingsworth Field in Oxford because of COVID-19 restrictions. The game itself would be business as usual between the longtime rivals.

Lane Kiffin replaced Matt Luke in December 2019 as head coach of the Ole Miss Rebels. In January 2020 Mike Leach took over at Mississippi State from Joe Moorhead as the Bulldogs' head coach.

November 28, 2020
Ole Miss 31, Mississippi State 24

	State	Ole Miss
First downs	23	24
Total plays	78	82
Total yards	479	550
Rushes/net yards	16/39	45/163
Passing yards	440	387
Passes (Att-Comp-Int)	45-62-0	25-37-0
Punts/yards	3/138	6/252
Penalties/yards	5/47	10/81
Fumbles/lost	1/1	1/0
Time of possession	32:27	27:33
Third-down conversions	3/14	8/18
Sacks by: Number/yards	2/10	1/5
Field goals attempted/made	1/1	1/1

Luke, a product of the Rebel football program as a former player, had struggled to recapture the winning ways the Ole Miss program had experienced during the Hugh Freeze era before things unraveled. Kiffin was hired to get the program back on track. A video by Ole Miss with a train moving through the landscape signaled that Lane Kiffin was arriving, even before the official announcement.

Moorhead had success at State—two seasons that ended in bowl games after two Egg Bowl victories. But it wasn't enough. Time would have revealed to everyone if he'd have been successful. But a new, veteran head coach would arrive not long after the calendar turned to the new year of 2020.

Leach was successful as a head coach in stops at Texas Tech and Washington State. The SEC, in this case Mississippi State, beckoned, and Leach answered the call. A new era had begun for MSU football.

Even with COVID-19 restrictions in 2020, the SEC chose to play football. But they decided on an all-conference schedule of games. The Egg Bowl was each team's eighth game of the season, rather than the usual season finale. Ole Miss hosted MSU with a 3-4 record, while the Bulldogs rolled into Oxford 2-5. The Rebels prevailed 31-24 before an announced attendance of 16,218 fans.

Ole Miss scored two touchdowns in the first quarter to lead 14-0. MSU scored two in the second period. Along with another touchdown for the Rebels in the second, the home team led 21-14 at intermission. There was no scoring in the third quarter, and both teams scored 10 points in the fourth for the final score—a 7-point Ole Miss victory.

The Rebels' first touchdown came on a Matt Corral pass of 48 yards to Dontario Drummond. The extra point by Luke Logan gave Ole Miss the upper hand. With only 16 seconds to go in the first quarter, Snoop Conner scored from the 1-yard line to extend the Rebels' lead. Logan's point after kick made it 14-0.

The Bulldogs found the end zone with 13:37 to go in the second quarter on a 6-yard pass from Will Rogers to Malik Heath. The extra point kick by Brandon Ruiz cut the Ole Miss lead in half. But it wouldn't be long before the Rebels answered.

An 81-yard catch and run to the end zone by Braylon Sanders on a pass from Corral pushed the lead back out for Ole Miss. With Logan's kick, it was 21-7 with 9:44 to go before halftime. But MSU would soon add more points.

On a 93-yard, thirteen-play drive, State scored with six seconds left on an 11-yard pass from Rogers to Heath. Ruiz made the kick, and the Bulldogs trailed only 21-14 at the half.

After a scoreless third quarter, the game was a thriller to the end. Logan connected on a 26-yard field goal early in the fourth quarter to increase the Ole Miss lead to 24-14. A Rogers-to-Austin Williams pass of 7 yards, along with a Ruiz extra point, pulled State to within 3 points at 24-21 with 7:51 to go. Both teams could still sense victory.

A Jerrion Ealy touchdown rush of 8 yards with 4:48 to go, and a Logan kick, gave Ole Miss a 31-21 lead. MSU added a field goal of 25 yards by Ruiz with 2:08 left, and the score was Rebels 31, Bulldogs 24.

MSU's Erroll Thompson (No. 40) celebrates during the 2020 Egg Bowl in Oxford. Courtesy of Mississippi State University Athletics

A short kickoff by State's Jace Christmann was downed at midfield. MSU was able to hold Ole Miss from any substantial gains on the drive, and a Mac Brown punt put MSU at its own 20 with only twenty-three seconds to go. Four plays later, including a long pass from Rogers to Geor'quarius Spivey, and State was in Rebel territory. On the final play of the game, from the Ole Miss 36, Rogers passed incomplete for Jaden Walley, and the Golden Egg was returned to Oxford.

"It's a really neat win," Kiffin said. "First time being a part of this rivalry, you could feel the energy from our fans, even though the stadium wasn't full, and our players with our sideline energy."

"I thought it was a pretty explosive game, and when that happens, nearly anything can happen," Leach said. "I thought the first half we missed some opportunities, some of them were self-inflicted, some of them the ball didn't really bounce our way. I thought we played extremely hard, and I thought we finished the game. We just didn't win the game. It didn't go our way."

Rogers's 440 yards passing in the game was a new MSU freshman record. He ended the game 45-of-61 in the passing department, the forty-five completions a new MSU single-game record. He threw three touchdown passes in the contest. Walley had nine receptions, a career-high in a single game for him.

After the 2020 Egg Bowl in Oxford, Rebel quarterback Matt Corral (No. 2) lifts the Golden Egg for all to see. Courtesy of Ole Miss Athletics.

Corral was also efficient, completing 24-of-36 passes for 385 yards and two touchdowns. Moore had twelve receptions in the game to lead Ole Miss. His eighty-six catches on the season, with more games still to play, was already a single-season record for a Rebel receiver.

"It's good to get the trophy back where it belongs," Kiffin concluded, with the Golden Egg nearby. "And let's keep it there for a long time."

2021

GAME 118

Davis Wade Stadium at
Scott Field, Starkville

The Rebels Get a Win with a Sugar Bowl Reward

2021 SCHEDULES

Ole Miss 10-3

RESULT	DATE	PF	OPPONENT	PA	LOCATION
W	September 6	43	Louisville	24	Atlanta
W	September 11	54	Austin Peay	17	Oxford
W	September 18	61	Tulane	21	Oxford
L	October 2	21	Alabama	42	Tuscaloosa
W	October 9	52	Arkansas	51	Oxford
W	October 16	31	Tennessee	26	Knoxville
W	October 23	31	Louisiana State	17	Oxford
L	October 30	20	Auburn	31	Auburn
W	November 6	27	Liberty	14	Oxford
W	November 13	29	Texas A&M	19	Oxford
W	November 20	31	Vanderbilt	17	Nashville
W	November 20	31	Mississippi State	21	Starkville
L	January 1	7	Baylor	21	New Orleans

Mississippi State 7-6

RESULT	DATE	PF	OPPONENT	PA	LOCATION
W	September 4	35	Louisiana Tech	34	Starkville
W	September 11	24	North Carolina State	10	Starkville
L	September 18	29	Memphis	31	Memphis
L	September 25	25	Louisiana State	28	Starkville
W	October 2	26	Texas A&M	22	College Station
L	October 16	9	Alabama	49	Starkville
W	October 23	45	Vanderbilt	6	Oxford
W	October 30	31	Kentucky	17	Starkville
L	November 6	28	Arkansas	31	Fayetteville
W	November 13	43	Auburn	34	Auburn
W	November 20	55	Tennessee State	10	Starkville
L	November 25	21	Mississippi	31	Starkville
L	December 28	7	Texas Tech	34	Memphis

Mike Leach and Lane Kiffin would square off in round two of their new rivalry on Thanksgiving night in 2021. The two head coaches, who had led major college football teams in several previous locales

[417]

MSU's Martin Emerson (No. 1) covers Ole Miss wide receiver Braylon Sanders (No. 13) in the 2021 Egg Bowl. Courtesy of Mississippi State University Athletics.

before becoming Mississippians, continued to build their programs in Starkville and Oxford respectively.

The site of this game was Davis Wade Stadium at Scott Field. Ole Miss was 9-3 and playing for its first ten-win regular season in program history. A spot as one of the teams in the Sugar Bowl, which would be the Rebels' tenth all-time appearance in the New Orleans classic, was the expected reward for an Egg Bowl victory.

Mississippi State was having a solid season and hosted the Rebels with a 7-4 overall mark. A twelfth consecutive bowl bid was already secured for State, and a win over Ole Miss would likely move the Bulldogs into a more prestigious bowl.

When the game was over, the Rebels were victorious by a 31-21 margin. With its tenth win safely in the ledger, the Sugar Bowl was indeed Ole Miss's postseason reward. The Rebels would play the Baylor Bears in the Superdome.

November 25, 2021

Ole Miss 31, Mississippi State 21

	State	Ole Miss
First downs	30	23
Total plays	80	78
Total yards	420	388
Rushes/net yards	21/84	44/154
Passing yards	336	234
Passes		
(Att-Comp-Int)	38-59-0	26-34-1
Punts/yards	2/93	2/87
Penalties/yards	8/75	11/73
Fumbles/lost	0/0	0/0
Time of possession	29:44	30:16
Third-down conversions	4/14	11/18
Sacks by: Number/yards	1/12	3/20
Field goals attempted/made	4/2	1/1

Sam Williams (No. 7) of Ole Miss chases MSU quarterback Will Rogers in the 2021 Egg Bowl. Courtesy of Ole Miss Athletics.

For the third time in its last four games in Starkville, Ole Miss came away victorious. Each win was under a different head coach.

In 2015, Ole Miss won 38-27 under Hugh Freeze and advanced to its ninth Sugar Bowl appearance. In 2017, the Rebels won 31-28 under Matt Luke but were not bowl eligible. In 2019, MSU defeated Ole Miss 21-20 at Scott Field.

With its loss in the 2021 regular season finale, Mississippi State finished 7-5 and traveled to Memphis to face one of Leach's former teams, the Texas Tech Red Raiders, in the Liberty Bowl.

Kiffin improved to 2-0 against State. Leach was now 0-2 vs. the Rebels.

Ole Miss had methodically built an insurmountable lead midway through the fourth quarter. When Matt Corral connected with Jerrion Ealy for a 15-yard touchdown pass with 5:35 to go in the game, the Rebels had basically put this one away. The extra point kick by Cale Nation was good, and the visitors led 31-13. Ole Miss fans were now making their reservations for New Year's in New Orleans.

"You can do things that are special, but it is really special when you can do something that has never been done before," Kiffin said of the ten-win regular season. "For this group of players and assistant coaches to do that is really cool."

Ole Miss running back Jarod "Snoop" Conner hurdles MSU's Martin Emerson (No. 1) and safety Fred Peters (No. 38) in the 2021 Egg Bowl. Courtesy of Ole Miss Athletics.

In the other locker room, Leach said his troops had to improve to take the next step.

"I thought that we marched it up and down the field, and if we play games by the stat sheet, then it looks pretty good," he said. "But the key plays that (Ole Miss) made that we didn't just became missed opportunities. It's unfortunate and you feel sorry for yourself, but you just have to get better."

Corral was excellent on this night, throwing 34 passes and completing 26 for 234 yards and one touchdown with one interception. He also scored a rushing touchdown.

MSU quarterback Will Rogers was also impressive in the Egg Bowl, passing fifty-eight times and completing 38 for 336 yards and a touchdown.

"We've said it multiple times this year," Rogers said of his offense that didn't keep pace with the Rebels' scoring marches. "At the end of the day, we have to finish drives in the end zone."

One of the opportunities State did not take advantage of and "finish" was after Ole Miss failed to convert on fourth and 1 at its own 34-yard line early in the game. Taking over at the Rebels' 33, MSU was only able to come away with a field goal of 34 yards by Nolan McCord six plays later.

A huge early momentum shift, after its defense stopped Ole Miss, did not result in what could have been a tone setter had there been a touchdown. And Rogers mentioned it.

"Us not scoring a touchdown on the first drive where they turn it over—it was pretty big," he said. "We have to finish drives."

Ole Miss tied the game 3-3 on a Cale Nation 25-yard field goal in the first quarter, but before the end of the period MSU was back out in front. Once again, State didn't score a touchdown, and the Bulldogs led 6-3 on a 29-yard field goal by McCord, capping a thirteen-play drive.

Ole Miss led by a 10-6 margin at halftime, the second-quarter touchdown a 1-yard Snoop Conner rush with 2:21 to go before intermission. However, the Rebels had done what Rogers said the Bulldogs didn't, and that was to finish an impressive drive of sixteen plays and 78 yards, eating 5:25 from the clock.

Ole Miss led 24-6 early in the fourth quarter on a 1-yard Conner run, plus a Nation point after, and a 4-yard rush by Corral, plus the extra point by Nation. There was 11:17 to go, and the Bulldogs had a lot of work to do in this one.

Rogers and company did get into the end zone on their subsequent drive, which began after State's Jett Johnson intercepted a Corral pass and returned it 48 yards to the Ole Miss 22-yard line.

In only two plays Rogers and his offense had a touchdown as he connected with Jaden Walley for 11 yards and a score. McCord's kick closed the gap to 24-13. There was 7:20 to go in the contest.

MSU's Scott Goodman kicked onsides, but the football only went 7 yards and the Rebels took over. Six plays later, with 5:35 to go, Corral connected with Ealy and, along with Nation's point after, the Rebels had that 31-13 lead.

State added a touchdown with 2:27 to go after a ten-play, 66-yard drive. Jo'Quavious Marks scored from the 11, and MSU's 2-point conversion try was successful. Ole Miss recovered an onsides kick of 16 yards by Goodman and took over at midfield with 2:26 to go.

After the MSU defense held and the Bulldogs got the ball back with 1:19 to go, Rogers had his offense at the Rebels' 3-yard line when time expired in the game.

"Not only is this a big win for our rivalry and Ole Miss, but we also go down in history because Ole Miss has never had a ten-win regular season," Corral said. "That is something special, and it speaks a lot for the people in this locker room."

2022

An MSU Victory That Only Days Later Resonated Much Differently

2022 SCHEDULES

Ole Miss 8-5

RESULT	DATE	PF	OPPONENT	PA	LOCATION
W	September 3	28	Troy State	10	Oxford
W	September 10	59	Central Arkansas	3	Oxford
W	September 17	42	Georgia Tech	0	Atlanta
W	September 24	35	Tulsa	27	Oxford
W	October 1	22	Kentucky	19	Oxford
W	October 8	52	Vanderbilt	28	Nashville
W	October 15	48	Auburn	34	Oxford
L	October 22	20	Louisiana State	45	Baton Rouge
W	October 29	31	Texas A&M	28	College Station
L	November 12	24	Alabama	30	Oxford
L	November 19	27	Arkansas	42	Fayetteville
L	November 24	22	Mississippi State	24	Oxford
L	December 28	25	Texas Tech	42	Houston

Mississippi State 9-4

RESULT	DATE	PF	OPPONENT	PA	LOCATION
W	September 3	49	Memphis	23	Starkville
W	September 10	39	Arizona	17	Tucson
L	September 17	16	Louisiana State	31	Baton Rouge
W	September 24	45	Bowling Green	14	Starkville
W	October 1	42	Texas A&M	24	Starkville
W	October 8	40	Arkansas	17	Starkville
L	October 15	17	Kentucky	27	Lexington
L	October 22	6	Alabama	30	Tuscaloosa
W	November 5	39	Auburn (Overtime)	33	Auburn
L	November 12	19	Georgia	45	Starkville
W	November 19	56	East Tennessee State	7	Starkville
W	November 24	24	Mississippi	22	Oxford
W	January 2	19	Illinois	10	Tampa

 le Miss hosted Mississippi State for the 2022 Egg Bowl in a free fall. The Rebels, once ranked as high as seventh nationally before the LSU game in late October, had lost their way.

A 45-20 setback to the Tigers in Baton Rouge on October 22, plus two losses in their next three games, meant Ole Miss was 8-3 entering the Egg Bowl after starting the season 7-0. The Rebels were 4-3 in Southeastern Conference play by late November when the Bulldogs arrived in Oxford.

Mississippi State was 7-4 at that point and 3-4 in SEC games. The Bulldogs were headed to another postseason bowl game, their thirteenth in a row. But a win at Ole Miss would help to make their season more successful.

The matchup again pitted longtime friends Lane Kiffin of Ole Miss and Mike Leach of Mississippi State against each other. The two head coaches had met twice in the Battle for the Golden Egg. Both times Kiffin and Ole Miss came away with victory.

On Thanksgiving night 2022 at Vaught-Hemingway Stadium, MSU won the game 24-22 as the Rebels continued their fall. Just a few weeks earlier, Ole Miss was in position to make a run at a spot in the Southeastern Conference championship game and a berth in the college football playoff. Those possibilities had long since vanished.

The year before, with an Egg Bowl victory in Starkville, the Rebels won ten games and played Baylor in the Sugar Bowl. But this season, after a 42-25 Texas Bowl loss in Houston to Texas Tech on December 28, 2022, their final record was 8-5.

By beating Ole Miss, Mississippi State vaulted into the ReliaQuest Bowl in Tampa, Florida, against Illinois. The Bulldogs defeated the Fighting Illini 19-10 on January 2, 2023, but sadly they did so without Leach. The Mississippi State head coach died on December 13, less than three weeks after his team's win at Ole Miss. The world of college football was saddened by his passing and stunned that one so much a part of the sport was gone so soon.

Just a few weeks earlier, it was the Egg Bowl that was front and center. It's always that way in Mississippi in late November. Leach and Kiffin led their troops onto Hollingsworth Field on the campus of the University of Mississippi for the 119th meeting of the two schools in football.

November 24, 2022

Mississippi State 24, Ole Miss 22

	State	Ole Miss
First downs	20	19
Total plays	77	78
Total yards	336	335
Rushes/net yards	37/97	39/78
Passing yards	239	257
Passes (Att-Comp-Int)	27-40-1	31-39-0
Punts/yards	5/236	6/270
Penalties/yards	6/47	4/20
Fumbles/lost	0/1	3/2
Time of possession	32:22	27:38
Third-down conversions	8/16	4/17
Sacks by: Number/yards	2/21	4/54
Field goals attempted/made	1/1	3/3

MSU's Emmanuel Forbes in the rain at the 2022 Egg Bowl in Oxford. Courtesy of Mississippi State University Athletics.

Ole Miss struck first, a field goal of 32 yards by Jonathan Cruz with 12:16 to go in the first quarter. But MSU was quick to respond, taking the lead on a 1-yard run by Jo'Quavious Marks, capping a ten-play drive of 61 yards. The extra point kick by Massimo Biscardi was good. State led 7-3. There was 8:17 to go in the first period.

The Rebels again drove downfield, but the Bulldog defense halted their effort. Again, Cruz connected on a field goal, this time a 33-yarder, and with 1:33 to go in the first period, Ole Miss trailed 7-6.

Kiffin is not a coach who likes to go the field goal route very often. But Ole Miss added its third 3-pointer to take a 9-7 lead with 12:04 to go in the second quarter when Cruz was good again, this one from a lengthy distance of 49 yards. The momentum was with the Rebels, but State's defense had still not allowed a touchdown in the contest. It appeared this game would be a battle to the end.

Things continued to head in the right direction for the home team, as Ole Miss scored again and increased its momentum in the big game. The Rebels moved out to a 16-7 lead when they finally found the end zone, but it wasn't easy.

The MSU defense stood tall inside the 10-yard line, and on fourth down at the 3-yard line, Kiffin elected to go for the score instead of kicking another field goal. The decision worked. Jaxson Dart connected with JJ Pegues for a

Mississippi State head coach Mike Leach, 61, exits Hollingsworth Field/Vaught-Hemingway Stadium in Oxford on November 24, 2022, after his MSU Bulldogs defeated Ole Miss in the Battle for the Golden Egg. It was Leach's last game to coach. He died of heart failure less than three weeks later. Courtesy of Mississippi State University Athletics.

touchdown. The extra point by Cruz gave the Rebels a 9-point lead. Only 1:55 remained until halftime.

But State didn't run out the clock. Will Rogers led the MSU offense 75 yards and connected with Lideatrick Griffin on a 19-yard scoring play. The extra point by Biscardi was good, and with eight seconds to go before halftime, the Rebels' lead was down to 2 points.

After a scoreless third quarter, a drive that began that period but spilled over into the fourth put MSU ahead. The Bulldogs took the lead on a 34-yard Biscardi field goal that made it 17-16. Later in the final quarter, State stretched its lead to 24-16 on a 22-yard touchdown pass from Rogers to Rara Thomas, along with the extra point kick by Biscardi.

But the Rebels weren't done yet. On a fifteen-play, 99-yard drive, Ole Miss scored on a 23-yard pass from Dart to Dayton Wade. The 2-point conversion attempt to tie the game failed, and there was 1:25 to go with MSU up 24-22.

An onside kickoff by Ole Miss was not successful, and Mississippi State claimed the victory to take the Golden Egg back to Starkville.

"This game had a season's worth of excitement in it," said Leach in what would be his last postgame interview with the press. "That was a wild game;

Bulldog Collin Duncan kisses the Golden Egg after the MSU victory in 2022. Courtesy of Mississippi State University Athletics.

it was a very up-and-down game. About the time you thought it couldn't get crazier, it did. It was a good game."

Kiffin said the outcome of this one was difficult to accept, especially after his program won the first two Egg Bowls in which he had coached.

"Really disappointed for our players, especially our seniors," he said. "Credit to Mississippi State. They played really hard."

Rogers, the MSU quarterback, was adamant about the importance of winning the game.

"It means everything," he said after he threw for 239 yards and two touchdowns in his first Egg Bowl victory after two losses. "It was my third shot. I kinda got tired of losing to these guys. Obviously, they're a really good football team."

Leach said the game reminded him of one he had coached in Oxford several years prior when he was at Texas Tech. His Red Raiders defeated Ole Miss 49-45.

"It was quite a day," he said, reminiscing about that game nineteen seasons earlier in 2003. "It was a fun day. It was a wild game, too."

Said the veteran coach of games at Ole Miss, "It's fun to win here."

Mike Leach had done a lot of winning in his seasons as a head coach. Nobody knew then that this Egg Bowl would be his last game to win, his last game to coach. After three decades on the major college sports scene, a memorable football life would unfortunately soon be at its end.

2023

Victory Means Another New Year's Six for the Rebels

2023 SCHEDULES

Ole Miss 11-2

RESULT	DATE	PF	OPPONENT	PA	LOCATION
W	September 2	73	Mercer	7	Oxford
W	September 9	37	Tulane	20	New Orleans
W	September 16	48	Georgia Tech	23	Oxford
L	September 23	10	Alabama	24	Tuscaloosa
W	September 30	55	Louisiana State	49	Oxford
W	October 7	27	Arkansas	20	Oxford
W	October 21	28	Auburn	21	Auburn
W	October 28	33	Vanderbilt	7	Oxford
W	November 4	38	Texas A&M	35	Oxford
L	November 11	17	Georgia	52	Athens
W	November 18	35	Louisiana-Monroe	3	Oxford
W	November 23	17	Mississippi State	7	Starkville
W	December 30	38	Pennsylvania State	25	Atlanta

Mississippi State 5-7

RESULT	DATE	PF	OPPONENT	PA	LOCATION
W	September 2	48	Southeastern Louisiana	7	Starkville
W	September 9	31	Arizona (Overtime)	24	Starkville
L	September 16	14	Louisiana State	41	Starkville
L	September 23	30	South Carolina	37	Columbia
L	September 30	17	Alabama	40	Starkville
W	October 7	41	Western Michigan	28	Starkville
W	October 21	7	Arkansas	3	Fayetteville
L	October 28	13	Auburn	27	Auburn
L	November 4	3	Kentucky	24	Starkville
L	November 11	10	Texas A&M	51	College Station
W	November 18	41	Southern Mississippi	20	Starkville
L	November 23	7	Mississippi	17	Oxford

The 120th Battle for the Golden Egg was set to take place on November 23, 2023, in Starkville. The host Bulldogs were having a difficult season. It had actually been a difficult twelve months.

Ole Miss's John Saunders Jr. dives toward MSU receiver Lideatrick Griffin in the 2023 Egg Bowl. Courtesy of Mississippi State University Athletics.

After the sudden illness and death of head coach Mike Leach just a few days after the 119th Egg Bowl, which had been won by Mississippi State 24-22 in Oxford, defensive coordinator Zach Arnett was elevated to interim head coach on December 11, 2022, then four days later to head coach with interim removed. The job was now his, although through unfortunate circumstances.

Arnett led MSU to a 19-10 ReliaQuest Bowl win against Illinois on January 2, 2023. But later in 2023, on November 13, two days after the Bulldogs lost 51-10 at Texas A&M to fall to 4-6 overall and 1-6 in Southeastern Conference play, MSU relieved Arnett of his duties. State elevated assistant coach Greg Knox to the interim head coaching

November 23, 2023

Ole Miss 17, Mississippi State 7

	State	Ole Miss
First downs	16	22
Total plays	67	75
Total yards	303	307
Rushes/net yards	28/96	49/211
Passing yards	207	96
Passes (Att-Comp-Int)	25-39-0	14-26-0
Punts/yards	8/326	8/345
Penalties/yards	4/56	6-/30
Fumbles/lost	0/0	0/0
Time of possession	28:03	31:57
Third-down conversions	4/16	4/16
Sacks by: Number/yards	1/9	1/1
Field goals attempted/made	0/2	1/1

position for the final two games of the regular season. Arnett had a 5-6 record in his eleven games as the MSU head coach.

Knox led State to a 41-20 win against Southern Mississippi in Starkville. Then it was time for MSU to get ready for another Thanksgiving night encounter with the archrival from Oxford.

Ole Miss was having a good season, similar to the one only two years before. In 2021, the Rebels won the Golden Egg battle 31-21 at MSU to finish the regular season 10-2 overall and 6-2 in the SEC. They were attempting an identical mark in 2023 in the Egg Bowl.

Mississippi State linebacker Nathaniel Watson celebrates after a play in the 2023 Egg Bowl. Courtesy of Mississippi State University Athletics.

Lane Kiffin was in his fourth season as the Rebels' head coach, and he was 2-1 in games against Mississippi State. His team was favored by 10 points in the contest when Thanksgiving rolled around with a clear, chilly late autumn night for football.

Under Kiffin, Ole Miss has been known for its explosive, high-scoring offenses. The 2023 version of that offense encountered some injuries along the offensive line that made things more challenging late in the season. MSU's defense had also played well, and the only SEC win for the Bulldogs was a low-scoring 7-3 victory at Arkansas.

Still, when the scoreboard showed Ole Miss with a 3-0 lead at halftime on a second-quarter Caden Costa field goal of 36 yards, perhaps many in the announced crowd of 60,412 were surprised. But it is the Egg Bowl after all, so expect the unexpected.

The first five Mississippi State drives ended with a punt. The first four Ole Miss drives ended the same way. On the Rebels' fifth drive, the score finally moved from 0-0 to 3-0. That's when Costa's kick completed a lengthy thirteen-play, 66-yard drive from the Rebels' 15-yard line to the Bulldogs' 19-yard line where on fourth down and 6 yards to go, the game's first points were recorded.

Both teams punted on their next possessions, and MSU finally got something going late in the second period with a ten-play drive to the Rebel 24.

The Ole Miss sideline sensing a victory during the 2023 Egg Bowl. Courtesy of Ole Miss Athletics.

Ole Miss players with the Golden Egg following the Rebels' 17-7 victory against Mississippi State in the 2023 Egg Bowl in Starkville. Courtesy of Ole Miss Athletics.

But Kyle Ferrie missed a 42-yard field goal, and the half ended with Ole Miss maintaining its slim edge.

The second half proved to have a bit more offense. Ole Miss got the football first in the third quarter, and in three plays had to do what was common in the first half—punt. The Bulldogs drove from their own 29-yard line in ten plays and took the lead on a quarterback Will Rogers keeper from 1 yard out. Ferrie was true on the point after, and halfway through the third period underdog MSU led 7-3.

The Rebels responded. Starting at its own 25, Ole Miss drove 75 yards in three minutes and forty-six seconds to retake the lead. Quinshon Judkins rushed for 2 yards right up the middle for the go-ahead score. Caden Davis was the kicker this time, and his extra point was good. It was 10-7 Rebels.

The Ole Miss defense then held MSU to three plays and a punt, and the Ole Miss offense went back to work. On the tenth play of a 71-yard scoring drive, quarterback Jaxson Dart found his tight end wide open down the middle for a 26-yard scoring play. Caden Prieskorn caught the pass and strolled into the end zone untouched with no Bulldog defenders near. The point after by Davis was good, and the Rebs led 17-7 in the fourth quarter with 13:26 to go.

The Rebels maintained control of the contest, and there was no more scoring for either team. Ole Miss head coach Lane Kiffin had positive comments after the battle.

"I'm really proud of our players," said Kiffin, as his Egg Bowl record improved to 3-1 and his overall record as the head coach of the Rebels stood at 33-15. "I thought our guys played great defense basically the whole night. We played well in the second half running the football, and we ended the game running the football."

After four Egg Bowl games, Kiffin knows the importance of the season finale. He also took a moment to remember Leach, his friend in coaching.

"Excited to get the trophy back," Kiffin said, after its one-year absence from Oxford. "That was really painful last year to lose that. If you're ever going to lose it—once we learned later on that it was Coach Leach's last game, maybe that was meant to be. I miss him. I missed him today. And we'll never forget him."

In the Bulldogs' postgame, Knox expressed his appreciation for the MSU seniors and the team's efforts.

"Every day we start with the word 'today,'" he said. "It's all about today. All we have is today. So we focused on today, and we tried to maximize the day. I thought they did that every day. I'm very, very proud of this group of guys."

Ole Miss head coach Lane Kiffin meets Mississippi State interim head coach Greg Knox after the Rebels' victory. Knox had coached on both sides of the Battle for the Golden Egg, having served as an assistant coach at Ole Miss in earlier years. Courtesy of Ole Miss Athletics.

Rogers had 207 passing yards on 25-of-39 attempts, allowing him to end the game with the most passing yards by an MSU quarterback in Egg Bowl history—1,222 yards.

An emotional Rogers said the Bulldogs, especially the seniors, stayed together and gave it their best.

"It would have been so easy for us to quit after everything we've been through on and off the field," he said. "You can say a lot of things about us, but we're not quitters."

Ole Miss senior safety Daijahn Anthony had a career-high fifteen total tackles, six of them solos, to lead the Rebel defense.

Dart, who was 14-of-26 for 96 yards and a touchdown through the air, said it was important for him and his team to return the Golden Egg to Oxford. "Last year was definitely a sour taste in our mouths with how it ended," Dart said. "We wanted to get the Egg back. This definitely means a lot to us."

It was the rushing attack that helped put Ole Miss over the top. The Rebels ran for 226 yards, while State only moved it 96 yards on the ground.

Leading the way for Ole Miss was Judkins, a sophomore who is one of two players in SEC history—the other Georgia's Herschel Walker in 1980 and

1981—with at least 1,000 yards and at least fifteen touchdowns in each of their first two seasons as freshmen and sophomores.

"It's a great milestone, and I'm just thankful and blessed to be in this position," said Judkins, who had 119 yards on twenty-eight carries with one touchdown in the 2023 Egg Bowl. "And I'm thankful for the guys up front that helped me get through the holes."

Ole Miss finished the regular season 10-2 overall and 6-2 in SEC games. A 38-25 win against Penn State in the Peach Bowl gave Ole Miss its first 11-win season in program history.

MSU was 5-7 overall and 1-7 in conference play.

Heading into the 2024 Battle for the Golden Egg, the official record book showed Ole Miss with 65 wins and Mississippi State with 46 wins, and there were six ties. Three of the games—two Ole Miss wins (2012 and 2014) and a State win (2018)—have been completely eliminated from the record book by NCAA rulings.

Appendixes

Fascinating Facts

The series between Ole Miss and Mississippi State is tied as the sixteenth-longest in-state rivalry in National Collegiate Athletic Association Division I-A.

Ole Miss and Mississippi State have played in seven cities on ten different fields. Thirty-five games have been played in Starkville, thirty-four in Oxford, and thirty in Jackson, on two playing fields in each city. Three games have been played in Tupelo, two in Greenwood, and one each in Columbus and Clarksdale.

Average score over 103 games = Ole Miss 17, Mississippi State 14. Total Points = 3,178: Ole Miss 1,729, Mississippi State 1,449. Touchdowns: Ole Miss 234, Mississippi State 199.

There have been thirty-two shutouts—seventeen by State, fifteen by Ole Miss.

Ole Miss's longest scoring streak is forty-nine games between 1947 and 1995. State's longest scoring streak is thirty-one games between 1972 and 2002.

Ole Miss's longest scoreless streak is five games between 1918 and 1921. State has never gone scoreless more than two games in a row.

The most consecutive victories is thirteen by State between 1911 and 1925. Ole Miss's longest win streak is six (1930–35 and 1947–52). Between 1947 and 1963, Ole Miss went seventeen straight games without a loss (fourteen wins and three ties).

In 1901, 1903, 1919, 1922, 1923, and 1940, State was undefeated prior to the game. In 1924, 1952, 1960, 1962, and 1963, Ole Miss was undefeated prior to the game. They have never met when both schools were undefeated.

Each team has scored more points in the second quarter than in any other:

	First	Second		Third	Fourth	Total
Ole Miss	357	598	316	493	= 1,764	
State	261	484	259	450	= 1,454	
Total	618	1,082	575	943	= 3,218	

These figures do not include games from 1901 to 1909, when play was in equal halves, not quarters; in those games, State scored 108 points, while Ole Miss recorded 88.

The most points Ole Miss has scored in one quarter is 42 in 1971. The most points State has scored in one quarter is 24 in 1974.

Twenty-six games have been decided by a single touchdown (5 points prior to 1912, 6 points thereafter) or less.

Of the ninety-one games not tied at the half, the team leading at that point has won seventy-three times (80.2 percent).

Of the one hundred games not ending in ties, the team scoring first has won seventy-three times (73 percent).

Four of the six ties occurred on November 30—1929, 1957, 1963, and 1968.

Three games have finished with 6-0 scores; State has won them all—1911, 1925, and 1941.

Five games have been decided by 1 point; Ole Miss has won them all—1926, 1928, 1945, 1983, and 1997.

There have been approximately 757 kickoffs. (Kicks must be estimated in 1902 and 1904, as scoring details are uncertain.)

Only 4 of those 757 kickoffs have been returned for touchdowns—one by State (1942) and three by Ole Miss (1935, 1964, and 1984).

Seven punts have been returned for touchdowns: five by Ole Miss (1932, 1937, 1948, 1983, and 2006) and two by Miss. State (1920, 2007). Also, each team has recovered a punt for touchdown (both in 1908). And each team has blocked a punt for a touchdown: Ole Miss in 1910, and A&M in 1919.

At least 384 individuals are known to have scored—204 for Ole Miss and 180 for State. (Names of scorers are not known in 1902 and 1904.)

About 3,700 lettermen have been eligible for play in these 106 rivalry games.

An estimated 2.9–3.0 million people—the same number as Mississippi's population in the 2000 census—have watched the 106 games in person.

The earliest meeting of the season occurred on October 18 (1924); the latest meeting occurred on December 7 (1918).

They have played on Thanksgiving twenty-five times, with Ole Miss winning fifteen times, State winning nine times, and one tie. Seven of the Thanksgiving meetings occurred in Jackson, where Mississippi State won four; ten occurred in Starkville, where Ole Miss won seven; and eight occurred in Oxford, where Ole Miss won four and there was one tie. On Thanksgiving, Ole Miss has scored 450 points, while Mississippi State has scored 350, for an average score of 18–14.

State and Ole Miss have played more games (106) against each other than any other opponent. The second-most-frequent opponent for each is Louisiana State, which State has faced 103 times and Ole Miss has played 98 times.

Milestone touchdowns in this rivalry:

	State	Ole Miss
No. 50	1919 (first touchdown)	1937 (only touchdown)
No. 100	1946 (second touchdown)	1959 (first touchdown)
No. 150	1983 (first touchdown)	1972 (sixth touchdown)
No. 200	2007 (first touchdown)	1990 (third touchdown)

The first passes were attempted in 1906, when forward passing was legalized. That year, Ole Miss tried nine and completed five, while A&M tried one and completed zero. A&M's first successful pass against Ole Miss came in 1908. Ole Miss recorded the first interception, also in 1908.

The first aerial scores came in 1915, when A&M recorded three. Ole Miss's first aerial score came in 1917.

Two men have been head coaches for both Mississippi A&M and Ole Miss:

Dan Martin	C. R. (Dudy) Noble
Ole Miss, 1901 and 1902: 1-1	Ole Miss, 1917 and 1918: 0-3
A&M, 1903-6: 1-2-1	A&M, 1922 and 1930: 1-1

Three players are known to have received football letters from both schools: Norvin E. (Billy) Green (Ole Miss, 1900; Mississippi A&M, 1901, 1902, 1903, 1904), Fletcher J. East (Ole Miss, 1915; Mississippi A&M, 1917, 1919), and Breck Tyler (Mississippi State, 1977, 1978; Ole Miss, 1980, 1981). None of the three scored.

The longest recorded drive is 105 yards, by A&M in 1908, when fields were 110 yards in length. The longest recorded drive since 1912, when fields were shortened to 100 yards, is Ole Miss's 98-yard march in 2004.

The longest play (and longest touchdown play) is 97 yards, recorded twice—an interception return by State's Jack Nix in 1938 and a kickoff return by Ole Miss's Lee Davis in 1984.

Seven games featured no rushing touchdowns: 1911, 1925, 1948, 1963, 1967, 1988, and 1996.

The largest deficit ever overcome is 16 points. Ole Miss has done it twice, winning after trailing 23-7 in 1983 and 16-0 in 2000.

Total Games = 120: Ole Miss has won 65 (including two forfeit wins but with two additional wins vacated), State has won 46 (with one additional win vacated), and there have been 6 ties.

Southeastern Conference Games = 90: Ole Miss has won 52 (including two forfeit wins but with two additional wins vacated), State has won 31 (with one additional win vacated), and there have been 4 ties.

Golden Egg Battles = 96: Ole Miss has won 59 (including two forfeit wins but with two additional wins vacated), State has won 29 (with one additional win vacated), and there have been 5 ties.

Games at a Glance, 1901–2023

Game	Year	Date	Site	Winner	Score	Overall Series			Attendance
						Ole Miss	Miss. State	Tie	
1	1901	Oct. 28	Starkville	A&M	17-0	0	1	0	N/A
2	1902	Oct. 25	Starkville	Ole Miss	21-0	1	1	0	N/A
3	1903	Nov. 14	Oxford	Tie	6-6	1	1	1	N/A
4	1904	Oct. 22	Columbus	Ole Miss	17-5	2	1	1	2,000
5	1905	Nov. 30	Jackson	A&M	11-0	2	2	1	5,000
6	1906	Nov. 29	Jackson	Ole Miss	29-5	3	2	1	5,000
7	1907	Nov. 28	Jackson	A&M	15-0	3	3	1	N/A
8	1908	Nov. 26	Jackson	A&M	44-6	3	4	1	5,000
9	1909	Nov. 25	Jackson	Ole Miss	9-5	4	4	1	5,000
10	1910	Nov. 24	Jackson	Ole Miss	30-0	5	4	1	5,000
11	1911	Nov. 30	Jackson	A&M	6-0	5	5	1	3,500
12	1915	Nov. 6	Tupelo	A&M	65-0	5	6	1	6,000
13	1916	Nov. 3	Tupelo	A&M	36-0	5	7	1	5,000
14	1917	Nov. 3	Tupelo	A&M	41-14	5	8	1	1,000
15	1918	Nov. 28	Starkville	A&M	34-0	5	9	1	N/A
16	1918	Dec. 7	Oxford	A&M	13-0	5	10	1	N/A
17	1919	Nov. 8	Clarksdale	A&M	33-0	5	11	1	3,000
18	1920	Nov. 6	Greenwood	A&M	20-0	5	12	1	4,500
19	1921	Oct. 28	Greenwood	A&M	21-0	5	13	1	5,000
20	1922	Oct. 21	Jackson	A&M	19-13	5	14	1	15,000
21	1923	Oct. 20	Jackson	A&M	13-6	5	15	1	8,000
22	1924	Oct. 18	Jackson	A&M	20-0	5	16	1	10,000
23	1925	Oct. 24	Jackson	A&M	6-0	5	17	1	10,000
24	1926	Nov. 25	Starkville	Ole Miss	7-6	6	17	1	11,000
25	1927	Nov. 24	Oxford	Ole Miss	20-12	7	17	1	14,000
26	1928	Nov. 29	Starkville	Ole Miss	20-19	8	17	1	14,000
27	1929	Nov. 30	Oxford	Tie	7-7	8	17	2	12,000
28	1930	Nov. 27	Starkville	Ole Miss	20-0	9	17	2	8,000
29	1931	Nov. 26	Oxford	Ole Miss	25-14	10	17	2	10,000
30	1932	Nov. 24	Starkville	Ole Miss	13-0	11	17	2	6,000
31	1933	Dec. 2	Oxford	Ole Miss	31-0	12	17	2	7,500
32	1934	Dec. 1	Jackson	Ole Miss	7-3	13	17	2	11,000
33	1935	Nov. 30	Oxford	Ole Miss	14-6	14	17	2	14,500
34	1936	Nov. 21	Starkville	State	26-6	14	18	2	20,000
35	1937	Nov. 25	Oxford	State	9-7	14	19	2	14,000

Game	Year	Date	Site	Winner	Score	Ole Miss	Miss. State	Tie	Attendance
						Overall Series			
36	1938	Nov. 26	Starkville	Ole Miss	19-6	15	19	2	15,000
37	1939	Nov. 25	Oxford	State	18-6	15	20	2	22,000
38	1940	Nov. 23	Starkville	State	19-0	15	21	2	26,000
39	1941	Nov. 29	Oxford	State	6-0	15	22	2	28,000
40	1942	Nov. 21	Starkville	State	34-13	15	23	2	16,000
41	1944	Nov. 25	Oxford	Ole Miss	13-8	16	23	2	8,000
42	1945	Nov. 24	Starkville	Ole Miss	7-6	17	23	2	18,000
43	1946	Nov. 23	Oxford	State	20-0	17	24	2	26,000
44	1947	Nov. 29	Starkville	Ole Miss	33-14	18	24	2	25,000
45	1948	Nov. 27	Oxford	Ole Miss	34-7	19	24	2	26,000
46	1949	Nov. 26	Starkville	Ole Miss	26-0	20	24	2	32,000
47	1950	Dec. 2	Oxford	Ole Miss	27-20	21	24	2	28,000
48	1951	Dec. 1	Starkville	Ole Miss	49-7	22	24	2	28,000
49	1952	Nov. 29	Oxford	Ole Miss	20-14	23	24	2	28,000
50	1953	Nov. 28	Starkville	Tie	7-7	23	24	3	35,000
51	1954	Nov. 27	Oxford	Ole Miss	14-0	24	24	3	36,000
52	1955	Nov. 26	Starkville	Ole Miss	26-0	25	24	3	35,000
53	1956	Dec. 1	Oxford	Ole Miss	13-7	26	24	3	34,000
54	1957	Nov. 30	Starkville	Tie	7-7	26	24	4	35,000
55	1958	Nov. 29	Oxford	Ole Miss	21-0	27	24	4	33,500
56	1959	Nov. 28	Starkville	Ole Miss	42-0	28	24	4	35,000
57	1960	Nov. 26	Oxford	Ole Miss	35-9	29	24	4	N/A
58	1961	Dec. 2	Starkville	Ole Miss	37-7	30	24	4	34,500
59	1962	Dec. 1	Oxford	Ole Miss	13-6	31	24	4	31,792
60	1963	Nov. 30	Starkville	Tie	10-10	31	24	5	35,000
61	1964	Dec. 5	Oxford	State	20-17	31	25	5	30,000 TV
62	1965	Nov. 27	Starkville	Ole Miss	21-0	32	25	5	35,000
63	1966	Nov. 26	Oxford	Ole Miss	24-0	33	25	5	30,000
64	1967	Dec. 2	Starkville	Ole Miss	10-3	34	25	5	21,000
65	1968	Nov. 30	Oxford	Tie	17-17	34	25	6	27,000
66	1969	Nov. 27	Starkville	Ole Miss	48-22	35	25	6	34,000
67	1970	Nov. 26	Oxford	State	19-14	35	26	6	35,000
68	1971	Nov. 25	Starkville	Ole Miss	48-0	36	26	6	35,000
69	1972	Nov. 25	Oxford	Ole Miss	51-14	37	26	6	33,586
70	1973	Nov. 24	Jackson	Ole Miss	38-10	38	26	6	43,556
71	1974	Nov. 23	Jackson	State	31-13	38	27	6	46,500
72	1975	Nov. 22	Jackson	Ole Miss	13-7	39	27	6	46,500
73	1976	Nov. 20	Jackson	State	28-11	40	27	6	46,500 *
74	1977	Nov. 19	Jackson	State	18-14	41	27	6	47,500 *
75	1978	Nov. 25	Jackson	Ole Miss	27-7	42	27	6	47,012
76	1979	Nov. 24	Jackson	Ole Miss	14-9	43	27	6	46,021
77	1980	Nov. 22	Jackson	State	19-14	43	28	6	62,250
78	1981	Nov. 21	Jackson	Ole Miss	21-17	44	28	6	61,153
79	1982	Nov. 20	Jackson	State	27-10	44	29	6	61,286
80	1983	Nov. 19	Jackson	Ole Miss	24-23	45	29	6	59,578
81	1984	Nov. 24	Jackson	Ole Miss	24-3	46	29	6	52,766 TV
82	1985	Nov. 23	Jackson	Ole Miss	45-27	47	29	6	48,705
83	1986	Nov. 22	Jackson	Ole Miss	24-3	48	29	6	44,500 TV

Game	Year	Date	Site	Winner	Score	Ole Miss	Miss. State	Tie	Attendance
84	1987	Nov. 21	Jackson	State	30-20	48	30	6	43,450
85	1988	Nov. 26	Jackson	Ole Miss	33-6	49	30	6	28,000
86	1989	Nov. 25	Jackson	Ole Miss	21-11	50	30	6	43,218
87	1990	Nov. 24	Jackson	Ole Miss	21-9	51	30	6	56,652
88	1991	Nov. 23	Starkville	State	24-9	51	31	6	41,200
89	1992	Nov. 28	Oxford	Ole Miss	17-10	52	31	6	41,200 TV
90	1993	Nov. 27	Starkville	State	20-13	52	32	6	40,328
91	1994	Nov. 26	Oxford	State	21-17	52	33	6	36,521
92	1995	Nov. 25	Starkville	Ole Miss	13-10	53	33	6	38,107
93	1996	Nov. 30	Oxford	State	17-0	53	34	6	23,678 TV
94	1997	Nov. 29	Starkville	Ole Miss	15-14	54	34	6	33,200 TV
95	1998	Nov. 28	Oxford	State	28-6	54	35	6	50,412 N TV
96	1999	Nov. 25	Starkville	State	23-20	54	36	6	41,200 N TV
97	2000	Nov. 23	Oxford	Ole Miss	45-30	55	36	6	48,871 N TV
98	2001	Nov. 22	Starkville	State	36-28	55	37	6	51,112 N TV
99	2002	Nov. 28	Oxford	Ole Miss	24-12	56	37	6	60,245 N TV
100	2003	Nov. 27	Starkville	Ole Miss	31-0	57	37	6	53,582 N TV
101	2004	Nov. 27	Oxford	Ole Miss	20-3	58	37	6	55,810
102	2005	Nov. 26	Starkville	State	35-14	58	38	6	53,655
103	2006	Nov. 25	Oxford	Ole Miss	20-17	59	38	6	57,658
104	2007	Nov. 23	Starkville	State	17-14	59	39	6	51,727
105	2008	Nov. 28	Oxford	Ole Miss	45-0	60	39	6	55,231
106	2009	Nov. 28	Starkville	State	41-27	60	40	6	55,365
107	2010	Nov. 27	Oxford	State	31-23	60	41	6	58,625
108	2011	Nov. 26	Starkville	State	31-3	60	42	6	55,270
109	2012	Nov. 24	Oxford	Ole Miss	41-24	61	42	6	61,005
110	2013	Nov. 28	Starkville	State	17-10 (OT)	61	43	6	55,113
111	2014	Nov. 30	Oxford	Ole Miss	31-17	62	43	6	62,058
112	2015	Nov. 28	Starkville	Ole Miss	38-27	63	43	6	62,265
113	2016	Nov. 26	Oxford	State	55-20	63	44	6	66,038
114	2017	Nov. 23	Starkville	Ole Miss	31-28	64	44	6	59,345
115	2018	Nov. 22	Oxford	State	35-3	64	45	6	56,561
116	2019	Nov. 28	Starkville	State	21-20	64	46	6	57,529
117	2020	Nov. 28	Oxford	Ole Miss	31-24	65	46	6	16,218
118	2021	Nov. 25	Starkville	Ole Miss	31-21	66	46	6	55,601
119	2022	Nov. 24	Oxford	State	24-22	66	47	6	62,487
120	2023	Nov. 23	Starkville	Ole Miss	17-7	67	47	6	60,412

Notes:
* Forfeited to Ole Miss by order of NCAA N = Night game
TV = Televised
N/A = Not available

Records by Playing Site

	# of Games	OM Won	State Won	Tie	OM Points	State Points
OXFORD						
University Park	1	0	0	1	6	6
Vaught-Hemingway Stadium/ Hollingsworth Field	40	23	14	2	788	594
TOTAL	**41**	**23**	**14**	**3**	**794**	**600**
STARKVILLE						
Fairgrounds	2	1	1	0	21	17
Davis Wade Stadium/ Scott Field	40	23	14	3	805	601
TOTAL	**42**	**24**	**15**	**3**	**826**	**618**
JACKSON						
Fairgrounds	12	4	8	0	100	147
Memorial Stadium	18	14*	4	0	387	285
TOTAL	**30**	**18***	**12**	**0**	**487**	**432**
OTHER SITES						
Columbus Fairgrounds	1	1	0	0	17	5
Tupelo Fairgrounds	3	0	3	0	14	142
Dorr High School, Clarksdale	1	0	1	0	0	33
Greenwood Baseball Park	2	0	2	0	0	41
TOTAL	**7**	**1**	**6**	**0**	**31**	**221**
TOTAL	**120**	**66**	**47**	**6**	**2,438**	**1,871**

Note: * Includes two by forfeit

Scoring

How They Scored

	Points by Touchdowns	Points by Extra Points	Points by Field Goal	Points by Safety	Total Points
Mississippi	1,491*	244	169**	2	1,906
Mississippi State	1,261***	187	157****	8	1,613

Notes: * Includes 18 touchdowns for 5 points each through 1911, and 216 touchdowns for 6 points each after that year.
** Includes 3 field goals for 4 points each prior to 1909, then 43 field goals for 3 points each after that year.
*** Includes 21 touchdowns for 5 points each through 1911, then 178 touchdowns for 6 points each after that year.
**** Includes 45 field goals recorded after 1909, when value of a field goal dropped from 4 points to 3 points.

Method of Touchdown Scoring

	Ole Miss	Mississippi State	Total
Run	160	157	315
Pass	90	73	162
Other	**25**	**19**	**43**
Lateral	1	1	2
Kickoff return	3	2	5
Punt return	5	2	7
Punt recovery	1	1	2
Blocked punt	2	1	3
Pass interception	10	7	17
Recovered kick	1	1	2
Blocked field goal	0	1	1
Fumble recovery	2	1	3
Fumble return	0	1	1
Total	**275**	**249**	**520**

Notes: Of the series' 451 touchdowns, 62.3 percent have come by rushing, 29.1 percent by passing, and 8.6 percent by other means. Ole Miss has scored 59.6 percent of its touchdowns by run, 31.0 percent by pass, and 9.4 percent by other means. State has scored 65.5 percent of its touchdowns by run, 26.7 percent by pass, and 7.8 percent by other means.

Extra Points

	Mississippi	Mississippi State
Kick (one point)	242	186
Run		
One point	4	2
Two point	2	5
Pass		
One point	2	4
Two point	2	2
Total number of successful extra points	252	199
Total points scored via extra points	256	204

Note: Details of the 1902 and 1904 games are not known, but it is estimated that Ole Miss had one extra point in 1902 and two extra points in 1904, all by kick. A&M had no extra points in either game.

Coaches

Twenty-eight men have coached Ole Miss in rivalry games; thirty-two men have coached Mississippi State.

Ole Miss	Record versus Mississippi State
Dan Martin, 1901–2	1-1
Mike Harvey, 1903–4	1-0-1
Tom Hammond, 1906	1-0
Frank Mason, 1907	0-1
Frank Kyle, 1908	0-1
Nathan P. Stauffer 1909–11	2-1
Fred Robbins, 1915–16	0-2
C. R. (Dudy) Noble, 1917–18	0-3
R. L. Sullivan, 1919–21	0-3
R. A. Cowell, 1922–23	0-2
Chester Barnard, 1924	0-1
Homer Hazel, 1925–29	3-1-1
Edgar Walker, 1930–37	6-2
Harry Mehre, 1938–45	3-4
Harold (Red) Drew, 1946	0-1
John H. Vaught 1947–70, 1973	19-2-4
Billy Kinard, 1971–72	2-0
Ken Cooper, 1974–77	3-1*
Steve Sloan, 1978–82	3-2
Billy Brewer, 1983–93	8-3
Joe Lee Dunn, 1994	0-1
Tommy Tuberville, 1995–98	2-2
David Cutcliffe, 1999–2004	4-2
Ed Orgeron, 2005–7	1-2
Houston Nutt, 2008–11	1-3
Hugh Freeze, 2012–16	2-2
Matt Luke, 2017–19	1-2
Lane Kiffin, 2020–	2-1

Mississippi State	Record versus Ole Miss
L. B. Harvey, 1901	1-0
Jerry Gwin, 1902	0-1
Dan Martin, 1903–6	1-2-1
Fred J. Furman, 1907–8	2-0

W. D. Chadwick, 1909–11	1-2
Billy Hayes, 1915–16	2-0
Stanley Robinson, 1917–19	4-0
Fred Holtkamp, 1920–21	2-0
C. R. (Dudy) Noble, 1922, 1930	1-1
Earl C. Able, 1923–24	2-0
Bernie Bierman, 1925–26	1-1
J. W. Hancock, 1927–29	0-2-1
Ray Dauber, 1931–32	0-2
Ross McKechnie, 1933–34	0-2
Ralph Sasse, 1935–36	1-1
Emerson (Spike) Nelson, 1938	0-1
Allyn McKeen, 1939–48	5-4
Arthur W. (Slick) Morton, 1949–51	0-3
Murray Warmath, 1952–53	0-1-1
Darrell Royal, 1954–55	0-2
Wade Walker, 1956–61	0-5-1
Paul Davis, 1962–66	1-3-1
Charlie Shira, 1967–72	1-4-1
Bob H. Tyler, 1973–78	1-5*
Emory Bellard, 1979–85	2-5
Rockey Felker, 1986–90	1-4
Jackie Sherrill, 1991–2003	7-6
Sylvester Croom, 2004–7	2-3
Dan Mullen, 2009–17	6-2
Joe Moorhead, 2018–19	2-0
Mike Leach, 2020–22	1-2
Greg Knox, 2023–	0-1

Note: * After forfeits of 1976 and 1977.

Team Records

Most points, one team—65, Mississippi State, 1915 Most points, both teams—75, 2000

Most touchdowns, one team—10, Mississippi State, 1915 Most touchdowns, both teams—10, 1969, 1985, 2000

Fewest touchdowns, both teams—2, 1903, 1909, 1926, 1929, 1937, 1945, 1953, 1957, 1963, 1995

Most extra points made, one team—7, Ole Miss, 1951 Most extra points made, both teams—9, 1969, 2000

Field goal attempts, one team—4, Ole Miss, 1906; Mississippi State, 1970, 1976, 1977, 1983

Field goal attempts, both teams—5, 1957, 1964, 1967, 1976, 1977, 1983, 1994, 2004, 2006 Field goals made—3, Ole Miss, 1906; Mississippi State, 1976, 1983

Field goals made, both teams—4, 1976, 1983, 1988, 1993 Total offense, one team—571 yards, Ole Miss, 1969 Total offense, both teams—950 yards, 1969

Most plays, one team—90, Ole Miss, 1949 Most plays, both teams—163, 1969 Fewest plays, one team—47, Ole Miss, 1945 Fewest plays, both teams—98, 1942

Fewest first downs, one team—1, Ole Miss, 1915; Mississippi State, 1925 Most first downs, one team—31, Ole Miss, 1969

Most first downs, both teams—50, 1969

Most rushing touchdowns—7, Mississippi State, 1915; Ole Miss, 1951 Most rushing touchdowns, both teams—8, 1951

Most rushing attempts, one team—80, Ole Miss, 1949 Most rushing attempts, both teams—112, 1973

Fewest rushing attempts, one team—25, Ole Miss 1946, 2005; Mississippi State, 1999, 2003

Fewest rushing attempts, both teams—56, 1966 Most yards rushing, one team—409, Ole Miss, 1972 Most yards rushing, both teams—583, 1952

Fewest yards rushing, one team—51, Mississippi State, 2008 Fewest yards rushing, both teams—123, 1985

Most passing touchdowns, one team—4, Ole Miss, 1988, 2008 Most passing touchdowns, both teams—5, 1969

Most passing yardage, one team—363, Mississippi State, 1978 Most passing yardage, both teams—585, 1988

Most pass attempts, one team—46, Mississippi State, 1978 Most pass attempts, both teams—86, 1988

Most pass completions, one team—25, Mississippi State, 1978 Most pass completions, both teams—42, 1969, 1988

Fewest pass attempts—1, Mississippi State, 1906, 1907

Fewest pass completions—0 Mississippi State, 1906, 1907; Ole Miss, 1916 Most interceptions thrown, one team—5, Mississippi State, 1972

Most interceptions thrown, both teams—7, 1940 Longest drive—105 yards, Mississippi State, 1908

Longest play—97 yards, Mississippi State, 1938; Ole Miss, 1984

Most fumbles—7, Mississippi State, 1951, 1954, 1978, 1981; Ole Miss, 1953, 1974 Most fumbles, both teams—13, 1954

Fewest fumbles, both teams—0, 1944, 1997, 2001, 2006 Most fumbles lost, one team—6, Ole Miss, 1974 Most fumbles lost, both teams—9, 1974

Most turnovers, one team—8, Mississippi State, 1972; Ole Miss, 1974 Most turnovers, both teams—12, 1974

Most punts, one team—23, Mississippi State, 1911 Most punts, both teams—37, 1911

Fewest punts, one team—0, Ole Miss, 1960 Fewest punts, both teams—3, 1961

Most penalties, one team—17, Mississippi State, 1985 Most penalties, both teams—26, 1985

Fewest penalties, one team—0, Ole Miss, 1917 Fewest penalties, both teams—3, 1925

Most penalty yards, one team—127, Mississippi State, 1995 Most penalty yards, both teams—196, 1985, 1995

Fewest penalty yards, one team—0, Ole Miss, 1917 Fewest penalty yards, both teams—15, 1925

Note: Very few figures available prior to 1933.

Individual Records

Most points	42—Laverne (Showboat) Boykin, Ole Miss, 1951
Total offense	318 yards—Tommy Pharr, Mississippi State, 1969; Kevin Fant, Mississippi State, 2002
Longest play	97 yards—Jack Nix, Mississippi State, 1938, interception; Lee Davis, Ole Miss, 1984, kick- off return
Most rushing attempts	40—Kayo Dottley, Ole Miss, 1949; Michael Davis, Mississippi State, 1993; D. J. (Deuce) McAllister, Ole Miss, 1998
Most rushing yardage	242—Dou Innocent, Ole Miss, 1995
Longest rushing play	90 yards—Fred Collins, Mississippi State, 1979
Most passing attempts	45—Tony Shell, Mississippi State, 1988
Most passing completions	24—Tommy Pharr, Mississippi State, 1969
Most passing yardage	340—Kevin Fant, Mississippi State, 2002
Most passing attempts combined	86—Tony Shell, Mississippi State (45), Mark Young, Ole Miss (37), and John Darnell, Ole Miss (4), 1988
Most passing yardage combined	585—Tony Shell, Mississippi State (224), Mark Young, Ole Miss (334), and John Darnell, Ole Miss (27), 1989
Most passing completions combined	41—Tommy Pharr, Mississippi State (24), and Archie Manning, Ole Miss (17), 1969; Tony Shell, Mississippi State (21), Mark Young, Ole Miss (19), and John Darnell, Ole Miss (2), 1988
Longest pass	84 yards—Omarr Conner to Ty Freeman, Mississippi State, 2004
Most pass receptions	14—David Smith, Mississippi State, 1969
Most yards receiving	194—David Smith, Mississippi State, 1969
Most interceptions	3—Rab Rogers, Ole Miss, 1934; Billy (Spook) Murphy, Mississippi State, 1946; Billy Stacy, Mississippi State, 1958; Jeramie Johnson, Mississippi State, 2005

Most points on kicks	13—James C. Elmer, Ole Miss, 1906
Most extra point kicks	7—Jimmy Lear, Ole Miss, 1951
Longest kickoff return	97 yards—Lee Davis, Ole Miss, 1984
Longest punt	80 yards—Rube Wilcox, Ole Miss, 1928
Longest punt return	78 yards—Ray (Little) Hapes, Ole Miss, 1937
Most field goals	3—Jim Elmer, Ole Miss, 1906; Kinney Jordan, Mississippi State, 1976; Artie Cosby, Mississippi State, 1983
Longest field goal	51 yards—Artie Cosby, Mississippi State, 1983
Shortest field goal	19 yards—Jim Elmer, Ole Miss, 1906; Artie Cosby, Mississippi State, 1983
Most tackles	23—Barrin Simpson, Mississippi State, 1999

Note: Very few figures available prior to 1933.

Scorers, 1901–2023

	Touchdowns	Extra Points	Field Goals	Points	Years
Mississippi					
Adams, Billy Ray	3	0	0	18	1960–61
Ainsworth, Greg	7	0	0	42	1971–72
Akin, William (Dooley)	1	0	0	6	1922
Allen, Charlie	1	0	0	6	1923
Allen, Gene	2	1*	0	14	1971–72
Ambrose, J. R.	2	0	0	12	1985
Baldwin, Randy	1	0	0	6	1989
Barbour, Calvin	1	1	0	7	1922
Barkley, Ross	1	0	0	6	2001
Bentley, M. C.	0	1	0	1	1929
Bernard, Dave	1	0	0	6	1936
Bettis, Adam	1	0	0	6	1999
Biddle, Taye	1	0	0	6	2005
Biggers, Neal	1	1	0	7	1930
Biles, Lacey	1	0	0	6	1926
Binkley, Les	0	8	3	17	1999–2000
Blair, Earl	4	0	0	24	1953–55
Blanchard, Don	0	2	0	2	1949
Bolden, Brandon	1	0	0	6	2008–11
Bowen, John (Bo)	1	0	0	6	1969
Bowen, John (Buddy)	1	0	0	6	1947
Boykin, Arnold Laverne (Showboat)	8	0	0	48	1950–51
Brewer, Johnny	1	0	0	6	1960
Bridges, Roy	1	2	0	8	1917
Bridges, Tony	1	0	0	6	2015–16
Britt, Oscar (Honey)	0	1	0	1	1942
Brown, A. J.	1	0	0	6	2016–18
Brown, Raymond	1	0	0	6	1956
Brown, Van	0	1	1	4	1967
Bruce, John	1	0	0	6	1944
Buchanan, Oscar (Buck)	1	0	0	6	1948
Burke, Jack	0	1	0	1	1931
Burke, Webster (Webb)	0	1	0	1	1926
Byrd, Ronald (Rocky)	1	0	0	6	1950
Carter, Fred	1	0	0	5	1910

	Touchdowns	Extra Points	Field Goals	Points	Years
Chumbler, Brent (Shug)	1	0	0	6	1970
Clay, Bill	1	0	0	6	1965
Cohen, Sollie	1	0	0	6	1927
Coleman, Pat	2	0	0	12	1988
Collins, Chris	3	0	0	18	2002–3
Conerly, Charlie	1	0	0	6	1947
Conner, Snoop	3	0	0	18	2019–21
Core, Cody	1	0	0	6	2012–15
Corral, Matt	5	0	0	30	2018–21
Cothren, Paige	1	4	1	13	1953–55
Courtney, Marvin	2	0	0	12	1990, 1992
Crawford, Eddie	0	1	0	1	1955
Crespino, Bobby	1	0	0	6	1960
Cruz, Jonathan	0	1	3	10	2022
Cunningham, Doug	2	0	0	12	1964–66
Curtis, Chester	1	0	0	6	1932
Dart, Jaxson	2	0	0	12	2022–23
Davis, Lee	1	0	0	6	1984
Day, Eagle	0	1	0	1	1954
Dennis, Mike	3	0	0	18	1963–65
Dottley, John (Kayo)	3	0	0	18	1949–50
Doty, Art	1	0	0	6	1961
Drummond, Dontario	1	0	0	6	2019–21
Ealy, Jerrion	3	0	0	18	2019–21
Ellis, Tim	2	0	0	12	1977
Elmer, Frederick W.	1	0	0	5	1903
Elmer, James C.	0	1	3*	13	1906
Elmore, Doug	0	1*	0	2	1959
English, Gino	1	0	0	6	1980
Felts, Leon	1	0	0	6	1969
Fields, Richard	1	0	0	6	1917
Flournoy, Maurice	1	0	0	6	1999
Flowers, Charlie	1	0	0	6	1959
Fourcade, John	2	0	0	12	1981
Fourcade, Keith	1	0	0	6	1982
Franklin, Bobby	1	1	0	7	1958
Gatlin, Todd	0	6	1	9	1980–82
Gibbs, Jake	3	0	0	18	1959–60
Goodloe, Willie	2	0	0	12	1985–86
Grant, Terrell	1	0	0	6	2013
Grantham, Larry	2	0	0	12	1958–59
Green, Allen	0	5	0	5	1960
Green, Marshay	1	0	0	6	2006
Green, Willie	1	0	0	6	1988
Green-Ellis, Ben Jarvis	1	0	0	6	2007
Greenich, Harley (Duke)	1	0	0	6	1942
Gunn, Joe	2	0	0	12	2001
Gunter, George	2	0	0	12	1933
Guy, Louis	1	0	0	6	1962
Haik, J. M. (Mac)	1	0	0	6	1967

	Touchdowns	Extra Points	Field Goals	Points	Years
Halbert, Frank	1	0	0	6	1961
Hall, Parker (Bullet)	1	0	0	6	1938
Hamley, Doug, Jr.	1	0	0	6	1973
Hapes, Clarence (Big)	1	0	0	6	1935
Hapes, Ray (Little)	2	0	0	12	1935, 1937
Hardy, Greg	1	0	0	0	2006
Haxton, Kenneth	1	0	1	8	1909–10
Haynes, Kirk	1	0	0	6	1931
Heard, Grant	2	0	0	12	2000
Heidel, Jimmy	1	0	0	6	1965
Hindman, Stan	1	0	0	6	1968
Hines, Reid	1	0	0	6	1986
Hinkle, Matt	0	2	0	2	2005
Hinton, Cloyce	0	4	2	10	1971
Hodge, Shay	3	0	0	18	2007–9
Hogue, Greg	0	3	0	3	1989
Holder, Jamie	1	0	0	6	1985
Hooker, Clyde	0	1	0	1	1944
Hooper, Kinny	1	0	0	6	1980
Howard, Jon	0	3	1	6	1984
Howell, Earl (Dixie)	1	0	0	6	1948
Huggins, Cleve	0	1	0	1	1906
Hutson, Earl	1	1	0	7	1933–34
Innocent, Dou	1	0	0	6	1995
Irwin, Billy Carl	0	4	2	10	1962–64
Jacobs, Brandon	1	0	0	6	2003
Jenkins, Eulas (Red)	1	0	0	6	1949
Johnson, Joe	1	0	0	6	1947
Jones, Bill	1	0	0	6	1969
Judkins, Quinshon	1	0	0	6	2022–
Kauerz, Don	0	1	0	1	1945
Kelly, Chad	3	0	0	18	2015–16
Keyes, Jimmy	0	6	1	9	1965–66
Khayat, Robert	0	7	0	7	1957–59
Kimbrough, Les	1	0	0	6	1978
Kinard, Frank (Bruiser)	0	1	0	1	1937
King, Perry	0	8	1	11	1968–69
Knight, Bob	1	0	0	6	1970
Kramer, Larry	3	0	0	18	1973
Kyzer, Sam	2	0	0	12	1929–30
Lane, Robert	2	0	0	12	2004–5
Langley, C. E. (Hoppy)	0	7	3	16	1976–79
Lavinghouze, Steve	0	13	4	25	1972–75
Lear, Jimmy	1	12	0	18	1950–52
Lee, Brian	0	5	2	11	1990–92
Lee, Church	2	0	0	10	1910
Lenhardt, Johnny	1	0	0	6	1938
Liggins, Jeremy	1	0	0	6	2014–16
Lilly, Lawrence	2	0	0	12	2003–4
Lindsey, Steve	0	1	0	1	1997

	Touchdowns	Extra Points	Field Goals	Points	Years
Lofton, Harol	1	0	0	6	1952
Logan, Ja-Mes	1	0	0	6	2010–13
Logan, Luke	0	6	2	12	2016–20
Lovelace, Kent	1	0	0	6	1958
Luke, Tom	2	0	0	12	1990
Malouf, Bill	1	0	0	6	1972
Manning, Archie	3	0	0	18	1968–69
Manning, Eli	1	0	0	6	2002
Masoli, Jeremiah	1	0	0	6	2010
Massengale, Kent	0	1	0	1	1938
Matthews, Bill	1	0	0	6	1966
McAllister, D. J. (Deuce)	3	0	0	18	2000
McCain, Bob	1	0	0	6	1944
McCall, John (Scotchy)	1	0	0	5	1909
McCluster, Dexter	2	0	0	12	2008–9
McDonnell, Gus	1	0	0	5	1906
McGee, Carlisle	0	0	2	6	1998
Metcalf, D. K.	1	0	0	6	2016–18
Miller, Romaro	1	0	0	6	2000
Mitchell, Steve	1	6	0	11	1909–10
Moffett, Tim	2	0	0	12	1983
Moley, Stan	1	0	0	6	1971
Moncrief, Donte	3	0	0	18	2011–13
Montz, Tim	0	4	5	19	1993–95
Moore, Elijah	1	0	0	6	2018–20
Mosley, Jamal	1	0	0	6	2011–12
Moss, Edgar	0	1	0	1	1903
Muirhead, Allen	1	0	0	6	1952
Mustin, Billy	2	0	0	12	1948–49
Myers, Riley	1	0	0	6	1971
Nation, Cale	0	4	1	7	2019–21
Nichols, Jonathan	0	13	4	25	2001–4
Oswalt, Bobby	0	7	0	7	1947–48
Owen, Bryan	0	14	6	32	1985–88
Owens, Darrick	1	0	0	6	1991
Pasley, Lea	0	1	0	1	1953
Patterson, Shea	2	0	0	12	2016–17
Patton, Houston	1	0	0	6	1954
Pegues, JJ	1	0	0	6	2022–23
Perry, Leon	4	0	0	24	1976, 1978–79
Peterson, Cory	0	1*	0	2	1997
Philpot, Cory	1	0	0	6	1992
Pilkinton, S. T.	1	0	0	5	1906
Plumlee, John Rhys	1	0	0	6	2019–21
Poole, Barney	2	0	0	12	1948
Poole, Jim	0	2	0	2	1970
Powell, Kelly	1	0	0	6	1983
Preston, Roell	2	0	0	12	1993–94
Prieskorn, Caden	1	0	0	6	2023–
Reed, James	3	0	0	18	1973–74

	Touchdowns	Extra Points	Field Goals	Points	Years
Renshaw, Paul	1	0	0	5	1908
Richardson, Bill	0	2	0	2	1935
Ritter, Andrew		1	1	4	2009–13
Rodgers, Rab	2	1	0	13	1933–34
Rone, Andre	2	0	0	12	1997
Rose, Bryson		7	4	19	2009–12
Ruby, Pete	1	0	0	6	1933
Salmon, Farley	1	0	0	6	1947
Sanders, Braylon	1	0	0	6	2017–21
Sanders, Vince	1	0	0	6	2011–14
Schneller, Bill	2	0	0	12	1938–39
Scott, Jeff	1	0	0	6	2010–13
Shene, Joshua	0	13	5	28	2006–9
Shows, Russ	1	0	0	6	1989
Smith, Claude M. (Tad)	1	1	0	7	1928
Smith, Ralph	1	0	0	6	1961
Sowder, Shawn	2	0	0	12	1987–88
Sowell, Bradley	1	0	0	6	2008
Stackhouse, Charles	1	0	0	6	2001
Stagg, Leonard	1	0	0	6	1942
Stribling, Bill	1	0	0	6	1950
Stringfellow, Damore'ea	4	0	0	24	2014–16
Studdard, Vernon	2	0	0	12	1969
Sullivan, Wes	1	4	1	13	1960–61
Summers, Markeith	1	0	0	6	2009
Sykes, Shawn	1	0	0	6	1985
Ta'amu, Jordan	2	0	0	12	2017–18
Teevan, Neil	0	3	1	6	1983
Thigpen, Ed	2	0	0	12	1987, 1989
Thomas, Andre	1	0	0	6	1981
Thomas, LeMay	1	0	0	6	1994
Toler, Ken	1	0	0	6	1979
Trotter, W. C. (Chuck)	0	1	0	1	1908
Turnbow, Guy	2	2	0	14	1930–32
Turner, Gary	1	0	0	6	1975
Turner, Tremaine	1	0	0	6	2003
Urbanek, Jim	1	0	0	6	1966
Veazey, Burney (Butch)	1	0	0	6	1971
Wade, Dayton	1	0	0	6	2022–23
Walker, Gerald	1	0	0	6	1928
Wallace, Bo	6	0	0	36	2012–14
Wallace, Mike	2	0	0	12	2008
Warner, Jack	1	0	0	6	1945
Walton, Jaylen	1	0	0	6	2012–15
Weatherly, Jim	1	0	0	6	1962
Wettlin, D. G.	1	0	0	5	1906
White, Brad	3	0	0	18	1931–32
Wilcox, Reuben (Rube)	1	1	0	7	1927
Wilkins, Jordan	4	0	0	24	2013–17
Williams, Don	1	0	0	6	1955

	Touchdowns	Extra Points	Field Goals	Points	Years
Williams, Freddie	0	1*	0	2	1976
Wilson, Bobby	1	0	0	6	1947
Wonsley, Nathan	4	0	0	24	1984–85
Woodruff, J. L. (Cowboy)	3	0	0	18	1957, 1959
Woodruff, Lee T. (Cowboy)	2	2	0	14	1927–28
Wunderlich, Gary	0	13	5	28	2014–17
Unknown	7	3	0	38	1902, 1904

Mississippi State

	Touchdowns	Extra Points	Field Goals	Points	Years
Allen, Henry	1	0	0	6	1919
Anderson, Jesse	1	1*	0	8	1987, 1989
Andrews, Keith	0	0	1	3	2004
Ballard, Vick	3	0	0	18	2010–11
Barkum, Melvin	1	0	0	6	1973
Barnett, Gene	4	0	0	24	1922–23
Bell, Devon	0	3	1	6	2012–14
Biggers, R. R.	1	0	0	6	1926
Billingsley, M. C.	1	2	0	8	1920
Bivines, Ray Ray	1	0	0	6	2001
Black, J. T. (Blondy)	4	0	0	24	1940, 1942
Blount, Lamar	1	0	0	6	1942
Bobo, W. H.	2	0	0	12	1916
Bond, John	2	0	0	12	1980, 1983
Bouldin, Jerry	2	0	0	12	1989–90
Bouie, Kevin	2	0	0	12	1994
Branch, Frank	1	0	0	6	1950
Broomfield, Corey	1	0	0	6	2009
Brown, Eric	1	0	0	6	1996
Brown, Ralph	0	1	0	1	1931
Buckley, Bill	2	0	0	12	1972
Bumphis, Chad	2	0	0	12	2009–11
Burke, Tom	0	2	2	8	1993
Burrell, Ode	1	0	0	6	1962
Canale, Justin	0	3	3	12	1963–64
Carlson, Adam	0	9	2	15	2005–7
Cassell, H. S.	1	1	0	7	1919
Chatman, Robert	1	0	0	6	1976
Christmann, Jace	0	10	2	15	2016–20
Collins, Fred	1	0	0	6	1979
Cosby, Artie	0	3	5	18	1983–86
Cross, Dennis	1	0	0	6	1936
Culpepper, R. H	0	1	0	1	1929
Culver, Bobby	0	2	1	5	1968
Cutrer, W. D.	1	0	0	5	1905
Dantone, Sammy	0	2	0	2	1960–61
Davis, Arthur	1	0	0	6	1953
Davis, Bryson	1	0	0	6	2005
Davis, Harper	2	0	0	12	1945, 1947
Davis, Michael	3	0	0	18	1992–94

	Touchdowns	Extra Points	Field Goals	Points	Years
Davis, Noll	1	0	0	6	1920
Dear, Malik	3	0	0	18	2015–19
Dees, Wilbur	0	1	0	1	1940
DePasquale, Derek		8	2	14	2009–10
Dixon, Anthony	3	0	0	18	2006–7, 2009
Dodd, Jimmy	1	0	0	6	1956
Dorroh, C. E.	1	4	0	9	1908
Ellis, Glenn	0	1	2	7	1970
Felker, Rockey	2	0	0	12	1974
Fitzgerald, Nick	8	0	0	48	2014–18
Fratesi, Joey	0	1	0	1	1978
Fugler, C. S.	1	0	0	5	1903
Furman, Harry (Little)	4	0	0	20	1908
Gaddy, T. L.	2	4	0	16	1915–16
Galloway, Tay	1	0	0	6	1991
Gardner, Chris	0	4	2	10	1991–92
Garrison, E.	1	0	0	5	1908
Gibson, Nick	1	0	0	6	2015–19
Granger, Hoyle	1	0	0	6	1964
Graves, Westin	0	11	2	17	2014–15
Gray, Donald	1	0	0	6	2015–17
Green, Marcus	1	0	0	6	2009
Green, Norvin E. (Billy)	0	1	0	1	1903
Griffin, Lideatrick	1	0	0	6	2020–23
Grindle, Terrell	1	0	0	6	2000
Grubbs, Lewis	1	1*	0	8	1970, 1972
Haddix, Michael	2	0	0	12	1980, 1982
Haley, Jesse	0	0	1	3	1934
Hardison, Bob	1	0	0	6	1936
Harris, Willie	1	0	0	6	1991
Harvey, L. B.	2	2	0	12	1901
Hazelwood, Brian	0	7	1	10	1995–98
Heath, Malik	2	0	0	12	2020
Henley, R. N.	1	0	0	6	1919
Herrington, Bob	1	1	0	7	1931
Hildebrand, Bill	1	0	0	6	1946
Hill, Billy (Tootie)	1	0	0	6	1961
Hill, Kylin	2	0	0	12	2017–20
Howell, Hubert	3	5	0	23	1917
Husband, Jason	1	0	0	6	2006
Inman, Tommy	1	0	0	6	1963
Jackson, I. M.	1	0	0	6	1915
Jennings, John	2	0	0	12	1995, 1997
Jennings, Morley	0	1	0	1	1911
Jiles, Cedric	1	0	0	6	2012–16
Johnson, Dennis	2	0	0	12	1975–76
Johnson, Harvey (Boots)	3	0	0	18	1939–40
Johnson, James (J. J.)	3	0	0	18	1997–98
Jones, H. T.	2	0	0	12	1915
Jordan, Chuck	0	2	0	2	1969

	Touchdowns	Extra Points	Field Goals	Points	Years
Jordan, Kinney	0	2	3	11	1975–76
Kelly, David	1	0	0	6	1960
King, Donald Ray	1	0	0	6	1981
Knight, Danny	1	0	0	6	1981
Koontz, Henry	2	0	0	12	1982–83
Lee, Donald	1	0	0	6	1999
Lenoir, R. L.	1	0	0	6	1929
Lewis, H. R.	1	0	0	6	1928
Lewis, Jameon	1	0	0	6	2010–14
Little, Stennis (Judge)	3	0	0	18	1920
Logan, Joel	0	3	5	18	1987–90
Magee, W. J. (Chick)	1	0	0	5	1911
Mallory, R.	4	0	0	24	1918 (2 games)
Marble, John	1	0	0	6	1931
Marks, Jo'Quavious	2	0	0	6	2020–23
Marler, Dave	0	0	2	6	1977
Marlin, John Michael	0	3	1	6	2001
Massimo, Biscardi	0	3	1	6	2018–22
Matulich, Wallace (Eagle)	2	0	0	12	1946–47
McCord, Nolan	0	1	2	7	2020–21
McDole, Mardye	2	0	0	12	1977–78
McGeorge, Hal	2	1	0	11	1905, 1907
McGowan, George	0	3	0	3	1921
McInnis, C. E.	3	0	0	15	1907–8
McKenzie, Duncan	1	0	0	6	1976
McNair, E. H.	2	2	0	14	1918
McWilliams, Tom (Shorty)	1	0	0	6	1946
McWilliams, W. K.	2	0	0	12	1917
Miller, Dicenzo	3	0	0	18	1998–99, 2001
Milner, Sammy	2	1*	0	14	1969
Moates, Jennings	1	0	0	6	1941
Montgomery, J. F.	1	0	0	5	1906
Moore, Arnold	1	0	0	6	1939
Moore, Dana	0	1	3	10	1980–81
Moore, Owen	1	0	0	6	1944
Morgan, Bob	0	5	0	5	1981–82
Moulds, Eric	1	0	0	6	1993
Murphy, Billy (Spook)	1	0	0	6	1942
Neil, James	0	0	1	3	1967
Nelson, Tim	1	0	0	6	1998
Nickels, Vic	0	5	2	11	1973–74
Nix, Jack	1	0	0	6	1938
Noble, C. R. (Dudy)	2	0	0	12	1915
Noble, Pete	1	0	0	6	1923
Norwood, Jerious	4	0	0	24	2005
Oden, C. S.	1	0	0	6	1915
Packer, Walter	2	0	0	12	1974
Pappenheimer, W. A.	1	0	0	6	1928
Parker, Jackie	2	3	0	15	1952–53
Patty, R. P. (Doc)	1	0	0	6	1924

	Touchdowns	Extra Points	Field Goals	Points	Years
Pearson, H. H	1	0	0	5	1901
Pegues, Derek	1	0	0	6	2007
Perkins, LaDarius	4	0	0	24	2009–13
Perry, Frank	2	2	0	14	1917–19
Phillips, Hank	1	0	0	6	1987
Pickens, W. H.	1	0	0	6	1928
Pickle, Ike	1	2	0	8	1936
Polk, Makai	0	2	0	2	2019–21
Polovina, Pete	0	1	0	1	1951
Prescott, Dak	5	0	0	30	2011–15
Quekemyer, R. K.	1	0	0	6	1919
Reed, Joe	1	0	0	6	1970
Relf, Chris	3	0	0	18	2007–10
Rhoden, Marcus	1	0	0	6	1964
Robinson, Josh	1	0	0	6	2011–14
Robinson, William (Sleepy)	1	0	0	6	1991
Rogers, Tim	0	1	1	4	1994–95
Rogers, Will	7	0	0	42	2020–23
Ross, Fred	1	0	0	6	2013–16
Ruiz, Brandon	0	3	1	6	2017–21
Rushing, Tom (Dutch)	2	0	0	12	1950
Russell, C. E.	0	3	0	3	1918–19
Rye, Jerry	0	0	1	3	1979
Saunders, W. B.	0	1	0	1	1922
Schwill, Otto	4	4	1	31	1915–16
Shaw, M. J.	1	0	0	6	1915
Shrader, Garrett	2	0	0	12	2019–20
Shuff, Ted	0	6	0	6	1942, 1946
Simmons, Crosby	1	0	0	6	1948
Sirmones, C. J.	1	0	0	6	1999
Sluder, Kevin	1	0	0	6	1996
Smith, Brent	0	0	2	6	2002
Smith, Chris	1	0	0	6	2009–11
Smith, David	1	0	0	6	1969
Smith, Don	3	1*	0	20	1985
Smith, O. L. (Shorty)	0	1	0	1	1928
Sobiesk, Evan	0	4	2	10	2012–14
Stainbrook, Max	0	5	0	5	1947–48, 1950
Steadman, Bill	3	0	0	18	1935–37
Stone, H. L. (Hook)	0	2	2	8	1924
Stone, L. H. (Dutch)	1	0	0	6	1927
Sudduth, W. P. (Heine)	0	1	0	1	1923
Tate, H. D.	1	0	0	5	1905
Taylor, Michael	1	0	0	6	1985
Thomas, Deddrick	2	0	0	12	2015–19
Thomas, Rara	1	0	0	6	2021–22
Thompson, Keytaon	2	2	0	14	2017–19
Threadgill, Bruce	1	0	0	6	1977
Trammell, Bubber	1	0	0	6	1957
Tribble, Bobby	0	2	0	2	1956–57

	Touchdowns	Extra Points	Field Goals	Points	Years
Tullos, Toxie	1	0	0	6	1940
Unger, J. W. (Doc)	1	0	0	6	1925
Vandevere, D. C.	1	0	0	6	1928
Verderver, Gil	1	0	0	6	1951
Vernon, Jackson	1	0	0	6	1918
Wade, Orlando	1	0	0	6	1987
Walker, Dontae	6	0	0	36	2000–1
Walley, Jaden	1	0	0	6	2020–23
Ward, Bernie	0	1	0	1	1937
Wells, Willie	1	0	0	6	1927
Westerfield, Scott	0	5	2	11	1999–2000
Williams, Aeris	3	0	0	18	2014–18
Williams, Albert	1	0	0	6	1987
Williams, Austin	1	0	0	6	2017–22
Williams, W. J. (Blondy)	1	0	0	5	1909
Wilson, De'Runnya	1	0	0	6	2013–15
Wilson, Elmer	1	0	0	6	1982
Wilson, Pat	1	0	0	6	1920
Windham, Lamar	1	0	0	6	1982
Wyatt, Matt	0	1*	0	2	1996
Young, J. C. (Spec)	1	0	0	6	1924
Zeringue, Lynn	2	0	0	12	1968–69
Unknown	1	0	0	5	1904

Notes: Touchdowns were worth 5 points until 1912. Field goals were worth 4 points until 1909.
* Two-point conversion, first allowed by NCAA in 1958.

Index

Kauerz, Don, 127
Kearney, Jack Rabbit, 60
Keenan, Frank, 100
Kelly, Chad, 389, 390, 391
Kelly, David, 173
Kelly, James, 147
Kelly, M. E., 53
Kennedy, John F., 178, 180
Kentucky, University of, 3, 251, 309, 360, 363, 408
Keyes, Jimmy, 187, 190, 191
Khayat, Robert (Bob), 163, 167, 169, 335
Kiffin, Lane, 413, 415, 416, 417, 419, 423, 424, 426, 429, 431, 432
Kimball, Hunter, 40
Kimbrough, Les, 230
Kimbrough, Orman, 13
Kinard, Billy, 207, 212
Kinard, Frank (Bruiser), 97, 103, 104, 203, 206, 212
Kinard, George, 113
Kincannon, A. A., 27, 28, 40, 42
King, Donald Ray, 237, 241
King, Perry, 196, 197
Kinnebrew, Earl, 33
Kirk, Dixon, 54
Knight, Bob, 204
Knight, Danny, 241, 246
Knox, Dawson, 406
Knox, Greg, 428, 429, 431, 432
Knox, Ike, 26
Koontz, Henry, 246, 248
Kramer, Larry, 213, 214
Kyle, Frank, 29
Kyzer, Sam, 82, 86

Lake, R. H., 55
Lane, Robert, 334, 338
Langley, C. E. (Hoppy), 223, 226, 230, 231, 235
Lavinghouze, Steve, 210, 211, 213, 214, 217, 221
Lawrence, Mike, 223
Leach, Mike, 413, 414, 415, 417, 419, 420, 423, 425, 426, 428, 431
Lear, Jimmy, 143, 145, 147, 150, 151

Lee, Brian, 278, 282, 283
Lee, Church, 33
Lee, Donald, 310
Lee, Tyson, 352, 356
Lenhardt, Johnny, 107
Lenoir, R. L., 82
Leonard, R. L. (Dutch), 52
Lewis, D. D., 194
Lewis, Jameon, 372, 379
Liberty Bowl, 181, 188, 197, 277, 279, 284, 348, 379, 419
Life, 109
Liggins, Jeremy, 382
Lilly, Lawrence, 330, 334
Lilly, T. J., 74
Lindsey, Steve, 303
Litkenhouse Rating System, 177
Little, Stennis (Judge), 59, 62
Lofton, Harol, 150
Logan, Ja-Mes, 362, 379
Logan, Joel, 265, 267, 268, 270, 273
Logan, Luke, 405, 409, 411, 414
Long, Juan, 286
Longino, Andrew H., 3
Look, 158
Louisiana State University, 3, 122, 128, 153, 169, 174, 232, 245, 248, 254, 309, 331, 359, 387, 388, 422, 423, 437
Louisiana Tech University, 246, 404
Louisiana–Lafayette, University of, 360, 408
Love, Jamerson, 378
Lovelace, Kent, 167
Lovelady, Matthew, 249
Lowery, Michael, 284
Luckett, J. E. (Jazz), 65
Luke, Matt, 397, 400, 404, 406, 408, 409, 411, 413, 414, 419
Luke, Tom, 273, 274, 278, 400
Luke, Tommy, 400
Lundie, Orlando, 253
Luster, Frankie, 273, 284, 288

Maddox, Carl, 232
Madkin, Wayne, 306, 307, 309, 310, 315
Magee, W. J. (Chick), 38, 40

About the Authors

William G. Barner (1926–2009), a graduate of University of Mississippi, retired as an advertising writer and lived in Atlanta, Georgia.

Danny McKenzie is a veteran Mississippi journalist and author of *Matters of the Spirit: Human, Holy, and Otherwise* and *A Time to Speak: Speeches by Jack Reed*, the latter published by University Press of Mississippi.

Jeff Roberson has written about sports in his home state of Mississippi for more than three decades. He is coauthor of *Midnight Train*, the life story of former Ole Miss quarterback and Songwriters Hall of Fame member Jim Weatherly. Roberson is currently an archivist and historian in the Ole Miss athletics department. He has attended more than forty Egg Bowls.